Organization and Management

THEORY AND PRACTICE

Gathorne V. Butler

Prentice-Hall International

Englewood Cliffs, New Jersey   London   Mexico   New Delhi
Rio de Janeiro   Singapore   Sydney   Tokyo   Toronto   Wellington

Library of Congress Cataloging in Publication Data

Butler, Gathorne V., 1927-
  Organization and management.

  Bibliography: p.
  Includes indexes.
  1. Management.   2. Organization.   I. Title.
  HD31.B863   1986   658   85-25650
  ISBN 0-13-641754-X (pbk.)

British Library Cataloging in Publication Data

Butler, Gathorne V.
  Organization and management.
  1. Organizational behavior
  I. Title
  302.3'5   HD58.7

  ISBN 0-13-641754-X (pbk.)

© 1986 Gathorne V. Butler

Prentice-Hall, Inc., *Englewood Cliffs, New Jersey*
Prentice-Hall International, (UK), Ltd, *London*
Prentice-Hall of Australia Pty Ltd, *Sydney*
Prentice-Hall Canada, Inc., *Toronto*
Prentice-Hall Hispanoamericana, S.A., *Mexico*
Prentice-Hall of India Private Ltd, *New Delhi*
Prentice-Hall of Japan, Inc., *Tokyo*
Prentice-Hall of Southeast Asia Pte Ltd, *Singapore*
Editora Prentice-Hall do Brasil Ltda, *Rio de Janeiro*
Whitehall Books Ltd, *Wellington, New Zealand*

Printed and bound in Great Britain for
Prentice-Hall International (UK) Ltd,
66 Wood Lane End, Hemel Hempstead,
Hertfordshire, HP2 4RG
by A. Wheaton & Co. Ltd, Exeter

1 2 3 4 5   90 89 88 87 86
ISBN 0-13-641754-X PBK

Contents

PART TWO
MOTIVATION

Contents

Contents

PART FOUR
ORGANIZATIONAL GOALS,
STRATEGY AND TACTICS

Introduction

The purpose of this introduction is to show teachers of management why this book is necessary. Students who find the vocabulary of this introduction is new to them are nevertheless advised to skim through it just to get some sort of 'feel' for the rest of the book. There the ideas (which the introduction treats in a sort of management shorthand) are fully explained. If students return to the Introduction after having read the book they will, I feel sure, be gratified by their newly acquired insights.

It is natural that Western writers of texts on business organization and management should tacitly assume that the subject is being studied with a view to applying it within a capitalist framework. But that does not justify those who fail to consider the crucial impact upon an organization's dynamics of applying to it capitalist *mores*. (*Mores* is a useful Latin word. It expresses in shorthand the customs and conventions which are essential to or characteristic of a community.)

No writer needs to tell us that he has assumed that we all breathe the same air. We can even stretch a point and say that a management writer is justified in omitting to point out to his readership that his ideas are based upon the *mores* of capitalism, since he is able to assume that his readership will not only recognize that fact but also share his beliefs. But it is just inexcusably bad scholarship if he doesn't even pause to consider the impact that those *mores* will have

(a) upon those people in the organization who do not share them, or
(b) upon those people who share them in principle, but who will object to specific proposals based upon them by which they are disadvantaged.

These *mores* dictate management initiatives. But until the *reaction* to each such initiative has been considered, we cannot speak of a *transaction* having occurred. These *mores* are therefore a major force in the dynamics of the organization. From the management standpoint they determine the nature of the goals which the organization is to seek, they determine the means by which it is to seek them, and (except in exceptional circumstances which we shall discuss later) they determine the moral values to be applied to all such activity. These *mores* are also central to the employee's reaction, irrespective of the form that takes. The employee may appeal to these same *mores* in his agreement or disagreement with management initiatives: though in the latter case he is more likely to challenge them. But either way the substance of the reaction centres upon the legitimacy or otherwise of the *mores*.

So good scholarship requires that a key consideration in any book on business organization and management should be the role played by capitalist *mores* in initiating action, in affecting reaction and thus in colouring transaction. Moreover, just because an author does not acknowledge that he himself has adopted a position in relation to these *mores* does not mean that he has not done so. If he had **not**, he could make no meaningful comment.

In all capitalist societies there exist certain infrastructures to perform the tasks which virtually everyone seems to agree it would be inappropriate to leave to market forces (defence, police, education, etc.). Such organizations as these are financed out of national and/or local taxes. Whether these organizations are operated by a local authority or by the authorities of the individual states which collectively form a federation, or by the authorities of a national state, is immaterial to the point I am making. In all instances they and the job they perform are taken out of the market-place and have become what for convenience I shall call a 'state' responsibility.

In Western Europe the majority of people (though by no means all) have sought to extend this list to cover certain welfare services, health care, unemployment benefit, old age pensions, and so on. Criticisms of such extensions to the list are more muted in Europe than they are in the United States. There the belief is more widely held that the less government interferes with what goes on, the better. This view that governments should, so far as possible, keep away from any action which might interfere with the free flow of market forces is referred to throughout this book by its commonly used French title of 'laissez-faire': (literally 'allow to happen').

American adherence to laissez-faire principles (which deny the state's social responsibility) has resulted in two basic themes in American management literature. The first is to extol the virtues of laissez-faire everywhere in the economy, including within the firm itself. *This theme falls into the error of understating the social role of the capitalist employer.* The second seeks to apply laissez-faire attitudes to businesses but to shield individuals from the competition and social indifference of this harsh doctrine. It therefore assumes that the untempered wind of market forces may freely blow anywhere other than within the firm. There the individual, for no better reason than because he is an employee, is to receive the care and attention denied by the laissez-faire state. *This theme falls into the error of overstating the social role of the capitalist employer.*

For me, as for millions of other Europeans, a capitalist economy which contains areas in which social need takes precedence over market forces, is the basic framework from which to work for the 'best' society. By 'best', we mean a society which is able to tolerate the greatest number of individual views... in short, a *pluralist* society. Such societies remain pluralist because, despite the many social obligations which are assumed by the state (and which are thereby subject to central funding and control) the main engine of the economy is decentralized. Even under Western European so-called 'socialist' governments, it is the economic activity of individual concerns (responding to the operation of market forces within a framework of enforceable contractual obligations) which powers the economy. Such decentralization of economic power is essential if pluralist political institutions are to be preserved.

Such capitalist economic pluralism, which is devoid of centralized planning and control, is possible only if there is an automatic integrative principle at work. There is. It is the 'invisible hand' of market forces. There is considerable truth in the criticism that capitalism's integrating 'invisible hand' will respond to the wishes of those with money, but ignore the needs of those without. That is precisely why most Europeans want two sectors within the system; one which uses the dynamics of the market-place to generate wealth and independence, and one which syphons off some of that wealth to be used to relieve distress, irrespective of the sufferer's ability to pay.

The impact of all the individual decentralized decisions in the competitive market sector have

(a) been the major means by which economic resources are allocated,
(b) generated the economic activity whose surplus has been taxed to pay for the other sector,
(c) fostered parliamentary democracy (as I shall explain later in this Introduction), and
(d) created over the centuries a world-wide trading network of great subtlety.

In avoiding gluts and shortages, capitalism has shown itself to be more responsive, and therefore more efficient than most centralized bureaucratic planning. Moreover, it motivates high output. To supplement the poor agricultural performance of Russia and China, both states have had to tolerate the operation of a capitalist subculture. While it remains to see what the future brings, in 1984 China initialled an agreement *to the effect that, when Hong Kong reverts to her in the 1990s, she would seek to harness capitalism's dynamism by a policy of operating capitalism and state socialism in tandem.* In December 1984 China appeared even to be denouncing Marxism, so perhaps she wishes to go beyond a mere tandem arrangement.

The term 'invisible hand' may by its poetic imagery invite mockery, but the reality it describes is both prosaic and practical. I, for one, am grateful that it has saved us for so long from the alternatives. These are: *(1) having no integrative principle, thereby producing the chaos of anarchy.* This, I feel sure, would be so unbearable that, if it did not result in a reversion to capitalism, then, out of desperation people would turn to *(2) imposing integration by centralized control.* This latter soon degenerates into totalitarianism.

I do not accept the viability of any hypothetical systems which have the alleged power both to overcome the chaos of anarchy and to sidestep the totalitarian evils of centralized control and to do both without resorting to the use of market forces. Unlike the 'invisible hand', such systems – usually variants on syndicalism – really **are** mysticism. It is relevant to note that the syndicalist aspirations of the anarchists in the Spanish Civil War were thwarted by the hierarchical discipline of the communists, and it is also relevant to note that at a Marxist conference in Venice held in the late 1970s the delegates from the West expressed their belief that Marxism could be pluralist, though those from the East recognized it could not.

Most American Organization and Management literature ignores the problems which result from managements basing their actions on capitalist *mores. In saying this I do not overlook the fact that the human relations and neo-human relations writing consists of little other than remonstrations against management's current style. This, however, only supports my claim. These remonstrations never suggest that such a change in management style will involve* **modifying capitalist objectives**. I can only conclude that, for such writers, management style is an *independent variable.* Indeed, as if to underline this independence of management style from capitalist objectives, *Robert Blake* and *Jane Moulton* (1964) make them, quite literally, independent variables. Their concept of management is to see it as a 'grid' which has **management style** on one axis, (under the label **'concern for people'**) and **capitalist** *mores* on the other (under the label **'concern for production'**). Furthermore, they infer that the best managers are able to maximize the values of both axes without compromise. Since the Second World War, these, and most other American liberal writers, have considered the capitalist system as though it were a neutral canvas on which the manager were free to paint in any style he chooses from Raphael to Renoir, from Poussin to Picasso.

There appear to be two possible explanations for such writers ignoring the impact on organizations of the *mores* of capitalism. One is that they have done so without realizing it. I find it more likely (and more generous) to assume the other. This is that they are seeking to avoid the topic in the hope of insulating capitalism from the criticism which, typically, it receives from Marxists. If this is their purpose, then they could not have performed a worse job. *By their refusal to argue that capitalism is a morally superior system, despite its warts, they have left the field open to the Marxist.* He points to the warts, he refuses to acknowledge that some of them would apply to any social system and therefore cannot be attributed to capitalism *per se*, and, of course, he makes no concession to capitalism's virtues.

But this is the negative damage that such writers do to the cause of capitalism. More significant is the positive damage that they do when they attempt to show that a conflict-free (and thus unitary) form of capitalism is possible. This of course is nonsense. But it is a nonsense that Marxists can exploit, for it lends credibility to the promised land of Marxist mythology. This is their belief that following the overthrow of capitalism, the 'dictatorship of the proletariat' will be a non-hierarchical and spontaneous mass-purpose, devoid of conflict, and thus not so much denying the validity of pluralist institutions as making them irrelevant.

If the general tendency for American liberals to see unitary organizations as desirable lends credibility to the above Marxist imagery of post-capitalist society, they are even more supportive of it in the specifics. For example, many liberal Americans suggest that hierarchy is unnecessary. *This fallacy finds its counterpart in the Marxist claim that hierarchy is not a universal requirement for any and every society, but simply an oppressive device of capitalism.* Similarly, many liberals hold a belief in the universal goodness of man. By so doing they not only deny all the evidence of history, but they make pluralism unimportant. This is not the same as the Marxist claim that the pluralism of capitalism is an **illusion**, yet if the liberals have made pluralism **unimportant**, the distinction hardly matters.

The interesting question we should ask is why any liberal who apparently believes these fallacies should take the trouble to hide the warts on capitalism. *I am a capitalist precisely because I recognize that hierarchies are essential. That being so I am fearful of the inhuman acts which those with unrestricted centralized powers have shown that they will perform in the name of humanity.* Of course, states whose governments already have achieved totalitarian powers can even harness capitalism, as we saw in Nazi Germany. But the Nazis gained power precisely because the economic events which followed the First World War, including reparations demanded of Germany, undermined capitalism there. Always the propensity is for a state which has centralized its economic planning to become totalitarian either by evolution or by revolution; not least because the levers of power are there to be grabbed. By contrast, the opposite is true of capitalism. For capitalism succeeds not only in diffusing economic power: it also diffuses the relationships of the separate hierarchies which wield that power. Such hierarchies are cross-linked by no more than the mutual benefits which result from trade: *links which are based not on **authority**, but on mutual convenience.* By this means the whole edifice can escape both the bureaucratic burden and the potential tyranny of centralized planning and control. For in the latter economic framework the 'separate' hierarchies may have functional specialisms: but they have no autonomy. They are locked into the authority structure of one huge totalitarian pyramid.

Yet none of these considerations (which are of such immense consequence to **me** in choosing a modified form of capitalism as my preferred economic system) would seem to have any logical significance for those American liberals who are able to convince themselves that hierarchies are not only unnecessary, but that human nature is essentially good. *On the contrary, their avowed beliefs make it illogical for them **not** to criticize capitalism. If non-hierarchical harmonious societies are a realistic option, what do they need with a system of impersonal market forces which inverts the liberal priorities? For such forces create economic and technical initiatives which dictate the nature of the political and social response. By contrast, liberal policy would prefer that political and social initiatives should dictate the economic and technical responses.* So we must ask the obvious question that this situation prompts. **Can it be that, at some subliminal level, the American liberal is fully aware of his own nonsense and recognizes that our pluralist institutions, by the grace of capitalism, are the greatest single bulwark against state oppression that we know?**

Whatever the answer to this conundrum, the price paid by American Organization and Management writers when they ignore the organizational impact of capitalism buys **nothing**. *The warts are **still** apparent. What they **do** succeed in doing is in making nonsense of their own scholarship and in the process denying capitalism its virtues.* It is precisely because people **do** have different interests and aspirations that the pluralist institutions, which capitalism naturally generates, are important. Pluralists assume that individuals and groups have the right to dissent. They therefore regard it as legitimate and even desirable that individuals or groups should identify where their own best interests lie and be prepared to fight for them.

It is one of the ironies of life that it should have been in the USA that writers should claim that the firm is properly a unitary institution: for it was the USA's founding fathers' regard for pluralist institutions which led them to write the 'separation of powers' concept into the Constitution. Yet, ironic as this twist most certainly is, it is not difficult to suggest why it should have happened. The idealization of laissez-faire capitalism, which occurs in American society as a whole, is entirely compatible with pluralism: but it is a doctrine which allows the state to justify placing the strictest limits on its social responsibilities towards the individual. Nor does the nature of the capitalist firm fit it to accept those social responsibilities which the state has refused. Were it to do so it would be engaging in a neo-feudal activity which is completely alien to the contractual and limited nature of all its dealings, and would, in any case, be beyond its resources to guarantee. Yet it requires little psychological insight to see why a socially concerned writer, whose heart ruled his head, should wish this role on to the firm.

Because I understand and even sympathize with the motive, it does not mean that I find the concept any less mistaken nor any less invidious in its end result. For the presumption that the firm could and **should** act in this way is used by writers of both the human relations and the neo-human relations schools to justify an assumption that the employee (if so treated) would identify with the organization's goals. There's the rub. *For by this series of apparently innocuous and even laudable moves, these theorists arrive at the position in which, in the name of social concern, they create a myth of unity. But its true effect is tacitly to deny pluralism within the firm because they deny the need (and with that the right) of the employee to hold a different view from that of the management.* (It is true that the neo-human relations writers sometimes pretend that it may be the employer who adopts the goals of the employee, but, in a key sentence in his book (which I reproduce in paragraph 10.3.33) Douglas McGregor shows the emptiness of this claim).

There is further reason to wonder that these writers should have developed, in support of their motivation theories, a myth that the most successful firms are those which enjoy a wholly co-operative internal ethos. For had they cared to look at the criteria by which organizational structures are segmented into departments and divisions, they would have seen that the opposite was true. Today's successful firms are even more conscious than their predecessors that organizational structures are essentially sectioned off in a manner which will concentrate the efforts of each section towards specific goals and towards using minimal resources in their achievement. It is never possible to know in **absolute** terms that resources used have indeed been minimal. *But, at least by using an accounting system which exposes when the section fails to achieve a standard equal to the best alternative internal or external source, management can know whether they are **relatively** sustaining any more than the minimal 'opportunity cost'.* If they find that a section is uncompetitive, they respond by eliminating the factor responsible. So (if for no other reason than this) the nonsense of claiming that the firm could, and should, be an oasis of co-operation in a competitive environment should have been easily recognized. Why in British business schools the neo-human relations myth should have been so readily adopted in the face of all evidence and *a priori* reasons to the contrary is a matter for speculation, but one I will not pursue.

A REVIEW OF CONTENTS

Part One of this book (Chapters 1 to 5 inclusive) attempts, with illustrations from management issues, to show the student why there is a 'management theory jungle', and to make the student aware that one of the causes is that each theoretician is seeking not only to deal with certain intractable problems which defy resolution, but to do so in terms of that part of socio-political spectrum of which he approves. So, for a full appreciation of the position of each theory in the tangle of the jungle, the student needs to understand

(a) the objective nature of the problem, and
(b) how the theorist's socio-political position affected
    (i) his perception of it, and
    (ii) the priorities of the 'trade-offs' he made in his response.

Once he has understood the ideology which explains why each school had a different concept of what goals were more desirable, what constraints were more stubborn, and what means were more efficacious, the student will at last be in a position to comment intelligently on contradictory claims. As for the manager, he needs to consider

(a) the social, technological, economic and political constraints in which he operates,
(b) the freedom that remains to him for choice,
(c) the justification he can make, both to himself and to others, for applying the concepts of one school rather than another, or his decision to hybridize his choice.

Only so can he feel that his stewardship is honest.

Part Two (Chapters 6 to 11 inclusive) deals with motivation. It accepts that motivation means getting the worker to co-operate in achieving management goals. However it denies the two extremes of:

(a) the Marxist view which assumes that the worker's natural role is to be in total conflict with management, and
(b) the view of the various 'content theory' writers who believe that, given the right ingredient(s), the worker will see everything through management eyes.

Morality and common sense suggest that the 'best' that can be legitimately hoped for, from management's standpoint, is that both they and the worker, while acknowledging that legitimate potential differences of interest exist, can find enough mutuality of interest most of the time. If so, it will be because the employee has come to terms with the constraints which hierarchies impose, as well as with the many technological and economic constraints whose inevitable existence is here described.

Part Three (Chapters 12 to 15 inclusive) deals with organization. It explains that the different theories of organization reflect an emphasis imposed by the theorist's perception of the problem to be solved. It acknowledges that there is some legitimacy in the human relations and systems attacks upon the 'mechanistic' elements in classical theory. Nevertheless, the main thrust of this part is to show that the *mores* of capitalism (and in particular the requirement for managements to seek to minimize opportunity cost) are met by classical concepts. They have therefore a perennial validity. Both the human relations and systems approaches would benefit from re-assessing the overly facile assumptions they have made in their criticism of classical thought.

Part Four (Chapter 16) deals with organizational goals, strategy and tactics. It suggests that cultural pressures have led to myths replacing the reality of the situation. The reality is that the goals of the organization are essentially those of management, while the goals of all other parties form the constraints within which management operates. This tends to focus (rather than diffuse) management goals. The myths, which have understandably (but mistakenly) been fostered by today's anti-elitist/pro-democratic ethos, are of three general types. Their respective claims are that:

(a) Organizations have a transcendent life of their own (which includes goal-setting).
(b) Organizational goals are a matter of consensus between interested parties.
(c) The typical organization is so big that top management are impotent. Experts of every status and buried deep within the firm (the techno-structure) have the real power.

These myths have just a large enough element of truth to be accepted. They are, however, almost wholly false.

The need for strategic planning and the manner in which existing organizational structures predispose the outcomes are also considered.

Acknowledgements

It is fitting that I should acknowledge first and foremost my debt to my wife. Perhaps it is because we have been married for over thirty years that I am so aware of the time which this book has stolen from our joint lives. Other than her, it owes its existence to four people. Mr Giles Wright is not only my editor, but it was he who, having seen some of my lecture notes for students, suggested that I should write the book. The person he chose as his reader commented on the first draft of the book with such aptness of criticism and depth of scholarship that I realized that it would have to be conceived differently...and started again from scratch. Only later did I find that this unknown scholar was an old friend whom I had first met when he was an extenal examiner to a course of which I was the tutor. I delight now to be able formally to thank him for his great help. He is Mr Michael Mumford, Head of the Department of Accounting and Finance at the University of Lancaster, Certified Accountant and both a liberal and a Liberal. My thanks are also due to Professor Tony Lowe of the University of Sheffield. It is a daunting undertaking to attempt a holistic approach to any subject. Doing so in the area of Organization and Management is peculiarly fraught with difficulty. Professor Lowe's conviction that (win or lose) my attempt was worth while was a constant source of encouragement. Lastly, the book owes its existence to my close friend and colleague, Mr Alfred Shmueli. I find writing an agonizing experience. It was he who cajoled me over the bad times and shamed me into getting on with it.

I do not hereby infer that any of these people necessarily identify with the sentiments expressed in this (doubtless) controversial book. Clearly those, and any faults the book may contain, are mine.

Apologia

My first apology is addressed to my women readers because, throughout this text I have used the words 'he' and 'him'. In the first draft of the book I deliberately referred to 'her/him' and '(s)he', (please note the priority), but colleagues who read this draft found the practice irritating. They approved my purpose but found that I had thereby confused the text. I started to re-write using only 'her' and 'she', but when I considered my readership it became, even for me, far too quixotic a gesture. For the lamentable fact is that the vast majority of students and practitioners of management at present are men. I therefore beg the forgiveness of my women readers. I do not want to add to the social injustices that you suffer: yet I do admit that my use of 'he' and 'him' adds another straw to the load of prejudice that you carry.

My second apology is for the use of the first person 'I' or 'we'. There are very good reasons for expressing ideas in an impersonal way; and this is something that most writers achieve by expressing themselves in the passive voice. Yet it is a practice that certainly makes the text less immediate and sometimes less clear. However, its most awkward outcome is in knowing what to say when the author wants to warn the reader that the view he has expressed, however true he feels it to be, is his **personal** attitude and **not** one that is generally held; or alternatively, how to refer to a **personal** experience. To maintain the formal style he then resorts to speaking about himself in the third person. This means that when he wants to say '*I think...*' he has to use such pomposities as '*it is the author's personal belief that...*'. In spite of this it is still important to keep the egocentricity within bounds. Thus, where I feel that if the reader and I were having a face-to-face discussion we would be likely to draw the same conclusions, I have used the word 'we'. For example, I might say, '*...we can infer from this evidence that...*'. When I feel that my views are idiosyncratic I shall use the word 'I' to underscore the fact. In a book such as this, which has many occasions to refer to various belief-systems, this is an important consideration.

PART ONE

Facing Up to the Theory Jungle

This part seeks first to show why there has developed a 'management theory jungle'. Secondly it searches for some basic concepts with which to discriminate between those theories which are of help to active managers and those which are not.

1

The management theory jungle

1.1 Why should there be a jungle?

1.1.1 Managers make things happen: that is their duty. Management therefore attracts people of a certain psychological make-up who want to get on with the job of running their organizations and who therefore begrudge the time involved in theorizing. In short, they are looking for a recipe that they can use with some assurance that it will work. Students who hope one day to be managers realize also that such a recipe would improve their chances of coping with the 'real' world. Moreover, such a recipe, in a succinct and stereotyped form, would make it easy to deal with examination questions in Management.

1.1.2 Yet when they come to study 'Organization and Management' no recipe emerges. Instead they are faced with a confusing interlacing of complex and often contradictory theories. It is small wonder that Harold Koontz (Koontz and O'Donnell, 1976; ch3) should survey the literature and refer to it as the 'management theory jungle'.

1.1.3 I believe that there is only one satisfactory way for the reader to cope with the 'management theory jungle'... and deal with it he must. For, although on occasion every manager and student has felt the urge to say *'A plague on all your theories: I just want to get on with the job'*, this is not a realistic option. The student cannot afford to do this because he has examinations to pass. Neither can the practising manager. I would ask the reader, at this stage, simply to accept this latter assertion, until we deal with its supportive arguments in Section 1.3.

1.1.4 The problem of finding a path through the 'management theory jungle' is made more difficult for students and managers by the nature of the two categories into which, apart from a few notable exceptions, most of the texts naturally fall. These are:

(1) Texts that are prescriptive. These are the work of authors who have identified some organization and management problem to which they think they have a solution. Because they are attempting to justify their claims their writing is propagandist in tone. This is understandable, but it can also mean that they can be tempted to overstate their case on occasion, or occasionally they may, as we shall see, avoid aspects which are pertinent but which their proposals will not resolve. If they do mention such problems, their usual line is to discount their significance, or alternatively to suggest that such a problem is not endemic, but is the temporary outcome of current bad management practice. On the occasions when prescriptive texts suffer from these shortcomings (and as we shall see these are many) they compound the problems facing the manager or student. They do so because they add to the theories which form the management theory jungle without being sufficiently convincing to eliminate from that jungle those theories that they were aiming to replace.

(2) Texts which are descriptive. These are written by authors who fulfil the useful function of giving a panoramic view of the texts of the prescriptive authors. But, unless they too are prepared to be prescriptive (for criticism requires us to be prescriptive) they will offer the reader no real means of comparative assessment. This may be thought by some to be academically desirable because it is dispassionate. Yet, in effect it presents to the reader what may be little more than a catalogue of those who have written on the topic: *'On the one hand Smith says this, while on the other Jones says that.'* Although such texts increase the reader's awareness of the **density** of the management theory jungle, they can be infuriating in that they so studiously avoid attempting to suggest which is the 'right' path.

1.1.5 Faced with this situation the student or manager has really only one piece of methodology that he can use to make any sense out of the confusion that appears to face him. This is to deal with the problem as he would deal with any other jig-saw puzzle that he was required to solve and for which he had no indicative finished picture from which to work. Just as in the case of a jig-saw some parts can be assumed to belong together because of their general coloration, so some bits of management theory can be seen as fitting together with other bits because they share the same 'coloration'. By that I mean that two or more concepts can be recognized as being consistent with a particular way of looking at things and therefore can be visualized as being different facets of a wider conceptual system.

Having put these bits of the jig-saw into a system he will look at the remaining pieces of theory in order to construct a further system: and so on from system 1 to system n. Of course, if he follows this way he will be left with the problem that none of these systems will interrelate. They will seem to be parts of different puzzles, precisely **because** the picture being presented by each system **is** so very different. With such an approach the problem of not understanding the basic diversity remains, but at least the student can find enough coherent material to pass an examination which asks superficial questions. But, because he still doesn't understand why all the bits of the picture **are** so different, he cannot construct any critique which will allow him to evaluate the relative merits of the different systems, one against the other. For the same reason, neither will the manager be able to select the theory upon which his actions will be based because he will have no means of knowing which is 'best', nor even what 'best' means in this context.

1.1.6 Before we go on to consider my claim that there is a better way of dealing with the management theory jungle – a term we shall continue to use because it expresses so well the tangle – we should also stress that it is a term with certain drawbacks. When we find ourselves in a real jungle the flora and fauna which surround us are alien to our experience. By contrast, however dense the management theory jungle may appear to be, the individual 'plants' that create it are far from alien, for they are not plants but theories, and however many there may be, and however difficult they may be to untangle, they are **human** concepts. They are the creation of the minds of men and women who are striving to identify and solve a relatively small number of problems which recurrently face all those who try to make sense of organization and management

1.1.7 As students and managers ponder on the vast diversity of the theories that surround them, they may find it difficult to credit that all this could be generated by so few problems. In particular, they may find it strange that theories that propose diametrically opposed actions could grow from the same root problem.

1.1.8 Yet it is so. This is why, if we are to hope ever to discriminate knowledgeably between the different theories, it is necessary for us to get back to the root cause of such diversity. For this return to the basic problem not only reduces the complexity which faces us (since there are fewer problems than answers) but it is only when we see the common problem that different theorists set out to resolve that we can compare and discriminate between their theories on the basis of how well, in our judgement, each succeeded.

1.1.9 Indeed, we might say that all of organization and management theory has stemmed from one single deep and intractable human problem. It is not a problem that has plagued only the theorists of twentieth-century organization and management. Every age and every society has had to come to terms with it, and its intractability lies in the fact that it has both a moral and a practical dimension. It is the fundamental problem of *What right does one section of society,* A, *have to use the means that it does to seek the goals that it does? In particular, what right does it have to induce other sections of society to become part of that means and also to expect those sections to refrain from such actions as* A *considers a hindrance to its goal achievement?*. Even if, in practice, *A* has managed to induce others to act in a manner of which *A* approves, this still does not dispose of the moral and practical questions which need to be resolved. Here are seven of them. I am sure the list is not exhaustive but it makes the point:

(1) What was *A*'s goal: was it clear and coherent?
(2) Was *A*'s **goal** legitimate, and if so, was it also the 'best' of the goal options?
(3) What does 'best' mean in this context?
(4) Was the **inducement** used by *A* legitimate, and if so, was it also the 'best' of the inducement options?
(5) What does 'best' mean in this context?
(6) Was the **technical** means chosen by *A* legitimate, and if so, was it also the 'best' of the technical options?
(7) What does 'best' mean in this context?

1.1.10 If such issues are central to the fundamental problem faced by management theorists, we need no longer wonder at the diversity of their answers. We could perhaps wonder at their temerity in attempting to answer the questions at all.

1.1.11 From what I have just said, we can see why a text which says 'On the one hand Smith says this, while on the other hand Jones says that' cannot help us to understand and compare theories. For it is only at the level of the root problem, and only if the commentator and the reader are prepared to bring their own value-systems into play, that any useful comparison can be made. We shall return to this question of value-systems shortly. What we need now to do is to understand that our insights to date have also determined our methodology as follows:

(1) We consider the theory in question and the action that the theorist is recommending.
(2) We look at the basic problem which the theory is supposed to help us to solve and identify those aspects of the problem that have been suppressed

or enhanced in order to 'sell' the theory. *(This is not cynicism. Just as every coin has a 'head' or 'tail', so every action has both good and bad outcomes).*

(3) We attempt to infer the 'frame of reference' within which the theorist is operating and which thus led him to enhance or to suppress the particular aspects that he chose to do. *(We shall consider what we mean by 'frame of reference' in Section 2.1. It could be many things – an ideology, a constraint imposed by technology, the models that are hidden in the use of language – in short anything that the theorist has used to construct a model of 'how-the-world-is' when he attempted to deal with the problem.)*

(4) We then repeat the process for all the competing theories.

(5) Finally we compare the various 'frames of reference' and decide which one we think to be the most valid. *(There is a problem associated with attempting to validate one 'frame of reference' relative to another, but in Section 2.2 I shall suggest that it is not insuperable.)*

1.1.12 Will such an approach be too demanding? Well, that is for the reader to decide. But the rewards for doing so are proportionately high. In my experience, good students are frustrated when they cannot integrate their knowledge of a subject. By contrast, when such students are able to make the apparently disparate theories 'fit' within a large integrated schema, they appear to find that a rewarding experience.

1.1.13 Yet even for those students who would not derive this gratification, the approach that I have suggested is still advantageous. For if they are able to understand the relationship between apparently contradictory theories they will be able to make a critical evaluation of each and thereby raise the general standard of their essay-writing.

1.1.14 The manager should find even greater rewards. He must always have sensed, however fleetingly, that the problem that he has faced, year in year out, are the fundamental issues of paragraph 1.1.9. Yet whereas previously the profusion of theories would have worried and confused him, now he can see that, thanks to the various theorists, he does not have to start, so to say, 'inventing the wheel all over again'. Even if his ultimate course is to adopt some hybrid model of his own, at least the theorists posed to him their alternatives: alternatives that gave him a 'head start' over the situation that would have existed is they had never written. His job now is to use the methodology in paragraph 1.1.11 in order to make his choice.

1.2 Authority problems peculiar to capitalism

1.2.1 We saw in paragraph 1.1.9 that in every age there have been general problems associated with the rights of one group to use another. Capitalism, however, has problems which are peculiar to itself. Marx visualized all historic social systems as having consisted of one class which exploited another. Now whereas, as is clear from my statement of the authority problem in paragraph 1.1.9, I am in agreement that groups have always exploited each other, I do not accept that it is as simple as the Marxist class emphasis would have us believe. As we shall see, members of the same class exploit each other, and members of different classes can form alliances. But that is something that will emerge later.

1.2.2 For the moment let us look at pre-capitalist society so that we may understand the essential difference that came in with industrial capitalism. The feudal lord clearly exploited his vassals. Nevertheless, at least in the early days of feudalism, both parties were bound to each other in a permanent relationship. It may have been unequal, but it was permanent: a cradle-to-grave involvement. In any event it was clearly not a contractual relationship that could be freely dissolved or renegotiated whenever one or the other party chose to do so.

1.2.3 I speak only of the era in which feudalism flourished. In the course of time this arrangement was abandoned. The reasons why feudalism's life-long interaction proved unsatisfactory to one or both parties need not concern us here. It is a contentious issue and not one we need to pursue. For we can agree that, whatever the cause, *a priori* it must have proved unsatisfactory, otherwise the relationship would not have been dissolved.

1.2.4 Vestiges of feudalism survive to this day in pockets of society, but they are clearly anachronistic in nature and therefore very rare. One such example would be the children's nannie who has been with a family for generations and who is now cared for by them in old age even though she has become an economic and social burden. Another would be the 'grace and favour' flats whch are located within the various British Royal palaces. These are in the gift of the Monarch to accommodate past servants of the Crown, whether they be nannies or widows of ex-Governor-Generals. But such patronage is alien to the spirit of capitalist so-called 'rationality'.

1.2.5 What is the spirit of rationality and from whence did it come? For our present purposes we don't need to become involved in deciding the answer to the second half of this question, other than to note that there are two basic theories. One is that the spirit of modern capitalism was the product of economic changes which became reflected in the values of protestantism (Marx), and the other is that the spirit itself is essentially that of a particular type of protestantism which became reflected in the economic life that it initiated (Weber). Whatever the cause may have been, the outcome is that *for the modern large-scale capitalist, the continued long-term economic well-being of his company is the main concern.* This continuance of the enterprise is the 'rational' goal to which he pledges himself and which becomes the focus of his attention.

1.2.6 It is important to note how this spirit differs from the greed of adventurers' capitalism, which exploited military conquest and piracy. We have only to think of the way in which an early Venetian doge would have used his profits from some trading venture in the East. Of course he might have retained enough capital to invest in another such venture, but that would have been no more than the actions of the first farmer who saved some of his harvest for 'seed-corn'. What our doge might have done was to build a palace to the glory of himself, or build a cathedral to the glory of God: but what he would not have done was to assume that the money that he had made must be ploughed back for the on-going growth and prosperity of the business.

1.2.7 By contrast, *the modern large-scale capitalist sees the long-term economic welfare of the organization as being **an end in itself.*** 'Rational' is the adjective from 'reason' and *this **end** is the **reason** behind modern capitalism.* (The reader might care to consider just how reasonable it is to adopt this attitude. It would be an omission on my part if I did not point out that making the business an **'end-in-itself'** must seem decidedly **irrational** to those persons whose culture would lead them to regard the organization as not more than a **'means-to-an-end'**!) Nevertheless, for the modern manager who is steeped in the 'rationality' of capitalism I maintain that there are two basic articles of faith, namely:

(1) *that the on-going well-being of the firm is of paramount importance,* and
(2) *that in pursuit of (1) management is obliged to minimize all known opportunity costs.*

1.2.8 Now if minimizing 'opportunity cost' is a basic tenet of capitalism then clearly the term needs to be thoroughly understood. It is a simple concept, but one that seems to cause both students and managers some difficulty. To understand it we need first to consider how we make decisions.

1.2.9 The many complex ramifications of decision-making are beyond the scope of this section. For our present purposes we need only to recognize the basic outlines of the process. In all considered decision-making we take the following three steps – even if sometimes the steps are performed very informally.

(1) We list the known available options from 1 to n.
(2) We consider the net advantages/disadvantages associated with each option relative to some scale of values that we had previously adopted, and rank the options according to that scale.
(3) We choose the highest ranking option.

1.2.10 It is noteworthy, and essential to our understanding of 'opportunity cost', to recognize that having taken one of the options, we are usually forced by that fact to relinquish all the other options that were originally open to us. For example, if I *actually* go into the city by train, I have, by that act, abandoned the original option of going by car. We should also note that all options have advantages and disadvantages. Travel by train has the advantage of allowing me to read on the train; but it may mean the jostle of the rush-hour crowds and the problem of making connections. Travel by car may be more comfortable; but there is the tedium of driving in heavy traffic and the problem of parking.

1.2.11 When I give up an option, I lose not only its disadvantages, but also its advantages. The loss of the advantage I might have had is the 'opportunity cost' that I suffer from giving up that option. It follows that we can never escape opportunity cost, for whatever we choose, there will always be some advantage associated with the discarded option which we shall lose. However, if we always choose the option which is highest on our scale of preferences, we will always minimize the opportunity costs we suffer *as represented by the values of that scale*.

1.2.12 The value scale that modern-day capitalism regards as valid is essentially economic. This is because only by sustained profitable operation can the firm hope to survive in a market economy. All other things being equal, therefore, the capitalist manager will choose the option which, over a sustained period, will minimize opportunity cost. (I do not suggest that there may not be occasions when, as we shall see, the manager may feel obliged to substitute values other than capitalist values. But there can be no doubt that, within the *mores* of capitalism, economic concepts are dominant.)

1.2.13 The effect of this concentration upon economic factors is bound to limit the degree of commitment to employees' interests that management can give, for by concentrating upon opportunity cost by the use of an **economic scale**, the manager is not necessarily minimizing opportunity cost in terms of a **social scale**, and certainly not in terms of the employee's scale of social values. For example, the loss-making section of a firm which cannot be made profitable (and which can be closed without creating a still greater threat to the survival of the firm) will be closed. If management were to keep it open, then the money that they could have saved by closing it would be a cost to the firm. This could have been avoided by taking advantage of the opportunity of the alternative course of action, namely closure. In other words, keeping the section open would not have minimized the firm's opportunity cost.

1.2.14 Of course, in the interest of humanity and of industrial peace, managements will redeploy workers when they can. But there is no neo-feudal 'grace and favour' concept that will induce them to support the worker in his search for a livelihood beyond a point of relatively minor inconvenience to the welfare of the firm. In recognition of this, and despite all the reasons that I shall elsewhere give for making capitalism my preferred system, it must be admitted that the articles of faith that I gave in paragraph 1.2.7 as fundamental to capitalism are a great handicap to the creation of any coherent motivation theory within the capitalist system. Let us consider why.

1.2.15 Under capitalism one group of people, senior management, attempts to engage in a co-operative exercise with two other groups of people, namely subordinate managers and workers. However, as we have seen, senior management's commitment to the other two parties must be of a very limited nature, because it is the on-going viability of the enterprise that senior management have at heart, and thus they cannot identify too strongly with the collective or individual welfare of their employees. Yet paradoxically, and despite senior management's limited commitment to the employees, that self-same prosperity of the firm demands that they should engage the hearts and minds of their employees in the furtherance of the goals of the enterprise. Additionally they must achieve this in the face of any adverse social effects suffered by the workforce as a consequence of introducing the most economic means of production.

1.2.16 For, although it is by no means the case that modifying the means of production to make it conform to the most economic practice will necessarily have an adverse effect upon the quality of life of the worker, there is evidence enough that it often does do so. When this happens, management's decision to improve efficiency by modifying the means of production will run counter to their other objective of motivating the worker who is operating under those conditions. The incongruities in this situation have stimulated many writers to offer to us 'solutions', but that same incongruity, I shall claim, has made most of their efforts fail.

1.2.17 So, the search for economic survival in a market economy leads us to the inescapable conclusion that *a priori* there is at least the potential for conflict between senior managers on the one side, and less senior managers and workers on the other. It therefore must follow that any theorist (myself included) who seeks to show how the workforce may be motivated has to mitigate or else deny the argument that I have just expressed. He can do this by denying the validity of the argument entirely, or else by claiming that the potential conflict can be countered. The nature of this counter-claim may be either (1) that potential conflict need never develop into actual conflict, or (2) that the potential for co-operation will act as a countervailing force which will neutralize the significance of any potential for conflict. I shall suggest that, although there will be many occasions when the employee does identify with the firm, the contractual nature of his relationship with the company (the latter being represented by management) casts its shadow at all times. It is the spectre at the feast.

1.2.18 Considering that this is a book which will argue the case for the morality of a certain form of capitalist system, what I have just written may sound strangely critical. But it is only one side of the capitalist coin. I shall later argue that it is capitalism's freedom to respond to market forces (within a framework of law which acknowledges and defends contractual relationships) which makes it possible to avoid the need for centralized *economic* planning and control. I shall also argue that, by doing so, capitalism is the only system which can stave off the drift into the centralized *political* control (i.e. totalitarianism) which must follow economic central-ization as night follows day. I am therefore a convinced capitalist.

1.2.19 However, we shall do no service to the cause of capitalism by white-washing the system's problems; but even more significant would be the moral and material damage which resulted from doing so. As individuals we should do damage to our intellectual integrity, and as members of society we would also fail to build adequate institutions to meet the needs of our society if we were to disguise from ourselves certain adverse implications which flow from the *mores* of capitalism. Of these two are particularly striking:

(1) The first is a macro-economic problem. Within capitalist society market forces will not necessarily allocate goods and services in a manner that matches the moral expectations of that society of what is socially just.
(2) The second is the micro-economic problem that we have already mentioned. This is that the worker realizes that it will not be **human values** which will determine his continued employment, but **impersonal market forces**, and this affects his relationship with the firm.

1.2.20 In Western Europe the first of these problems has resulted in governments, of both left- and right-wing nature, intervening to create areas within the economy in which social need is not subject to market forces. In general, this approach has been less attractive to Americans, whose cultural tendency has always been towards 'rugged individualism' as an ideal. Consequently they have tended to be suspicious of any government 'tampering' with laissez-faire capitalism. Although I shall claim that the American reluctance to deal with the macro-economic problem has influenced their management writings, it is the micro-economic problem that has most affected their theories.

1.2.21 This micro-economic problem has dominated American management literature for almost a hundred years. It has done so because of the convolutions they have gone through to avoid accepting that it exists and is endemic. In one of the Sherlock Holmes detective stories the significant clue is not that a dog barked on the night of the crime, **but that it did not**. So too, we must attach the greatest significance to the manner in which their literature is flawed **by their refusal to admit that worker/management relationships are conditioned by the ever-present threat to the employee's livelihood of impersonal market forces.**

1.2.22 Not only does this threat hang over the employee as menacingly as the sword which hung, suspended by a single hair, above the head of Damocles, but the resentment that this engenders, which cannot be directed against anything so nebulous as 'market forces', is directed against management. In this there is some justice: for although those same market forces threaten management as much as they do the worker, marketing is part of management's responsibility, and even in the deepest recession **some** firms survive. In any instance where the firm's survival is ensured by partial dismissal of staff, those dismissed see the act as an arbitrary managerial decision. To some extent the same is true even when a firm goes into liquidation, as has been shown by the many occasions when protesting redundant workers have organized 'sit-ins' and other activities.

1.2.23 What makes the employee feel that such management decisions are arbitrary is that he senses that the code being used by management is alien to him. I do not suggest that he recognizes and takes exception to the standards of economic opportunity cost which management has applied (although some may do so). But he **does** recognize that all the reasons that **he** would give for maintaining the format of the firm are of no avail *because they are not considered sufficiently relevant.*

1.2.24 Now this is all so obvious that for it to be excluded from most American Organization and Management literature is very striking indeed. Certainly if we are to understand that literature and the theories it contains, we need to ask the question 'Why didn't the dog bark in the night?' In all the contradictions that exist among these theorists, why should the one thing upon which they are all agreed be a fallacy? For, with a few notable exceptions (such as Robert Hoxie) who stand out because

(a) they are so very different from the general run, and
(b) they have largely been ignored,

American theorists have claimed that there is no reason why the employer and the employee should not be in complete accord in a well-managed company. This claim runs like a thread through the work of people as diverse as Taylor and McGregor, who are normally seen as fundamentally at odds, and goes back, at the very least, to Taylor's paper to the American Society of Mechanical Engineers delivered in 1895.

1.2.25 Such unanimity about a fallacy suggests one or more of the following causes:

(a) independently or collectively, all the writers in question have taken a conscious decision to promote the fallacious concept because, whatever their differences, they have decided that the intellectual dishonesty that that entails is less than the good it does: in short all decide that they are justified in telling a so-called 'white-lie'; or
(b) they have independently and unconsciously adopted an assumption, and their unanimity of thought springs from their common cultural heritage which promotes the assumption and blinds them to the fallacy.

These are, so to speak, the possible positive reasons for such unanimity. Either may be reinforced

(c) when some very strong cultural taboo is at work, which makes any criticism of the fallacy seem improper. This may be because the fallacy itself is surrounded by such taboos, or because pointing out the fallacy might threaten some associated concept which is taboo. (For example, Galileo's acceptance of the theory that the Sun and not the Earth was at the centre of the then known universe was not only seen as a diminution of the Earth's significance, but also a diminution of man's significance in the order of things and particularly in the relationship in which he stood to the Creator. The Catholic Church of the day therefore made the whole subject taboo.)

1.2.26 I suggest that, to some extent, all of these causes have played their part in the widespread creation of the management fallacy that management and workers do, can, or should have identical goals. For example, the phenomenon can be explained in terms of reason (a) above, because of the need to motivate employees. Since, by definition, the word 'motivation' in management literature involves getting the employee to work towards the goals of the employer, there would be a strong impulse for writers to suggest that 'goal congruence', that is agreement upon objectives, is possible within the company. Such an impulse is made all the stronger in a society which seeks, as a matter of principle, to create institutions which are as democratic in their functioning as practical limitations will allow. In the case of reason (b), it is easy to see how sloppy thinking could shift the emphasis from the true situation (namely that the state of the company's fortunes will affect both management and worker), and to assume that this is the same thing as the fallacy (namely that management and worker interests are therefore identical). The third reason is also not difficult to understand, and is one with which many of us can sympathize. This is the fear that any criticism of any aspect of capitalism is seen as undermining the 'American way of life'. Such criticism, even from those who like myself are committed to capitalism and seek only to improve its functioning, is therefore also considered taboo.

1.2.27 *If he had not known it previously, the reader may by now have realized that theories are not only biased by the value-judgements of the theorist, but that, if he is to choose between theories, he must do so on the basis of his own value-judgements.* I would claim that the most fundamental shortcoming of our educational system is that it fails to make the majority of people aware of this, and in saying this I do not exclude graduates. Consequently, many managers and students of management have been known to suggest that, if theories involve these value-laden elements, they would be better off performing value-free actions and limiting themselves to 'practical' things. Yet it is a fallacy to imagine that theory and practice can be separated or that either can be value-free. To establish this we shall therefore turn next to these two issues.

1.3 The need for management theory

1.3.1 Practical people, and managers are essentially practical people, are given to saying, 'Ah! Yes! That's all very well in theory: but in practice....' The remark is an indication that the manager wants to get the theoretician off the stage so that he, the manager, can get on with his act.

1.3.2 Now we too shall have occasion to throw bricks at particular theories: indeed we have already indicated that, since most management theories are trying to reconcile elements which have a greater or lesser degree of incompatibility, we expect to throw bricks at quite a few. But what is fundamentally wrong with making a remark which contrasts theory with practice is that it invites us to infer that the actions of the manager are, in some way that has not been specified, theory-free.

1.3.3 This they are not: this they could never be. Every purposive act can be regarded as an attempt to produce some desired end, which we shall denote as B, by some means, which we shall call A. But it must be obvious that anyone who acts in such a way is exhibiting his belief in a causal relationship: namely a relationship in which action A will, directly or indirectly, produce result B.

1.3.4 So in the very act of managing, the manager demonstrates that he is a theorist who holds certain beliefs about how the world is. In the sphere of economics Keynes (1936; p.383) made the same point:

> the ideas of economists and political philosophers both when they are right and when they are wrong are more powerful than is commonly understood. Indeed the world is ruled by little else. Practical men, who believe themselves to be quite exempt from any intellectual influences, are usually the slaves of some defunct economist.

1.3.5 It follows (as I promised in paragraph 1.1.3 to show) that managers cannot escape theory if they are to make decisions of any type. This remains true whether these decisions are to do with the long-term strategic goals of the organization, or the decisions which need to be taken to overcome the short-term considerations of each day's operating problems, or whether they are concerned with the type of administrative arrangements necessary to implement either of the other two types of decision. For the act of all decision-making is the act of choosing from a range of actions which have theoretically related consequences. Therefore 'good' decisions (by which I mean decisions whose consequences most conform to the ideals of the decision-maker) will only be likely to result if the decision-maker (in our case the manager) has taken the following steps:

(a) He has assured himself that he has identified a sufficiently comprehensive range of theoretical models as will make it improbable that any significantly more advantageous course of action has escaped his notice.

(b) In so far as it lies within his power, he has challenged the assumptions upon which those models were founded.

(c) He has developed a set of criteria, that is to say value-laden models which embody a view of the way things should be, that he can apply to the range of options he identified in (a) above.

(d) He has used the criteria in (c) (modified by any unique circumstances or general policy) to choose from the range in (a).

1.3.6 The process is shown in Figure 1.3(a). In this example the manager has seen options A and B. By his filter he has come to the conclusion that A is much to be preferred. Option C is an option he neither saw nor considered even though there exists the possibility that it would have been the best option. This is why we argued that the manager should welcome as many theories as he can, providing he has the means of rationally discriminating between them.

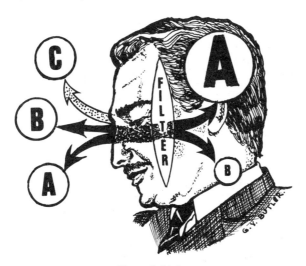

Figure 1.3(a)

1.4 The problem that deciding between theories requires us to introduce our own value-judgements

1.4.1 We saw that the decision-maker could only choose his preferred course of action by applying some yardstick or other to the options that he had available to him to discover which of them was the 'best'. But 'best' in what way? 'Best' at what cost? 'Best' for whom? All decisions involve us in defining and justifying, if not to others then certainly to ourselves, by what criteria we conclude that this goal is **better** than that goal, or this method is **better** than that method.

1.4.2 The same is true of any course of action we may advocate. However delicately or obliquely we may prescribe such action, the very fact that we are doing so shows we hold certain values to be important, and equally (in that particular context at least) that these values rank more highly for us than do other values.

1.4.3 Deciding to do one thing rather than another is a 'normative' act. Advocating that someone should do one thing rather than another is a 'normative' statement.

1.4.4 What do we mean by 'normative'? Normative is the adjective from 'norm' and a norm is that standard of behaviour or course of action which a particular individual or particular group of people regard as being right and proper in particular circumstances. Because of these implicit moral overtones the man in the street tends to recognize that such questions as 'Should murderers hang?' or 'Should abortion be legal and available on demand?' are likely to get a response that will depend upon the respondents' normative response to deeper questions.

1.4.5 Such questions might take the form 'Do I believe that human life is sacrosanct?' 'Do I really mean to appeal to some Absolute and Divine standard, as the word "sacrosanct" would imply, or was that just a sloppy English usage?'. Clearly our decisions are frequently conditioned by norms which are buried deep within us and may be quite unconsciously operating upon our judgements: an issue that we shall discuss in the next chapter. At the moment my concern is simply to get the reader to recognize that all decision-making is normative in character. Moreover, since few norms are accorded universal approval, we owe it to others, and to our own personal integrity, to examine the social, technological, economic and political norms which underlie all our decision-making.

1.4.6 The reason why I am stressing the existence of norms in all decision-making is that it is frequently unrecognized: surely a circumstance that raises questions about our educational system. Let me illustrate this with two quotes from third-year Honours Degree students in Management:

Student A: '...But I don't see **why** one has to define the sort of society one wants to bring about before one can decide upon what economic strategy a government should follow...'

Student B: '...All that **I** want to do is to show how French Railways are better than British Rail. **You** (the tutor) are the one who keeps on bringing in value-judgements...'

1.4.7 However, there is a further reason for my having stressed the normative nature of decision-making, for it presents the manager who reads this book with a problem which the student can avoid. Even after we have exposed the various frames of meaning which explain the diverse theories that have been propounded, the student can still adopt a non-allied stance. He can lift the level of his work by his new-found capacity to explain what prompted the theories without being forced to choose between them. For him there is still the luxury of philosophizing about the issues in the happy knowledge that, for a little while at least, he can enjoy sitting on the fence.

1.4.8 The position of the manager is quite different. Even if, as a result of understanding the frames of reference from which the theories spring, he is able to understand their diversity, he still has to make a positive choice from among them if he is to act. Yet where does the truth lie? According to the account given in the New Testament (John ch.18), Christ is reported as having said to Pontius Pilate, 'Everyone who is of the truth hears my voice'; to which Pilate is reported to have remarked 'What is truth?'. Given the context and the role that history chose for Pilate, his remark is often interpreted as being a piece of deep-dyed cynicism. Yet, faced as the poor man was with the truths of Rome, the truths of Christ's accusers, and now by the truth of Christ himself, is there not another interpretation? Would it not be as arguable (and certainly more charitable) to recognize in this remark the despairing cry of a man who was drowning in a sea of relativism? Faced with the 'truths' of all the theorists, is this also the unhappy fate of the manager also? It is to this problem that we now turn.

OM-B*

2

What makes one theory 'better' than another?

Nature and Nature's laws lay hid in night:
God said, Let Newton be! and all was light.
Alexander Pope (1688–1744)

It did not last: the Devil howling 'Ho!
Let Einstein be!' restored the status quo.
Sir John Collings Squire (1884–1958)

2.1 Can we not split theory into 'facts' and 'value-judgements'?

2.1.1 If I am right in suggesting that the reader of this book is more likely to be a 'doer' than a philosophizer then it is more than likely that by this stage he is asking himself why I don't at least sort out the facts from the theories. Unfortunately it's not as easy as that. Indeed, if that thought had crossed the reader's mind it would illustrate a misapprehension about the way that we take in so-called 'facts' from the world we inhabit. Whether in the 'hard science' of physics or the 'soft science' of.sociology (and management has obvious links with both) there are no 'facts' that are free of interpretation by the human mind.

2.1.2 I would not agree with those who would have us believe that there is no significant difference between such 'hard' and 'soft' sciences. The physicist draws conclusions about what is going on in the **objects** he studies. By contrast, the sociologist draws conclusions and propounds theories from analysing the behaviour of the **subjects** that he studies. *But they are subjects and and not objects.* This makes the whole study more difficult than that of, let us say, physics. Let us consider why this should be so.

2.1.3 It must be self-evident that a sociologist cannot make any sense of what is happening in the world of the people whom he is studying unless he is able to get inside their skins and see that world with their eyes: that is to say, their 'frame of reference'. Yet, unless he is merely to become one of them he must also be able to step back into another 'frame of reference', that of the sociologist, in order to achieve the very necessary perspective from which to operate as a scientist. The issue is thereby complicated to a degree not experienced by the physicist. But worse is to follow.

2.1.4 The people being studied are not insulated from the knowledge of the conclusions which the sociologist has reached. As an example let us take the concept of alienation. We shall later consider the different emphasis that various writers give to this word, but in one sense or another, all are implying that the alienated person is at odds with the world, with his fellow-men, and not least with himself. Again, although the emphasis can change from writer to writer, most sociologists suggest that placing a person in the sort of intellectually undemanding repetitive type of work that abounds in industry has a tendency to create alienation. This is a view which has become axiomatic, though it is one which we shall later question. At the moment, however, I merely seek to make the point that, true or false, the concept seeps back on to the shop-floor and enters the consciousness of the worker who is the subject of the study. It therefore becomes part of the frame of reference which he applies to the world and of his perception of himself within that world. There is therefore *a priori* reason to believe that the original theoretical conclusion reached by the sociologist will seep through to the frame of reference of his subject, and (to the extent that it materially affects the subject's future actions) become a self-fulfilling prophesy.

2.1.5 This slippage between frames of reference makes the methodological problems of the sociologist very difficult, although we could be forgiven for finding the difficulties made more so by the sociologists' choice of vocabulary; for example, Giddens (1976) finds it necessary to refer to this slippage as a 'double hermeneutic'.

2.1.6 Not that the ground of 'hard science' is so very much firmer. Indeed, the earthquake caused by Einstein's theory of relativity at the beginning of this century was strong enough to bring down the whole edifice of Newtonian physics. And secondary shock-waves were to follow, triggered by other scientists and philosophers who have warned us against ever trying to recreate such an edifice ever again.

2.1.7 For the whole approach to science in the nineteenth century, which was to try to pile up a mass of incontrovertible knowledge, is now perceived by most scientists as being a mistaken goal. Worse still, it is seen as being a goal which is fundamentally alien to the true spirit of enquiry which must be maintained if science is not to degenerate into dogma. This is one of several reasons advanced by Popper for abandoning the traditional approach to science known as induction, for the *psychological* result of attempting to prove a theory right is to become unscientifically protective towards it. Popper's approach, though it is not free of criticism, has a distinct advantage in this respect, for he advocates that the scientist should try to prove his theory wrong, rather than to prove it right. Popper's supporters would claim that this is not only *psychologically* superior, but also that it is also *logically* and *methodologically* so. (We shall touch on these issues in a moment, but if the reader is interested in a lucid readable text on Popper then Magee (1973) is such a book.)

2.1.8 Although it is always easy to be wise after the event, there were at least two reasons why, even in the nineteenth century, they might have suspected that the pillars of Newtonian science might crumble, no matter how firm they then appeared to be. The first was that, as Magee says (1973; p.29), 'it can be logically demonstrated – and had been long ago by Leibniz – that any finite number of observations can be accommodated within an indefinitely large number of different explanations'. It follows that just because the observed facts fit the explanation that the scientist proposes in his theory, it does not mean that the same facts could not equally be used to support an entirely different theory.

2.1.9 The second warning had come from Kant in the eighteenth century when he had pointed out to us that we cannot obtain any knowledge of the real world except by means of our five senses. Yet the stimuli that we so receive by means of those senses requires us to manipulate them in some way. In consequence we can never really know the world as it is: we can only know our interpretation of that world as perceived through those manipulated stimuli.

2.1.10 These then are the reasons that we cannot split the world into 'fact' and 'theory'. This is why the laws of Newtonian science had been proved wrong after 200 years of so-called 'verification'. For they had not, as everybody supposed, come from the world of 'facts'. They had come from the world of Newton's imagination.

2.1.11 So, partly because more than one theory will fit the 'facts' and partly because those 'facts' are the modified and interpreted stimuli that our senses have received, we should approach all theories, whether in 'hard' or 'soft' science, very warily. This does not mean that we should abandon theory; for, as we saw in Section 1.3, without theory we should be incapable of rational action. What it does mean is that we should approach each theory with a humble awareness of our very tentative grasp upon the truth.

2.1.12 Incidentally, the realization that the same set of observations could be used to substantiate more than one theory is the reason why Popper's approach of trying to prove a theory wrong, that is to say to 'falsify' it, is *logically* superior to trying to prove it right. There is an asymmetrical relationship, because if the observations do not support the theory then it must fall, whereas if the observations do support the theory it doesn't necessarily stand.

2.1.13 The reason why Popper's approach of attempting to 'falsify' theories instead of trying to 'verify' them is claimed to be *methodologically* superior is seen if we consider that we can boil a million pans of water at 100°C at sea-level and learn nothing. It is only when we take the pan up the mountain that we find that it boils at a lower temperature because of the lower atmospheric pressure. Yet, if we do not *methodologically* attempt to falsify the theory, and therefore to take the water up the mountain as part of a methodological programme which attempts to *disprove* that water will always boil at 100°C, we shall only make such a discovery by blind chance.

2.1.14 Thus our attitude to theory, like our attitude to so many other things, proves to be most realistic when it is ambivalent. We need to develop theories to guide our steps, yet anything less than a healthy scepticism for all theory, whether in 'hard' or 'soft' science, will itself be unscientific.

2.1.15 We therefore return to the problem we posed at the end of paragraph 1.1.11. If we were to attempt to expose the 'frame of reference' of each theorist in order to decide which one we would choose to adopt as the basis of management action, are we put in the position of having to find some sort of platform, some 'super frame of reference' from which to judge? Secondly, in default of finding and justifying such a platform, are we bound to wallow in a sea of relativism? It is to these questions that we next turn.

2.2 The Gordian knot of relative 'frames of reference'

2.2.1 We said earlier (paragraph 2.1.3) that the sociologist needs to get inside the skins of the people he studies and then to climb back into his own skin for the purposes of assessment. Suppose that we are sociologists who have succeeded in getting into the skin of an African witch-doctor and of seeing the world with his eyes. Only so could we make sense of his frame of reference. How did we do this? We did it by accepting his yardsticks. Any other yardstick would, by definition, make the witch-doctor's actions meaningless mumbo-jumbo. The difficulty is that if we accept his yardstick, it can *never* be mumbo-jumbo! We have pre-ordained that he will always be right. But worse is to follow.

2.2.2 If we go through exactly the same procedure with a Harley Street physician we shall equally always prove him right. Now comes the sixty-four thousand dollar question: *'How do we choose between the witch-doctor's truth and the physician's truth?*, or, more generally, *How do we mediate between different frames of reference?* Such a question is frequently seen as requiring us to build some 'super frame of reference' from which to dispense justice. This sounds like a very unlikely possibility.

2.2.3 Yet if, as is often suggested, there is no possibility of justifying the basis upon which we can attribute a greater truth to this third frame of reference than we did to the other two, then the methodology we proposed in paragraph 1.1.11 will meet an insuperable problem. For there we instructed the manager to compare the various frames of reference and decide which one we consider to be the most valid. It now appears possible that he will not be able to comply with the very thing that we asked him to do!

2.2.4 By now the 'practical' student or manager will be incensed; and rightly so. It is not difficult to imagine them refusing even to contemplate the idea that, if a parent has a sick child, he would have any problem in deciding whom to send for, witch-doctor or physician. For, if there really **is** no way of mediating between frames of reference, that would be the result... but of course that is precisely the reason I chose this example: to commit the reader to the belief that it **is** possible to mediate between different frames of reference, even though it is difficult. Yet, that having been said, I must warn the reader that if he were philosophically to attempt to justify choosing the physician's frame of reference in preference to the witch-doctor's, with arguments which did more than rely upon his cultural affinity to the one rather than the other, he would find it incredibly difficult.

2.2.5 After acknowledging the difficulty, I suspect that most philosophers would conclude that **some** mediation between frames is possible. Pears (1971; p.19) does so. He was referring to this very same problem in the field of philosophy itself, for, given **his** frame of reference of what philosophy was about, Bertrand Russell was completely unable to appreciate the later work of Wittgenstein. Yet, despite their different yardsticks Pears dares to believe that some mediation between their frames of reference should have been possible. He says;

> The predicament...occurs in many places where criticism and evaluation are needed. Something has to be measured, but when we set about the task, we find that the first thing to be done is to select the right scale of measurement. But what is the right scale? If there is no objective way of arriving at the answer to this question, how are we to start? It would be harsh to judge a work by some totally alien standard, but it would be silly to allow it to dictate the standard to be used simply with a view to its own success. Everything is the size that it is, and extreme tolerance will end in tautology and banality.

2.2.6 Interestingly enough, although Pears is seeking to mediate between philosophies and **not** management theories, he proposes, (pp.19–20), the identical means of resolution that I proposed, namely, to go back to their roots.

> ...[T]he predicament is not quite as difficult as it appears to be...[T]he different ways in which the rival claimants have developed from their common origin can be described and to some extent justified. So when they try to shout each other down, we need not listen. We can ignore the bedlam, and attain some degree of objectivity by tracing the divergent ways in which they have developed from a single starting point.

This then is **our** philosophic justification, and we believe it will be more than vindicated by what the process turns up in the course of the book.

2.2.7 Such vindication will often speak to us with the truth of a parable, not unlike the incident in one of G.K. Chesterton's novels. A young man is 'sent down' (expelled) from Oxford for chasing a don over the roofs of the college while armed with a revolver. The incident ends with the don clinging precariously to a pinnacle and begging for his life. Since it is a typical Chesterton story there is a twist. The don is the tutor of the young man and a nihilist philosopher. Nihilism is a philosophy of the most negative scepticism which the young man was sure was wrong but against whose arguments he was intellectually helpless... until he thought of this way of getting the don to renounce the validity of negativism. And what a superb argument it was despite its simplicity! Chesterton, a staunch Catholic, has made his point and none of his readers can ever again regard nihilism as the repository of truth – for we see the fundamental absurdity of its claims.

2.2.8 The reader may feel that there could be no such parallel to the Chesterton story in management theory. I believe that there is an almost exact parallel in the work of the **neo-human relations school** of writers. The late Abraham Maslow was the founding father of this school and in the Appendix to this book I have commented at length upon his theory. However, I wish to anticipate some of my comments there, and suggest that Maslow's is a view of society which invites us to apply to it the Chesterton treatment. For, whereas nihilism was absurdly negative, Maslow takes such a positive view of life that it reaches levels that can also be little short of absurd. Among other things, we shall see that he implies that anyone in American society who seeks to gratify his need for safety has little legitimate reason for doing so and must be suspected of being neurotic.

2.2.9 Now it is true that Maslow's style of writing is such that it could be argued that he never really meant this because of various little disclaimers in the text. I shall attempt to give enough quotes in the Appendix to allow the reader to judge for himself. For my part, I find it difficult to avoid the conclusion that he believes that no healthy American has any legitimate unsatisfied safety needs, since there is nothing to fear. It seems to be an ideal case for the Chesterton treatment. We might ask ourselves such questions as 'I wonder if Maslow ever locked his door?' 'I wonder if he ever walked down dark alleys with $10 bills sticking out of his pocket?' 'I wonder whether he was ever one of the mass of unemployed?' The result of such questions would certainly be to impress upon the reader that, whether it was Maslow's intention to adopt this position or not, it is certainly a position which, if adopted, could rightly be regarded as absurd.

2.2.10 Moreover, we shall see that Douglas McGregor (of whom Maslow approves and whose work is based upon Maslow's theories) ignores the whole issue of safety as a motivator, even though the philosopher Hobbes (who wrote in 1651) saw safety needs as being man's main motivator and the reason why man was prepared to make himself subservient to, and to be bound by, a higher authority. Hobbes's claim is that man deliberately reduces his own liberty in order to induce others to do the same (Hobbes, 1973; p.65). By this means he avoids 'continuall feare, and danger of violent death: And the life of man, solitary, poore, nasty, brutish, and short.' It is for this reason that Hobbes regarded it as a second law of nature (Hobbes, 1973; p.67) 'That a man be willing, when others are so too, as farre-forth, as for Peace, and defence of himselfe he shall think it necessary, to lay down his right to all things; and be contented with so much liberty against other men, as he would allow other men against himselfe.'

2.2.11 When one tries to explain the existence of trade unions without including some reference to a search for safety, it is clear that the neo-human relations position, which, by the most likely interpretation **denies** the need to seek safety, and by the most generous interpretation **ignores** the need, is on either count somewhat absurd. Indeed, if the reader ultimately is brought to choose between McGregor's position and mine, it will be his sense of the absurd that will mediate between our two frames of reference. However, it would not be fitting to leave this topic without a word of warning.

2.2.12 Alexander the Great sidestepped the puzzle of the Gordian knot. He sliced through it with his sword. If we are to mediate between frames of meaning we have to avoid the maze of relativism. Only by getting back to the basics of the problem and then by slicing our way through with our sense of absurdity can we make any reliable judgements. But we must beware. Absurdity is a two-edged sword. Once upon a time it was absurd to believe that the Earth was round. The assumptions in our own conceptual models may be absurd, and never more so that when they are **unconscious** assumptions.

2.3 The dangers of unconscious modelling

2.3.1 It would not be surprising if readers who have not been exposed to any writing concerning the nature of perception should find it difficult to believe that there can exist any amount of unconscious bias. It is therefore very important that any such reader should be converted to a realization of the extent of such bias as quickly as possible, and for two reasons:

(i)   If he is not convinced of the extent of such bias he will not seek for it as diligently as he should, either in his own or in other people's thought.

(ii) If he is not convinced of it he will tend to attribute any distortion to the **conscious** bias of its author, thereby doubting the intellectual integrity of an honest writer. It was Popper who pointed out that objectivity in science is not achieved by the objectivity of the scientist, but by the fact that he publishes and exposes his ideas to the attacks of others. It is not conceivable that any significant number of theorists would be dishonest. It is even more inconceivable that they would then publish. There are exceptions. The human skull with the ape-like jaw and known as the 'Piltdown Man' (since it was found at Piltdown in Sussex in 1912) was discovered after over 40 years to have been a complete hoax. But I am not suggesting that we do not challenge any and every theory. I only suggest that we assume intellectual honesty in the theorist.

I must declare an interest in getting students to look for unconscious modelling beyond the good that it does them. That is the good that it does me. Many of the views I have discarded over the years have been dropped because my students rightly concluded that my models were also due for a challenge. Here is an example. Bureaucracy is a particular type of authority system which we shall discuss in paragraphs 9.5.7 and 8. In common with many textbooks on the topic I used to teach that in bureaucracies nepotism is not only rare, but few people **suspect** the system of being corrupt.

The naivety of this statement caused one of my students from a developing country to peal with laughter. After some discussion I realized that he was absolutely right in his contention that bureaucracy is a marvellous machine for transmitting the *norms* of the top people. If they are corrupt then bureaucracy is a marvellous machine for the spread of corruption. It has been our good fortune in the West that most bureaucracies have been headed by relatively honest people. Needless to say, my original inference, namely that bureaucracies are *in essence* not corrupt, has long since been dropped from my lectures!

2.3.2 But perhaps the best way to convince the reader of his own unconscious modelling is to give him an exercise to perform. This is to examine the models hidden in a typical school history question, namely 'What were the causes of the French Revolution?' Now this question is 'loaded'. The examiner has, perhaps unconsciously, put a bias into the question. If the reader did not discover this bias and were to accept the question at its face value, then he would also have accepted this same bias. (Incidentally, in dealing with this problem it is quite unnecessary for the reader to need to know any history other than that there **was** an event called the French Revolution in which the monarchy was overthrown in favour of a republic.) Here is the problem: 'What **is** the bias, and how **does** the way the question is posed introduce that bias?'

2.3.3 I would suggest that the reader pauses at this point for a few minutes to attempt to solve this problem before continuing.

_____ P A U S E   F O R   D E L I B E R A T I O N _____

2.3.4 I do not doubt that there is more than one hidden model in the problem. It is therefore entirely possible that the reader has seen something other than the example that I shall present. Nevertheless it must be conceded that the question invites us to view society as **static** – sitting, as it were, like a vase on a table and requiring some external agency (such as a clumsy cat) to knock it off.

2.3.5 Yet such a view is highly questionable. Would it not have been at least as appropriate a view (if not better) to have seen society as existing in a precarious state of dynamic equilibrium? It is then better expressed by the imagery of a circus troupe on the high-wire than by the imagery of the vase and the clumsy cat. If the examiner who set the question had seen the issue in **these** terms then he would have asked an entirely different question, and perhaps one that would lead on to far more significant answers from the students being examined. He might then have had the insight to ask 'What combination of forces preserved the stability of French pre-Revolution society **for so long?**'

2.3.6 This, as we can see, is the complete inversion of the other question. Moreover, it too could be seen to contain hidden models. 'What exactly do we **mean** by "society"?' is a very interesting question. Indeed, in paragraph 2.3.22 I shall refer to a publication entitled *The Corporate Report*, and I shall there suggest that it was the failure to identify what is meant by the word 'society' which was largely responsible for the fact that its authors were unaware of the confusion of their models or the failure in the logic of their argument. For all language is full of hidden models which will entrap the unwary; yet it would not be surprising if the reader were unaware of this 'coloration' that language lends to ideas: after all, it took one of the most gifted philosophers of this century half a lifetime to realize it. Magee (1978; p.126) says that 'Russell...tells...how, until he was in his mid-forties – by which time he had done all the philosophy for which he is most famous – he "had thought of language as transparent".'

2.3.7 But language is far from transparent: at best it gives the coloration of a stained-glass window, while at worst it refracts and distorts ideas to an incredible degree. The *Bullock Report* (Bullock; 1977) advocated that industrial democracy should be promoted by worker participation on the boards of the companies in which they worked. For reasons that will emerge as we look at the problems of organization and management, I am opposed to such a move. That, however, it not the point at issue here. The question to which we address ourselves now is that of whether the language then used created hidden models *which, quite unconsciously, distorted the issues.* Although the Bullock proposals never came to anything at the time, the basic issue keeps reappearing, with the Social Democratic Party making it a part of their political platform in 1982 and the Labour Party doing the same in 1983. Moreover, since it is an issue that impinges on the central problem of all societies (as outlined in paragraph 1.1.9), it is a problem which we must assume will continually arise.

2.3.8 The *Bullock Report* (1977) suggested that, for companies over a certain size, worker-directors should be able to participate, as of right, in running the companies in which they worked. Bullock (1977) advocated that they should have as many seats on the board as those directors who represented management, while there would also be an unspecified number of independent directors. This arrangement became known in management jargon as the '$2x + y$' formula: that is to say x management-directors, x worker-directors and y independent directors.

2.3.9 The response to the *Report*'s publication was to engender a spate of articles and letters in every type of journal in the United Kingdom. These came from all quarters and were often expressed in terms of considerable passion. Yet, so far as I am aware, in all this flurry of activity no one suggested that both the confusion and the passion were the result of the word 'participation' having muddied the pool.

2.3.10 This is because the word 'participation' is a model. It is not a 'neutral' word: on the contrary, it is highly charged with particularly attractive 'value-meanings'. Many words have this quality; 'mother-love' is such a word. If I were to declare myself against 'mother-love' I should be considered a monster. Similarly, those who were **against** 'participation' were treated as monsters by those who were **for** it. What was not recognized was that this problem was caused by the very use of the word 'participation' which prejudged the whole issue.

2.3.11 'Participation' carries within itself the concept of two or more parties, who are fundamentally agreed on the basic aims which they are seeking to achieve, and who have got together to discuss any minor matters of difference such as the detailed ways and means which will be used to achieve this common goal. The concept of participation crept into management language under the subtle, but extremely powerful influence of the neo-human relations school. We shall deal later with the detail of this school's approach to the problems of management. At this point I merely wish to register that the approach assumes that there need be no conflict between management and worker, providing that management confers adequately with the worker. There are therefore at least four implicit assumptions in this approach. The first is that management's position is that which any 'reasonable' person would adopt, providing that he had had it properly explained to him. The second is related to the first, and is that all men of good will will think alike. The third is that conflict is therefore avoidable, and the fourth is that that it should therefore be so avoided. It is, in fact, a strongly unitary view of the way the world is. This word 'unitary' and its contrasting concept of 'pluralist' need explanation before we discuss further the concept of 'participation'.

2.3.12 Those who believe that the various factions in society have a right to their perspective of 'the-way-the-world-is' are **pluralist**. Those who believe that there is only one valid view are **unitary** in their attitude. This is not the place to follow up all the implications of these two concepts, other than to warn of the dangers of unitary views. More aspects will emerge during the course of this book. All I will ask the reader to consider now is how he would answer these questions:

(1) *Does he believe that people will, given freedom, develop different perceptions of the-way-the-world-is?*
(2) *Does he feel so convinced of his own view of the-way-the-world-is that when it differs from theirs he is prepared to say that they are mistaken and he is right?*
(3) *If he feels that they are wrong but finds them still stubbornly clinging to their beliefs, is he prepared to tolerate their attitude or will he make them conform by force of any kind? (This includes passing legislation to outlaw them or the practice of their beliefs.)*

Now clearly some views and some practices will not be tolerated in society because of their inherently immoral nature in the eyes of the generality of people in that society. But the dangers are surely apparent. Unitary attitudes are the highway to most of the hells that man has created on this planet. Moreover, most of these hells were created for the best of reasons. As Magee says (1973; p.91):

> although the practical consequences of reactionary and Utopian theories are
> societies like those of Hitler and Stalin the desire for a perfect society is not
> rooted in wickedness, but the reverse. The most horrific excesses have been
> perpetrated with sincere moral conviction by idealists whose intentions are
> wholly good; like those, for example of the Spanish Inquisition.

2.3.13 In the realms of management theory, unitary views usually reduce to the question 'Is the view of management the only valid one?' If the reader answers 'Yes!' to that question, then let him beware of the path he is treading. We shall further develop this issue later. Meanwhile, let me declare an interest. I have a very clear idea of what for me constitutes the 'best' society. It is *that society that can tolerate the greatest number of individual views.*

2.3.14 It would be wrong to claim that those who were in favour of the Bullock proposals were all unitary in their views and all who were against were pluralist. Those trade unionists who were favourably disposed towards the Bullock proposals were those who saw the proposals as offering to the employees the means whereby they could obtain a grip upon the levers of industrial power. Of these, some would doubtless have been unitarist and seeking a way to put power solely into the hands of the workers. Others would have been pluralists, seeking only sufficient power from the proposals as would redress the balance of power between capital and labour to a point that they thought more appropriate. Clive Jenkins, the General Secretary of the Association of Scientific, Technical and Managerial Staffs, and a member of the Bullock Committee, was one who argued thus (Jenkins, 1977).

2.3.15 From my analysis of the reasons why many trade unionists opposed the proposals, they would appear to have fallen into two groups. The first of these contained both unitarists and pluralists. The main objection of this group to the proposals was because they wanted to obtain more power but they were unconvinced that the proposals would achieve that end. The second group was made up almost exclusively of pluralists, and the nature of their objection was one which finds enormous and widespread support among British trade unionists, and, as we shall later see, has been cogently argued by Clegg. This group maintained that if worker-directors (who were assumed to be union representatives) joined such a board, then, *to the extent that they **did** co-operate, they would have lost their true and traditional function.*

2.3.16 Hugh Scanlon, the retiring president of the Amalgamated Union of Engineering Workers, having made this point, wrote as follows, (*Sunday Times* 29 Jul. 1978): 'It is an essential fabric of our democracy to have free and independent trade unions to represent all employees' views under private enterprise. Moreover this independence can be best maintained through the machinery adopted by workers to represent their views, namely, collective bargaining.'

2.3.17 Whether pluralist or unitary in his view, virtually every manager was opposed to the proposals. Even the Bullock Committee itself was split, with three of its members who were company chairmen dissenting from the majority report. These managers, in their minority report, objected that the Committee had only been asked **how** and not **whether** there should be worker-directors. The most frequent criticism of the proposals expressed at the time by managers was that the boardroom would be changed from a place in which those with similar norms co-operate (for it has been shown that shareholding and non-shareholding management have similar *mores*), to a battlefield ravaged by ideological differences during which the firm is wrecked by lack of direction.

2.3.18 All of this historical commentary is offered as background material to make clear the importance of the hidden models in language. For, although those managers and trade unionists who objected to the Bullock proposals gave arguments to defend their positions, they nevertheless found themselves being pilloried as reactionaries. This was basically unjust, and clearly many of them felt it to be so. Yet to judge from the speeches and correspondence of the time, none of them seemed to see what it was that had put them in such a false position. The culprit was the word 'participation' which, as we saw in paragraph 2.3.11, is a value-laden word which presumes that the 'participants' share the same goals.

2.3.19 Yet we have already seen that this is can clearly not be the case. Managers are basically committed to serving the long-term interests of the company and, when circumstances make this necessary, may do so at the expense of the employees' interests. Employees are committed to serving their own interests and, when circumstances make this necessary, may do so at the expense of the company. Consequently, neither the managers nor the union representatives who opposed the Bullock proposals could honestly answer 'Yes!' to the question with which, in effect, they had been faced. This was 'Are you for, or against, warm, cuddly, sociable participation? Answer "Yes" or "No"!' No wonder they were frustrated. It was a trick question and hopelessly loaded.

2.3.20 From the managers' standpoint they sensed that if they voted for 'participation' they might get 'power-struggle'. From the union standpoint it nullified all their historic claims to opposition and made their past opposition appear sterile and illegitimate. Either way these two camps were being asked a totally loaded question and the loading was all in that one value-laden word.

2.3.21 The lesson is not that people are as intellectually dishonest as asking such a loaded question would appear to make them. The lesson is that the world is full of such language traps which are only of late being recognized. One psychiatrist (Laing, 1965; p.20) complains that we shall never be able to deal with the totality-of-someone-as-a-person so long as the very language of psychiatry and psychoanalysis 'split men up verbally'. For by using the language we do we get a 'shattered Humpty-Dumpty who cannot be put together again by any number of hyphenated or compound words: psycho-physical, psycho-somatic, psycho-biological, psycho-pathological, psycho-social, etc., etc.'. How far this all seems from Russell's early belief that language is 'transparent'!

2.3.22 The sloppy use of the word 'participation' during the Bullock controversy was (as I have suggested and will later amplify) caused by the equally sloppy acceptance of the unitary views of the neo-human relations writers. I equally believe that, only the adoption of these writers' views, with the corresponding denial of the existence of any valid conflict situations, could explain the failure in elementary logic in *The Corporate Report*, which is the subject of our next example. I shall argue that such a basic mistake could not have been perpetrated unless its authors had visualized 'society' as *a relatively homogeneous institution of a unitary character in which sectional interests are to be considered invalid.* The totalitarian implications of such an image are frightening. They are all the more so if one believes, as I do, that its authors had absolutely no realization of what they **had** implied.

2.3.23 *The Corporate Report* (ASSC, 1975) is clearly normative in character in that it deals with what a company's accounts **ought** to contain when reporting to the interested parties in society. Nor should it be criticized upon those grounds, for it is entirely proper that the accounting bodies of the UK should concern themselves with the ethical norms of their profession. The report was the product of the Accounting Standards Steering Committee, whom they instructed to look into the matter of what should be reported and to whom.

2.3.24 In their *Report* the Committee listed the various interested parties in society and gave the reasons why they might have an interest in the company's affairs. So far, so good. But then the *Report* takes the absolutely illogical and gratuitous step of equating this 'interest in knowing' with the conclusion that such an interest confers 'the right to know'. But clearly there are many things that I have an interest in knowing that I can conceive no possible reason for my having the right to know. The failure in logic is so ridiculously obvious that we have to explain how a number of intelligent people could get together and make it without at least one of their number realizing that they had done so. For example, it is in the interest of a potential car-buyer to know that a new model is about to come on the market. This knowledge will allow him to avoid buying the new but obsolete stock which is in the pipeline between the manufacturer and the general public. However, if the manufacturers and dealers are not to be left with a damaging amount of stock which can only be sold at sacrificial prices, it is in their interest to maintain silence about the new model. Do they have such a right? I believe that they do. But in any event they are entitled to expect a reasoned argument before losing such a right. Yet nowhere in *The Corporate Report* do we find an argument which shows why such a firm should lose this right.

2.3.25 *The Corporate Report* does not indicate whether such an example as the one I have given would come within the scope of reporting, but it certainly claims the right to spread its net wide, and, in any case, the example will stand for parallel examples which could be considered as certainly within the *Report*'s sphere of interest and of recommendation. Nor can we accept the fact that it is a 'discussion document' as reason for not laying out the full case for discussion. It is clear that this error in logic is a blind spot for which we must attempt to account. To maintain that it is **not** an error in their logic it is necessary to maintain that everyone in society should adopt an identical viewpoint. If that were so it would be logical to apply the following rationale to the ethics of their profession:

(i)   Accountants owe prime allegiance to the good of 'society' ('society' being undefined but its meaning conceived of as some relatively homogeneous body which transcends sectional interest).
(ii) Such a view of society means that, even if there are sectional interests, they are illegitimate.
(iii) Since they are illegitimate their appeals for confidentiality are, *ipso facto*, illegitimate and need not be discussed.

For my part I am convinced of two things. The first is that this indeed was the thinking which underlay *The Corporate Report*. The second is that it is more than likely that none of those committee members would be very happy about the totalitarian overtones contained in this denial of sectional rights. In other words, the report was created by people who were, at that time, holding unconsciously the beliefs in (i) to (iii) above, because the euphoria from neo-human relations 'brotherhood' concepts had anaesthetized their critical faculties.

2.3.26 It is clear therefore that, whether we are aware of it or not, we have each adopted a value-loaded way of looking at the world. In many books this highly personal way of seeing things is referred to by a somewhat forbidding title: it is known as a person's *'Weltanschauung'*, (pronounced 'velt/an/sh/ow/ung'). We too will use this German expression because there is no English equivalent expression with quite the same meaning. When we do so it will contain the following concepts.

2.3.27 To make sense of the world, each of us needs to create for himself a pair of very special 'spectacles'. Wearing these 'spectacles' is vital to us, for without them we would be quite incapable of arranging and giving meaning to the stimuli that we receive from the world about us, and without that capacity we couldn't cope. Yet these same 'spectacles' also distort and colour the way that we see things. This distortion is the price we pay in making sense of what is 'out there'. For in the process of trying to create a coherent interpretation of what we see, we are driven to choose certain 'sets' or 'clusters' of ideas which are mutually compatible. The corresponding action is that we also reject other ideas which, had they been introduced, would have proved to be incompatible. The effect of this is that the value-laden elements in the individual's *Weltanschauung* corroborate each other, so reinforcing his belief in the validity of his vision precisely because the contrary elements that would have introduced doubt have been filtered out. It is therefore necessary to have a shorthand way of saying all of this, and *Weltanschauung* has the advantage of being difficult to overlook.

2.3.28 Because this is part of the human condition, no writer can avoid feeding into his work elements that reflect the values which, consciously and unconsciously, have gone into his *Weltanschauung*. Yet what one person will value, another will not. It is therefore in the nature of things that such elements in any writer's work should be the subject of controversy, and in evaluating the pros and cons of such a controversy it would serve no useful purpose to pretend that the specific statement or position which a writer had adopted was independent of an underlying, more general, set of values. To pretend that this were so would be like pretending that the spots had a significance which was independent of the measles that caused them. So, although the specific writer's work may help to diagnose his more general *Weltanschauung*, we must turn to the latter if we are to discover anything meaningful in the evaluation of competing theories.

2.3.29 For the writer and reader alike, this situation has far-reaching implications. It means, for example, that it would be absurd of the reader to regard the introduction of such coloration into a writer's work as something to be deplored...for how can that which is inevitable be regarded as either wilful or improper? On the other hand, neither party can ignore that the coloration exists. There is little a writer can do about any unconscious values he may have adopted. But in so far as a writer's propositions are a reflection of the consciously adopted values of his *Weltanschauung*, he has a moral obligation to expose to his readers any such values of which he is aware. The reason why he has this duty is that, if he does not, he is either inviting his readers, by default, to imagine that his statements are value-free, or alternatively he is putting them to the quite inexcusable trouble of attempting to discover for themselves what his assumed values are. This they can only do obliquely, for they have nothing more to guide them than the inferences that they can draw from his text.

2.3.30 It is perhaps surprising that more writers do not do this, for, once a writer has fulfilled his obligation to make his *Weltanschauung* explicit, he will have 'paid his dues' to the cause of being intellectually honest with himself and his audience. That done, there is no reason why even the most punctilious of academics should not be a propagandist for a particular viewpoint. Consequently one would have thought that (unless writers are ashamed of their respective belief-systems) more of them would have welcomed the freedom to be propagandist that such openness granted to them. Nor, in the light of what I have just said, do I think I need to explain further why this is the position which I have adopted. As we have seen, there is no way in which an author can avoid the problem of his work being value-loaded. That being so, the only matter in doubt is whether those who do not make their position explicit have failed in their obligations to their readers by accident or design.

2.3.31 I have so far spoken of the individual's *Weltanschauung*, and we have seen how that it is both inevitable and value-laden. However, it is not perhaps surprising to find that certain ways of looking at the world are more common than others. We have seen that it is a requirement of a person's *Weltanschauung* that the concepts it contains should 'fit' well enough to produce models of the world with enough internal consistency to permit him to function. For this reason he is selective in the concepts he accepts or rejects. Consequently, when those who share a common *Weltanschauung* become aware of it and begin publicly to express their identification with those views, it is not surprising that they form a mutually supportive group, giving a title to the perceptions that they hold and seeing them as alien to those of other groups with different views.

2.3.32 I shall maintain that this is how ideology is born. I make the point for two reasons. The first is that the meanings given to the word 'ideology' are so many and varied that if someone chooses to use it he must, in fairness to his audience, define precisely what he means by it. The second is in order that the reader will understand that, unless I specifically qualify a particular use of the word, its meaning in this book is entirely neutral. This is an important point to make because these days 'ideology' is used more often than not disparagingly. Yet if by my definition it is a universal phenomenon, and we are all ideologists of one sort or another, then it must in this book be seen as neutral.

2.4 Dealing with ideological concepts in Organization and Management

2.4.1 To say that we use the word 'ideology' neutrally does not mean that every ideology is equally true or false, so we still have the problem of how to choose between them. We are therefore back to the problem of mediating between frames of reference which we discussed in Section 2.2. There I suggested that the answer was to look at the basic problem that was being considered, and to regard the various theories in terms of how well they dealt with the problem, using as a criterion our sense of the absurd. Yet this, in effect, merely pushes the problem back one stage further, unless we can justify that same 'sense of the absurd'.

2.4.2 The disparagement that is normally associated with the word 'ideology' most commonly implies that there **is** an absurd gulf between 'reality' and the views which the person has espoused, which makes both the person and the views false and arbitrary. From what we have so far said it is clear that, although the ideology and the person may exhibit these characteristics, it can never be the case that they can be condemned *purely and simply* for having a value-laden view of the world, since there is no such thing available to them as a value-free alternative. That being so, to demonstrate that any ideology was absurd would require us to show one or more of the following conditions:

(1) that it failed in its own internal logic, or
(2) that it required us to deny a truth as a condition of its operation, or
(3) that it required us to believe in something fantastic as a condition of its operation.

2.4.3 However, of these three objections only the first could ever claim any degree of demonstrable objectivity, for what represents 'truth' or what is 'fantastic' is dependent upon the standpoint of the commentator. Does this mean we are back to the problem of being lost in a slough of relativism? I think not. First of all, if I were to ignore all the problems of perception and interpretation which attend any attempt to get at the truth, I should be declaring my belief in what Bronowski (1973; p.367) so aptly called 'monstrous certainty', and which he so rightly identified with totalitarianism. There is nothing wishy-washy in insisting upon the legitimacy of doubt. Secondly, although I admit that those with another standpoint might find my position as absurd as I find theirs, yet this does not means that there is nothing to choose between our respective views. For I shall seek to identify to the reader the reasons for the respective standpoint differences, and couple this with an explanation of why I consider mine preferable. Given the problems of knowledge, there is no highway to

'Truth'. But by reviewing the major alternatives it is probable that one will have greater appeal to the reader than the other(s). If so, he will avoid the distress and/or inertia which often accompanies the feeling that 'everything is relative'. But I suggest that he is being offered more than this psychological crutch. What he gets is a reasoned basis for contrasting and comparing the values and assumptions which his position applies to social, technical economic and political 'facts' with those applied by others.

2.4.4 There is a certain class of ideology which claims to transcend our existing experience and to demand that its disciples make an act of faith which may well fly in the face of current evidence. To a certain type of individual the transcendent nature of the claims has tremendous appeal. But for myself (and I trust, for the reader) though such ideologies are not necessarily false, their position is such that they invite scepticism. Such ideologies, for reasons I shall now explain, I term *Mosaic-myth ideologies*.

2.4.5 Using the definition of ideology that I gave in Section 2.3, it would be true to say that everyone adopts one ideology or another. But (using that same definition) it would not be true to say that every one of these ideologies will claim to be able to show us the way to a new and better society...a promised land. Some do however, and therefore, by my definition, they form a subset of ideologies in general. Lewis S. Feuer (1975; p.105) whose definition of the word 'ideology' is different from mine and relates only to this subset, claims that 'every ideology [of this type] ...incorporates a variant of the Mosaic myth, a conception of an elite, a historically chosen class and an emerging higher society'. For this reason I have picked up his imagery and chosen to refer to the ideologies of this subset as 'Mosaic-myth' ideologies. It is the nature of things that Mosaic-myth ideologies, with their strong emphasis upon what society 'should' be like, will be more prone to contrast their vision of the future with the experiences that we have encountered in present society. This being so, sceptics typically require those who support such ideologies to explain why, to date, we have seen no evidence to indicate that if we follow their path, we shall come to the promised land. It is scarcely surprising that we should find that all Mosaic-myth ideologies should stress the **falseness of our experience to date** and the truth of a whole new experience that awaits us when we reach the promised land.

2.4.6 Now, although the transcendent nature of such a gospel is the thing that makes it appeal to its adherents, it must be said that this denial of current experience does little to reassure the sceptic, particularly when he finds that all evidence from current society which does not support the new vision is usually declared invalid. Thus American liberals, whose vision of the promised land contains the belief that conflict is both undesirable and eradicable, strongly renounce the validity of any current evidence which might suggest that it is neither. Marxists similarly go so far as to declare that capitalism has created in those who do not accept their position a 'false consciousness' of reality. By so doing, they destroy the validity of all who would challenge their 'monstrous certainty,' and of any evidence that might be used by that person to do so, because his 'false consciousness' has determined what he selected as evidence and how he interpreted it.

2.4.7 Such denunciation of existing evidence does not make Mosaic-myth ideologists necessarily wrong. But it does make their position less easy to justify than that of theorists who are less cavalier and selective in their use of admissible evidence. Such evidence from existing society as they are prepared to consider valid is usually no more than a description of some distasteful feature, coupled with the claim that, when we enter the promised land, that feature will disappear. This makes such Mosaic-myth ideologies vulnerable, for if it can be demonstrated that the feature which they criticize is universal in character and would be found in any society, irrespective of that society's conformation, then the utopian element in the ideology and the falseness of some of its claims are exposed.

2.4.8 For example, 'hierarchy' is a feature of existing society which most people appear to dislike. Yet I claim it is a universal feature of every society. That being so, I maintain that the liberal and Marxist assumption that hierarchies are unnecessary, and that they therefore should and would be abolished in their respective promised lands, must cast doubt upon their overall positions. Another shared liberal and Marxist weakness is their frequent refusal to acknowledge the extent to which the freedom to organize industrial working practices is subject to severe technological constraints: constraints which, short of abandoning the product in question, will largely condition (rather than be conditioned by) the character of the organization and society in which the product is made. (When I later demonstrate the objective character of those constraints, the reader may ascribe the error to technical ignorance. In the case of the liberals this may be so. Their thoughts are sometimes too lofty to understand the determinant quality of technology. But the Marxist recognizes only too well that under capitalism the hierarchical and technological actualities of production determine also our psychological conditioning and/or social institutions. It is therefore particularly perverse of them to imply, without showing how, that under socialism it will be the psychological conditioning and social institutions which will allow the worker to escape from the determinants of technology and hierarchy. Other similar erroneous claims made by Mosaic-myth ideologists will be dealt with progressively throughout this book: but so important are these errors concerning hierarchy and technology that we shall consider them forthwith.

3

The role of hierarchy and technology in organizational design

An organization is the rational co-ordination of the activities of a number of people for the achievement of some explicit purpose or goal, through division of labour and function, and through a hierarchy of authority and responsibility.

E. H. Schein (1970; p.9)

3.1 Hierarchy

3.1.1 There are many ways of looking at organizations, which, given the respective frame of reference of the observer, would justify him in choosing to emphasize, to de-emphasize or to ignore certain characteristics. Equally, however, there are certain aspects of organizations that are so fundamental to *any* thought on the subject that their omission must result in a distorted perspective.

3.1.2 Such a distortion would occur, for example, if we were to imagine that we were free to choose whether, or whether not, to have hierarchy. Schein (1970), quoted above, clearly believes that hierarchies are essential to **all** organizations in that he makes hierarchy part of his definition of what **constitutes** an organization. I would agree with him, However, for a variety of reasons some writers on organizations have chosen to ignore or even to deny the existence of hierarchies. Still others have implied that where hierarchical structures exist they are the vestigial remains of an anachronistic style of management that a more enlightened age has jettisoned. Such a denial of an ingredient essential to organizational theory is reflected in the errors that they later build into their own models because of its omission. The first essential concept therefore is that of hierarchy.

3.1.3 It would be grossly unfair to suggest that there are no organizational theory writers who are prepared to state that hierarchy is an absolute prerequisite for all organizations. We have seen how Schein has made his position clear, and Simon is another. Tannenbaum, in a book entitled *Hierarchy in Organizations*, (Tannenbaum, Kavčič, Rosner, Vianello and Wieser, 1974) expressed the view that hierarchy was a universal feature of organizations. Katz and Kahn (1978; p.312) quote Tannenbaum with approval and find his beliefs to be 'consistent with our... discussion of the defining characteristics of organizations, in which we postulated an authority structure as essential to decisionmaking and its implementation in collectivities'. This list is obviously by no means inclusive of all such literature. Yet, that being said, it is amazing how few management textbooks even have a reference to hierarchy. The reader is invited to check this by a flip through the subject index at the back of the books in his library, where he will almost certainly find that the majority of the books do not even give the word as a subject title. Where the word appears its related text is often concerned with Maslow's 'Hierarchy of needs' (which has nothing to do with this issue but refers only to his belief that human beings attempt to satisfy their different types of need in a particular sequence). In those instances in which the word **is** associated with organizational structures, the related text often reveals that the author considers that hierarchical structures are not characteristic of **all** purposeful organizations but only of **some**, and that even the existence of these is to be regretted in that they are evidence of a reactionary management style that more enlightened managements have, by implication, allegedly outgrown.

3.1.4 Writers who, if pressed, might agree that hierarchies are a universal feature still manage to give the impression that they are not. Burns (1963), in the course of pointing out the differences between 'mechanistic' and 'organismic' systems of management, highlights differences in the nature of those systems which I consider valid and well worth saying. I also doubt if he would deny the need for hierarchical controls in all organizations. If that is true then it is unfortunate that the description of mechanistic management systems has, under the sixth item, the phrase 'Hierarchical structure of control, authority and communication'; while the corresponding item under organismic management systems has the phrase 'A network structure of control, authority and communication'.

3.1.5 Now there is, without doubt, a world of difference between hierarchical control which denies any initiative to people who are lower in the hierarchy, and hierarchical control that allows great freedom to take initiatives within prescribed limits. We shall later consider the way in which the company Data General gave considerable autonomy to a group of young men to design and build a new computer in record time, using an approach which Burns would call organismic. We shall also see that it still required hierarchical control to ensure a successful outcome. I would agree with Katz and Kahn (1978) when they identify three basic management functions and I would also claim that these functions demand a hierarchical framework to make them possible. They are (1978; p.91):
(1) *the co-ordination of substructures,*
(2) *the resolution of conflicts between hierarchical levels,* and
(3) *the co-ordination of external requirements with organizational resources and needs.*

3.1.6 Such a widespread aversion to discuss hierarchies, if they truly **are** an essential feature of all purposive organization, requires an explanation. The omission only begins to make sense if we perceive that for most liberal and Marxist writers 'hierarchy' is a dirty word. In respect of liberal thinking it is perhaps helpful to allow the late Arthur Koestler, whose humanitarian credentials were generally regarded as impeccable, unequivocally to declare (Koestler, 1975b; p.50) that a 'society without hierarchical structurings would be as chaotic as the random motions of gas molecules flying, colliding and rebounding in all directions'.

3.1.7 In a sense there is an inevitable hierarchy in the very act of creation which makes it a basic concept of nature. Let us consider Bronowski's statement (1973; p.349):

> ...Evolution is the climbing of a ladder from simple to complex steps, each of which is stable in itself... I call it *Stratified Stability*. If the stars had to build a heavy element like iron... it would be virtually impossible. No. A star builds hydrogen to helium; then at another stage in a different star helium is assembled to carbon, to oxygen, to heavy elements; and so step by step up the whole ladder to make the ninety-two elements in nature

What he is describing is a tree-like structure or hierarchy at the heart of creation.

3.1.8 Koestler (1975b; p.45) (while acknowledging his debt to Simon for it) has 'elaborated' the story of two fine watchmakers, Bios and Mekhos, the former of whom prospered and the latter of whom failed. Koestler explains why. 'Mekhos had assembled his watches bit by bit… thus each time he was disturbed in his work and had to put down a partly assembled watch, it fell to pieces and he had to start again from scratch.'

3.1.9 'Bios, on the other hand, had designed a method of making watches by constructing, for a start, sub-assemblies of about ten components, each of which held together as an independent unit. Ten of these sub-assemblies could then be fitted together into a sub-system of a higher order: and ten of these sub-systems constituted the whole watch.' Koestler points out that the method has two advantages. Firstly, that Bios didn't need to keep going back to scratch when he was disturbed, and secondly, that Bios' product was (Koestler, 1975; p.47) 'incomparably more resistant to damage, and much easier to maintain, regulate and repair, than Mekhos' unstable mosaic of atomic bits'. Koestler concludes that, although we may not know what other life exists in the universe, we may safely assume… *it must be hierarchically organised*'.

3.1.10 He continues, 'If we look at any form of social organization with some degree of coherence and stability, from insect state to Pentagon we shall find that it is hierarchically ordered.'

3.1.11 Now clearly if this is true, not only must it be that the concept of hierarchy should be central to all organizational theory, but also it must be a matter of our existing experience that even the most democratic of purposive organizations must be hierarchical. In the light of this, how can we account for the many books that will only shamefacedly and grudgingly admit to it, those that ignore it, and even those that deny it?

3.1.12 The answer lies in the social problem with which we stated in paragraph 1.1.9. One way of eliminating the problem of group A attempting to get group B to achieve the goals of group A with all its elitist overtones would be to deny the need for hierarchies in the first place. Such writers therefore are not convinced of the need for hierarchies from **current** evidence because they have a vision of a **better** society.

3.1.13 Now Heaven forbid that we should not all hope for that! But this better society in the case of most liberal and Marxist writers is tied in to a view of the perfectability of man which in turn is coupled with the presumption that in this state of new-found grace mankind will have no need of hierarchies.

3.1.14 Both liberals and Marxists tend to see hierarchies as no more than a mechanism for dealing with conflict; they therefore conclude that, once the causes of conflict have been eliminated, there will be no further need for hierarchy.

3.1.15 We should not, of course, follow them into this fallacy. Hierarchical structures are not a by-product of conflict alone. So far as I am aware, my feet and my hands live in happy accord, yet they are still co-ordinated by my head in hierarchical fashion. Many a spastic would wish that he had such a degree of hierarchical control over his limbs.

3.1.16 We shall later show why these naïve beliefs in the perfectability of man are so dangerously totalitarian in the end. For the moment it is enough for us to understand that the causes of conflict are seen by both liberals and Marxists as circumstantial. In no way is it the product of flawed nature in man and in no way are the circumstances which cause it inevitable. Both therefore propose that a change in circumstance will issue in the millennium. The Marxist, for example, assumes that having got rid of class conflict he will have got rid of the cause of all antagonisms and therefore the need for hierarchies. Quite what the organization of society will then be is disguised under such vague concepts as 'the dictatorship of the proletariat'.

3.1.17 Aron points out that the concept of the proletariat in power will get rid of neither hierarchy nor antagonism. He says (1968; p.174),

> [T]he mass of factory workers cannot be confused with the dominant minority which exercises power. Consequently, the expression 'the proletariat in power' is merely a symbolic way of referring to the party or group of men claiming to represent the masses. As for the non-antagonistic society, the problem is that in a society in which there is no longer private ownership of the instruments of production, by definition there is no longer any antagonism connected with this ownership; but there are men who exercise power in the name of the masses. There is therefore a state which performs the administrative and directorial functions indispensable to any developed society. A society of this kind is not characterized by the same antagonisms as a society in which there is private ownership of the instruments of production. But a society in which the state, by means of economic decisions, largely determines the condition of each and every man may obviously be characterized by antagonisms between groups, whether these be horizontal groups – peasants versus workers – or vertical groups – those at the bottom and those at the top of the hierarchy.

3.1.18 For Aron therefore, as for us, hierarchical structures have a universal quality that no change in regime will eradicate. I think that there is also a further point that needs to be made. Where, as Aron says, 'economic decisions... determine the condition of each and every man', there will be antagonisms. Moreover, although Aron applies his remarks to an imaginary Utopian post-revolutionary society, the pre-revolutionary world of capitalism is also one in which economic conditions determine the condition of each and every man. Ours too is therefore a world of antagonisms, principally generated by the very real fear of being disadvantaged economically. The search for safety in capitalist society seems to me to be more like prudence than the neurosis that Maslow appears to regard it as being, and which I criticize in the Appendix to this book. Let us therefore now turn to Koestler again to take a positive view of hierarchical structures and their relationship to healthy organizations in a healthy society.

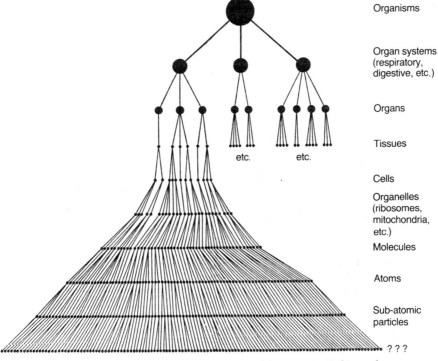

Organisms

Organ systems (respiratory, digestive, etc.)

Organs

Tissues

Cells

Organelles (ribosomes, mitochondria, etc.)

Molecules

Atoms

Sub-atomic particles

? ? ?

Figure 3.1(a) Schematic representation of the organismic hierarchy (Reprinted by permission of A.D. Peters & Co. Ltd).

3.1.19 We will start with a schematic presentation of organisms as given by Koestler (1978; p.28–9) and reproduced here in Figure 3.1(a). What we see is the typical pyramidal shape that we have come to expect of organizational structures; as we shall later see this shape is fundamental to all hierarchical structures. As we descend the hierarchy of the organism we come first to the various organ systems. Notice their specialization, the respiratory system, the digestive system, and so on. Then as we continue down the hierarchy we go from organs, to tissues, to cells, to organelles, to molecules, to atoms, to sub-atomic particles, and on to 'who-knows-where?'.

3.1.20 At each level in the hierarchy the members form a quasi-independent whole.

> [At] the lowest level observable through the electron microscope, we come upon...organelles which are...systems of staggering complexity. Each of these minuscule parts of a cell functions as a self-governing whole in its own right, each apparently obeying a built-in code of rules. One type... of organelle looks after the cell's growth, others after its energy supply, reproduction, communication, and so on. ... The activities of a mitochondrion can be switched on or off by controls on higher levels; but once triggered into action it follows its own code of rules. It cooperates with other organelles in keeping the cell happy, but at the same time each mitochondrion is a law unto itself, an autonomous unit which will assert its individuality even if the cell around is dying. (Koestler, 1978; p.30.)

3.1.21 Let us now turn from organisms to the human parallel of an organization which has been formally set up to achieve certain goals. Koestler recognizes that at every stage in the hierarchy the members of that stage have an ambivalent relationship with the rest of the organism. Looking upward, they perceive themselves to be parts of a larger structure; looking downward, however, they perceive themselves to be 'wholes' which are served by the lower parts of the hierarchy. Because of this ambivalence Koestler (1978) refers to them as 'holons'. This term is itself a combination of the two aspects. The term 'holism' was coined by the South African statesman Jan Smuts in 1926 to indicate 'wholeness' in things. The suffix '– on' is taken by Koestler from physics and indicates 'particles' as in electron, proton or neutron. Putting the two concepts together implies this dual image of their nature. In Roman mythology there was a god called Janus, who had two faces. Every level in the hierarchy, claims Koestler, is a 'Janus-like holon'. Facing upward it is a part; facing downward it is a whole.

3.1.22 If we take Koestler's comments seriously, and I do, then we shall need to think in a radically different way about organizations from the manner in which they are described in most management textbooks. We shall realize that, to the extent that the group or individual at a certain level in the hierarchy see themselves as forming a quasi-autonomous whole, they are self-assertive. To the extent that they see themselves as parts of a larger structure, they are integrative. There is therefore a polarity in their perception that must be kept in balance. I regard it as the job of top management to ensure that a healthy dynamic equilibrium is maintained so that the parts of an organization become neither too assertive nor too compliant.

3.1.23 If any part of the organization becomes overly self-assertive, either in response to stress or alternatively because the controlling influence of the due higher authority in the organization has been too weak to be effective, then such assertion can only be at the expense of the organization as a whole.

3.1.24 The opposite tendency is equally dangerous, for when the power of the whole, as exemplified in strong centralized control, is so great that the parts are dragooned into an integrative conformity, then their autonomy and individuality is so eroded as to create an unhealthy dependency.

3.1.25 It is a useful exercise to take the work of an author who is not a management theorist, but who is a trained and observant journalist, in order to see (a) how complex organizations whose purposive activities are at the frontiers of technology must be organismic in character, and (b) how they must also be hierarchical. We therefore turn to the book by Tracy Kidder (1982) entitled *The Soul of a New Machine*. The book forms a marvellous case-study precisely because it is so obviously an attempt to record the process 'as it happened' and so has none of the self-consciousness of most case-studies. I have no doubt that it is the way that the account rings true that won it the 1982 Pulitzer prize for non-fiction.

3.1.26 Kidder's description of the traumas and joys of conceiving and developing and eventually giving life to a new 32-bit minicomputer illustrates the two characteristics of hierarchies as expressed by Koestler. The first is the self-assertive qualities which are beautifully encapsulated in the fantasies of one of the engineers about his ideal job. 'In it,' says Kidder (1982; p.66), 'he goes to work as a janitor for a computer company whose designs leave much to be desired. There, at night, disguised by mop and broom, he sneaks into the offices of the company's engineers and corrects the designs on their blackboards and desks. Dreams of pure freedom were not uncommon.'

3.1.27 The fact is that, even in this most suitable situation for engaging the hearts and minds of the staff in identifying with the company (and how much easier that is than for a worker who spends his day on an assembly line putting wheels on cars), the computer engineer would not necessarily serve the goals of the company best unless he were restrained. Kidder makes us recognize the essential need for that restraint, but also its demotivating nature.

3.1.28 The boss of the project was named West.

> West reviewed all the designs. Sometimes he slashed out features that the designers felt were useful and nice. He seemed consistently to underestimate the subtlety of what they were trying to do. All that a junior designer was likely to hear from him was 'It's right', 'It's wrong', or 'No, there isn't time'. To some the design reviews seemed harsh and arbitrary and often technically short-sighted... [I]t is the most talented engineers who have the hardest time learning when to stop striving for perfection. West was the voice from the cave, supplying that information: 'Okay. It's right. Ship it.' (Kidder, 1982; p.110.)

3.1.29 Over and over again, despite the flexibility of the relationships that such a project demanded, Kidder identifies the need for control and for hierarchy. For example, there was a strong need to co-ordinate the meanings contained in the microcode, particularly since, to allow greater versatility, certain coded messages would mean one thing to one part of the machine, and something different to another. A man named Holland was in charge of this. Those young men who used the microcode either worked on software and were known as the 'Microkids' or hardware and were known as the 'Hardy Boys'. It is helpful in understanding the following passage to know this and also to know that the equivalent result can sometimes be achieved by modifying the associated software or hardware of a computer.

3.1.30

> The possibilities for creating microcode full of internal contradictions were virtually unlimited. Holland drew up rules – of grammar, as it were – to make sure that the code and the hardware would fit together and to prevent each microprogram from interfering in some subtle way with any other. He saw to it that every microcoder consulted the others when making a change in a microverb. The microverbs and rules for their application he put into a book, called UINST. U stands for 'micro' and INST for 'instruction set'. ... UINST became a battlefield. Its contents changed every week... [The Microkids] would discover something... that was hard to do in microcode, and deciding that it should be done in hardware, they would insert in the next issue of UINST this wish for a change. The Hardy Boys were on guard ... and finding this new item, declare, 'No way we can do that in hardware.' And it was back to bargaining again. (Kidder, 1982; p.144).

3.1.31 I suggested in paragraph 3.1.22 that, if we were to adopt Koestler's view of the hierarchy as being comprised of Janus-like holons with their ambivalent self-assertive/integrative propensities, then the job of top management would be to maintain these polarized tendencies in some sort of healthy dynamic equilibrium. Kidder, with the eye of a journalist, and no management theory bias, records this state of affairs, paradoxes and all.

3.1.32

> Control seemed to be nowhere and everywhere at once. It was an almost tangible commodity, passed from hand to hand down the hierarchy of the group, and everyone got some. West gave Alsing responsibility for getting the microcode done on time. Retaining ultimate authority, Alsing let Holland assume almost complete technical command; and after establishing general rules and while keeping an eye on them, Holland gave each Microkid reign over a portion of the code. (Kidder, 1982; p.144.)

3.1.33 We shall develop the implications of maintaining this dynamic equilibrium between the integrative and self-assertive elements of hierarchy progressively throughout this book, since it is central to many derivative notions as, for example, centralization/decentralization and many other structural and operating concepts. For now, let us consider a second essential constituent of organizational thought, namely a model of the organization which will allow us to visualize the nature of organizational 'trade-offs', and the central role of technology in those trade-offs.

3.2 The key role of technology in determining organizational design and operation and the possible 'trade-offs'

3.2.1 One of the strangest and most revealing classifications in management theory refers to certain theorists as 'contingency theorists'. What is meant is that these theorists regard organizational design as contingent upon circumstance. In other words, they see management theory less as a body of knowledge with universal application, and more as a set of concepts which may be applicable when circumstances permit, but which would need to be modified when circumstances change. What is revealing about this classification is that it invites us to contrast these theorists with another class of theorist, who, it implies, maintain their theories and corresponding practices, irrespective of circumstance. Yet the idea that management theory and practice could conceivably be independent of circumstance is fundamentally so ridiculous that any 'non-contingency theorist' would lose all credibility.

3.2.2 Even those factors which are **always** present do not diminish this argument. Purposive organizations will, for example, **always** be hierarchical. But the nature of the hierarchy can vary dependent on circumstance (as can other factors). It therefore follows that *there will be unique elements or unique combinations of elements in every situation* and my original objection to the term 'contingency theorist' is not lessened by the universal nature of such concepts as hierarchy.

3.2.3 So what we need to find is some model of the firm which will enable us to see the interrelationships between the various elements which compose the organizational system, and thus be able to see the various 'trade-offs' that we are required to construct to make that system. (By 'trade-off' I refer, of course, to the relinquishment of alternative options, which, as we saw in paragraph 1.2.11, accompanies the act of choosing a particular option, and which thereby creates opportunity cost.)

3.2.4 Such a model would serve two distinct functions. The first arises from our *a priori* assumption that organizational design must be contingent upon circumstance, and not least on the nature of the technology being used. That being so, we need a model of the firm which will make clear to us the constituent factors which modify organizational design (including technology), and the nature of the interaction which takes place between them. This is to clarify our own vision.

3.2.5 However, a second significant function of such a model is that it will serve as a tool with which to identify the ideological leanings of the respective theorists we encounter. I pointed out earlier (paragraphs 1.2.15 and 16) that organizations tend to suffer from certain basic inconsistencies because their social, technological, economic and political elements are frequently at odds with each other. Let us assume that we could find a model which represented the organization as a total system, but which allowed us to identify its constituent elements and their interactive nature. Then if any theorist were to provide a 'solution' to the problem of the inconsistencies by emphasizing one aspect at the expense of another, we would be able to recognize that he had done so. Moreover, by seeing what he had chosen to emphasize and what to de-emphasize we should be able to deduce a great deal about his value system and the sort of bias we should look for in his work.

3.2.6 Fortunately we do not need to invent such a model: it has been done for us by Stanley H. Udy (1970). It would be no surprise if Udy's model is unknown to the reader. To some extent this is because there is no apparent correlation between the significance of an idea and its popularity. To some extent it appears to be Udy's own fault in that his own commentary on his model fails, to my mind, to do justice to the concept: it is after all difficult for the modern manager to relate to examples associated with buffalo-hunting! Yet, having said that, it is extraordinary to me that the fundamental significance of Udy's model should have been so widely ignored.

3.2.7 I find it desirable to elaborate Udy's model to bring out those subtleties that he either did not see or ignored, but which, either way, he did not develop. However, before doing so let us acknowledge the seminal aspect of his model by reproducing it in its original form in Figure 3.2(a).

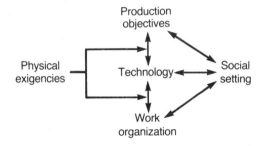

Figure 3.2(a) The work system and its constraints.

3.2.8 It seems to me that the model identifies the problems of organizational trade-offs very well. Clearly there are characteristics associated with any product that make it more appropriate to use one technology than another, and which rule out completely the use of certain technologies no matter how appropriate they may be for other products. There are therefore only a few technologically feasible ways of making any product; or, as expressed in Figure 3.2(a), there are 'physical exigencies' between the 'production objectives' and the 'technology' which limit our options.

3.2.9 Similarly, there is a type of work organization which is appropriate to a certain technology, and which constrains the nature of the organization in question. Although E. L. Trist's work in this area seems principally to have been directed to illustrating that efficiency is dependent upon having created the best combined socio-technological system, he seems also to imply that technology is less of a determinant of work organization than is commonly supposed. I shall argue that the few examples which he and others have given to illustrate this claim tend to be special cases with characteristics that are amenable to a certain flexibility, and are not to be assumed to have universal validity. This we will discuss in Chapter 4. In the meantime let us regard technology as a determinant of organization.

3.2.10 Let us illustrate this with an example. The old technology of newspaper printing was a complex business. The reporter's typewritten article was edited and then sent to an operator whose job it was to set the article in raised type. Although this process has been speeded up since the early days of printing, yet in effect the advance was only a quicker means of assembling the type than had existed for hundreds of years. It consisted of a series of hoppers – one for each letter – attached to a keyboard like that of a typewriter and operated by the man who set the type. Pressing the appropriate key opened the gate to its associated hopper and allowed the machine to deliver a piece of type into the row of type that the operator was setting. Part of his responsibility was to ensure that the left- and right-hand margins of the columns of type lined up: a requirement that meant that he also had to use his judgement about creating such spaces in the text as would ensure this result. This he did by inserting additional pieces of blank type, as necessary, in each line of type. When each article was finished, the set type would be locked in a large frame which represented a page of the newspaper.

3.2.11 For centuries such a frame of type would have been inked and covered with the page that it was to print. Both would then have been put in a press and the raised inked characters would have done the actual printing. But in the twentieth century such presses would be far too slow, and the rotary presses that every reader must have seen in dozens of Hollywood films came into use. To make this possible the type had somehow to be transformed from its flat-bed form and assume a cylindrical shape to fit the print-rollers.

3.2.12 To achieve this transformation the flat frame of type was covered with a heavy-weight sheet of a card-like material. Both were then put into a press which forced the undersurface of the card on to the raised type. This created indentations in the card which corresponded to the type. The card was now bent into a semicircle and put into a mould which was then filled with molten metal. When cooled, this semicircular copy of the original typeset face, together with a similar one, would be used to make up the print-roller of the printing press. It will be seen, therefore, that the above technology required considerable skills and many of the aspects of a foundry. It was a technology of long standing and had been built on the social legacy of the printing guilds. Such erosions of skill that might have crept in over the recent decades had been discounted by the mystique and the working practices that an aggressive union had been able to introduce with managers who feared that any industrial disputes would mean loss of circulation and advertising revenue.

3.2.13 Nevertheless, the work organization (subject to any qualification we might add on overmanning) was appropriate to the technology being used. However, a combination of competitive pressure and rising costs meant that many newspapers became ever more financially unsound. This situation coincided with technological breakthroughs in two areas. Firstly, it was possible to use a word-processor to create a printed copy of the reporter's article in the same format as that which had previously been done by the typesetter. Now the reporter could not only do it himself, so making the typesetter superfluous, but he could quickly modify his article in accordance with his editor's alterations by use of the word-processor's flexibility which would allow the original article, stored in its memory bank, to be modified. Secondly, if a facsimile of the final page of the newspaper were created by pasting together the articles, then, by photographing this on to a flexible plate which could be wrapped around a printing-machine roller, all the foundry-like work of the existing system would be eliminated. The effect upon costs would be dramatic if the work organization appropriate to the new technology were introduced.

3.2.14 However, the effect upon that same work organization would be nothing short of traumatic, for the necessary labour would not only be dramatically reduced, but it would be reduced both in skill and mystique. Some of the workforce would not only have been made physically redundant, but the rest would endure the trauma of being forced to recognize that they had lost much of their claim to being skilled. When we consider the history, for example, of *The Times* newspaper following their attempt to introduce such technological change, we are forced to ask whether, even if the affair could have been better handled, any management of such a major nationally distributed daily paper – given the combined circumstances of the time – could have obtained the voluntary acceptance of the change from the workforce. Such changes had been managed in some small-scale provincial newspapers, but some of the elements there were different enough to swing the balance. I believe that the problems that followed the attempt to introduce the new technology, which included a year-long strike, were inherent in the situation. Udy's model, by stressing the link between the technology and the work organization, will lead us to question the facile approach of the neo-human relations writers. McGregor, for example, in his chapter advocating 'participation' (1960; pp.124–131) ignores completely the conflicts that can be caused by traumatic changes in technology, while by advocating 'job-enrichment', Herzberg gives us few occasions on which we would conclude that this advice might be technologically impossible.

3.2.15 What now of the links between product, technology and work organization on the one side, and society on the other? In a market economy a firm is principally aware of 'society' as the activity of competitors, the reactions of customers and the intervention of governments. Products may be banned or require modification. Anti-pollution laws have already banned the use of certain fuels in smokeless zones. Specifications of the maximum permissible levels of toxic gases from exhausts exist in many countries. Certain sprays and pharmaceuticals are banned. There are strong pressure-groups alien to certain technologies, which become all the stronger when there are alternatives. The anti-nuclear lobby which is seeking the banning of nuclear power stations derives some of its following because alternatives such as hydro-electric schemes and coal-fired schemes are available. It would appear, if I may be forgiven a little cynicism, that society is more likely to intervene in safety measures, if thereby it does not put the product that it desires at risk.

Societies have a habit of ignoring conditions which can only be altered at the cost of banning, or of making more expensive, the goods available to them. Short of going over to robotics, it is technologically and economically difficult to eliminate either danger or dehumanizing monotony from certain industrial operations: so most societies have, to date, accepted that this is so and have adapted their moral and legal responses accordingly. With regard to the attitude to dangerous work, we can contrast the strict requirements concerning the design and operation of the 'clicking presses' which cut the upper-leather of a shoe with the minimal requirements which apply to cutting its leather sole on a 'revolution press'. Let us consider this example. In both instances a shaped knife is used. This knife is placed on a piece of leather and, when struck by a single blow from the press, it cuts out its shape in the leather. An analogy would be the way a pastry cook, using a shaped tinware or plastic tool, cuts gingerbread-men from a rolled-out piece of dough. Designing an upper-leather press which incorporated safety features was relatively easy. The arrangement was as follows. The knife was placed in position, the operator removed his hands, and to ensure that he had done so the machine was triggered by a two-handed device. But attempting to cut the large, tough, and often very wavy sole leather hides posed a different problem. Such leather made it difficult to maintain the position of the knife during the cutting stroke unless the knife was held in place. The solution adopted was to make the knife deep enough to allow the operator to keep both hands under the press during the press-stroke in order to steady the knife as he triggered the machine's stroke with his foot. Faced with this situation the UK factory inspectorate made the two-handed safety mechanism a compulsory feature of all clicking presses even as they were accepting the almost nonexistent lower safety features of the revolution press. So the enforcement of safer practices by law often awaits management initiatives to produce a more desirable alternative before it can become a reality. Moreover, when the issue is not a matter of safety, but one of humanizing work, there is no legislation at all and any initiative must come from management.

3.2.16 The most common way of making motor cars is by means of a conveyor belt. We have long seen Detroit as a symbol, but a brutish symbol of the twentieth century. We recognize that, for all its ingenuity the moving conveyor belt is dehumanizing and only really suitable to the use of robotics: this is why we laughed so much at Charlie Chaplin in his film 'Modern Times'. Laughter is often the product of a mental comparison with the event which we see and our conception of the way things **should** be in a well-ordered world. We laugh at Charlie's antics, not in spite of, but **because** of his bitter message. The same aspect of the situation that angers Chaplin, *the incongruity of it all*, is precisely what makes us laugh. Our laughter is caused because of the clownish antics that Charlie had to get up to to cope with an inhuman machine: but we recognize also that his true nature as a human being is also under attack. We laugh in order not to cry.

3.2.17 For the benefit of those who have not seen the film it may be helpful to recall the related sequence. Charlie is standing by the conveyor belt with a spanner gripped in each of his hands. Before him passes at high speed a constant stream of identical but unidentifiable chunks of cast metal, from each of which protude a couple of nuts. Charlie's job, the ultimate purpose of which is as unidentifiable as the metal chunks themselves, is to give these two nuts a half a turn with his spanners as they go by. In due course the end of the shift arrives and the bemused Charlie wanders into the street, still holding his spanners and twitching convulsively, only to be confronted by an enormous woman. Her bosom is bedecked by two strategically placed buttons, and Charlie, conditioned to perform his mindless operation, advances upon the terrified woman with his two spanners.

3.2.18 If society is not always prepared to intervene to create constraints upon the organization, this means that it leaves managements with the problem of deciding whether they have any moral obligation to do more than is legally demanded of them. For if a management goes beyond the minimum demanded either by law, or by irresistible pressure from some other party such as a trade union, then what **was** a constraint has, in effect, been transformed into a goal. We shall consider the relationship between goals and constraints in detail in a moment. In the meantime we have said enough about the role of society relative to the firm to explain one of several reasons why I chose to adapt Udy's model and to give below, in Figure 3.2(b), my own version of the organization-system model.

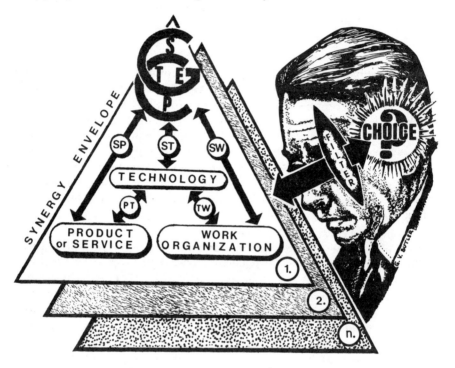

Figure 3.2(b) My model of the organization-system.

3.2.19 The first thing to note is that the 'social setting' of Udy's model has gone. Udy's social setting was used by him to illustrate that different societies will have certain work organizations which are appropriate to them and some that are not. He had pointed out (Udy, 1970) that no product is produced unless it is socially valued, so that nowadays there is little demand for horse-drawn buggie whips. Technology cannot be divorced from its social setting, hence there were no aeroplanes in ancient Greece. Finally the work organization must be appropriate to its social setting, so that Udy assures anyone who doubted it that limited liability companies did not exist among the indigenous Australian aboriginals.

3.2.20 We shall not dispute any of these truisms, but it is more useful for us to consider the firm as an organism attempting to survive in its social environment by seeking those goals which will permit this within a framework of constraints. Both goals and constraints will have social, technological, economic and political dimensions. This accounts for the symbol at the top of my model in which the 'G' represents the goals, the 'C' the constraints, and the S,T,E,P the respective social, technological, economic and political dimensions they exhibit.

3.2.21 It was no accident that the 'G' of goals should have been placed at the top of the model. Formal organizations are, in fact, set up for the very purpose of achieving certain goals. It is true that, in the light of experience, those original goals may be modified or abandoned for others. This can happen because of social, technological, economic or political changes either within or without the organization. Nevertheless, at any given time and until its death, an organization exists to accomplish its goals. If we forget this, whether we are engaged in the act of management or we are contemplating the theory , we shall be allowing the tail to wag the dog. To remind us of this I have placed the 'G' for goals symbolically at the very top of the model.

3.2.22 In Part Four we shall consider the problem organizational goals in some detail, for it is an extremely contentious topic that requires considerable discussion to do it justice. The only point I wish to make here is that I shall maintain that at any time an organization has a number of goals, with the complication that any attempt to achieve one goal may, to a greater or lesser extent, be counter-productive to the achieving of another.

3.2.23 I have already implied that a constraint is imposed by others, whereas a goal is imposed by oneself. It is important to make this point, for my experience is that students commonly see all constraints as being different in character from the goal that they obstruct. Sometimes this is true. If I were to try to sail to New York from London, my general direction would be westward. However, to begin with I should have sail eastward down the Thames, that is to say in entirely the opposite direction, because my goal, to reach New York, was being frustrated by a constraint of a different character, namely the intervening land-mass of Southern England.

3.2.24 Yet frequently goals and constraints are almost identical. If a trade union's pressure forces a management to pay more in wages to their employees than they would freely have done, then such wage-rates are a constraint. However, if, for whatever reason, that management chooses to pay its workers more than the negotiated minimum, then such wage-rates would be a goal. Either way it is the same thing, the wage-rate, that is both constraint and goal.

3.2.25 Sometimes it is almost impossible to decide which is which. If a company had been contemplating a takeover, but chose to refrain because of the possible intervention of the Monopolies Commission – even though this eventuality was by no means certain – are we describing a goal or a constraint?

3.2.26 Goals and constraints manifest themselves in terms of social, technological, economic or political issues, which not only pervade the environment, but also invade, or else find their origin within, the boundaries of the company: for, to paraphrase the poet Donne, 'No firm is an Island entire of it self...'. For example, if our competitor develops a technological improvement which will give to him a competitive advantage, dare we not respond? Alternatively, if our own research department has discovered some new advantageous process, dare we not adopt it?

3.2.27 There are, of course, examples of managements attempting to maintain the status quo in the face of such breakthroughs, but they most frequently come to grief in the process. Britain's steel-making history during the latter part of the nineteenth and the earlier part of the twentieth century is a case in point. When high-quality steels could only be produced from pure haematite ores (i.e. before the invention of the 'basic' process) British pure ore deposits were nearing exhaustion. So British steel men were prudent enough to invest in pure ore deposits in Spain and Sweden, and also to invest in the shipping fleet to transport the mined ore.

3.2.28 However, the 'basic' process made possible the use of the more commonly available phosphoric ore deposits. It was a British invention which did not require any great implementation, since it only required that the existing Bessemer or Siemens furnaces were lined with bricks of heat-resistant material rich in metal oxides, called 'basic', and that they additionally added 'more basic, silica of limestone to the metal during the heating. The basic dephosphorised the material leaving steel as pure as any of the other (acid) processes had done' (Stern, 1962; pp.63–64).

3.2.29 Once this invention, the work of a British police-court shorthand writer called Sidney Gilchrist Thomas, had become public knowledge there was obviously going to be more competition from Germany and the USA as they developed their own phosphoric ore deposits, but to some extent the fact that they overtook Britain in the 1890s was surely because the British did not take up this invention. Stern sees British failure to do so as being because they 'deprecated developments which detracted from the value of these investments', referring of course to the deposits in Sweden and Spain and to the ships. Just how blind they were to the need to change is illustrated by another of Stern's comments, for it must be recognized that by 1901 the 'basic' process had been known for 22 years. 'Only 17 per cent of British steel was produced by the basic method in 1901; it needed the cutting of shipping lanes in the first world war to bring home to British steelmakers the debt of gratitude which they owed to Gilchrist Thomas.' (Stern, 1962; p.64.)

3.2.30 A further moral we may draw is that in the 'depreciation of assets' (an accountancy concept) we cannot presume that a piece of equipment will continue to be of use to us for the whole of its physical life, for long before it is actually worn out it may be more economic to scrap it and to re-equip with more modern equipment. Not to do so would place us in the position of accepting the opportunity cost of using the outdated equipment, which, as we have seen, runs counter to the capitalist ethic.

3.2.31 It would be wrong to mention only the technological aspect of goals and constraints, for there are, of course, also economic, political and social dimensions to the issues. Readers should have little difficulty in imagining all manner of changes of an economic or political nature: changes in interest rates, protective tariffs, import licence restrictions, nationalization, etc., spring immediately to mind. But social changes may be less readily obvious as creating threats or opportunities within or without the firm, so that a couple of instances may help.

3.2.32 Some years ago I was associated with the parent board of a company which had several divisions. One of these divisions was at that time making a profit but the parent board had received an offer to buy the division from the group as a going concern. The price was reasonable: but should they sell? I believed that they should because I thought that I detected two social changes were about to occur which would adversely affect the profitability of the division.

3.2.33 The division in question manufactured uniforms of various sorts, but their biggest turnover came from supplying school uniforms. However, my forecast was that if the grammar-school system was about to be superseded by the comprehensive-school system then the probability was that that market would die. My reasoning was that the comprehensive-school system had largely been introduced by people whose objection to the grammar-school system had mainly been that they considered it to be socially divisive. This being so, I could not believe that they would not equally consider school uniforms to a separatist feature and therefore also socially divisive. If I were right, then my calculations showed that the loss of so much volume in turnover would put the division into financial loss. But there was also another social change which threatened a loss.

3.2.34 This was that about 95 per cent of the labour in the division was female. Although I hoped that legislation was pending to rectify the iniquitous pay differentials between men and women, yet it would be a cost which could not be passed on to the mothers of comprehensive-school children, nor could the firm afford to absorb such a cost. The prospective purchaser was really interested in the plant more than our market, and could possibly pass on such costs in the selling-price of his product (well-cut, up-market trousers). Socially and economically it seemed right to sell, for the future of the workforce also seemed more secure if transferred to this purchaser, who had a good marketing image and a wide spread of retail customers.

3.2.35 If the reader refers again to Figure 3.2(b) on p.58 he will see that in that model the management must choose a complete system of (1) product or service, with (2) its associated technology, with (3) its associated work organization as a means of achieving (4) the S,T,E,P goals of the organization within constraints. (There seems no reason why we should not adapt Udy's model to cover service industries as well as production industries, since even service industries are commonly associated with an appropriate technology and work organization.) I shall attempt later in the book to justify why I consider that the choice of system and of goals should be the prerogative of management. For now I only wish to point out that management's choice is restricted to mutually compatible combinations: that is to say, whatever system management adopts must be accepted as a totality.

3.2.36 An example will perhaps be useful in clarifying this. If a desirable product, cheap eggs and poultry, requires a technology which is thought to be undesirable (say battery hens) then that, together with its associated work organization, is an integral system. If we choose to get rid of the undesirable element, namely keeping hens in batteries, all well and good. But then we must accept the consequences of the change in terms of its associated product and work organization. If, for example, we had chosen to adopt the technology of keeping the hens on a 'free range' basis, then we should reconcile ourselves to getting a 'free range' product which will have the undesirable characteristic of making the eggs and the poultry that we produce by this method more expensive. This is what I mean when I say that the management must choose a complete system as a totality. The management will survey the various systems options, 1,2,...,n, and, by means of the values contained in their ideology, and also in the light of the implications of any constraints that they perceive, they will choose what they see as the 'best' total organizational system. For this reason I have shown management as making their choice only after putting the options through a 'filter' of the kind just described.

3.2.37 Further, it will be noticed that I have indicated in Figure 3.2(b) that each system will have a 'synergy envelope'. We shall deal with the concept of synergy in more detail in Part Four when we consider organizational strategy. What I mean by it in this context is that the combined effects of all the parts of any system may be extremely fortuitous, and in effect give us a totality that is greater than it would have been reasonable to expect from their sum. We might express it as '2 + 2 = 5'. Of course, sometimes the factors might tend to interact in a way that makes the total effect less efficacious than we might have supposed, so that we could say '2 + 2 = 3'. The first of these we shall regard as 'positive synergy', and the second as 'negative synergy'. The synergistic way in which the elements combine will affect the perception of management in deciding which system to choose.

3.2.38 Finally, I wish to point out that not only are the means of achieving an organization's goals to be considered as variables, to some extent the goals themselves are to be considered variable. This is because all planning is an iterative process in which ends and means alternate in modifying each other in successive actions and reactions. An example may make this clearer.

3.2.39 Suppose that I start off by planning to achieve goal A. I calculate that, in order to be able to achieve this goal I shall need certain corresponding resources, which we can label as resources A. However, it is conceivable that in the course of this exercise I found that an alternative goal A1, which was far more desirable, existed and that the resources that it would require, resources A1, were scarcely more than the resources required for goal A. Such a disproportionate increase in return for so little increase in financial and social costs would then be so worth while from a cost-benefit standpoint that it would be irrational not to switch goals to A1.

3.2.40 Alternatively, I may have found that goal A2 is only marginally less attractive than goal A but that the resources that it would require, resources A2, are much cheaper or much less anti-social than those required for goal A. Again it would then be more rational to switch to goal A2.

3.2.41 We conclude therefore that management is always attempting to obtain the greatest cost-benefit from the total system in terms of their value-judgements. It can be expressed in the following formula in which the symbols are those used to indicate the links in Figure 3.2(b) on p.58, and VJ represents management's value-judgement in each case.

(VJ) (max. cost-benefit) = (VJ) (PT+ST+TW+SP+SW+G(STEP) +C(STEP)+synergy).

3.2.42 We shall find this model particularly useful when we apply it to theorists who claim to have found a simplistic remedy for organizational problems, because it will expose their value-judgements by highlighting what they suppressed to make their theory fit. As we shall see, Frederick W. Taylor inferred that a person would not mind being treated as a social isolate nor being used 'instrumentally', that is to say doing machine-like repetitive work, providing that he was paid enough. He therefore emphasizes society's need for the product, and claims that even if the technology or the work organization required to manufacture it have unattractive elements, the people can be 'bought off', and will still be happy with the arrangement. Similarly, when Frederick Herzberg specifies 'job-enrichment' we can see that he has emphasized changing the work organization without ever considering whether the firm can accomplish this. For we are able to recognize the very real possibilities that (a) the technological constraints may make such alterations to the work organization impossible, or (b) if the alteration is technically possible it may nevertheless incur such additional costs that any product so produced could not survive in a market situation.

4

Technology as a determinant of organizational design

Things are in the saddle,
And ride mankind.
R. W. Emerson (1830–82)

4.1 Why technology has been an ideological football in management theory

4.1.1 According to Greek legend, Theseus used a thread to find his way back out of the Minotaur's labyrinth. But we cannot hope to unravel the complexities of the 'management theory jungle' by following a single thread of influence. This section is a case in point. In it we shall consider a whole area of management theory that we will neither understand nor be able to criticize unless we consider jointly two strands, namely technology and motivation.

4.1.2 Because certain aspects of technology are as near 'brute fact' as anything in this life **can** be, I could have chosen to present them in a completely factual manner and in a self-contained section labelled 'Technology'. But if I were to do so I should be failing to show why something so straightforwardly 'factual' should have given rise to so much ideological disagreement in management theory; a disagreement which caused the neo-human relations motivational theorists to deny the reality of these self-same technological 'facts'.

4.1.3 To understand the discrepancy between the 'facts' of technology and their denial by such theorists, we have a choice. Either we can

(a) *follow the motivation thread and introduce technology as a cross-thread in the overall web of ideas,* or
(b) *follow the technology thread and introduce motivation as the cross-thread.*

But either way, our understanding of the matter is conditional upon the two threads crossing. Of these two options I have two strong reasons for choosing (b):

(i) Because our knowledge of 'truth' is tentative, when we seek to disentangle 'fact' from 'interpretation' we should start with the foundation of those 'facts' which seem to be most 'brute'. Being least subject to differing interpretations, these are less likely to lead us into error. I maintain that the 'facts' of technology are less contentious than those of motivation.
(ii) Approach (b) is more in line with our approach to the problem of how to choose between ideologies. This, we said, was to start with the basic problem and consider how well the respective 'solutions' dealt with the issues which the problem raised.

4.1.4 It may be asked why technological considerations should impinge at all on the issue of how employees can be motivated. From management's standpoint the issue would seem to resolve itself into a two-part question:

(a) *'What is it that our employees really want of us?'* and, (assuming that management have learned the answer to that)
(b) *'How can we so arrange things that in his efforts to fulfil his needs the worker freely does the things necessary for the firm's survival?'*

But technology constrains the possible arrangements which can be made. It does so because of two factors. Firstly, 'technology' is only another way of saying 'how-we-get-the-job-done'. Secondly, other than when an organization is set up for the participants' benefit, all purposive organizations give 'getting-the-job-done' greater importance than 'keeping-the-participants-happy'. I claim that managements have a moral duty to keep the workforce as happy as possible, and they may thereby even make it easier to get the job done: but it has to be admitted that no purposive business organization has the *primary* objective of maximizing employee satisfaction. Even providing its product or service is not its major mission. No business continues indefinitely to supply a product or service nor to employ people to do so if that involves financial loss. The sole exception is when the loss-making product or service is seen as a necessary subsidy to some other profit-making part of the enterprise.

4.1.5 So we can restate management's goals as being the following:

(1) *To fulfil the survival needs of the organization and to use the product or service as a means to this end.*

Thereafter, and only sequential to or incidental to the achievement of (1):

(2) *To satisfy the needs of the worker.*

Let us amplify what this means. The survival needs referred to in (1) involve the firm in finding a technology which will be

(a) *capable of making the product or providing the service,*
(b) *socially acceptable,*
(c) *politically acceptable,* and
(d) *economically viable.*

Only then, and within the constraints that these other demands have created can we stipulate that it should be

(e) *capable of satisfying the needs of the worker.*

When we developed our model of organization (Figure 3.2(b)) we found no reason to presume that society would permit all the possible technological options with which to create the product or service. Of those options which were socially permitted, managements (following their capitalist *mores*) will choose the most cost-effective. To expect that the work organization which results from all these prior claims will also ideally suit the needs of the employee is to lean heavily upon coincidence.

4.1.6 So there is almost bound to be a mismatch between those conditions of work which are determined by technology and those which, given a free choice, the employees would prefer. To admit that this is so is relatively easy for the pluralist. As we saw (Section 2.3) the fact that the employer and employee both have an interest in the survival of the company does not blind the pluralist to their legitimate differences of interest. For him, therefore, any mismatch between what might be seen as 'the ideal work organization' and the work organization as shaped by technological and economic factors is no more than a specific example of this general problem.

4.1.7 The same is not true of those unitarists who comprise the vast majority of American theorists. These (as I said in paragraph 1.2.24) are united in the fallacy that there is no reason why the employers and employees of a well-managed company should not be in perfect accord. To acknowledge any mismatch between the conditions of work imposed by a firm's technological/economic constraints, and those conditions of work to which the worker would otherwise aspire, threatens the *Weltanschauung* of such writers. They take flight in the only way possible. The first group of theorists accept the technicological/economic constraints but deny that the effect of these upon the work organization is important. The second group accept that the work organization is important but deny that the technological/economic aspects are really as constraining as the evidence shows. The absurdity of both positions is something we shall now consider.

4.1.8 Frederick Winslow Taylor (1856–1917) was the most famous of those unitarist American theorists who accept that technological/economic factors are determinants of the way organizations are designed and operated, but who maintain their unitarist position by denying that the employee will be unhappy with the resulting work organization. Indeed, Taylor's claim was that the employee would be *positively happy* with any and every situation which technological/economic factors determined, providing that the pay was right.

4.1.9 In the course of Chapters 7 and 8 I shall seek somewhat to rehabilitate the memory of F. W. Taylor. For too long he has been the whipping-boy of ill-informed idealists. I hope to illustrate that if Taylor had not been born, someone else would have filled his role. The needs of the time were far too insistent to be ignored. It was our good fortune that F. W. Taylor was the man who matched that moment. Even Taylor's greatest enemy, and he still has many, could not (with truth) doubt his stature. But his technological and administrative genius is overlaid by psychological absurdity. Taylor insisted that, providing the worker's pay was right and the amount of work he was required to do had been scientifically measured, the worker would welcome entering into an individual commitment with management in which he would happily perform the most monotonous work in a manner and at a rate which would be determined by management. Such a claim makes certain assumptions about human nature that are usually referred to as those of 'economic man'. 'Economic man' is supposedly prepared to enter into this personal deal with management irrespective of any repercussions such a deal might have on his fellow workers. It assumes that the worker is essentially individualistic or (as some would interpet it) a selfish 'loner'. Secondly, he is supposedly prepared to perform the most meaningless work if asked. This latter characteristic, if true, would mean that the worker was 'instrumental' in his attitude towards his work in a two-fold fashion: he would be instrumental because he allowed management to use him like a tool, no more than the extension of the machine he operated; and he would be instrumental because his work would be motivated by no better reason than to use his pay as the instrument with which to purchase other satisfactions.

4.1.10 We have yet to consider how accurate a description of human nature that is. I would claim that it is in error. However, there is one thing of which we can be certain. Right or wrong, it is not a vision of man likely to endear Taylor to liberal democrats. To them, Taylor's assumptions about human nature are unforgivable. This is the first of the two main reasons why his genius is disputed. The second is that (from the 1960s onward) management theory was to fall into the hands of psychologists and sociologists who do not know enough about technology to appreciate the genius of Taylor's contribution. I shall try to make good this omission.

4.1.11 Yet it must be admitted that, if Taylor had been a man of different character, he could have avoided most of this calumny. His essential claims make lesser (and altogether much more reasonable) demands on his audience. To restrict himself to these lesser claims was a course he was logically free to adopt: but given Taylor's visionary zeal for a unitary society it was one which he was psychologically incapable of following. I shall expand on this aspect when in Chapters 7 and 8 we discuss Taylor and his concept of 'scientific management'. This more reasonable position would have been to have argued that, if certain technological requirements create unattractive working conditions, then, at the very least the worker deserves to be compensated for that circumstance. If Taylor had limited his claims to this, it would have had an undoubted morality.

Frederick Herzberg claims that money will not compensate the worker for the satisfactions that he loses when he is asked to do mindless work. Yet even Herzberg must surely agree that paying more for it is more moral than not doing so. Taylor's mistake was to put his case in positive terms rather than the negative terms I have used above. His language invites us to believe that the worker is prepared to connive with management in the cheerful destruction of his own psychological and social aspirations. It is Taylor's absurd image of the worker welcoming the destruction of his own humanity for thirty pieces of silver that Michael Rose found to be so grotesque. Such a worker, said Rose (1978; p.62), would be 'a monstrosity: a greedy machine indifferent to its own pain and loneliness once given the opportunity to maim and isolate itself'.

4.1.12 But if Taylor's attempt to resolve the inherent conflict between the demands of technology and the needs of the workforce is absurd, it is no more absurd than the claims of psychologists and sociologists who deny the constraints of technology and economics. By vague statements about the power of 'job-enrichment' to eliminate conflict, they are making a claim of monumental absurdity. For their claim infers that there will always be enough technical elasticity in the system to permit the job content and the work organization to be adjusted to an extent that will meet the worker's social and psychological aspirations. They are indulging in exactly the same sort of self-delusion that Taylor did and for exactly the same unitary reasons. *In the area of the system that Taylor understood he had come to recognize that there was insufficient flexibility to meet the demands of the total system...He therefore presumed that there would be enough flexibility in the area that he did not understand. They have done precisely the same. He was wrong...and so are they.* They are principally members of the neo-human relations school of writers.

4.1.13 We shall deal with the neo-human relations school at some length during the course of this book, and we do so here only to show how negative is their interest in technology. The basic thesis of the neo-human-relations school is that what the worker wants more than anything is the opportunity to grow and develop. This is the vehicle which they visualize will bring an end to industrial conflict. They assume that if the worker is allowed responsibility and meaningful work, his attitude towards the firm will become entirely positive, and indeed he will come to share the goals of management.

4.1.14 The reader will recognize that, even if these writers are correct in their basic belief that a desire for personal 'growth' is the main motivating force in people (a vision of human nature which is usually referred to as 'self-actualizing man') it still does not get over the fact that in a capitalist situation both the employer and the employee will recognize that the worker is not only a resource, but he is also a potential liability. So even if the basic thesis about human nature were true, there would be no reason to doubt that some management decisions would place the worker's interests secondary to other conflicting interests, nor that this will cause the worker to feel resentment.

4.1.15 For this reason, even if management themselves accepted the vision of 'self-actualizing man' it would be absurd for them to expect the worker to agree with decisions which went against his personal interest. It could be argued that management's refusal to allow workers to 'participate' in making such decisions was management's mute tribute to the worker's ability to make independent and intelligent evaluations. We certainly would not be free to assume the opposite, namely that it was mute evidence that management regarded the worker as passive, unambitious and irresponsible. Yet this was the position adopted by Douglas McGregor; and it was McGregor who (by applying to the management arena the ideas of the psychologist Abraham Maslow) started the neo-human relations movement.

Well we shall see (in Chapter 10) that McGregor was clearly a very naïve man and that this was only one of a number of fundamental errors which he made. He was wrong (I shall claim) even in his interpretation of Maslow. But what concerns us most here is that he inferred that management had no good reason to limit the employee's freedom of expression whether that limitation arose from the use of hierarchical structure or from the use of certain technologies. According to McGregor there was therefore only one conclusion to draw from such limitations... and he drew it. Such practices were clear evidence of a widespread management attitude, which was contemptuous of the inherent ability, intelligence and moral fibre of the people they employed. To this attitude he gave a label, 'Theory X'.

4.1.16 Indeed, it is this naïve assumption that such practices are wilful and unnecessary that prompts McGregor's righteous indignation: as well it might, had it been so. Here is a sample of his anger:

[This] assumption of the 'mediocrity of the masses' is rarely expressed so bluntly [as I (McGregor) have just done]. In fact, a good deal of lip service is given to the ideal of the worth of the human being. Our political and social values demand such public expressions. Nevertheless, a great many managers will give private support to this assumption [of the mediocrity of the masses] and it is easy to see it reflected in policy and practice. Paternalism has become a dirty word, but it is by no means a defunct managerial philosophy (McGregor, 1960; p.34).

4.1.17 Frederick Herzberg, another member of the neo-human relations school, focused his attention of the qualitative aspects of the worker's job. His assumption was that if the worker's job were 'enriched' it would increase his motivation. Indeed, claimed Herzberg, only so could the worker be motivated. Those things extrinsic to the job, such as pay, wouldn't do it. Only if he were able to identify with his job because he saw it as meaningful and demanding could he feel a sense of commitment to doing it and doing it well. Herzberg, like all the other neo-human relations writers, allows the reader to infer that such identification with his work will bring the worker also to identify with the aims of management.

4.1.18 If we ignore some of the more contentious aspects of Herzberg, it seems to me that there is little to be said against (and much to be said for) his formula for management action. It seems to me that if it **is** physically and economically possible to make a worker's job more 'meaningful' (and if the worker would welcome the change), then management have a moral duty to make that change. *It may be true, as the old adage says, that 'that which cannot be cured must be endured'. But to allow a situation to be endured because we just did not **care** enough to change it, would be (if I may be permitted* *the language of those of us who believe in such things) sinful.* What would make it so would not be the objective conditions. It would be the wholly gratuitous and wilful nature of the act: it is this wilfulness that would make it an offence against the personality of another human being.

4.1.19 In Chapter 10 I shall explain my doubts concerning both the truth and the morality of the neo-human relations school's claims that the worker could and should be brought to share the views of management. But from what I have just said, it must be clear that I regard the policy of job-enrichment as having a value which is independent of those claims. *However, what I do most certainly dispute is the neo-human relations school's frequent implication that job-enrichment would be relatively easy to accomplish were it not for the mental attitude of the management concerned.* Indeed, they use management failure to implement job-enrichment schemes as evidence that managements adopt the attitude which McGregor labelled 'Theory X'. Herzberg himself may not have claimed that job-enrichment is easy: but, as I shall show in a moment, some of his disciples have done so. Moreover, to what (other than the belief that managements are deliberately withholding job-enrichment) do we attribute the plaintively didactic tone which Herzberg adopts in the title of one of his articles? It reads 'One more time: How do you motivate employees?' (Herzberg, 1968).

4.1.20 Yet the truth is that even the most sympathetic managements can find it impossible to enrich many jobs. It follows that by making a case for job-enrichment, Herzberg has done far more to emphasize that a problem exists than he has to offer a solution to it. It is high time that someone said so. Here then is a statement that I shall substantiate by the contents of sections 4.2 and 4.3:

*Job-enrichment is only technically and economically feasible in a limited number of situations which can be classified. In such situations it is an approach which is likely to be as commercially successful as, because of its humanity, it is desirable. Indeed, where it **is** applicable there is likely to be a congruity of interest between satisfying the worker and the shareholder. Nevertheless, in many industrial situations, which can also be classified, job-enrichment is neither technically nor economically viable. I believe that when I have explained these classifications the reader will share with me the belief that probably the majority of industrial jobs **cannot** be enriched. That being so, although the manager should use job-enrichment whenever he can, he cannot afford to regard it as the only answer to the problems of motivation. If it were to prove so, we would all be in deep trouble.*

4.1.21 Before we turn to the technical limitations on job-enrichment I need to make good my promise to demonstrate that the literature does indeed erroneously claim that job-enrichment is a process which is hindered more by management attitudes than by technical difficulties. I have chosen to do so by quoting an article written by Sirota and Wolfson and quoted in Gellerman (1974; pp.109–118). Gellerman himself introduces the article, and warns the reader that interest in job-enrichment (1974; p.109) 'must be tempered with a realistic appreciation of the difficulties that are likely to be encountered in actual practice. Job enrichment is, after all, an intervention in an existing system, and as such is likely to encounter the typical misunderstandings; lack of attention and enthusiasm and outright resistance that greet all interventions – at least initially.' But he makes no mention of any technological constraints.

4.1.22 In the Sirota and Wolfson text (which follows Gellerman's introduction), among eleven problem areas, such as those of 'ideology', they only write this one small section on the technological barriers to job-enrichment, (p.114). 'Because there are real and encompassing constraints imposed by the technology with which work is done, the changes that ideally should be made in jobs would often (especially in manufacturing operations) require considerable investment in new equipment or facilities.' (Notice the hint creeping in that it is recalcitrant management that is **really** to blame. They then become completely won over to this view by their own rhetoric as they continue.) (p.114) 'Unfortunately, job-enrichment is still seen by most managers as too "iffy" a proposition to warrant large-scale expenditures on its behalf.' (Implying that management could if they would.) 'And there is not much that the enrichment practitioner can do about that.' (Lucky him!) 'But there is another side to this obstacle about which a great deal can be done – the belief that the technology makes any change impossible for large classes of jobs.' (A belief that I shall justify.) '...or, if possible perforce trivial. The Maytag, Motorola and Non Linear Systems experiences (p. 115) refute this belief, proving that even within the limits of assembly line technology significant modifications in work can be made.' (I shall later demonstrate why certain types of assembly work are among the few which are amenable to job-enrichment.) 'It is the demonstration of the feasibility of enrichment that is among the first tasks of the enrichment practitioner.'

4.1.23 It is the sting in the tail there that causes so much damage because most people would take that to mean that if job-enrichment can be demonstrated in one area, then by analogy it must be possible in another. That is quite decidedly untrue. Indeed, the biggest constraint upon job-enrichment is undoubtedly that imposed by the nature of the associated machinery. Nor is this an issue that can usefully be discussed in vague generalities, even if that has been the approach of most authors to date. The only way to come to grips with the topic is by a detailed study of machine characteristics. We shall find it helpful to categorize all machinery into two classes: 'special purpose' and 'general purpose'. By 'special purpose' machinery I mean machinery that performs a particular operation in order to produce a particular product. A weaver's loom is an obvious example but in every industry there are many such machines whose function would only be known to those actually working in the industry. By 'general purpose' machinery I refer to machinery which does a limited operation, but could perform that operation upon a variety of materials to make a variety of products. Most engineering machinery is of this type, with lathes, drills, planes, etc., being common examples. We shall consider these classes in turn to discover the constraints that each puts upon job-enrichment.

4.2 The constraints that 'special purpose' machinery places upon 'job-enrichment'

4.2.1 It is interesting to note that the historical development of most 'special purpose' machinery follows a characteristic and classic pattern: not what we might have been led to expect from the incredible variety of such machinery which has resulted from the many specialist operations for the many specialist products that we manufacture. Yet it is the very degree of such specialization that has created the common pattern of development.

4.2.2 Even prior to mechanization (say) in the eighteenth or nineteenth century, that same operation would have been performed as a short-cycle repetitive action by the use of some specialist tool or simple machine. The advantages for the manufacturer of such repetitious work were well known for generations. Josiah Wedgwood (1730–95) had advocated such practices in the pottery industry with the chillingly memorable phrase 'Make such machines of men as can not err!' But without doubt it was *The Wealth of Nations* published by Adam Smith in 1776 (the same book which we shall find became the 'Bible' of laissez-faire capitalism) which was to popularize and promote short-cycle work. Yet even before that date several simple high-volume products were made in this way as the case of Wedgwood illustrates. Adam Smith's example was taken from the making of pins. 'One man draws out the wire, another straightens it, a third cuts it, a fourth points it, a fifth grinds it at the top for receiving the head; to make the head requires two or three distinct operations; to put it on is a peculiar business, to whiten the pins is another; it is even a trade by itself to put them into the paper.' (Smith, 1970; Vol. 1, p.5.)

4.2.3 There are three aspects I wish the reader to note about this system. Firstly, it leads to what is known as a 'product layout'. This is when the operations are strung out in the sequence in which the product is made. In its most extreme form such a system becomes a conveyor-belt type of production. Secondly, any equipment used is likely to be 'special purpose'. Thirdly, once such a production line has been set up it requires virtually no management to run it. It therefore was extremely popular with the earliest capitalists in that it could be put under the control of a 'charge-hand' who could run the system and allow the entrepreneur to get on with the business of social climbing with the local 'squirearchy', an ambition which the profits financed. He would have been despised for being 'in trade' so that anything which distanced him from the day-to-day running of the plant would have been welcomed by him. In addition to the system freeing the entrepreneur from the duties of management, it had further aspects to recommend it to him.

4.2.4 The first was in terms of quality. We have already noted that Wedgwood saw such short-cycle work as a means to consistency of product quality…'Make such machines of men as can not err.' But the real economic gains that accrued from the system were not from quality, but from two other aspects that gave high volume at low cost.

4.2.5 In the first place the system gave a great boost to productivity because the operator became highly dexterous in the performance of such a repetitive job. Secondly, not only did it allow the scarce skills to be reserved for the high-quality work that they were capable of doing, but it also meant that the less skilled parts of the job could be paid for at a lower rate. Obviously even without the tie-up with machinery these two advantages would have tended not only to create short-cycle work, but also to make it economically non-viable for *any* manufacturer in a market economy to avoid such methods if his competitors had chosen to employ them, an influence that to this day dominates those industries in which long-cycle work would be *technically* possible but is not *economically* possible. We shall later consider precisely such a case when we look at mass-production tailoring.

4.2.6 However, our present interest is in the way in which 'special purpose' machinery has constrained the application of 'job-enrichment'. The link between such machinery and the short-cycle operations of Adam Smith is this: once the machine builder has seen these short-cycle jobs he had no difficulty whatsoever in imagining how to mechanize them. On the other hand, more complex longer cycles were too great a challenge for him. So the short-cycle jobs became mechanized. In every industry the 'special purpose' machinery that has proliferated has done so as a result of the previous method having been reduced to a few simplistic movements under the axioms of Adam Smith.

4.2.7 Yet such operations would not have been mechanized if that act would not yield higher productivity. This higher productivity logically must imply that an already short operation cycle was made shorter still. Not only that, but whatever slight variation in method that might have been possible in a short-cycle hand operation has now almost certainly gone. The scope for method variation in the simple act of feeding a machine is limited in the extreme, and I challenge anyone to 'enrich' such a job without great economic loss. Indeed, having come so far with mechanization, the next logical stage is to make the feeding of such machines robotic. That, however, is not to **enrich**, but to **dispose of** the job.

4.2.8 On the few occasions that 'special purpose' machinery has proved amenable to job-enrichment, one of two special conditions has applied.

(1) The 'special purpose' machinery used has been so cheap that the firm can afford to have it stand idle while the operator abandons it to use yet another piece of 'special purpose' machinery. Volvo's decision to move away from making cars on a conveyor-belt system to a system known as 'group working' must mean that the specialist tools are used less intensively, consequently, for any given level of car output, many more of these tools must be bought by the firm to offset the length of time that each will be standing idle.

(2) Alternatively, the 'special purpose' machinery must be able to operate without the continuous presence of any single attendant. The occasions when the Tavistock Institute of Human Relations have beneficially changed the social organization of the workforce have primarily been in this category. What made their modifications possible was that the machinery was not **intimately** coupled to the activity of the operator. E. L. Trist's work in coal-mining was facilitated by the existence of a large team of men associated with the coal-cutting equipment. This enabled Trist to modify the social arrangements of that workforce since quite clearly they were not all closely tied to the 'special purpose' machinery which was being employed. In the same way A. K. Rice was able to alter the working patterns of operators tending looms in the Ahmedabad textile mills in India, for the looms were automatic, and therefore, *although they needed to be serviced, they did not require the constant attention of any single operator who was tied to them by the needs of the machine.*

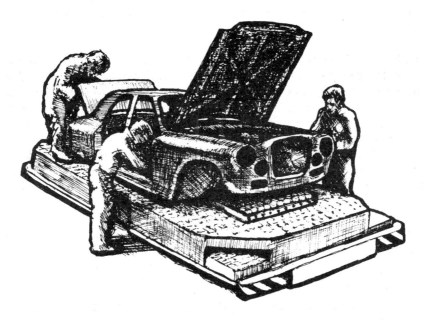

Figure 4.2(a) Group working at Volvo's Kalmar plant.

4.2.9 Interestingly enough, so vague has been the analysis concerning the circumstances in which 'special purpose' machinery is amenable to job-enrichment that even those commenting on the topic confuse the two conditions without (apparently) recognizing that they have done so. Car assembly at Volvo is, as I indicated, made possible by allowing relatively inexpensive equipment to stand idle. The manner in which a car is transported around the Volvo factory at Kalmar, thus allowing successive groups to work on each car, is shown in Figure 4.2(a) and according to most commentators the results have been beneficial. H. G. Jones (1983; p.79) claimed that applying the same principles elsewhere in Volvo has been equally effective. For example, he wrote that in one of their sub-assembly plants in Olofström, which lacks the glamour of an 'immediately evident sophisticated end product' and where the work was 'potentially noisy and heavy', it was found that labour turnover 'which has been as high as 40 per-cent has now been reduced to an average of less than 10 per cent – and in some sections to between 2 per cent and 3 per cent'.

4.2.10 In this other example Jones may be right to suggest that the same enrichment principle applied, namely that of electing to increase the interest of the worker's job at the cost of using equipment less intensively in a longer work-cycle.

But he also infers that the same principle is responsible for the increased output of the press shop. **He does this despite the evidence that he gives for there being more intensive use of equipment there.** Here are his words, (p.79): 'As for productivity, an important measure in a metal-working shop is the number of press-strokes per hour: throughout the period of group working at Olofström, there has been a steady improvement in the works average from 290 to 350.' If a change in group practices increased output in this manner it seems almost certain that it would have been a change of the **other** kind which I identified, namely **changing the nature of the interface between the group and the machinery being worked as exemplified in the Trist and Rice studies.** Such confusion of models in the mind of one interested enough to write on the subject gives some indication of how vague the more general literature is when discussing this area of technology.

4.2.11 As I have already indicated, the most famous examples of adapting the mode of working of teams of people associated with high-use machinery come from the Tavistock Institute of Human Relations in London, who have conducted many assignments of this type though it is not clear that they recognize themselves that their work has fallen into a specific category. A. K. Rice, whose work in Ahmedabad we noted in paragraph 4.2.8, was a member of that Institute. He used, as we saw, the latitude in how the operatives who tended the machines might be deployed to modify the nature of this organization and achieve a 21 per cent increase in productivity and a drop of 59 per cent in damaged cloth.

4.2.12 However, probably the best-known example of the work done by members of the Tavistock Institute is that of E.L. Trist in the mining community of County Durham, where the introduction of coal-cutting equipment into the mines had destroyed the old 'hand-got' system of autonomous work-groups of the type which will be described in paragraph 8.3.4. In the interest of greater efficiency the new equipment was essential. But because this new system, which Trist refers to as the 'conventional' Longwall organization, had destroyed the old 'hand-got' *social* relationships, it never achieved its *technical* potential. Trist and his associates (notably K. W. Bamford) modified the social system to attempt to put back some of the previous autonomous quality of the 'hand-got' relationships. The modified system, which they referred to as the 'composite' Longwall organization, had a marked effect upon the efficiency of the 'socio-technical system', as the figures in Table 4.2(a) show.

Table 4.2(a) (Data extracted from the text of Trist, Higgin, Murray and Pollock, 1963; pp.122–125)

	Conventional Longwall organization	Composite Longwall organization
Productivity (expressed as a percentage of coalface potential after due allowance for haulage system efficiency)	78.00	95.00
Percentage of shifts whose duties were unfinished in the allotted time	69.00	5.00
Absenteeism (expressed as a percentage of possible attendances)		
no reason given	4.3	0.4
sickness and other	8.9	4.6
accident	6.8	3.2
total	20.00	8.2

4.2.13 I wish to make it absolutely clear that I am not disparaging job-enrichment. Each example to which I have referred has not only been a commercial success story but has been so because of its humanizing elements. The point that I wish to make is that *each had* **necessarily** *to fall within the two special categories* (paragraph 4.2.8) *of 'special purpose' machinery or they would never have been technically possible at all.* This is a vitally important concept that appears to have been overlooked in the general euphoria surrounding these examples. In cases where the operator is employed to do no more than to stand by a machine and service it, managers are quite unable to alter the method of working in any way that could be considered at all analogous. It would therefore be completely immoral to load such a manager with a sense of guilt because he has not enriched such a job; yet I would suggest that texts such as Sirota and Wolfson's (quoted in paragraph 4.1.22), whether intentionally or not, will do precisely that unless the manager can be shown the hollowness of their claims.

4.3 The constraints that 'general purpose' machinery places upon 'job-enrichment'

4.3.1 What then of the constraints imposed by 'general purpose' machinery? By this term I refer to the relatively simple basic machinery which performs a single operation, but which, because of its wide range of machine settings, can be used in the manufacture of a wide range of products.

Such machinery may even be able to be used upon a variety of raw materials.

4.3.2 Almost any machine in an engineering works would be an example of this type. It will help if we regard them all as using different techniques to knock bits off a block of material. By starting with a different block and by knocking off different bits of it in different ways, the product range can be infinite. The material in the block may also be changed: ranging from steel, brass, aluminium, etc., to non-metals such as wood and plastics. These machines perform such simple operations as turning, boring, grinding, milling, shaping, planing, broaching, pressing, sawing and drilling. Yet with these operations, and a few others that I haven't mentioned, engineers make all the artefacts of that industry: a range which is capable of infinite variety, including machines to make machines.

4.3.3 Now although a machine of this type can be used for a great range of products, it might nevertheless take quite some time to adjust it for the job it has to do in any particular instance. This process is known as 'setting' the machine and the time taken to do it is known as 'set-up time'. It is very common in this sort of work to find that the set-up time is very much longer than the time taken to do the actual operation itself. For example, it may take me 15 minutes to set up a drilling machine and only 0.5 minutes to drill the hole that I set it up to make. It should be obvious that there is the most limited opportunity for 'job-enrichment' in the act of drilling a hole which takes 0.5 minutes to perform.

4.3.4 More than that, however, the reader should note that, to be economic, the operator would have to perform that same operation several times over and to drill a 'batch' of that particular product. Table 4.3(a) demonstrates why:

Table 4.3(a) The effect of batch size in reducing the impact of set-up cost

(a)	(b)	(c)	(d)	(e)	(f)
Set-up time	Operation time per occasion	Batch size	Total running time (b) × (c)	Total time (a) + (d)	Average time per operation (e) ÷ (c)
15.0	0.5	1	0.5	15.5	15.500
15.0	0.5	10	5.0	20.0	2.000
15.0	0.5	100	50.0	65.0	0.650
15.0	0.5	1000	500.0	515.0	0.515

4.3.5 I have entitled the above table using the term set-up **cost**, rather than set-up **time** because, for an 'hourly-paid' worker, time and money are directly proportional to each other. Indeed, we do not even have to know the rate of payment to know that each operation in a batch of 1000 will be thirty times cheaper than it would be if the batch size had been 1, because $15.5 \div 0.515 = 30.1$.

4.3.6 Hence this is one of the economic pressures determining the 'optimum batch size' (OBS) referred to in management textbooks. Of course, if this were the only criterion the OBS would be infinitely large. Clearly that would create difficulty in terms of the 'holding-cost' of such a batch. Indeed, from the holding-cost standpoint, the smaller the batch the better. Somewhere between the two lies the optimum size. This is where the set-up cost and the holding-cost are equal, so giving a minimum combined cost. This is the basis of calculating the OBS. The importance of this phenomenon to the debate on 'job-enrichment' should need no elaboration. When operating such 'general purpose' machinery, engineering and other workers are *condemned to performing short cycles and, moreover, to performing such cycles on a repetitive basis.* To do otherwise would not be economic. Job-enrichment in such a situation is limited. It consists only of allowing the worker to set up his own machine and to check that the resultant output is up to specification. This, I believe, all managements should allow; but it is little enough, and certainly too small a thing to claim the sort of job satisfaction that one of my sons, a production engineer, expressed about **his** job: 'I'd pay them to let me do it.' Yet in preaching the gospel of job-enrichment as the way to industrial peace, nothing short of this latter attitude is a credible solution: and even that will not succeed in eliminating the differences that arise from the worker being both resource and liability to capitalist managers.

4.3.7 To my mind, it is a pity that job-enrichment has been shackled to such idealistic nonsense on the one hand, and has been over-sold as being universally applicable on the other. For in those cases where job-enrichment **is** possible it often makes good sense commercially as well as being a humanizing element. At one time in industry the setting up of the machinery was seldom done by the operators. Instead it was done by men who specialized in this function and who were appropriately known as 'setters'. They thereby robbed the operatives of even such little job-enrichment that setting up might have given to them. Yet employing specialist setters is not as economic a use of total labour as might at first appear to be the case. Let us see why.

4.3.8 When any two resources come together to be used in conjunction, it usually implies that there will be an under-utilization of one or the other.

This is caused by the probability of a mismatch occuring. Let us illustrate this by considering ships coming into a set of docks. Either all the docks will be full and the ships will be queuing to get in, or some of the docks will be empty, awaiting ships. Seldom will the 'ideal' match occur of no ships queuing and all docks occupied.

4.3.9 It follows that one of management's most important and most frequent problems is to decide which, of any two resources that must be used in conjunction, should be *deliberately underloaded* so that the other resource is unlikely to be idle as a result of queuing. The degree of underload required to achieve this is often very great. Students will doubtless study 'queuing theory' as part of their business statistics training, so that I intend here to give no more than a descriptive insight.

4.3.10 I have already said that most machines in a machine-shop operate by knocking off bits of metal. In each case they use a tool to do it, and that tool gradually becomes blunt and needs sharpening. Let us assume that the operators sharpen their own tools. (Taylor would have had a fit at this suggestion; but more of that later.) Let us also assume that there is only one grinding wheel in the department. Since tool wear will be irregular, the men will approach the grinder at 'random' intervals of time. Perhaps when a man arrives there will be no one using the machine, perhaps someone else will be using it, or perhaps someone will be using it and one or more people will already have formed a queue to do the same. The statistical probability of this latter case happening gets greater, the more that the grinding machine is in use during the day. If its use gets much higher than about 60 per cent, queues become commonplace.

4.3.11 So it is with setters. If they are loaded to 100 per cent it is likely that they will not have finished setting up enough of the free machines before the operators who have completed their previous job start to queue. Moreover, using setters requires that the factory has many 'free' (i.e. unoccupied) machines. Otherwise when a setter was working on a machine its associated operator would have to wait. It follows that the cost of having 'setters' is not simply the social cost to the worker, who is denied the opportunity of setting up his own machine; it is also the cost of purposefully keeping those setters underemployed and the cost of proliferating the number of machines in the department. The latter increases both space and capital requirements.

4.3.12 I know of several firms who still use setters because of the 'backlash' of job-enrichment. In spite of the disadvantages of having setters, these firms have gone back to it because the operators were so bored with the actual job of production that they spent an inordinate time tinkering with the setting of their machines. I feel sure that there should have been some way of dealing with this problem other than a complete reversal to the practice of employing setters.

4.3.13 To sum up, on general purpose machines, where the set-up cost is disproportionately high compared to the cost of performing the operation, then short-cycle repetitive work is technically and economically unavoidable. It can be relieved (but no more than relieved) by allowing the operative to set up his own machine, and it will probably pay to do this. Only if set-up time can be made insignificantly short and the machines made flexible enough to be multi-purpose could the average engineering workshop worker be given long-cycle work which approached the integrative nature of that done by the old-time craftsman. But, apart from any other objections, I doubt the technical and economic viability of making a machine that is, say, a drill and a lathe and a milling machine.

4.3.14 Future development, by computer-controlled setting of machines, is likely to result in a smaller value of 'optimum batch size'. Nevertheless, because operation 2 is unlikely to be similar in character to operation 1 (by that I mean that if operation 1 is drilling then operation 2 may be milling), the work will still need to move to the next machine for the next operation. This suggests some other costs which are related to batch size in a similar way to the cost of setting up a machine. These are the costs of producing the paperwork associated with the batch, the costs of transporting the batch, and the costs of checking the batch's progress through the various operations to the finished product. In all these cases these costs, when considered as costs per unit, tend to be inversely proportional to batch size in just the same way as set-up costs are. It costs no more to produce the paperwork for an order calling for 1000 items than it does to produce one that calls for 10. It costs no more to move a box containing 1000 items than it does to move the same box containing 10, and it costs no more to check what has happened to that box whether it contains 1000 or 10. Of course, one of these days computers and computerized transportation systems may make what I have just written obsolete. However, I believe that when that day dawns the whole problem of worker monotony will have become irrelevant. For I find it inconceivable that the peripheral aspects of production should have reached the degree of sophistication required by that sort of system without the job itself being performed by robots.

4.3.15 In the meantime I'm afraid that (beyond allowing the operator to set up his machine) 'general purpose' machinery is not amenable to job-enrichment.

OM-D*

4.3.16 There is one 'general purpose' machine that is in common use on which the 'set-up' cost is minimal, and which therefore could perform a series of cycles without going beyond the bounds of economic credibility. Moreover, its operation is so basic that it is able to perform extremely long cycles before the product has cause to move on to another type of machine. I speak of the factory equivalent of the domestic sewing machine. If we think of, say, manufacturing a man's suit jacket, there are certain operations that will require certain specialist machines, button-holing, felling, overlocking, plonker-basting, etc. There are, moreover, 'special' sewing machines: machines which involve the same principle as the 'flat-bed' sewing machine which we are considering, but which have the bed of the machine replaced by an arm or a pillar to facilitate positioning the work. Nevertheless, having said all of that, the flat-bed sewing machine is probably responsible for over 80 per cent of all the work in the making of a jacket for a man's suit.

4.3.17 Yet even here, in a situation in which the conditions are favourable (perhaps even uniquely favourable) for job enlargement, and thereby perhaps for job-enrichment, I know of no firm that does so on a production basis. (Design departments sometimes use highly skilled girls to 'make-through' a garment: but this is for the convenience of such an arrangement: it is not done for economic reasons.)

4.3.18 I was concerned enough with this problem to attempt 'making-through' when I was Chief Executive of a men's suiting company employing some 2000 operatives (almost all young girls). My experiment failed on three counts while I felt myself to be mocked by the supercilious ghost of Adam Smith, who had known all along that it would do so.

(1) For whatever reason (and at this stage I don't want to get into a discussion as to whether a process of socialization had predisposed the operatives to low-achievement attitudes), few wanted to learn anything longer than a 2½ minute cycle. This was despite the fact that, in addition to the added job-interest factor, I was prepared to pay a premium for their flexibility.

(2) For a girl to acquire the skill to perform a 2½ minute cycle to an adequate standard of output and quality took 6 weeks. Although this period shortened slightly as a girl learned other operations, the training cost per operation was still considerable. This was set against a culture which created a labour turnover which was outside our control. In the mining villages of North East England, from where our employees came, a girl usually married at about 18 or 19. If her husband was a miner, which was often the case, he probably worked shifts. He therefore expected his

wife to be there when he returned: or so it was alleged. I suspected a 'macho' attitude concerning who should be the bread-winner also existed. So, if a girl came to us at 16 we were lucky to get three years' work from her before she left. Even 6 weeks' training out of 150 weeks represents a considerable training cost at 4 per cent. Extending the period of training for the same period of employment would raise this percentage.

(3) In the factory as a whole we achieved an output of one jacket for every 3⅓ hours of attendance time. This is therefore a measure of the productivity that was attainable by the *average* girl within our factory. This was achieved because in the making of any one jacket, eighty different operations were performed by eighty different girls, each one performing a 2½ minute operation on average. We have seen (paragraph 4.2.5) how dexterity increases with repetition. Given our technology, even the most exceptional girl could not have 'made-through' a jacket to the quality required by us in 3⅓ hours, and I beg the reader to accept my assurance that that was so. Yet not only did we achieve this level or productivity year in and year out; we did so (in effect) with the talents of the average girl in our employment.

4.3.19 This is another issue that I feel that the neo-human relations writers have not faced honestly. Their emphasis upon job-enrichment does not acknowledge the fact that thanks to short-cycle repetitive work there are people with minimal marketable talents that are making a living and who can have pride in their ability to support themselves. Some years ago I read a moving book by Carlo Levi about the desolation of life in Southern Italy. I needed to be reminded of the author's name but I remembered very clearly the title. It was *Christ stopped at Eboli*. The implication was that after you passed Eboli on your way south you went back into another age. It was not just a time-slip into the economy of the Middle Ages; it was into a virtually pre-Christian era.

4.3.20 Around the late 1960s Scandinavian suit-manufacturers found that inflation was getting the better of them. For all their superbly 'engineered' tailoring methods, their labour costs had risen to such an extent that they were being driven out of the export markets that they had for so long dominated. So they closed down their Scandinavian plants and took their money and their 'know-how' to such places as Southern Italy. There, thanks entirely to management skills and to the principle of teaching a 2½ minute cycle to peasants who had been left in degradation and illiteracy for centuries, they were producing, within weeks rather than months, superb merchandise for sale in the West End of London.

4.3.21 Of course this was no act of philanthropy. Since there were no competitive employers in the area, I imagine that wage-rates were low. But let us try to imagine the change to that area, and the general attitude that the workers would be likely to have towards such an employer.

4.3.22 The reason why I have chosen such an extreme example to make my point is that it says positively what is offensive when said negatively. However, let us not duck the issue: let us say it negatively. What skills does a 16-year-old girl in a mining village in the North East of England have that could be tapped by an enterprising management in such a way that the girl would feel vitally fulfilled, and which would produce a competitively marketable product of any type that one could care to name? There is another aspect of this question also that needs to be answered. Are we prepared to say that workers who are forced by circumstances to perform short-cycle repetitive operations (and there are millions of them all over the world whose situation cannot be improved unless they move on to other work) must ultimately become alienated from their own nature and from the world at large? The evidence is by no means as cut and dried on that subject as Marxists and neo-human relations writers would have us believe. But this is something to pursue later.

5

Life is full of ambiguities: theories that presume otherwise are immature, false ... and popular

Why is all around us here
As if some lesser god had made the world
But had not force to shape it as he would?
A. Tennyson (1809–92)

5.1 Admitting that truth is often ambiguous is a liberating experience

5.1.1 In the last chapter we saw how there are usually two or more threads which we need to follow in order to extricate ourselves from the management theory jungle. But this was no great problem, even when the various threads led in different directions. Indeed, it gave us certain cross-bearings by which to estimate the shape and dimensions of the maze.

5.1.2 On the one hand, we saw that neo-human relations writers claim that people will be most motivated when they can achieve psychological 'growth' from what they do. We did not consider the validity of this claim, but I would doubt if the reader did not sense its considerable intuitive appeal. (We can see how a baby delights in its new achievements, and the euphoria which accompanies having (say) passed a driving test is a common experience.) If such growth were thought to be a major motivator, we can readily see that the logical policy to follow would be job-enrichment. We therefore have no difficulty in understanding why such theories should exist.

5.1.3 On the other hand, neither have we any difficulty in seeing the technological and economic limitations to job-enrichment (imposed by the use of 'special purpose' and 'general purpose' machinery) are as near 'brute facts' as anything in life can be. This does not cause us to question the neo-human relations belief in 'growth', but it does bring us to question their claim that job-enrichment is widely applicable. Nor does it necessarily bring us to question their basic honesty, for we can see how it is quite likely that neo-human relations writers would lack any conscious awareness of the strength of the technical limitations to job-enrichment. These would be hidden from them by their non-technical backgrounds and by their enthusiasm for the Mosaic-myth element in their ideology which caused them to focus their eyes on the promised land and caused them to miss more immediate, mundane, inconvenient factors.

5.1.4 So, it is the very pulls of the contradictory elements in the situation that allow the mature-minded reader to know the nature of the issues and why the maze is the shape it is. He has developed valuable insights into the minds of the neo-human relations writers but equally he has gained an insight into the mind of Taylor. He now has no difficulty in seeing why Taylor (whose knowledge of technological constraints was as great as his hope for a world of high productivity and industrial peace) should have incorporated in his own ideology a Mosaic-myth element, namely that cash would settle all differences.

5.1.5 I hope and trust that the reader shares with me the feeling that the conclusions reached above:

(a) have some claim to objectivity, and
(b) say something which will help the manager to determine what practical steps he might usefully take.

If he shares this reaction with me then there are two observations that are important to make. The first is that we reached these conclusions because we were able to turn up enough 'factual' substance to feel that we had come to grips with the reality of the situation. It is this realization which quietens our misgivings that the approach has to be dependent on a subjective assessment; namely our 'sense of the absurd'. For to have denied the validity of our conclusions would have required us to be intellectually dishonest. In other words, in practice, far from being diffident about our ability to sense the absurd, we reached the point of insisting on the right to do so. This tends to support Pears's claim for the objective properties of the approach. He said, it will be remembered (paragraph 2.2.6), that 'when [rival claimants] try to shout each other down, we need not listen. We can ignore the bedlam, and attain some degree of objectivity by tracing the divergent ways in which they have developed from a single starting point.'

5.1.6 The second thing to note is as follows. If the conclusions we reached would be of use to the practising manager (and I suggest that they would), it is not a usefulness that is dependent upon a *resolution* of the issues. For the issues were *not* resolved. Any usefulness that it contains arises from the value of having the issues clearly stated, even though within that statement there are contradictory elements and ambiguities. It may sound odd to speak of a clear statement of ambiguities: but it is not so, for the word 'ambiguity' is itself ambiguous, in the sense that it can have one of two meanings. It can mean 'uncertain': but it can also mean 'equivocal'. For example, there is nothing uncertain about the clear statement that the Christian believes simultaneously in the following two concepts:

(i)   human nature is corrupt;
(ii) human beings are built in the image of God.

This represents an ambiguity not of the **uncertain** kind but of the **equivocal** kind. Moreover, the actions which flow from it are also clear enough. Indeed, it is the clarity of this particular equivocal vision of man which explains the two-part response which I and many others adopt.

Our response to to (i) is to seek to avoid centralized control. Sharing Lord Acton's belief that 'power tends to corrupt and absolute power corrupts absolutely', we support capitalism because its natural pluralism makes totalitarianism less likely.

Our response to (ii) is to seek to modify capitalism and to attach to it some sort of social 'safety-net' because we believe that those hurt by the blind operation of market forces are entitled to some protection – an entitlement which stems from their worth as human beings.

5.1.7 If, therefore, reality may involve us in adopting models which are (a) objectively valid but (b) contradictory, and if the actions which flow from adopting those models enable us to cope better with life than we otherwise would have done, such a conclusion is vitally significant to dealing with the management theory jungle. Indeed, it brings into question the whole philosophy of assuming that if we could only find the right single thread, some unambiguous, key, simplistic theory, we should get clear of the maze.

5.1.8 I have no doubt that there are those who would debate the proposition that if we could attain to a high enough platform from which to perceive 'Absolute Truth' (whatever that may be) we should find all contradictions were resolved. But that is so metaphysical a concept as to be beyond the speculation of this book. What I am prepared to stipulate and to defend is the concept that 'truth', when it is defined as 'the most honest expression of reality to which humans can aspire', is frequently ambiguous. We see this when, in an attempt to encapsulate truth, we are forced to develop such hyphenated contradictions as are present in the word 'love-hate'. Yet which of us would deny that that ambivalent expression is the truest description we could apply to some of our relationships?

5.1.9 All of this brings me to a consideration of some of the simultaneous (yet contradictory) developments which have occurred in the history of Western societies and of their organizations during the last two centuries. However mutually incompatible these have been, and whatever difficulties that mutual incompatibility may place in the path of obtaining a 'solution' to the problems of organization and management, we cannot jettison either if, each is valid. Life would be a great deal 'tidier' and far less tense if we were to eliminate the awkward bits and develop an '**either…or**' approach, But I assume that the reader shares my view that we are not free to do that. Intellectual honesty demands that our approach to management and organization should embrace as much of the truth as we can encompass. In short, we must hold fast to a '**both…and**' appreciation of the issues involved… contradictions included. The developments to which I referred are shown graphically in figure 5.1.(a).

5.1.10 In Figure 5.1.(a) I have shown seven different changes which have taken place in society and organizations over the course of the last two centuries. The factor I have chosen to place at one end of each of the seven continua could be regarded as the antithesis of the factor at the other end. Yet in no instance is the reader to suppose either that the left-hand factor of the continuum ever existed in its extreme form, nor that we have attained, nor shall ever attain, the right-hand extreme of the continuum. With that qualification, I suggest that the polarized qualities of the chosen factors are useful in identifying the general direction of shift.

5.1.11 It may help to explain the manner in which I suggest that these continua should be used by making some comments upon one of them. I think that most people would agree that there has been a shift in government policy and practice from regarding laissez-faire as desirable to regarding intervention as desirable. We shall have occasion to qualify this, for in the area of social welfare (such as sickness and unemployment relief) the

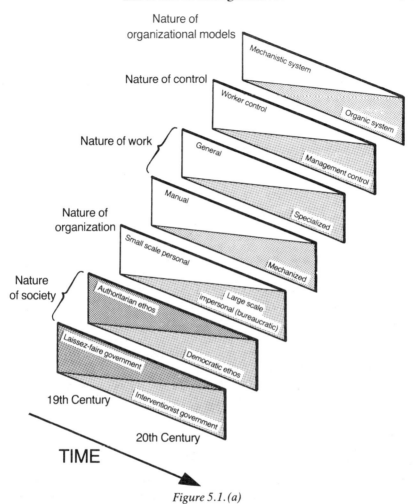

Nature of
organizational models

Mechanistic system

Nature of control

Worker control

Organic system

Nature of work

General

Management control

Manual

Specialized

Nature of
organization

Small scale personal

Mechanized

Nature
of society

Authoritarian ethos

Large scale
impersonal (bureaucratic)

Laissez-faire government

Democratic ethos

19th Century

Interventionist government

20th Century

TIME

Figure 5.1.(a)

governments of Western Europe have gone much further down the road of
intervention than has that of the USA. (I shall later claim that it is reaction
to this situation that has caused some American writers to pretend to the
firm having an exaggerated social role in its dealings with the worker, and
others to pretend to it having none at all.) Nevertheless, even in the United
States, the general drift from laissez-faire to interventionist government
holds good. To demonstrate this we need only instance US legislation fixing
maximum allowed levels of toxics from car exhausts.

5.1.12 This move towards interventionist government has been only one of two major shifts in the nature of society. The other is that society has shifted from a past ethos in which authoritarianism was the norm to the present one in which democratic values prevail. But even here we begin to catch a sense of contradiction in these two shifts. For interventionist governments take action because, if they did not do so the parties involved would not have chosen to act as the Government desired they should. If that were not the case there would have been no need for intervention in the first place. So interventionist government is basically paternalistic in character: but what is this other than adopting an authoritarian line for allegedly good motives?

5.1.13 These ambiguous developments in society are matched by different but related ambiguities in organizational developments. Earlier organizations were smaller and more personal than those which were to follow. Smallness is often characterized as preferable. Yet such firms were often associated with sweat-shops and the worst forms of entrepreneurial exploitation. This is scarcely surprising in a world in which authority was vested in the entrepreneur by reason of his economic position; a position which laissez-faire attitudes not only permitted him to abuse if he so chose, but also justified him in if he did so. On the other hand, it is commonplace to regret the later growth of organizations as creating for the worker, by that very size, a dehumanized world of impersonal bureaucratic structures and ethos. Yet, as we shall see, that the same impersonality springs, not least, from a genuine attempt to be fair: to deal with people by categories and to use consistent and known rules. So the effects of increased scale are not wholly bad, and we are again presented with ambivalent imagery.

5.1.14 It is chiefly because large-scale operations are able to achieve economies of scale that today's worker can afford to buy from an immense range of good-quality cheap goods which, had they even existed, would have been far beyond the economic means of his or her forebears. But this social gain has demanded that a social cost be paid. Scale, of itself, has little to recommend it and, of itself, develops few economies. The exceptions to this arise in those few instances involving huge capital equipment projects, as, for example where, relative to its capacity, a bigger furnace or a bigger rolling mill is cheaper to build and to operate than a number of smaller plants. Certain overheads are more easily recovered from scale also. But, generally speaking, the more important vehicles by which such economies are achieved are the twin means of specialization and mechanization. To speak of the 'economies of scale' is mainly to acknowledge that, increased scale leads to more instances in which these two devices of specialization and mechanization can be used. But their use is extremely ambivalent in its social outcome. Mechanization has reduced much manual drudgery, but it has done so in a context which, as I said, involved a social cost which has been generally acknowledged and deplored.

5.1.15 For the nature of work has moved from being general and manual to being specialized and mechanized, and with that change the worker has lost autonomy and control. Not only does specialization bring with it the possibility that the work will become monotonous, but specialization poses the problem of how the various specialisms are to be co-ordinated. For without such co-ordination these specialisms would never succeed in their ultimate purpose of achieving the organization's goals. We shall find that there are many reasons why the job of co-ordinating is given to someone whose position is higher in the hierarchy than that of the person performing the specialism: but however justified this may prove to be, the net effect is to move control upward from worker to manager. So the direction of these developments runs counter to that of the shift in society away from authoritarianism and towards democracy. We cannot be surprised if the ambivalence caused by this contra-flow of ethos results in frustration and conflict.

5.1.16 Lastly, there has been a general tendency away from looking at organizations as mechanistic systems and towards seeing them as organic systems. By that I mean that early 'classical' theory tended to regard the organization as a construction set, the purpose of which was to achieve a type of mechanistic efficiency by means of a pyramid of specialist functions. The most efficient form and shape to give to this pyramid was supposedly to be derived from certain organizational 'principles'. The ambivalence here is two-fold. The first results from those who support the 'systems' approach having overstressed the extent to which their 'organic' imagery is to be regarded as the antithesis of the previous 'mechanistic' imagery.

5.1.17 By this I do not wish to deny the value of the 'systems' vision, which has many legitimate advantages over the cruder mechanistic imagery. Their approach is to view the firm as an organism which is attempting to survive in a hostile environment. To do that, the firm must do what an organism does: namely, monitor the threat and then modify its behaviour and even its own physical characteristics in order to cope with that threat. This shift of emphasis is highly significant and is to be welcomed, not least because it has extended the boundaries of the 'system' beyond those inferred by the earlier and more 'mechanistic' concepts. We have already seen how Trist's work in coal-mines led him to insist that the organization is a socio-technical system. In so doing he made us aware that we needed to change our way of looking at things; in particular, to recognize that if the system as a whole is to be efficient then we must extend the boundaries of our perception of what makes it efficient. So expressed it becomes a nonsense to ignore, as had previously been the case, those conditions which were necessary for the efficient operation of the human 'subsystem' namely the worker.

5.1.18 But systems writers have largely overstated their case. In their anxiety to show that their vision differs from the mechanistic they have stressed this polarity to such an extent that they have created confusion for the manager and lost credibility. For example, when systems writers are true to themselves, they accept the need for hierarchy. Yet that is not the message that most managers receive. So the manager who perceives the need for hierarchy believes that he has fallen from grace with the 'systems' approach and lapsed into 'mechanistic' concepts. Thus his attitude towards the mechanistic/systems controversy becomes unnecessarily confused. This then is the first (and gratuitously unnecessary) ambiguity which this switch from mechanistic to organic imagery has aroused.

5.1.19 However if systems writers were to modify their approach and were to take the line I am about to suggest, they would not escape ambiguity. I believe that 'systems' theory has become seduced with its own anti-mechanistic propaganda; I suggest that those involved need to backtrack to the point at which they began to infer that certain concepts vital to the success of systems thought, such as hierarchy, should be labelled 'mechanistic' and be renounced as heresy. However, if they were able to do so, I must warn that the effect would only be to substitute yet another ambiguity for the current one. Currently the ambiguity is between the reality of the situation and the exaggerated claims of systems writers. If they do as I suggest, the new ambiguity will occur because sometimes truth will be defined in 'mechanistic' terms, and sometimes in 'systems' terms. Yet such ambiguity has been common in the history of science, and is a reflection of honest endeavour. The puzzles of the electron, wrote Bronowski (1973; p.364) led to the

> quip among professors... (because of the way that university timetables are laid out) that on Mondays, Wednesdays, and Fridays the electron would behave like a particle; on Tuesdays, Thursdays and Saturdays it would behave like a wave... The world... shifts under our gaze, it interacts with us, and the knowledge that it yields needs to be interpreted by us. There is no way of exchanging information that does not demand an act of judgement.

5.2 Why the ambiguity of figure–ground oscillation is essential to Organization and Management theory

5.2.1 The title of this section has singled out Organization and Management theory as needing this 'figure–ground' oscillation. However, my hope is that, by the end of this section, the reader will see that this particular form of ambiguity is essential to our perception if we are to be able to cope successfully in any area of human activity. Only because this book is concerned with Organization and Management are we treating this need as if it specifically relates to these areas. Indeed, the image that I shall use for illustration purposes (Figure 5.2.(a)) is a diagram which frequently occurs in texts concerned with the general psychology of perception, though it occurs also in texts on management. Its purpose is to highlight the way in which each of us imposes upon the stimuli that he receives from the world some patterning, or framework. This is an issue that we discussed in section 2.1 and there is certainly no need to repeat it here.

Figure 5.2.(a)

5.2.2 But even if we accept, as is generally held to be true, that there is more than one way of interpreting 'facts' and even if one admits that these interpretations will be conditional upon the 'frame of reference' that each person brings to bear, I still find it at odds with our experience of life that most textbooks emphasize that such perception will be **either** in one framework **or** the other. They thereby imply that we have very limited capacity to switch frameworks. Figure 5.2(a) can be seen as **either** a white vase on a black ground **or** as a pair of black-silhouetted heads on a white ground. But it is obviously *also* possible to recognize that it is **both** a vase **and** a silhouette (though our perception may have to oscillate in time from one to the other).

5.2.3 To my mind, although there are many strong and obvious reasons for emphasizing the **'either...or'** relationship, there are equally strong reasons for emphasizing **'both...and'**. These have either gone unnoticed or their value has been discounted. I would maintain that the result of this neglect has been to distort management theory into simplistic parodies of what really happens.

5.2.4 Now it is certainly important to emphasize the 'either...or' element in human perception, for we know that a person will tend to resist the introduction of new concepts which threaten to invalidate his existing frame of reference. I have deliberately used the word 'threaten' because we all find a sense of security in the existing picture of the world which we have formed and in which we have somehow managed to make things hang together into some sort of sense. We therefore cherish deeply this patterning which forms our 'cognition', *'Weltanschauung'* or 'ideology'. Now along comes this piece of data that doesn't seem to fit, and which, if allowed in, would call the whole of our cognition into question. Small wonder that we check against our existing cognition before we decide whether to accept new data or not.

5.2.5 It is important for the educationalist to recognize that students will not accept information that causes too much trauma for them in making it 'fit', just as it is important for the manager to realize that his workforce may also reject information that does not 'fit'. He can be almost certain that they will do so if to accept the information would require them to make changes in their existing world which would be so great as to be traumatic. Communication does not take place until the person with whom we have tried to communicate has accepted our message: it is not the **transmission** but the **reception** of the message that constitutes communication. The manner in which educationalists now instinctively avoid references to 'teaching' but instead speak mainly of 'learning' is only one of many consequences of this realization.

5.2.6 If I am presented with a piece of information I have three possible responses.

(1) I can check it against my existing knowledge and recognize that it is

something that I already know. It is therefore redundant information and no learning takes place.

(2) I can check it against my existing knowledge and find that its acceptance will do so much violence to my view of the world that I reject it. I usually find some reason for discrediting the information in order to maintain and defend my existing world in the face of this attack. In this case no learning takes place.

(3) I can check it against my existing knowledge and find that, although it will mean some rearrangement of my world (the dropping of this, the emphasis of that, the de-emphasis of these, etc.), yet I can afford to do this because the resultant changes will not be so great as to be traumatic. I therefore do so. Then, and **only** then, does communication and learning take place.

5.2.7 This is why the teacher or the manager must be very conscious of the *Weltanschauung* of his audience. He must not to try to sell them anything which, given where they now stand, will be too outlandish for them to accept. To change a person's *Weltanschauung* radically will generally require us to do so by a series of steps. We thus accomplish the big shift by a series of small shifts, none of which is too great for them to handle. This is not a patronizing act, for what we have just described is part of the human condition which applies to the communicator as much as anyone else, and to ignore it would be as foolish as driving a car into a brick wall because we refused to believe that it was there. Indeed, one of the thoughts uppermost in my mind in writing this book was the nature and sequence of the presentation, not merely to present the issues in some logically related sequence, but also to present them in such a way that the reader had the opportunity to make any progressive minor shifts in *Weltanschauung* that might be necessary so that he could accept any possible major shift in *Weltanschauung* that its contents might require of him.

5.2.8 All of this explains why we all have a tendency to adopt only one frame of reference, and also why most textbooks go to some pains to suggest that, given alternative explanations for certain phenomena, our response is likely to be to gravitate to one or the other, dependent upon our prevailing frame of reference. That is to say, we choose on the basis of 'either...or' rather than that of 'both...and'.

5.2.9 Now whereas this may be true, it sells the human race short, for it does not recognize our capacity as adults to live with ambiguity. Neither does it recognize our innate need to oscillate from one frame of reference to another when we feel that each of them encapsulates some of the truth while neither of them does so completely. Not then to oscillate would violate our integrity. Moreover, it ignores the many situations in which the person's sense of security is the greater when he **does** switch from one frame of reference to another, as is the case with many workers.

5.2.10 We saw in Section 1.2 that the *mores* of capitalism require that managements adopt an ambiguous attitude in their perception of the worker, and a similar ambiguity was likewise induced in the worker's perception of the management. The extent of their mutual need does indeed encourage co-operation, but it does not disguise their potential conflict: a conflict that will occur when one and/or the other attempts to change the status quo in favour of their particular interests. This frequently occurs when some change in the environment is perceived by one or the other as requiring a change in company practices. Alternatively, it can occur when, even in the absence of such stimuli, the aspirations of the parties change sufficiently to make them so dissatisfied with the status quo that they demand change.

5.2.11 The worker in a capitalist situation is frequently driven to see that he must prepare against such a contingency by increasing his future bargaining power. He therefore joins a trade union to ensure that when the conflict comes he will be in as strong a position as he can be to meet the threat. But he does not then normally behave as though he were at war with management. Generally he achieves satisfaction from his work precisely because it **is** a co-operative venture. Indeed, when he sees his trade union leaders using their position to wage an ideological war against capitalism, that too he regards as a threat.

5.2.12 The worker therefore oscillates between two frames of reference. But this is an uncomfortable experience for him, so that he does so as infrequently as possible. This is the reason why agreements made between unions and management are usually for a considerable period. Wage reviews, for example, are seldom more frequent than once a year. But it would be a travesty to suggest that this ambivalence is not perpetually lurking at the back of the worker's mind, nor that, just because he has co-operated with management for a long period, he will not, in response to some stimulus, switch into an unco-operative mode of behaviour.

5.2.13 Equally the Marxist view that the worker has a **constantly** hostile attitude to management cannot be maintained, even by those spreading such propaganda. The drawing in Figure 5.2(b) is a sketch that I made from a photograph on a Marxist poster. The photograph is a very well-known one and, I believe, was taken in Wigan in the 1930s. It is of a despondent man 'on the dole'. The purpose of the poster (printed in 1982) was to attack capitalism's failure to cope with unemployment: and this is certainly the biggest single problem in the capitalist system. However, the irony of the situation is that the man's almost palpable misery is precisely because he has been excluded from the very system with which they would have us believe that he has absolutely no affinity.

Figure 5.2(b)

5.2.14 It is noteworthy too that most trade unionists reject this unambivalent Marxist condemnation of the whole capitalist system. Instead they seek only to get the best deal that they can within the existing system. This has long been acknowledged by both Marxists and non-Marxists. Allan Flanders (in McCarthy, 1972; pp.17, 18) reviews the Marxist claim that unions 'by their nature are tied to capitalism' and so 'can [only] bargain with society but not transform it'. Flanders agrees that union policy consists of 'doggedly sticking to their immediate ends and refusing to be captured by any political party; but he strenuously denies the Marxist claim that this cannot be the means of changing society. Indeed, he maintains that the unions have already succeeded in doing so. 'That they may be right', he adds, 'in preferring reform to revolution and unity to discord never crosses the mind of [their Marxist critics].'

5.2.15 So no one really doubts that trade union policy is to live in an ambivalent posture within capitalism in which they challenge its *mores* but accept the basic system. The only issue is whether this ambivalence is to be condemned. Leftists condemn it for watering down their radicalism. Rightists condemn it because, while offering no coherent alternative system, they see it as gumming up the works of the one we have. Those in the middle of the political spectrum often regard the outcome of trade union ambivalence, which frequently amounts to a call to go 'full speed ahead with all brakes on', with amused contempt. The wide popularity of the late David Low's political cartoons owed much to the way the public took to their hearts his vision of the TUC (Trades Union Congress). This he always depicted as an amiable and not very bright cart-horse. Yet there is another dimension to Low's vision. Of the people who approve the way in which capitalism's economic decentralization promotes political pluralism (and if one includes all who instinctively sense it, there must be millions), few would claim that unbridled market forces need no apology, modification, or restraint. So they are seeking for the best of two worlds, a 'both...and' reconciliation of value-systems whose incompatible elements will defy resolution and thereby create ambiguity for those making the attempt. Some may find this leads them to ambiguity of the 'uncertain' kind when they begin to doubt the fundamental wisdom of adhering to capitalism. Others, like myself, are led to the ambiguity of the 'equivocal' kind. We recognize the irreconcilable nature of the two value-systems between which we are oscillating but we cling tenaciously to both.

5.2.16 Most supporters of capitalism experience at least some ambiguity towards it. However, they sense (and rightly) that politico-economic systems can inflict worse things on people living under them than the tensions of ambivalence. The ambivalence towards capitalism arises, as we have seen, from conflicting standards. On the one hand, the sheer indifference of laissez-faire market forces to social need affronts our humanitarian instincts. On the other hand, we need an integrative power which will not tyrannize us; which role the 'invisible hand' of market forces is uniquely able to fill. No other system than capitalism could be so diffuse, decentralized and reactive to the changing wishes of those with the money to be customers. I am convinced that more people than is commonly supposed recognize that their fundamental choice is between

(a) an ambiguous relationship with capitalism on the one hand, or
(b) (i) the unambiguous chaos of anarchy or
    (ii) the unambiguous order of totalitarianism.

Given these options, some may either renounce capitalism or alternatively suffer the 'uncertain' kind of ambiguity concerning what they should feel. Yet a surprising number are mature enough to live with the 'equivocal' kind of ambiguity, and face the 'both...and' need to oscillate between two different value-systems, neither of which they are prepared to relinquish.

5.2.17 All of this brings us back to Low's TUC cart-horse. Low's popularity showed that his public shared his amusement and even his irritation at the knots into which trade unionists often tie themselves. Yet I believe that there was a widespread recognition that the TUC's bumbling arose in large measure because it shared their own ambivalence. It might be committed to calming the fears and meeting the aspirations of the membership of its affiliated unions, but it was committed to doing so while clinging tenaciously to the pluralist advantages which derive from capitalism. That is not a formula for incisiveness, but it is a stance which can evoke sympathy, and this I believe it did. Low's public were able to identify with the general aspirations of the TUC precisely because these reflected their own: namely to find some means of solving the ambiguities within capitalism. Herein lies its ultimate ambiguity. For it is not a problem that is going to be solved, yet neither is it a problem from which those of us who are pluralists can walk away. Few of Low's public (who accepted his image of the TUC as a none-too-bright cart-horse) could therefore have ever thought it capable of solving the dilemma, yet they did hold that same cart-horse in affectionate esteem for its benign intentions and its sheer tenacity in attempting, year after year, to reconcile the irreconcilable. Just how tenaciously, if ambivalently, most trade unionists cling to the capitalist system is underlined by certain issues raised during the course of the miners' strike of 1984.

5.2.18 These issues centre around the legitimacy of trade unions to enter the political arena. In one sense it was likely that at some stage, irrespective of the personalities involved, an industrial dispute in the coal industry would raise 'political' issues. The coal industry had for decades been in public ownership. So the National Coal Board, in addition to managing the industry, were also agents of the Government. Moreover, the industry had been making enormous losses which could only be met by government subsidy from taxation and the Coal Board's chairman had been appointed by the Prime Minister to make the industry profitable. It was therefore likely that, in any confrontation, the executive of the National Union of Mineworkers (NUM) would claim that the National Coal Board were only puppets and that their real enemy was the Government. Given the personalities on the NUM executive and the fact that the government of the day was Conservative, any strike would therefore have 'political' overtones.

5.2.19 So, precisely because these 'political' overtones would be sure to surface in any miners' strike, it cannot be to these overtones alone that those trade unionists who criticized the NUM's executives intentions as 'political' were alluding. Moreover, whatever they meant by 'political', it was clear that they felt it to be **outside the legitimate range of trade union activity.** (We are less concerned here with the motives of the NUM executive than with an insight into what their fellow trade unionists meant by the word 'political' and what it was that made such 'political' intentions 'improper').

5.2.20 From the context of the statements, we can infer that these critics of the NUM executive had reached one or both of the following conclusions:

(1) That the attack upon the Government was not incidental to the solving of an industrial problem, but that the industrial problem was the opportunity for the attack. (We need not pursue this charge, though we should note that coming from their fellow trade unionists it has greater weight than if it had been made by management. Our interest is in the second conclusion below.)

(2) That any actions which are not consistent with a policy of seeking to define and to solve problems within the framework of capitalism do not constitute legitimate trade unionism. (This is implicit in the pejorative manner in which they used the word 'political', and the further implication that it ought to be possible to achieve the legitimate objectives of trade union members within the existing political framework).

5.2.21 To the extent that these critics typify the attitude of the average trade unionist, their ambivalence highlights a basic ambivalence in the movement. Many of these critics were union officials whose day-to-day work largely consisted of attempting to persuade management to adopt values **other** than those of market forces in specific cases. We therefore might reasonably have expected them to see in the NUM's demands **the logical conclusion of their own arguments.** For the NUM case undoubtedly argued for values other than market forces: indeed, it amounted to a claim that the mines should be insulated from market forces in order that they might be operated for the primary benefit of the miners. Yet those trade unionists who criticized the

NUM's executive did not do so because the latter stood for values which they themselves often sought to invoke. They did so because it expressed those values so unequivocally that it required them to abandon their second (simultaneously held) belief system; namely that of capitalism. For as I said earlier, most trade unionists seek not to deny the validity of market forces and the capitalist concept of minimizing opportunity cost, but only to modify it by other and more human concepts. To these critics the NUM executive's strike position was 'political' *precisely because it made no such concession.* Indeed, within capitalism (that is to say in any industry not taken into the 'public sector' by nationalization) the terms demanded by the NUM would have been economically impossible to fulfil and therefore ridiculous to demand. Even if the Coal Board agreed to them this would still not be cause for trade unionists generally to rejoice, for the two possible outcomes of such a deal would both be troublesome, as follows:

(1) Unless the Government wrote a blank cheque to cover subsidies, the Board could not honour any agreement made on the miners' terms. This the Government was unlikely to do, and at the first breech of the agreement everything would be back at square one, except that the situation would be yet more explosive.

(2) If the Government were to agree to honour such an arrangement (however unlikely) the rest of society, including other trade unionists, would have to pay for the unique advantages which the miners enjoyed.

5.2.22 It was the starkly (and even crazily) unambiguous position of the NUM which made some other trade unionists label their cause as 'political'. For the miners' position simply refused to acknowledge market forces. As a pluralist I too share Allan Flanders's approval of those trade unionists who operate within the capitalist framework to reform capitalism rather than to revolt against it (paragraph 5.2.14), and I am grateful that they form the majority. Yet no one can doubt the ambivalence of their position. *For they offer piecemeal opposition to specific situations **as and when they are created by the operation of market forces**. Moreover, the rationale for this opposition is almost invariably that, **in the case under consideration**, a value-system should prevail which is based upon more 'humane' values than those associated with allowing market forces (together with their associated policy of minimizing economic opportunity cost) to operate. The ambiguity of such trade unionists lies in that, until the next specific case under consideration they adopt a position in which they appear to accept, albeit tacitly, the general principle of allowing the market forces in society to operate.*

5.2.23 Before I close this catalogue of reasons why 'both...and' concepts are essential to appreciating the reality of organization and management, I must emphasize that without the ability to think in terms of 'both...and' (that is to say, to oscillate between different frames of reference) we could never hope even to design an organization.

5.2.24 There have been three basic approaches to organizational design; the so-called 'classical', 'human relations' and 'systems'. I do not wish to anticipate what I shall later have to say about these approaches, but a short review is essential to make the point. The primary concern of the 'classical' approach (so called because it was the earliest of the formal approaches and flourished between the two World Wars) was to determine what type(s) of specialization and hierarchy would optimize the efficiency of organizations. There is some truth to the claim that the approach to the use of specialization and hierarchy in classical theory was very mechanistic. Inevitably and rightly, therefore, this gave rise to the objection that the classical approach paid too little regard to the people in the organization, seeing them only as 'cogs in the machine'. This omission certainly justified some form of 'human relations' approach, not as an 'either...or' substitute for specialization and hierarchy, but as a 'both...and' modifier of those concepts. For, in making room for the needs of people, neither the need for specialization nor for hierarchy could legitimately be jettisoned. Despite this the human relations approach to organizational design came eventually to do both. *(It should be noted that whenever motivation is discussed management theory used the term 'human relations' in a precise way to mean the school of concepts associated with Elton Mayo. In sharp distinction to these, the motivational ideas of Douglas McGregor are the basis of 'neo-human relations' theory. However, when applied, as now, to organizational design the term 'human relations approach' is commonly used in a somewhat vague way which will cover almost any concept which stresses the significance of the human factor in organization design.)*

5.2.25 The historical development of the main theories which comprise the 'human relations approach' to organizational design is inextricably entwined with a particular Mosaic-myth ideology with its roots in American culture. Not all theories are Mosaic-myth ideologies: but all Mosaic-myth ideologies are theories. As such they share the same starting point as all other theories. This, as Popper has shown, is the need to solve a problem. In the case of Mosaic-myth ideologies the 'problem' is always 'dissatisfaction with the status quo of organized society', and the 'solution' is always some 'promised land'. This particular Mosaic-myth ideology arises from the American wish to humanize their society without interfering with the free operation of market forces. *The ideological promised land to which this directs them is one* *in which everybody accepts that it is socially and economically desirable that there should be the greatest degree of competition outside the firm: but that they equally accept that any competitive or contentious elements within the firm are wholly undesirable, both socially and economically.*

5.2.26 Although this myth is nowadays treated by most business schools throughout the world as if it were axiomatic, it is far from being so. Indeed, as I shall show, successful organizations insist that no department or division has a right to survive unless it can offer goods or services which are competitive in price and quality with those of the best external supplier. Yet despite clear evidence that this myth has, in practice, suffered universal rejection, to date there has been little attempt to provide any theory which explains or even acknowledges the discrepancy. This lack is itself mute testimony to the appeal of the ideology, for it indicates a widespread reluctance to do anything which will undermine its axiomatic status.

MAYOISM (HUMAN RELATIONS)

5.2.27 Mayoism's growth was fostered by the problems of motivating employees. In management theory 'motivation' is synonymous with 'getting the worker to share the goals of the organization'. When, in the 1920s and 1930s, Elton Mayo and his associates were concerned with the problem that the workers were not behaving as management intended, they did not blame it on the effect of hierarchy and specialization. Theirs was an autocratic age and they were no less autocratic than anyone else. So they tried to sell the idea that the way to get over the problem was to keep hierarchy and specialization but to make the firm equivalent to being the 'family' of the worker. The authoritarianism would remain, but now it would take the guise of a paternalistic interest in the worker to which he would respond in a filial manner. This 'family' concept fitted the Mosaic-myth, and gave further justification to regarding competition between people or departments as taboo.

McGREGORISM (NEO-HUMAN RELATIONS)

5.2.28 By the late 1950s and early 1960s such implicit authoritarianism was socially unacceptable. Nevertheless, the change in approach introduced by the neo-human relations writers did nothing to challenge the basic Mosaic-myth: the concept of competition within the firm remained anathema. What the neo-human relations writers offered was their vision of the firm in which, because hierarchy and specialization had largely been eliminated, people were not only given room to grow, but in the process became co-operative.

So the ideas of the neo-human relations school, for all that they were diametrically opposed to the patronizing ideas of the human relations school, served to perpetuate the same Mosaic-myth ideology.

5.2.29 There is a particular irony in the fact that the neo-human relations 'either...or' approach, which made the relinquishment of hierarchy and specialization the price of industrial peace, should have appeared when it did and that it should have met such academic approval. For at the very same time that neo-human relations ideology was being adopted as the received wisdom of our business schools, the **real** world of management was undergoing an unprecedented shake-up. Never before had interest in organizational design been more intense, and never before had entrepreneurs like Charles Clore used the principles of hierarchy and specialization to such dramatic effect as when they used them to stimulate internal competition. This was largely done by creating a structure which would allow the divisions of the firm to become independent 'profit-centres' and departments to became identifiable 'cost-centres'. By this practice, not only would those divisions or departments which were uncompetitive be exposed, but because they were identifiable self-contained entities which had a limited interface with the rest of the organization, disposal of such entities as could not be made competitive would cause minimal disturbance to the remainder of the organization.

5.2.30 It is clear from this that, even if we accept that 'classical' theory was lacking in concepts which would adequately cater to the needs of people in organizations, it was not realistic of the human relations theorists to attempt to satisfy these needs at the expense of all other organizational considerations. What the situation called for was a 'human relations' approach which would be 'both...and'. It should accommodate to the concepts of hierarchy, specialization and economic competitiveness, but ensure that in the process the needs of the employee were identified, and so far as possible (within the limits imposed by these three constraining factors) that those needs were incorporated into the design and operation of the organization. I do not wish here to anticipate my detailed criticism of the position to which the human relations approach has brought us. Yet I need to state my conclusions here in order to show the harm that can result from 'either...or' concepts: in this case the proposition that (1) either a manager uses hierarchy and specialization and is 'bad', or (2) he does not and is 'good'. For the simplistic and false assumption of the neo-human relations school is that specialization and hierarchy are the unnecessary trappings of an outmoded management style. It is because these assumptions have been incorporated into the human relations approach to organizational design that the approach has been such a failure in this, its prime task of maintaining corporate competitiveness. Nevertheless, propositions which make organizational nonsense can create ideological images that are still politically potent even when they are false. It used to be said of international economics, that if America sneezed, Europe caught a cold. The history of the human relations approach to organization is similar. President Calvin Coolidge encapsulated much of his countrymen's ethic in a statement that was pithy, even by the standards of 'Silent Cal'. It was 'The business of America is business.' Free from interventionism, American managers have astutely sidestepped the attack on hierarchy, and have succeeded in making the attack on specialization and their attempts to deal with it the focus of attention. We have seen that job-enrichment can only successfully be applied when certain conditions (which I specified earlier) exist. Yet when so applied, job-enrichment can be immensely successful. By contrast, interventionism in Europe is historically more commonplace. So the moral fervour with which European academics and politicians embraced the view that specialization and hierarchy are unnecessary features of reactionary managements led (tragically and inexorably) to the drafting of interventionist legislation aimed specifically at reducing managements' hierarchical powers. American theorists sneezed, but it was European management that caught the cold.

SYSTEMS

5.2.31 The systems criticism of classical theory seems also to have an element of truth but then by overstatement to tend to lapse into parody. It may well be that, by its emphasis upon specialization and hierarchy, classical organization theory sometimes came to place undue emphasis upon the achievement of **departmental** rather than **organizational** efficiency. However the typical 'systems' imagery of the way in which 'classical' managers operated usually sees them as having been so brainwashed by 'classical' concepts as to be unable to see that they were committing two most rudimentary faults: faults which call their stewardship into question. These are as follows:

(1) Classical managers concentrated upon departmental efficiency to such an extent that they failed to perceive that the success of the total enter-prise lay not in optimizing the operation of each department, but in optimizing the operation of all departments in conjunction. They are supposed not to have perceived that this might require the sub-optimal use of certain departments in order that the operation of the organization as a whole might be optimized.

(2) Classical emphasis is supposed also to make those managements who

adopt it
(a) inward-looking, and
(b) rigid.
(The usual systems jargon for indicating that 'classical' managers ignored the environment in which they operated and so failed to adapt is to say that they regarded their organizations as 'closed systems'. By contrast, systems managers, being aware of both, are supposed to regard their organizations as 'open systems'.)

5.2.32 The purpose of this exaggerated representation by systems theorists of the shortcomings of 'classical' managers is made, of course, to enhance the claim that systems thinking is (a) essential, and (b) different. I do not deny that there are positive advantages to be derived from formally regarding the organization as an organism which needs to be aware of, and respond to, environmental changes. But by suggesting that the 'classical' approach concentrated upon the bits of the organization with no reference to the whole or to what was happening around it, 'systems' writers invite us to believe that they have a completely different frame of reference.

5.2.33 The imagery that they conjure up is of a 'systems' manager who, when he designs an organization, conceives of it as an undifferentiated entity, ideally suited to its environment. This entity he will (by implication) split into specialist subsystems only to the extent that such splits do not jeopardize the inherent co-ordination of the original undifferentiated system. In effect they imply that we have an 'either...or' choice between the 'classical' approach (which allegedly thinks in terms of 'bits'), and the 'systems' approach (which thinks in terms of 'wholes'). But this is a false proposition based upon a caricature of both approaches. It is not simply false in the sense of being wrong: it is false in the sense of being beyond our intellectual or psychological ability to think exclusively in terms of *'bits'* **or** *'wholes'*. We have to think in terms of both *'bits'* **and** *'wholes'*, as indeed have all organizational theorists, including the much-maligned 'classical' school. Let us see why such 'both...and' thinking is inescapable.

5.2.34 If I were to ask the reader to think about a hospital, but **not** to think about the various specialist activities that take place there, such as the casualty department, the pathology laboratories, the wards, the operating theatres, etc., would he be able to do it? In other words, *can we even conceptualize a hospital in a completely undifferentiated way and as a totality without getting involved in thoughts about the specialisms that it will contain?* On the other hand, is there any sense in thinking about the specialist departments that I have just mentioned, as well as the many that I have not, without thinking of their interrelatedness? The same would be true of whatever one chose to design. The specification for an internal combustion engine must be related to its ultimate use. In isolation from the car, boat, aircraft, fire-pump or whatever totality for which it is designed, an internal combustion engine is just so much junk.

5.2.35 But if we cannot think serially from the whole to the part, or from the part to the whole, are we lost? Not a bit. We manage to oscillate between the two quite happily, using each in turn to show the possibilities and the limitations of the other. In fact if it were not for our inherent ability to do this with such facility that we are virtually unconscious of our skill in doing so, there would be no need for me to make this point. It is the reader's very facility to switch frames that disguises from him that he has habitually done that. He sees 'both...and' and not just 'either...or'. Yet in making this criticism I do not wish to belittle the impact made by general systems theory, not only in the realms of management, but in all walks of life. It is one of the most revolutionary concepts of the twentieth century as we shall acknowledge in Section 15.1. However, as far as management goes my belief is that its most significant impact has been upon the relationship between the firm and its environment rather than between the relationship between the firm and its own specialisms, where the need to modify the functional splits of classical theory had already been acknowledged by such features as matrix organizations even before most managements were aware of systems concepts. This is a matter, though, for later discussion.

PART TWO

Motivation

This part seeks to show why the basic motivation theories developed. I will claim that the problems of getting the workers to identify with the objectives of the capitalist firm have given rise to six basic responses.

(1), (2), The denial that workers, when fully conscious of their own interests, will ever identify with the firm's objectives. Such a position is typically, but not exclusively Marxist. Hence it applies to (1) 'Marxist man' and also to (2) 'Hoxie man'.

The next three responses are all unitary. They each claim that, as long as the job contains a particular ingredient, the worker will identify with the goals of the firm. In each of these three responses the ingredient is different (reflecting, I shall claim, the theorist's own ideological values rather than those of the employee). Nevertheless, because all three believe that their chosen ingredient will solve the problem, they are collectively known as 'content' theories. They are:

(3)   The belief that money is the ingredient: the so-called 'economic man theory'.

(4)   The belief that comradeship is the ingredient: the so-called 'social man theory'.

(5)   The belief that achievement is the ingredient: the so-called 'self-actualizing man theory'.

The sixth response claims that workers can share to some extent the goals of the firm, but only as part of a dynamic and volatile marriage which can flip to and fro between conflict and co-operation. There is *no general body of literature that has adequately stressed this ambiguity: though there is a body of literature which has stressed that the dynamics of the **process** of motivation are more important than the statics of any particular **content**. Such writtings are collectively referred to as 'process' theories. I find this term too vague. It is a term which hints at (but fails to stipulate) the ambiguity of the employee's attitude towards the firm. It similarly implies (but fails to claim) that such ambiguity is legitimate. But if such ambiguity is a legitimate attitude for the employee to adopt, then 'process theories' are essentially rooted in pluralism. To make clear (a) the ambiguity and (b) the right to be so, I have given this response a name which I have borrowed in part from Arthur Koestler. I call it:*

(6)   'Political holon man theory'.

To evaluate the above responses we shall need from time to time to digress into ideological, technological and organizational considerations.

6

The first and second of the six responses to the problems of motivating the employee and an overview of the remainder

Whence are we, and why are we? Of what scene
The actors or spectators?
P. B. Shelley (1792–1822)

6.1 The first response – the Marxist denial of the morality of motivation

6.1.1 Right at the start of the subject of motivation we run into a problem of definition. There is no doubt that 'motivation' in Organization and Management literature has a different, and indeed a much narrower meaning than it does in the field of general psychology. In our subject area it is synonymous with 'getting the worker to identify with the goals of the organization'. The difficulty lies in specifying what is meant by 'the goals of the organization'. Who or what is meant by 'the organization' and by what right should its goals be considered to constitute a 'given' with which the worker should identify? Some capitalist writers have claimed that organizations acquire an impersonal life of their own which transcends the people in them. It **is** therefore (in their view) possible to speak of 'organizational goals'. Others deny this and claim that people alone are capable of setting goals. Some say these goal-setting people are the management. Others deny this, claiming that goals result from the negotiated 'consensus' of everyone involved with the organization: not management alone. We shall deal with these issues in Section 16.1. For the moment I would ask the reader to accept the outcome of that future discussion.

There I shall argue that the goals of capitalist organizations are currently set by their managements, albeit within a framework of constraints. I shall also make a plea for management's right to continue to set them. But it is a right which is under increasingly widespread attack from liberals as well as Marxists.

6.1.2 The problem of such a 'right' is a philosophic minefield. Historically the 'natural rights' of Man have been used to justify many courses of action. The American Declaration of Independence is an example. Such 'natural rights' are usually buttressed by some *a priori* appeal to a humanist or religious precept which specifies how men and women are intended to interact with the rest of creation and especially with each other. When the precept claims religious authority (as when the Declaration of Independence claims Man's rights are 'inalienable' because they are 'endowed by [our] Creator'), each person's rights are assumed to flow from our mutual relationship to God.

6.1.3 In practical terms, the rights enjoyed in a society are a reflection of the opinions of those who have the power to govern. Dependent upon the constitution of that society these opinions may, or may not, be representative of the majority view. But in either case it is safe to assume that someone will make use of the 'natural rights' argument either to bolster or to attack the nature of the 'rights' which that society permits. So far in our society the 'right' of managements to set goals, and thereafter to attempt to induce workers to act in such a manner as will achieve those goals, is widely accepted.

6.1.4 The basis upon which these managerial rights are legitimized in the eyes of the general public would appear to be something like this:

(i)   The survival of the firm is seen as being beneficial to society in general and/or to specific sections of society in particular.
(ii)   The survival is seen as being the main concern of management, or, to put it another way, they are seen as having fewer conflicting interests.
(iii) Management are supposedly the most qualified persons to recognize which action(s) will be most likely to contribute to the firm's continued survival.
(iv)   The combination of (i) to (iii) is held to be sufficient reason to legitimize management's prerogatives.

6.1.5 Now, in common with the majority of people in the Western democracies I see this as being the way that management's position becomes recognized. It is the basis on which I too accept its legitimacy. By contrast, the Marxist, while agreeing that this indeed is the way in which management's position within capitalism becomes recognized, would claim that such recognition was not legitimate since, in his view, it would be the product of 'false consciousness'.

6.1.6 In paragraph 2.3.32 I defined our use of the word 'ideology' as neutral, and as meaning any *Weltanschauung* which claimed widespread support. I did so because definitions vary. The Marxist use of 'ideology' is not neutral. Only the proletariat see the realities of life. The other classes, by contrast see only their 'ideologies': 'the false image a social class has of its own situation and of society as a whole' (Aron, 1968; p.177). For the Marxist, therefore, my acceptance of the legitimacy of management is caused by my bourgeois false consciousness. I am deceived by my view of the world. Moreover, because capitalism is the dominant system, Marx would claim that it can get its ideas 'legitimized' more easily because it can disseminate them more easily than is possible for other classes. Giddens (1971; p.41) sees 'little objection' to the Marxist generalization 'that consciousness is governed by human activity in society', nor to the belief that 'the dominant class is able to disseminate ideas which are the legitimation of its position of dominance'.

6.1.7 But, unless we were to believe that all hierarchical control must be wrong simply because it *is* hierarchical control, then there is no reason for us to believe that the views of the dominant class are necessarily wrong. They may be so: but not **simply** because they are the dominant views.

6.1.8 This brings me to one of many reasons why I could not, in a book on management, let the Marxist attack on capitalism pass unheeded. If, as I have argued, all societies and all purposive organizations require a degree of hierarchical control, then to ignore the Western Marxists' claim that such control is unnecessary and that in a post-revolutionary society there would be no such control would mean that I was encouraging that error by default. Such an omission would be intellectual dishonesty on my part.

6.1.9 The Marxist position is to deny all managerial authority within capitalism. Firstly, he sees the whole system as invalid in that it is geared to producing those things that the market will pay for rather than to fulfilling the requirements of the needy. Secondly, he claims that because the aims of the firm are those of capital accumulation (as described in paragraph 1.2.13 in which the employee is little more than a resource, and a disposable resource at that, the worker will come into total conflict with the management.

OM-E*

6.1.10 It may well be, the Marxist would say, that the majority of people in the Western world see the position of the capitalist manager as being legitimate on those grounds which are listed in paragraph 6.1.4. Doubtless the managers themselves also see these same arguments as endorsing the legitimacy of their position.

6.1.11 But, says the Marxist, both are wrong. Their view of the world has been coloured by their 'false consciousness'. Only the view of the workers, the proletariat, is 'true consciousness' and that view, according to the Marxist, is one of implacable hostility. Nor will evidence of co-operation between management and worker lead the Marxist to accept the legitimacy of the capitalist manager's right to manage. For the Marxist it would be evidence only of the power of the capitalist to force the worker to abandon his 'true' perspective either by brainwashing ('embourgeoisement') or economic pressure.

6.1.12 I wish to point out that my many references to Marxism arise not from any wish to be polemical for its own sake, but because, in the course of this book, I am obliged to justify my preference for capitalism over Marxism if I am to justify my belief that a capitalist manager has a claim to moral authority. The frame of reference of the Marxist I shall refer to as the 'total conflict unitary frame of reference' in that he sees only the workers' views as valid, and then only when they favour revolutionary attitudes. The Marxist image of the worker I have called 'Marxist man'. Marxist man's attitude can have no relevance to 'motivation theory' within the meaning that term has acquired in the Organization and Management literature of the West. For, as we shall see in the next section, all such 'motivation' theories are based upon a belief that, at least to some extent, the workers' goals and the goals of management have something in common. Indeed, this is the very complaint of the Marxist concerning trade unions. By negotiating with capitalism, even if in opposition, the trade unions have (for the Marxist) given a spurious legitimacy to the idea that the goals of the employers and the employees are in some way reconcilable. Motivational theory goes further and concludes that there must be a congruency of goals between the various parties which (in spite of any differences that there may also be) makes mutual agreement possible and desirable: so they reject it.

6.2 The second response – the Hoxie denial of the practicality of motivation

6.2.1 I said on the title page of Part Two that not all those who deny management's right or ability to motivate workers are Marxist. R. F. Hoxie (writing in 1917) appears to have granted management's right to try, but to have denied that they would be able to pull it off (McCarthy, 1972; ch.3). It seems fair to label his attitude as the 'total conflict pluralist frame of reference'. (We shall consider Hoxie's ideas in paragraphs 9.1.12 to 14) I have called Hoxie's vision of the worker 'Hoxie man'.

6.2.2 (Liberals who question management's right to dictate policy usually do so only because they see it as an unnecessary cause of friction which can be avoided by consensus. They therefore properly belong in a specific positive category, – namely the fifth response of Section 6.5 – and not in this negative category.)

6.3 The five conceptual frames of reference which contain the six responses

6.3.1 We have just seen that it is possible for motivation theory to be denied by people who have two distinct frames of reference. The Marxist frame of reference did so because, though they did not always doubt management's **ability** to motivate the employee on those occasions when the latter had been led into 'false consciousness', they did doubt management's **right** to do so. In Hoxie's case this situation appears to be reversed. He does not so much deny management these rights as defy them successfully to claim them.

6.3.2 The converse is also true. Two or more different responses can emanate from the same frame of reference. I have already identified four positive responses from theorists as to how managements might succeed in motivating the employee:

> economic man,
> social man,
> self-actualizing man, and
> political holon man.

Yet I shall argue that all four of these responses, and any others which the future may bring, must be grounded in one of three frames of reference. This is because only these frames of reference contain an element vital to all motivation theories. This element is the assumption that, at least in some measure, the worker will share the goals of management. I make this point strongly because it sometimes appears that there are writers who feel that one day we shall discover some new framework that will transform all our concepts. In exactly such a manner did the alchemists of the Middle Ages hope to find the so-called 'philosopher's stone' that would turn base metals into gold. They seek in vain. Past, present and future theories of motivation will fall into one of three frames of reference to which I have given the following titles. The names chosen are intended to be striking but they are intended to be accurate, they are **not** intended to be flippant. These titles are as follows.

(1) 'The daddy-knows-best unitary frame of reference.'
(2) 'The all-pals-together unitary frame of reference.'
(3) 'The love-hate pluralist frame of reference.'

6.3.3 If we put all these concepts together and add the Marxist vision of the worker and that of Hoxie, the result may be depicted as in Table 6.3(a).

Table 6.3(a)

	Motivation denied because it is considered:		Motivation considered valid in the advocated circumstances of the response		
	Immoral	*Impractical*			
frame of refer- ence	total- conflict- unitary	total- conflict- pluralist	daddy- knows- best- unitary	all-pals- together- unitary	love- hate- pluralist
response	first	second	third fourth	fifth	sixth
	Marxist man	Hoxie man	economic social man man	self- actualizing man	political- holon man

6.4 The 'daddy-knows-best' unitary frame of reference

6.4.1 A résumé of this view would be as follows. *Management and workers are bound together in a co-operative exercise: but the workers are too wayward to recognize either this or the consequential underlying unitary character of the relationship. They must therefore be prevented by managerial control – and in their own best interests – from committing the dysfunctional acts to which they are prone. Moreover, since management's viewpoint is the only valid viewpoint, such coercion as may prove to be necessary is no less valid than the rights of a parent to chastise a child.*

6.4.2 I shall seek to demonstrate that it is not unfair to attribute this view to Taylor's 'economic man' model (which we will arbitrarily date from around 1910) nor (though this may surprise some readers), to Mayo's 'social man' model (which we will date as about 1930). The only way in which, it seems to me, they can be said to differ is as a result of their different perceptions of the actual content of what would motivate the worker. Because the satisfaction of the worker's goals as perceived by Mayo demanded a warmer-hearted response from management than did the worker's goals as perceived by Taylor, it follows that Mayo's attitudes are usually seen as being more culturally acceptable. But, as I shall hope to demonstrate, this did not make his attitudes any the less unitary or paternalistic than those of Taylor: they were simply more kindly in their expression.

6.5 The 'all-pals-together' unitary frame of reference

6.5.1 A résumé of this view would be as follows. *Management and workers will share the same goals freely because there are no basic differences that could cause conflict providing that management can fully communicate its point of view. Such conflict as may exist is the product of misunderstanding brought about by faulty communication on the part of management.*

6.5.2 This view is grounded in a view of human nature as 'perfectable': 'every day in every way we are getting better and better'. However, to this questionable premise is added another equally questionable one. This is not necessarily and logically related to the first, but experience teaches us that many people find enough psychological linkage between the two ideas to regard them as related. This second premise is that 'all people of goodwill will naturally agree on the same things'. The perfectability-of-man theory is enormously attractive because of its idealism. We shall find that it has thus engaged the heart of Marxists (who, however, claim that this can only happen after the corrupting power of capitalism has been removed) and liberals (who see no such need for the elimination of capitalism, but do see a need for those in authority to initiate freer and more trusting relationships). On these latter grounds Abraham Maslow published a theory of motivation (Maslow, 1970 (first edition, 1954)) which Douglas McGregor endorsed and applied to organizational theory (McGregor, 1960), and which forms the concept of 'self-actualizing man'.

6.5.3 At the level of the state, the claim that all people of good will are bound to think the same way has always led to tyranny. We see this in the Eastern bloc countries, we saw this in the McCarthy era in the United States. This is a theme we shall develop later: but even here the reader will doubtless instinctively recognize its dangers. For if we insist that all men of good will will think alike, and we meet opposition, it is not difficult to argue that those opponents cannot, by definition, be men of good will and that they therefore need to be silenced.

At the political level it has led to Russian political prisoners being committed to psychiatric hospitals, and at the organizational level it has led to the denial of the validity of trade union views by managements and governments of East and West.

6.5.4 However, in order that this book should not lose its focus, when we engage in discussion at the organizational level we shall limit discussion to considering whether the 'all-pals-together' concept is a model which is helpful or unhelpful as a representation of organizational reality. (We shall conclude that it is unhelpful.) Only when we look at complete social systems shall we concern ourselves with the relationship of this concept with that of tyranny. This approach is useful in maintaining the focus of the book, which is one of my concerns. However, there is another justification in that unitary attitudes at the level of the organization do not threaten society with the evils of tyranny as they would at the level of the State. This is because, in a market economy, there will be a natural pluralism **between** the competing firms. Only when they form tyrannical non-competitive agreements will this be a problem, and such non-competitive practices should be possible to curb. (An example of such a practice is the one-time policy of the lending banks to refuse work to employees who left one of their competitors: a policy obviously designed to cripple the bargaining power of the employee who, if he moved at all, was reduced to moving outside this cartel.)

6.6 The love-hate pluralist frame of reference

6.6.1 A résumé of this view would be as follows. *The frame of reference of the management sees their authority as stemming from their ability to keep in being an enterprise that fulfils a morally acceptable need in society by providing certain goods and services to society. That a need exists is evidenced by the preparedness of people to pay for these products or services. That the satisfaction of this need is legal and to that extent 'moral' is evidenced by the permissive or encouraging attitude of government which either positively or by default allows such commerce. However, the frame of reference of the workers (though different) is also valid. The workers recognize, quite rightly, that management cannot be wholly committed to them, for, necessary as they are as a labour resource, they are nevertheless a liability upon cash resources in exchange for that same labour. The workers therefore respond to management's ambivalence towards them by adopting a corresponding ambivalence towards management. To the extent that the management have created a situation from which the worker may profit either economically, socially or from a sense of fulfilment, the worker feels constrained to identify* *with the firm's interests. To the extent that the worker perceives that, at any time, his extension of and even his retention of these rewards might be put at risk (as when those rewards are seen as jeopardizing the future of the firm), he feels constrained* **not** *to identify or to co-operate with management. To maintain these disparate interests both parties are anxious*

(i)   *to affirm their basic belief in co-operation, while*

(ii) *attempting to legitimize both to each other and to society at large, that certain rights are contractually theirs and that in consequence of any infringement of those rights, they would be justified in invoking certain specific sanctions.*

6.6.2 The very ambiguities of such a frame of reference require that all the parties should be conscious of the need to 'give-and-take'. Only so is it possible to preserve the essential stability of the system that will permit it to survive and enable the participants to benefit from its survival. Management's attempts to motivate therefore consist in maintaining the dynamic stability of the system by balancing the social/technological/ economic factors in such a manner as will secure the system's continued vigorous growth.

7

The third response – 'economic man', or Taylor's version of the 'daddy-knows-best' unitary frame of reference

7.1 The vocal anti-Taylorite theorists of academia

7.1.1 When Frederick Winslow Taylor died in 1915 his work was the centre of public controversy: yet today it is not. Such knowledge that exists about him in management circles does so because it has seeped through from the world of management academics. Where it has not, few know his name. Even in academic circles there is no controversy: how can there be? He has no supporters. Yet despite this we are left with the strange phenomenon that the barrage of academic ridicule directed at his view of the worker's social and psychological make-up continues unabated. Taylor's belief, that providing that the worker were paid appropriately he would be content to enter into an individual contract with the firm and to perform such routine repetitive movements as management should specify, is referred to in the short-hand jargon of management theory as the 'economic man' concept. This belief comes in for enormous criticism. For it implies, by the individuality of the deal, that the worker will be prepared to give up his social aspirations and, by the instrumentality of the deal, that the worker would be prepared to renounce the satisfactions that more stimulating work might have given to him.

7.1.2 All of which raises the interesting question: 'If Taylor, who died in 1915, got it all wrong, why does he still generate such interest that every other academic feels the need to dance on his grave? This obsession with him in the academic world is particularly puzzling for those students who have already been out in the 'real world' of industry. For there, as they point out, no one uses the term 'Taylorism', or the name which Taylor applied to his system: 'scientific management'. One particularly intelligent student said of this latter term 'If I had ever met it I would certainly have remembered: it's so **quaint!**'

Figure 7.1(a) F. W. Taylor

7.1.3 But the academic world is right to be concerned with Taylorism. Modern management practice may not be called that (nor given the more 'quaint' term of 'scientific management') but the spirit of Taylor and the use of techniques which he developed (or which were developed by others in that same spirit) form the warp and weft of modern-day management practice. For Taylorism is a spirit which stems from the application of capitalist principals, and in particular, the principle of minimizing the firm's economic oppportunity cost.

7.1.4 This introduction of market forces into the very fabric of the firm is likely to create internal conflict. The very essence of Taylorism (and of modern-day capitalism) is to harness market forces and attract more business to the firm by ensuring that its product or service has more economic worth to the consumer than does that of its competitor(s). This in turn means the firm must adopt a technology which minimizes the use of resources. Yet it is also clear that this approach, which makes economic and technological considerations the determinants of the system, requires that employees make whatever adjustments which the system requires for it to function effectively. This may well put them under considerable strain. When this strain has resulted from having to lower their economic social and/or psychological aspirations, it may well be accompanied by lower morale and perhaps open hostility. Consequently it is a problem with which academics **should** rightly be concerned.

7.1.5 Unfortunately that concern has taken the form of simply inverting the problem. Academic teaching of management and organization is now dominated by sociologists and psychologists who only see the human problems that Taylorism presents but who either do not know, or do not want to know, about the economic and technical constraints. In the main I think it is genuine ignorance. McGregor, for example, clearly did not see that economic and technical constraints force managements to adopt the practices of Taylorism. He attributed these practices to nothing more profound than managerial élitism. McGregor therefore concluded (as we saw in paragraph 4.1.16) that these practices demonstrated only a management belief in 'the mediocrity of the masses'. Consequently, although he conceded that 'a good deal of lip service is given to the worth of the human being' he felt that this was only because 'our political and social values demand such public expression'. Nevertheless,' he concluded, 'a great many managers will give private support to this assumption [of the mediocrity of the masses] and it is easy to see it reflected in policy and practice. Paternalism has become a nasty word, but it is by no means a defunct managerial philosophy.' (McGregor, 1960; p.34).

7.1.6 The reader will notice the tone of outraged morality. This is typical of the tone of much neo-human relations literature. It has the unfortunate effect of warning off potential opponents unless they are prepared to risk the implication that they have low ethical standards. Perhaps this highly immoral use of 'moral blackmail' is the reason why the many scholars who could have countered this naïve nonsense have failed to do so.

7.1.7 There is a further thing to note about this high moral tone. It is very didactic. Perhaps it is inevitable that those who are didactic become paternalistic. Perhaps it is that those (like McGregor) who believe that Taylorism is essentially 'paternalistic' feel that that justifies them in adopting their own brand of paternalism. Whatever the reason, no one is more paternalistic than a liberal academic. Let me offer an example. Taylor and Gilbreth were the joint founders of a technique called 'work study', a system for devising the 'best' method of doing work and then of measuring it. It is a technique which a competitive manufacturing concern ignores at its peril. Yet, under the paternalistic censorship of psychologists and sociologists, few indeed are the Organization and Management courses which have work study in their syllabus. When we reflect that the existence of that future manager's firm may be jeopardized because he lacks this knowledge, it seems to me that there can be few actions more paternalistic or more questionable than that of the syllabus designer who deliberately omits this topic. If, on the other hand, the omission is because he does not recognize work study's importance, then that raises questions concerning the limitations of the tradition in which he himself has been trained.

7.1.8 There is one aspect of the attack on Taylorism that I find particularly odd. It is the apparent lack of insight into Taylor's mind on the part of those psychologists who have challenged his views. I should have expected that a psychologist, on finding that Taylor was making the absurd claims about human nature which are inherent in the concept of 'economic man', would have asked himself 'Why?' 'Why did this relatively intelligent man make some of the absurd statements that he did?' I should have expected that a psychologist would also be fascinated with Taylor's obvious desire to build a conflict-free world. For it was clearly this aim that led him into his major absurdities. Let us consider some of the 'double-talk' in Taylor's writing. It was in 1878 that he went to the Midvale Steel Company and was subsequently made 'gang-boss'. They were violent times and times of depression. Morison (1965; pp.768–769) gives us the flavour of the age.

> ...For a decade after 1867 the anthracite coal-mining section of Pennsylvania around Mauch Chunk and Pottsville, was terrorized by a secret miners' association called the Molly Maguires, composed mostly of Irish Catholics. They burned property, controlled county officials and murdered bosses and supervisors who offended them. Finally...the murderers were brought to trial and ten were hanged in June 1877...In the same year there were serious race riots in San Francisco against Chinese immigrants who...[kept] wages down. This problem was solved by a series of Chinese exclusion acts. The year 1877 was very rough. When the four Eastern through railroads...announced a wage cut of 10 per cent, second since the panic of 1873, the unorganized railroad

employees struck and were supported by a huge army of hungry and desperate unemployed. Traffic was suspended on the trunk lines and every industrial centre was in turmoil. In Pittsburgh, Martinsburg and Chicago there were pitched battles...

7.1.9 It is against this background that we must consider the fact that Taylor's life was threatened. (Taylor, 1967; p.51.) '[I] was told that if [I] continued to [walk home along the lonely path by the railroad] it would be at the risk of [my] life.' [I] answered '[I] proposed to walk home every night right up that railway track, that [I] never had carried and never would carry a weapon of any kind and that they could shoot and be damned'. This was the culmination of a long 'war' (Taylor, 1967; p.48) between Taylor and the workmen as he tried to introduce his system. He tells us of the lengths that the men went to to break his system and the lengths that he went to to ensure that they would not succeed in doing so. Despite which he continued to insist – in a way that would be hilariously funny were it not for the sad implications – that there was no fundamental conflict between him and the men. He tells us in graphic detail how they would deliberately break their machines to blame him. He tells how he cut wages, lowered rates, fired, hired black-leg labour and yet through it all he expects us to accept, as I believe that he did, these incredible words: 'in most cases [it was] a friendly war because the men under [me] were [my] personal friends.'

7.1.10 Clearly this piece of classic self-deception is the act of a man who is trying to build a *Weltanschauung* with pieces that won't fit. Clearly also he is making these ridiculous claims that it wasn't a real war because he's a man with a mission. He wants a wealthier society, but not at the price of conflict: so he denies the conflict.

7.1.11 There is a direct parallel between this early fantasy and that in Taylor's later work. For he tries there also to claim that it is possible to build a total socio-technical system which will be conflict-free. It would be conflict-free, said Taylor, because there would be goal congruence between management and worker. The efficiency of the worker would be so great, thanks to management having found the 'one best way' of doing the job, that profits would be more than adequate to satisfy the worker's demand for high wages and the shareholder's for high dividends. So great would the total cake be that the traditional conflict about the apportionment of it between the two 'sides' of industry would disappear.

7.1.12 This then is the reason for his insistence that the worker acts and reacts as 'economic man'. He is trying to build a socio-technical system of peaceful endeavour with pieces that won't 'fit'. But if they don't fit there will be conflict. He therefore tries to make them fit by claiming that we don't have to worry about the nature of the technology or work organization that a product requires, for it is a matter of indifference to the worker providing he is appropriately paid.

7.1.13 Ironically, the last people to understand Taylor's motives appear to have been the psychologists. Surely they at least suspected that Taylor had found that the economic and technical constraints that the manufacturing system has to face were highly intractable? Why else did they imagine that he constructed his vision of man: of a worker who was happy to adapt to any situation that he met, so long as the money was right? The more absurd they found his claims about man's nature to be, the more they should have suspected technological difficulties of a highly intractable nature. They did not.

7.1.14 Let us use my model of the organization in Figure 3.2(b) on page 58 in order to see the nature of the problem in general terms. Let us start with the assumption that society values a particular product. This means that the link 'SP' in that figure will be positive in value. Even so, its related technology could still be undesirable, thereby giving a negative value to 'PT'. Similarly, the technology may so constrain the work organization options, by the link 'TW', that we cannot create a socially desirable work organization. For the brute fact is that just because we value a product does not mean that its associated work organization will also be socially desirable. That could only be guaranteed in all cases if it could be shown that the technology was an intervening variable with vast flexibility. A flexibility that was so great that, however great the range of possible products might be and however small the range of socially attractive work organizations, the technology would still have the flexibility to create a feasible link. Yet the constraints imposed by technology are, as we saw in Chapter 4, highly inflexible. That being so, there will inevitably be occasions when socially desirable products can only be economically produced by workers whose jobs contain features which are less than ideal. In short, some degree of exploitation of the worker would appear to be technologically and/or economically necessary, with the inherent conflict that such a situation must generate.

7.1.15 I have already quoted McGregor's attack on management. So flexible does he imagine the technical aspects to be that he never even considers them as a constraint. On the contrary he is at the greatest pains to have us believe that the problem is in no way technical: it is psychological.

The fact that modern-day management practices are an extension of Taylorism does not lead McGregor to wonder whether Taylorism has any validity. It leads him to conclude that such managers have (in essence) a personality problem which distorts their view of human nature. This is why operations remain specialized and why organizations remain hierarchically controlled.

7.1.16 McGregor's contribution to the debate is to claim that, if only management would change in their outlook, then this would lead to a change in their practices, and the result would be a change for the better in the whole industrial scene. I wish to make entirely clear that I concur with the view that hierarchies should operate with as democratic a style as possible and also that, within the limits that technology imposes, the worker should be offered the greatest possible amount of 'job-enrichment'. But in each case we need to acknowledge that there are limiting factors. McGregor does not. Neither does Herzberg, who supports McGregor's attitude (for they are both disciples of Maslow). Herzberg is the father of 'job-enrichment', which advocates among other things that short-cycle repetitive work – which was advocated by Taylor but which is alienative in character – should be replaced by more significant tasks.

7.1.17 There is no need for me to reiterate the economic and technical problems associated with job-enrichment. These were covered in Chapter 4. All I wish to do here is to call them to the reader's mind to mitigate any criticism which he might make of Taylor, or indeed of present-day management.

7.1.18 Like Taylor, the modern manager is subjected to competitive technological and economic pressures. By this statement I do not mean to suggest that, if either of them were released from competitive pressure, they would necessarily be induced to relax their Taylor-like practices. That is probably not the case with modern managers. It was certainly not the case with Taylor. With modern managers I say that it is 'probably' not the case because we cannot judge. The standard of competition is so high that achieving the highest efficiency of which the firm is capable is probably the same thing as being better than the competition, and this latter requirement is essential if a firm is to survive in a free market.

7.1.19 Being better than the competition was just as essential in Taylor's day: but then the competition was so inefficient that it was not very hard to stay ahead of it. Indeed, one of the reasons he gave for firms *not* taking up his system was that the abysmally low standard of competition made it possible for extremely inefficient firms to make a living, and so get by without 'scientific management'. Consequently, although I claim that technological and economic constraints led him to make the absurd social claims that he did, I readily agree that these constraints were largely of his own making.

7.1.20 To that extent his position differed from that of the modern manager whom economic and technological pressures greatly constrain. Yet in agreeing that Taylor created the very pressures which painted him into a corner and caused him to make his absurd claims about 'economic man', I am not suggesting that we should regard him as a free agent who could choose to modify these demands at will. I am convinced that, since he saw his system as the only means by which to raise the general material welfare of mankind, he felt that he could not escape a moral obligation to adopt it and get others to do so.

7.1.21 It was his system's capacity to deliver the goods that drove Taylor on, and which is the thing which has driven all other Taylorites on since his day. He was arrogant; he was paternalistic; he had little compassion for the individual, for the fall of the sparrow. But in his attempts to improve life for the greatest good of the greatest number – that utilitarian doctrine which is morally right in principle but so desperately dangerous to individual freedom in practice – he was a sincere and altruistic idealist. This made it psychologically imperative for him to hang on to his system in the face of seemingly intolerable opposition with an equally fierce tenacity.

7.1.22 In a postscript to a letter written in August 1912 (Del Mar and Collons, 1976; p.20), he makes this comment. I have quoted it in full.

> PS One more thought on this matter. The only way to make the world happier in a material way is to increase the riches of the world, that is, the material things that are useful to man; and all of these come from two sources only – from what is produced by the earth or comes out of the ground, and what is produced by man. An important fact to bear in mind is that more than nineteen-twentieths of all the wealth in the world is consumed by the poor people, and not by what are called rich people.
> Any increase, therefore, in productivity of the individual simply increases the wealth of the world to that extent, and nineteen-twentieths of this increase goes straight to the poor people.   F.W.T.

7.1.23 However noble this sentiment may be, Taylor's paternalism was offensive to some people even in his own day. Hoxie, for example, was highly critical of the unitary nature of all such paternalism, for, by adopting a 'daddy-knows-best' stance in his style of management the manager is denying the validity of the workers' standpoint. Yet it must be stressed that in Taylor's day such people as Hoxie were probably in the minority. Patronage was so much part of the spirit of the age that it was not only viewed as legitimate by many managers, it was frequently seen as legitimate by the very workers they patronized. Nor was such authoritarianism confined to the industrial scene, as the sordid story of the way that the authorities treated suffragettes bears witness. To some extent the First World War acted as a watershed, for the sacrifices of the common people and the atrociously inept conduct of that war by the various 'high-commands' made authoritarian patronage more questionable than ever before. It was no accident therefore that the first vote to be given to any woman in Britain was in 1918, for that was the year in which the war ended. Similarly, although the federal nature of America made their corresponding story a much more mixed affair, it was not until 1920 that Article XIX of the US Constitution universally guaranteed this right to women.

7.1.24 This brings us to a most anomalous situation that requires explanation. As this century has worn on, the average man and woman in Western society has demanded an ever increasing 'say' in the running of his or her own life. There has therefore been a steady movement **away** from patronage. We should expect from this that Taylorism would have raised greater and greater antipathy. **Yet the reverse is true in practice**. Workers and unions were prepared in the early days to fight Taylorism 'tooth and nail' and they did so to such effect that they actually succeeded in getting it thrown out of various plants.

7.1.25 Today Taylorism in its wider aspects is tolerated by both workers and unions. It is true that they sometimes try to block Taylor-type proposals in a somewhat desultory fashion: the halting of this incentive scheme, the abandonment of that work study concept. From the 'slippage' between the academic frame of reference and the factory floor they know all about the anti-Taylor arguments. Yet most of the time the purpose to which they put this knowledge is simply as a bargaining-counter in wage negotiations. They do not try to stop Taylorism in its tracks as they did in Taylor's day. *Why should industrial practice have moved in an opposite direction to that of the general social tide?*

7.1.26 *It is because Taylorism (whatever our reservations may be) is here to stay. Taylor, so to speak, 'let the genie out of the bottle', and it is beyond our power to get it back.* For better or worse we have to learn to live with Taylorism, because it cannot be un-invented any more than the atomic bomb can. Nor is that so only within the capitalist system. Ever since Lenin introduced it, Taylorism has been a part of Eastern bloc Communism. For Taylorism to vanish would require some entirely new system to emerge. Of course there are those who believe this will happen: the alternative-technology buffs, or those Western type Marxists who believe in some vague sort of syndicalism. Such life-styles may be possible in some rural developing community. However, so long as our present industrialized society exists to make our current manufacturing processes a real option – by that I mean that as long as society as we know it hasn't crumbled – I do not believe that the average Westerner would trade the material goods that Taylorism produces for some 'alternate technology' that would run counter to all the premises of high production in Taylorism. The actions of the workers and the unions in electing to live with it even as they criticize it are evidence to this effect.

7.2 The non-vocal (but *de facto*) Taylorites of industry

7.2.1 The efficient conversion of resources is so much a reflex action for a manager that he often does not even stop to consider his actions as having any philosophic foundations. But of course, like all rational actions, they have. Yet if he did stop to think about it he would recognize that the argument that legitimizes his right to act, which I set out in paragraph 6.1.4, comes from a concept of there being a mutuality of interest between the needs of society and the continued existence of the firm to meet these needs. Now whereas it is sometimes possible in this process for the manager also to meet the needs of the employee, yet sometimes it is not: the two aims may be incompatible.

7.2.2 Looking at the degree of authoritarianism that exists in management I would claim that it is strongest in those managers who, like Taylor, have a utilitarianist concept. They therefore are more ready to interpret the needs of society as an imperative. Since (they argue) those needs will not be met other than by the continued survival of their firm, the survival of their firm becomes vital to society. (Of course, this is not true, because the demand would merely shift to their competitors. At this stage, however, they are able to retort 'And what good would that do for our present employees: they would be thrown out of work?' This leads to the 'firm' being viewed not as the aggregate of the people within it, but as an abstract concept, a vehicle for satisfying the needs of society, of which the collective needs of the employees represent a subset. Service to the 'firm', this abstract entity, becomes management's goal. Consequently, to a greater or lesser extent, the welfare of the 'firm' as an abstraction becomes the 'greatest good of the greatest number', and of paramount importance to the manager. It will be remembered that I said that this was the first of the basic articles of faith of the modern manager (paragraph 1.2.7). The other was that in pursuit of the firm's welfare the manager is obliged to avoid all known opportunity costs.

7.2.3 Also in paragraph 1.2.7 I said that these were the articles of faith of capitalist managers: and so they are. But that does not mean that they have not also become articles of faith for managers in the communist Eastern bloc just as Taylorism has been since the time of Lenin.

7.2.4 This brings me to the question of the political bias in Taylorism: for there is quite a strong one. Indeed, that bias is one of the reasons that I have throughout tended to avoid the term 'scientific management' (which is the term that most books use when speaking of Taylor's system). Taylor told the chairman of the Special Committee of the US House of Representatives that was convened in 1912 to study his system that 'scientific management' was his preferred title for the system. He though it better than 'the Taylor system', on the grounds that the movement was too great to be attributed to one man, and better than 'the task system', because he thought that that name had too severe a ring to it. 'Scientific management', however, met his approval.

7.2.5 I have not used the term, because I cannot share his approval of it. In the first place it seeks to impart to the system a quite spurious claim to 'objectivity'. Such a claim makes clear to us how little philosophic insight Taylor and his followers had. But more than that, 'scientific management' carries implications that the system is 'politically neutral'. This brings me again to the question of the political bias in Taylorism, for 'neutral' it most certainly is not.

7.2.6 Nor is this 'political neutrality' merely implicit in the title 'scientific management'. It was a claim which was actively put forward by Taylor's disciples. Their claim was based upon the evidence that Taylorism was not only acceptable to many Americans who identified with certain democratic values; but it was also acceptable to the extreme left (Lenin), and the extreme right (Mussolini). Surely, they argued, such approval across the political spectrum, from Left to Right and from democracy to dictatorship, was living proof of Taylorism's political neutrality?

7.2.7 In terms of the normal political categories in which we tend to operate, this claim appears valid. But politics are fundamentally an expression of a particular philosophy applied to society. In that sense all three of the above political systems have a common thread, that of utilitarian philosophy: the greatest good of the greatest number. This is alien to caring for the individual. Each expresses that lack of concern differently. The dictatorships may care for his welfare but not his freedom. The democracy may care for his freedom but not his welfare. All regard him as in some way expendable. So there is a political bias towards 'society' and away from 'the individual' in all three. As we have already seen, this same bias is also present in Taylorism. So although it was not for that reason alone that Taylorism was largely rejected in Britain, prior to the Second World War, yet there can be no doubt that the 'political' aspect of its unitarian bias **was** a factor. I hesitate to attempt to isolate any other factors for its rejection, for they have a subtle interactive quality that is as important as the factors themselves, an interaction that Judith Merkle (1980) has caught marvellously. They do, however, include snobbishness towards science and towards the technocrats of uncertain origins who practised it, a strong neo-feudal class system and a strongly unionized workforce.

7.2.8 Merkle is also correct in suggesting that elements in British society with 'reformist' aims had already pre-empted certain of the 'reformist' aims of Taylorism. With the sugar gone, the rest of the pill was less attractive. *(Either because she is American or because she is writing for Americans she refers to these elements as 'British Socialism'. Yet they included elements that we in Britain would not label 'socialist'. In this she shares the general American tendency to regard as 'socialism' almost any form of capitalism that is not completely 'laissez-faire'. I shall refer to this again, but for us in Britain it has a gently comic aspect. For if 'socialism' were defined by US usage I should imagine that the majority of the British Tory Party would prove to be 'socialist'. This makes her labelling questionable, but not her analysis.)*

7.2.9 Although Merkle does not specifically state that it was the politically unacceptable elements in Taylorism's utilitarian philosophy that caused it to be rejected in Britain (namely that it has no real concern for the fall of the sparrow), all her comments breathe this meaning. In the following passages that I quote she is at pains to infer that some degree of concern for the individual employee was allowed to temper, for various reasons, British management's search for 'efficiency'.

7.2.10

[M]anagerial progressivism in Britain had developed out of the Quaker strain of thought that stressed the duties, as well as the rights, of the employer, resulting in the general philosophy that industry had broad social functions beyond profit-seeking. Such management pioneers as Joseph and B. Seebohm Rowntree, or Edward Cadbury, had investigated the evils of sweated labour, poverty, and drink; they had come to the conclusion that bad labour conditions had brought about lower standards of productivity and higher levels of force. It followed, then, that industrial conflict was not simply the product of 'agitators', and that trade unions had a legitimate place in the industrial order. This communal emphasis in industry led to a conscious rejection of Taylorite individualism, and of the differential piecework schemes that the unions had denounced as punitive. (Merkle, 1980; p.225).

7.2.11 Merkle also lays considerable stress, as I have, upon the extent to which the First World War created great social changes in its aftermath. Not least of these were that the attitudes of the Quaker 'welfare' employers now appeared to be less distasteful to other industrialists than they had previously. These other industrialists were now prepared to

make some compromise with organized labour. By its very nature such a compromise would require the rejection of Taylorism. It involved a delaying action for the demands of workers' control and a search for alternative methods to undermine [*sic*] the labour movement. Such alternatives had certain requirements: they had to provide a new basis of legitimacy for owners' control (humanism and leadership led the list ahead of 'dehumanizing' science as sources of legitimacy) and, eschewing visible techniques of control such as Taylorism, they had to provide subtle, psychological means of manipulation and propaganda in the interest of higher worker output. The result was that British Management began to cultivate a sort of proto-human relations school of management thinking even before the works of Elton Mayo (Merkle, 1980; p.229).

7.2.12 Again, in discussing the manipulative element in this situation and in relating it to Mayo (with her hint that Mayo too was manipulative), Judith Merkle shows the insight which her whole book evidences. The only questionable elements in it for me are two-fold:

(1) Her criticisms sometimes seem to imply an understable yearning for a non-hierarchical world, and a less understandable tendency to believe in its possibility.
(2) She seems to see Taylorism as essentially tied to totalitarianism whereas I see it as working equally well for the laissez-faire manager. Moreover, the evidence is in my favour, for I do not believe that she can substantiate her implication that totalitarianism is Taylorism's natural home. At the level of the plant manager, Taylorism fits both Right-wing and Left-wing totalitarianism and laissez-faire concepts.

7.2.13 I do not seek to deny that many Taylorites ultimately came to regard it as a bit nonsensical to have 'scientific' management at the level of the individual enterprise (what economists call the 'micro-level') if the economy were in chaos at the national (i.e. 'macro') level. Here is Sandford E. Thompson (an early President of the Taylor Society) on the subject. (Del Mar and Collons, 1976; p.207): 'Means will be found in the coming years for adjusting the volume and the flow of goods to all consumers just as surely as it has been worked out in the factory.' This is clear advocacy of centralized planning in the totalitarian mould.

7.2.14 But even such evidence does not validate a claim that there is a **necessary** connection. Indeed, even if it could be shown that the inherent logic of Taylorism **must** lead on to centralized planning (which I do not believe that it does), experience teaches us that the majority of Taylorite managers, including Taylor himself, have been able to build a personal *Weltanschauung* which ignores completely any such logic. Most Taylorite managers today would strongly resist any move towards centralized planning of the economy, preferring to rely upon market forces. This is because Taylorism can have a tremendous appeal to managers who operate at the micro-level but who believe in laissez-faire government. It even has an appeal to those who accept a market economy that is generally 'free' but in which certain pockets of 'welfare' flourish: but I shall say more of that later.

7.2.15 Few readers will have any difficulty in seeing why Mussolini's fascist state would find Taylorism attractive. M. Rokeach has shown (Reich and Adcock, 1976; p.24) that fascist values renounce freedom and equality in favour of authoritarianism and elitism. It follows that, although I deny that there is an innate tendency for Taylor to adopt fascism, there is a tendency for fascism to adopt Taylor.

7.2.16 Rokeach tries to make a distinction between fascism and Leninist communism. He claims that both deny freedom, but that communism values equality. By that token, communism should adopt authoritarianism but avoid elitism. Well, perhaps it is possible to have a non-elitist authoritarian system: but if it is, I can only say that it doesn't seem to have happened yet. To show what blood-brothers Mussolini and Lenin were I should like to quote some of Merkle's comments upon the latter and to echo some of Lenin's own words which she has quoted. The latter illustrate not only Lenin's approval of Taylorism, but also his utter disregard for any of the participative decision-making that might reasonably have been expected in a social system that pays lip service to egalitarianism.

7.2.17 Judith Merkle points out (1980; p.112) that Lenin 'demanded that

the economy [of Russia] be rebuilt by making capitalist science serviceable
to a socialist regime. In particular, strong administrative measures were
required to eliminate shortages by raising labour productivity through **the
reestablishment of labour discipiine**.' (My emphasis.)

7.2.18 Merkle goes on to quote Lenin as follows:

> We must organize in Russia the study and teaching of the Taylor system and
> systematically try it out and adapt it to our purposes. At the same time, in
> approaching the task of raising the productivity of labour, we must take into
> account the specific features of the transition period from capitalism to
> socialism, which, on the one hand requires that the foundations be laid of **the
> socialist organization of competition** and on the other hand **the application of
> coercion, so the slogan 'dictatorship of the proletariat' shall not be desecrated
> by the practice of a jelly-fish proletarian government.** (Merkle, 1980; p.113; my
> emphasis.)

7.2.19 Merkle adds her own comment to this autocratic piece of double-talk
'This method', she says, 'could not be adopted, however, without directly
overriding the workers' committees in the factories and their trade unions:
like their Western counterparts they had been bitterly opposed to
Taylorism, and they sensed the imminent betrayal of labour interests and
union independence by the party.'

7.2.20 What Lenin's and Mussolini's totalitarianism have in common is the
morality of the beehive. The 'State' becomes the embodiment of society and
its dictates are claimed to be the ultimate in morality, for they are supposed
to bring about the utilitarianist's goal, that of 'the greatest good of the
greatest number'. At the level of the worker, as at the level of the worker-
bee, compliant performance of a prescribed task is the highest service. The
difference, of course, is that the worker-bee is by its very nature a cloned
creature. What totalitarianism tries to do is to 'clone' people by techniques
of social conditioning.

7.2.21 Yet is is highly significant that we seldom use biological imagery
when discussing the way in which societies use people instrumentally. Our
more common imagery is mechanistic. We speak of 'cogs in the machine'.
Totalitarianism could not keep control unless it adopted a 'bureaucratic'
model of society. As we shall later see (paragraphs 9.5.7–8), bureaucracy is
extremely mechanistic in character. Weber, who wrote at great length on the
characteristics of bureaucracy and other authority systems, describes
bureaucracy as a 'well-oiled machine'. So there is a strongly mechanistic
element in totalitarianism. But – and this may be strange though to those

who see a philosophy advocating an unplanned economy as 'rugged individualism' – *there is a strong mechanistic model underlying laissez-faire also.* This I shall explain in a moment.

7.2.22 The net result is that both totalitarian and laissez-faire societies tend to produce managers in Taylor's own mould, namely autocrats who arc convinced of their own moral rectitude. In both instances this springs from regarding the economy of the society in which they live as a 'machine' which will only operate efficiently if each and every enterprise is closely controlled by its managers. In the case of their own enterprise this means themselves.

7.2.23 It is easy to see why the bureaucratic totalitarian state should breed such personalities: men who self-righteously regard workers as pawns. In the first place, such a man regards even himself as a piece in the chess-game of the economy: he too is an instrument. His position is relatively lowly in the state hierarchy. From that low vantage-point he can have no idea how dire, or otherwise, any deviation from the master-plan might be. This limits his discretion, so he obeys and expects others to do the same. But it is not only from practical necessity that he acts so; he also perceives it as a moral obligation. Conditioned to regard the 'state' as being synonymous with 'society' and thus to conceiving the *dicta* of the state as expressing the will of that society, he concludes that the independent will of the worker is a threat to social order which it is his moral duty to eradicate.

7.2.24 Nothing could appear more alien to rugged individualism than the above confirmity. Yet the laissez-faire manager shares the same preoccupation with the efficiency of the firm, the same distrust of the independent will of the worker, and the same self-righteous attitude towards having adopted such a patronizing *Weltanschauung.* Let me not be misunderstood: I am not saying that this is a position that he has no valid reasons for adopting. At this stage I am merely recording the situation and pointing out its similarity to that of totalitarian management.

7.2.25 If we analyse why the actor John Wayne was such a box-office pull during his life, and a TV cult-hero after his death, it is because he epitomized rugged individuality within the capitalist system. His films had always the same plot. Given guts, the individual can conquer the stupidity of authority and the hostility both of Nature and of man. Small wonder that he has a heroic image for those whom the mechanism of our society has trapped into routine confirmity.

7.2.26 Yet there is an irony in the philosophic justification of the 'maverick' roles that Wayne played. *This is, that (whether they know it or not) mavericks too are cogs in the machine.* This is because, when all the mavericks have done what suits their own purposes, the result will be the 'best' society. This may be a strange idea, deliberately made yet stranger by the way that I have expressed it, but it is the philosophic justification for laissez-faire attitudes, and has been so since Adam Smith gave the idea general currency when in 1776 he published his book *An Inquiry into the Nature and the Causes of the Wealth of Nations.*

7.2.27

'Every individual is continually exerting himself to find the most advantageous employment for whatever capital he can command. It is his own advantage, indeed, and not that of society, which he has in view. But the study of his own advantage naturally, or rather necessarily, leads him to prefer that employment which is most advantageous to society.' (Smith 1970, Vol 1, p.398.)

7.2.28 This claim of Adam Smith, namely that, given the opportunities open to him, the entrepreneur will, by choosing his own good, indirectly choose what is good for society, is the basic idea behind the doctrine of the 'invisible hand'. This is to rely upon market forces to supply the integrative principle in society. It is not centralized planning which ensured that London had no shortage or glut of bread today. It is that the production was regulated by each capitalist bakery individually and delicately balancing the risks of losses caused by overproduction and the loss of opportunity which would occur from underproduction.

7.2.29 As I said in the Introduction, the invisible hand is a concept that is often treated flippantly as though it were mysticism and/or condemned because it supplies what people can afford rather than what they need. It is certainly not mysticism. Its practicality is demonstrated by the way it regulates the economies of the Western world. As to its being a mechanism which is indifferent to social need, this is undoubtedly true. The device is therefore amoral. For that reason most of us in Western Europe are (as I said in paragraph 5.2.16) equivocal about it. We would question making it the *sole* means of allocating resources. Yet, that having been said, even those Western European governments which choose to call themselves 'socialist' still use the invisible hand of market forces as the main mechanism for resource allocation. Only in specific areas of social concern do they intervene to give the invisible hand a push in a direction in which it would not otherwise go.

7.2.30 With the proviso that the hand may need such a push from time to time, we can rebut the claim that it is *im*moral to use this amoral device. Marxists, of course, will argue otherwise. Others who might join them are those who are interested in obtaining a government subsidy for a service or a good at the expense of the rest of us; for it is in the nature of subsidies that someone in society has to pay for them. When it comes to providing money from the public purse for the things from which everyone can benefit, defence, and health and welfare services, everyone would want the priorities changed, and there is a strong anti-nuclear lobby, but few object to all such expenditure in principle. On the other hand, giving subsidies to protect certain industries would, I suggest, be more frequently challenged in principle. A case can be made for certain subsidies by non-Marxists...and even by non-socialists. The grounds are that the industry forms part of a national infrastructure which is socially or strategically important to maintain. Yet, without subsidy, this industry either

(a) would be unable to survive competition, or
(b) would be unable to bring its product or service on to the market at a price which the public could afford. They would then be driven to forgoing it, or using less desirable alternatives. [Cheap frequent (subsidized) commuter travel, for example, may reduce car-traffic congestion.]

7.2.31 Yet, that being said, it is remarkable how many middle-of-the-road and right-wing socialists (disenchanted as they are by the way nationalized concerns have swallowed tax-payers' money in the form of subsidies, or have used their monopolistic powers to raise prices, or both) no longer preach the cause of nationalization. Sampson (1982; p.80) claims that 'after 1956, Anthony Crosland's book, *The Future of Socialism* became the revisionists' bible, spelling out the merits of the mixed economy, the limits of nationalisation and the need for higher growth rates to finance more welfare'. Indeed, even non-capitalist societies find that they need some yardstick which will perform one of the functions of market forces, namely to identify and eradicate opportunity costs. If they do not, the rest of the people in that society will end up paying for the inefficiency that this represents. For example, if the general public of any society, capitalist or non-capitalist, had the choice between subsidizing miners to get coal from difficult pits rather than having them dig a hole elsewhere, I suspect that (particularly if the new hole would be within commuting distance of the existing mine) they would be unsympathetic to the subsidy.

7.2.32 Nor, I suggest, would they find that the miners' cause was enhanced by a proposal made by the National Union of Mineworker's president, Arthur Scargill. He was speaking in support of the two issues in the 1984 miners' strike: namely that no job should be lost in the industry and that no pit should be closed other than on grounds that it was now unsafe or exhausted: in effect a claim that whatever it costs to mine coal in a particular mine, that cost must be paid. He suggested that the market for the coal so mined could be expanded by giving winter coal to old people who might otherwise suffer from hypothermia. This emotive linkage of concepts is a very transparent conjuring trick. Even if old people should be provided with heat out of the public purse, its source doesn't have to be coal, nor does it have to be the most heavily subsidized coal one can find. His suggestion was an inversion of reality. The more of society's limited resources that are consumed by extracting coal from uneconomic pits, the less will there be for other purposes. That being so, it is possible to question the morality of allowing inefficient pits to absorb resources which might, among other things, have been used to subsidize the elderly.

7.2.33 Subsidies are always an attempt to prevent the operation of the invisible hand. This was the reason that the European Parliament, under the provisions of its Common Agricultural Policy subsidized its agriculture and viniculture. But the entirely predictable result was that they created the infamous 'butter mountain' and 'wine lake'. Such embarrassing gluts are bound to occur when subsidies encourage production above the ability of the public to consume. For, if demand is inelastic, reducing the price will not get rid of such surplus, and, in any case, artificially low prices will only increase the compensatory size of the subsidy next time around. On both counts the butter needed to be 'dumped' somewhere it could not leak back into Western Europe. So it was sold behind the 'Iron Curtain' at far lower prices that Western Europeans had to pay. In effect, subsidies which might have gone to those in need in Western Europe went to finance the Russian economy. Some may question the morality of that. At a more mundane level, given the arms race between East and West, they might also find it strategically questionable for the West thereby indirectly to have funded Soviet missiles.

7.2.34 So moral rectitude is not the attribute solely of those who denounce the use of the invisible hand. Moreover, there is a moral reason for its use which I find compelling and which I mentioned in the Introduction to this book. It is that its use brings the majority of society's hierarchies together in a loose federation within which they retain their own autonomy. In 'planned economies' all economic activity needs to be integrated so that it forms a huge totalitarian pyramid, bound together under centralized authority. By contrast, this loose federation of autonomous structures makes the levers of economic power, and thus of political power, too diffuse to be easily grabbed by any one group. This happy circumstance, which for a variety of reasons is now under threat, is our greatest natural defence against arbitrary centralized tyranny. Long may it remain so.

7.2.35 All capitalists therefore see it as important to respond to market forces in a way which will minimize opportunity cost, but none do so as fervently as the laissez-faire capitalist. He is the manager least likely to have compassion for the employee who falls victim to market forces. All managers find, from time to time, that their responsibility to preserve the company by minimizing opportunity cost brings them into conflict with the interests of certain employees. If they do not shrink from this, neither do they avoid some sense of guilt. By contrast, the laissez-faire capitalist may well perform the same duty with an autocratic and self-righteous attitude. For the rider to Adam Smith's theory is that managers who do not place the interest of the firm above everything are failing, not only in their obligation to that firm, but also to society. For only by concentrating upon the firm's self-interest can the 'best' society emerge. But the self-interest of the firm requires that it should survive. In manufacturing this makes producing goods for sale the firm's paramount duty. So the laissez-faire manager, justified by these reasons in his complete single-mindedness will emphasize the link 'SP' in my model of the organization in Figure 3.2(b) on page 58 and will de-emphasize the other links in the system. This is precisely what I claimed that Taylor did. The circle is therefore complete and Taylorism and laissez-faire management are seen to be quite as mutually compatible as Taylorism and totalitarianism.

7.2.36 Merkle claimed, and I would agree with her, that Taylorism in Britain was resisted prior to the Second World War. Attempts were made by some managements, particularly in the depression of the 1930s (when depressed profits made cost-cutting a common reaction), to bring in some form of work study. (This precise term was not used then, but in fact that was what it was.) Of course such savings in labour-cost in a stagnant market can only come from cutting total hours paid, i.e. redundancy. Again the workers and the unions rejected it. Echoes of the 1930s came to me as I started upon a work study assignment in the early 1950s. The foreman, a kindly man but with a perverse sense of humour, said solemnly to me on my first day, 'Would you mind coming with me Mr Butler?' I agreed and to my wonderment was taken into the ladies' toilet. He pointed gravely at a small window and looked at me with a face of deep melancholy. 'It must be twenty years ago', he said, 'that we had the Bedaux boys in here doing the same sort of job you're doing. I thought that you'd like to see the window that they escaped through.' He continued with his sad, dead-pan stare. Then with a sigh he added ominously, 'Well, you never know!'

7.2.37 Charles E. Bedaux developed his own form of work measurement about 1911. The system need not worry us. It had some interesting technical aspects, but it is now, so far as I know, completely obsolete. However, its use during the 1930s to cut costs by getting the same output from fewer workers added fuel to the anti-Taylorite attitudes of both workers and unions upon which Judith Merkle has already commented. Reaction was often fierce: a circumstance to which the toilet window was mute witness.

7.2.38 During the Second World War, however, most workers and trade unionists were more ready to accept work study. (By then this was the term that was in common use. The name had largely been adopted to give a new respectability to the technique that 'time and motion study' and 'the Bedaux system' and all such other terms had lost.) Moreover, although it would be fallacious, I think, to suggest that the worker had sunk his differences with management in a fervour of patriotic zeal, yet there may have been an element of that. This element could easily be exaggerated, however. For a variety of complex reasons there is a tendency for union membership to rise in wartime. We do not have to consider these reasons: we need merely note that a rise in union membership is not compatible with the claim that patriotism has led the worker to feel a kinship for management. A more likely reason for the acceptance of work study in the 1940s and 1950s was probably the boom conditions. Increased efficiency therefore did not give rise to the redundancy of the 1930s but to higher wages from the increased output. It was a sellers' market.

7.2.39 The result of this general interest in – and application of – Taylorism was that the general level of managerial ability rose sharply. This tendency for competitive managerial ability to rise is an irreversible process. An increase in the quality of our competitor's managerial ability calls for a response from us. Our increase calls for a response from him. It is a one-way ratchet. There is no going back. Nowadays it is extremely difficult to credit that when I started my consultancy career in the early 1950s there were fewer British firms, in my experience, that had budgetary control than did not. During the whole of that decade I only came across two or three firms that had standard costing apart from those to whom I introduced it. Accountancy was seldom an instrument for plotting the future course of the firm. Frequently it did no more than to chart the wake that the firm had left behind it when the annual accounts were produced. Even these were, as often as not, 'wrong' in that they frequently, in those naïve days, underestimated the value of the assets employed in the business: a situation that was to enrich

Charles Clore and others.

7.2.40 Taylorism therefore sneaked into Britain very late. It was allowed in by the workers and their unions under the boom conditions of the Second World War and the cold-war aftermath, when returning ex-service men and women had their lives to re-build. So as consumers they bought, and as workers they produced. These factors kept the economy buoyant. Yet, once introduced, Taylorism's ratchet-like effect makes it unrealistic for either management or workers to drop it without putting their firm at risk... so they don't.

7.2.41 A further development had, by this time, made Taylorism more acceptable to the British. This was that the State was either implementing, or insisting upon the firm implementing, 'welfare' obligations towards the worker which previously had not existed or else had only been implemented on a voluntary basis at the firm's expense. Enforced 'cushioning' of the employee removed some of the moral tension from management's more unpleasant responsibilities. Indeed, my own view is that it allowed the British manager to be more honest in handling such matters than his American counterpart. Language can be very revealing. The British manager says to the worker 'I'm afraid that I've got to make you redundant.' The American manager goes through the pretence that the initiative has come from the employee. Somewhat hypocritically he says 'I'm afraid that I've got to let you go.'

7.2.42 I think it is important to recognize the way in which the average European's cultural approach to 'welfare' concepts differs from the average American's. I believe it is true to say that the right wing of the political spectrum in all the European countries is more prepared to envisage a 'laissez-faire' society than the centre or the left wing. Yet my experience is that even the typical right wing European is less happy with completely 'laissez-faire' policies than is an American of the centre. Why is this?

7.2.43 Of course we can only speculate. Possibly it is that Europeans have a feudal legacy in their culture that makes caring for others more of an obligation. The number and the quality of the 'voluntary' welfare services in Britain today is evidence of this. Possibly it is because anything that can have a 'socialist' label affixed to it causes so much agitation for some Americans that they just 'turn off' and even refuse to think about the issues. Perhaps it is also a fear that 'welfare' will undermine the Protestant work ethic and ruin the moral fibre of their society. Whether a society that refuses to care for the disadvantaged can be said to have a good moral fibre is another question.

However, as an avowed capitalist who would deny that he was a socialist, let me give my own view of the matter which I am sure is shared by the majority of European managers. This is that a capitalist society

(1) can only regard itself as civilized, and
(2) can only allow the blind forces of the market to operate, if it also
(3) provides adequate welfare facilities to help those people whom the system hurts.

I do not doubt for one minute that there will be some who take advantage of such a situation. I am sure also that the level of benefit can be so high that it is a disincentive to self-help. The question that has to be answered is 'Do you want to live in a society that does not provide a safety net for those whom the free market makes socially disadvantaged?' Most Europeans would answer 'No!'

7.2.44 Throughout the world, therefore, by a gradual process of assimilation, from Milwaukee to Moscow and to Manchester, Taylorism has spread. Despite the consistently bad publicity it has received, its effect on productivity has been positive enough for not only managements but also workers and union officials to make their peace with it in one form or another. I shall not consider further the position of the Moscow manager. His requirement to achieve the maximum productive use of his resources means that the issues are the same as those facing the manager in Milwaukee and Manchester. The difference is that he does not have their economic yardsticks.

7.2.45 Some of these managers may not even realize that it is Taylorism which pervades the tools of their trade. How many managers who daily use 'Gantt charts' know that the name derives from Henry L. Gantt, one of Taylor's followers? Yet such basic techniques as work study, production control, and budgetary control are Taylor's children. The refinements within those techniques give us a whole specialized management lexicon: standard minute values, rating, critical path analysis, optimum batch size, variance, etc. Yet it is all a direct inheritance of Taylor's system. For the modern manager these techniques are more than the mere tools of his trade. They are an expression of his professionalism and his belief that with their aid he can benefit his firm in particular and society in general.

7.2.46 That being so, Taylorism has become part of his intellectual integrity. He could no more renounce the use of such techniques than he could renounce his whole being. This is the major reason why, despite all the sermons from the likes of Douglas McGregor, the manager still persists in his allegedly 'unregenerate' ways. One of the disadvantages that the neo-human relations school has suffered from adopting its high moral tone now emerges. This is that it has blinded them to the possibility that the actions of others can be inspired by as moral an intent as their own. As for the outcome of those respective actions, that of the neo-human relations school is not above reproach.

7.2.47 My personal belief is that they have done enormous harm. For since the neo-human relations cult takes pride in condemning so-called 'mechanistic efficiency', it has, as much as any other single cause, been responsible for eroding the manufacturing base of the British economy. So strong has pressure been from this particular lobby that, not only (as I said earlier) do many 'management' courses in our polytechnics and other institutions make no reference to work study, but 'professional' institutions, whom one could have hoped would have had a more realistic approach to the problems of managerial control, have been bamboozled into following suit. To single out that there was no mention of 'work study' in the 1983 'Organization and Management' syllabus of the Association of Certified Accountants, is only to illustrate a failure which is far more widespread. But I do feel that professionals should have shown more realism.

7.2.48 Work study has two aspects, both of which are offensive to the neo-human relations school: (1) method study, and (2) work measurement. Method study precedes work measurement because it is obviously pointless to measure a poor method.

(1) Method study offends them because, not realizing the limitations of job-enrichment (which we dealt with in Chapter 4), they have made it their chosen vehicle for motivating the worker. Since the method study engineer (on behalf of management) chooses the method to be adopted, this limits the worker's initiative and blocks job-enrichment. (We saw in Chapter 4 that such a block is probably there in any case – imposed by the technology.)
(2) Because among its many other uses, which we shall list in paragraph 7.2.50, work measurement can be the basis of incentive schemes, this too is anathema to them. This is because they reject the validity (one could even say the right) of the worker to work for extrinsic reasons, such as to earn money, when he should be doing it for job satisfaction. In the jargon, he should not have an 'instrumental' attitude towards his work. I have already mentioned (paragraph 7.1.7) the phenomenon of paternalism in liberal thought. If the worker appears content with a situation that **they** perceive as being 'instrumental', then he has no right

to be so. They match Taylor's paternalism exactly: but they are 180
degrees out of phase with him. He claims the worker **should** be happy
being instrumental, they insist that he **should not.** Each believes that
they know better than the worker what he should want of life.

7.2.49 In a moment I shall list the purposes to which work measurement is
put, in order that the reader will be able to see how essential it is to the
practising manager or accountant. After reading through the list, I believe
that the reader will confirm that assessment. If so he may feel, as I do, that
the whole issue raises certain fundamental questions. I accept that it is the
right, indeed even the duty, of academics to point out to their students the
philosophic implications of work measurement and its mechanistic
overtones. Yet, as I said in paragraph 7.1.7, the arrogant paternalism that is
displayed when they deny the student the right to know anything about it at
all, because to do so would offend their own tender consciences is, to me,
culpable. For the price of their action is to send the student manager or
accountant out into a world in which he will be required to fulfil certain
functions but for which he will not have been equipped. The way to hell, as
always, is paved with good intentions. Of course the final irony of the
situation is that these are the very people who accuse others of 'paternalism',
as the reader will recall from McGregor's words in paragraph 7.1.5. I deny
that they have this right to such blatant censorship.

7.2.50 The purposes of work measurement and the standards derived from
it have been set out by the International Labour Office as follows, (ILO
1957; pp.195–196):

   (a) To compare the efficiency of alternative methods. Other conditions being
        equal, the method that takes the least time will be the best method.
   (b) To balance the work of members of teams in association with multiple
        activity charts so that each member has an equal task to perform.
   (c) To determine in association with man–machine charts the number of
        machines an operative can run.

The time standards, once set, may then be used:

   (d) To provide information on which the planning and scheduling of production
        can be based, including the plant and labour requirements for carrying out
        the programme of work and the utilization of available capacity.
   (e) To provide information on which estimates for tendering selling prices
        and delivery promises can be based.
   (f) To set standards of machine utilization and labour performance which can
        be used for any of the above purposes and as a basis for incentive schemes.
   (g) To provide information for labour-cost control and to enable standard
        costs to be fixed and maintained.

In other words, work measurement provides the basic information necessary for all the activities of organizing and controlling the work of the factory in which the time element plays a part.

7.2.51 It may well be that the reader is not too sure about what some of these uses imply in detail, but my hope is that he will at least get some sort of 'feel' for the economic importance of the technique which will induce him to study the subject so that even if he himself is not applying it, he can appreciate what it involves. For if capitalism requires that we apply the concept of minimizing 'opportunity cost', then work study is of the essence of capitalism. For its whole purpose is to apply certain formalized techniques to the objective of achieving particular purposes within a certain time-scale, but to do so in a manner which will minimize the combined costs of the material, machinery and labour resources consumed.

7.2.52 Indeed, that is a definition which, though it applies to work study, could equally be used to define what constitutes efficient management, whether that management is capitalist or non-capitalist. All the techniques of Taylorism (which include work study, budgetary control, production control, and many others) are amenable to this definition. It also represents a definition of the purpose behind applied research in industry. Indeed, it was in experimenting to establish the factors and relationships which optimize metal-cutting that Taylor discovered high-speed steel. To choose, as many critics do, to emphasize the role of Taylor's personality in all this while making light of the intractable nature of the problems he tackled is to distort the picture, belittle the man, and bedevil our own efforts to find solutions. It would be foolish to deny that Taylor's own personality contributed greatly to the coloration which Taylorism acquired. But to emphasize that is to disguise that the things he did needed doing. If Taylor had never lived, the task he set himself would still have been there waiting for someone to undertake. Perhaps it would have helped if that someone had been of a less obsessive disposition than Taylor. Such a person might have avoided some of the antagonisms: but who knows? I suspect that the fundamental clash between the impersonality of capitalism and the personal needs of the worker would have made such antagonisms inevitable. In which case, perhaps we should be grateful that Taylor's obsessive, blinkered approach allowed him to persevere where the tenacity of many another would have crumbled. Whatever the course of history might have been, it seems to me that from our vantage-point in the last decades of the twentieth century, we can gain some understanding of those factors which determined the road which the last two centuries of technological development have taken. Chronologically and figuratively Taylor stands at the centre of that development. I hope to show not only that Taylor's work was essential to his era: I hope also to show that all subsequent developments in management techniques are but a postscript – dictated by him but signed in his absence.

8

Technology *is* Taylorism

8.1 Why technology affects both organizational structures and motivation

8.1.1 No one writing on this topic can fail to pay tribute to the seminal work of Joan Woodward. It was she who first claimed (Woodward, 1958) that technology determined in large measure the structure and spirit of an organization. By 'technology' she was not referring to such differences as whether one was working with one material or another, on one machine rather than another, or producing one product rather than another. The differences she chose loosely to refer to as 'technology' were whether one

(1) was manufacturing single unique products or small batches,
(2) was making a product in volume by large batches or 'mass' production, or
(3) was engaged in such near-continuous processes as are associated with chemicals, etc.

8.1.2 I do not fully agree with Joan Woodward's categories as I shall explain later (paragraph 15.8.3), but I certainly concur with the principle that certain types of production are determinants of organizational structure and ethos. Perhaps the doubts I have about the manner in which she splits her categories have caused others to doubt the whole principle of the determinant nature of technology rather than simply to ask whether it should not be modified. If so it is a pity.

8.1.3 The reason that I suggest that her insight has not received the merit it deserves is that (along with E.L. Trist and a few others) she has been put into that strangest of categories – the category of 'contingency theorist'. Such a title means 'theorists who believe that circumstances alter cases'. Yet who doubts such a truism? If such theorists deserve a special category, then who are the 'non-contingency theorists' who believe that no matter what the circumstance the case remains the same? Of course there are none. This leads me to conclude that it is not the significance of contingencies *in general* that is in doubt: merely the significance of such *technological* contingencies as these theorists have identified. If so, that doubt needs to be dispelled, even if the technological categories need to be more closely defined.

8.1.4 This chapter will concentrate in the main on the economic and technical aspects of those categories I consider significant. In Sections 15.8 to 15.12 we shall expand on their organizational implications. The three categories of technology which I consider significant are subsets of Woodward's first two major groupings. We shall not concern ourselves with her third main grouping. My categories are:

(1) Making a product in volume by continuously passing the work along a fixed chain of operations (product layout).
(2) Manufacturing a number of products in parallel by intermittently moving batches of each product between machines. These machines are not laid out in any particular sequence but each group performs a particular manufacturing process which differs from the process which each other group performs (process layout).
(3) Making large single units such as a ship, a dam, a motorway, etc. (large-scale jobbing).

8.1.5 I shall claim that those who possess the technical knowledge to understand the ramifications of these three different manufacturing systems cannot resist a common conclusion. This is as follows: *The requirements of these three manufacturing systems mean that distinctive features arise in each. Consequently the spirit and structure of an organization engaged in continuous production on a 'product layout' will differ* (a priori) *from one engaged in batch production on a 'process layout'. Similarly, both of these will differ from one engaged in large-scale jobbing. Furthermore, except for minor variations caused by specific differences in product and culture, an organization in any one category of 'technology' will share its salient structure and ethos of other organizations in the same category.*

8.1.6 Our travel along the road of technological development starts in about 1780 because that was the era of the Industrial Revolution in England. So dramatic were its social effects that few people have recognized that for the following hundred years industry got along with precious little management at all. But by the time that Taylor went to Midvale, industry's problems had become so acute that nothing less than a quantum leap in management skills would suffice to meet them. Taylor, on behalf of us all, made that leap. This new requirement in management is my first historical justification for Woodward. Prior to Taylor's day no manufactured products had demanded that general-purpose engineering machines should produce batches of standardized products by means of a 'process layout'. Now, in the late nineteenth century, they did. But it was a requirement for which no previous experience had prepared us. We needed a Taylor if it was ever going to work. *This circumstance alone should indicate how right Woodward was to argue the significance of technology.* However, I anticipate. Let us go back to 1780 to start our review of industrial development.

8.2 Industrial development during the century before Taylor

8.2.1 What happened in Taylor's America was part of a process which started a hundred years previously in Britain. The staggering social changes in Britain over the period (known as the Industrial Revolution) resulted from many contributory factors. Yet there is a tendency for some commentators to simplify the issues and to deny what others would emphasize. It should not surprise us that a commentator's vision should reflect his ideology, but we should at least be on our guard if he minimizes factors which must be significant in order to emphasize the uniqueness of his interpretation. The main split lies between commentators who incline to the views of Marx and those who incline to the views of Weber. But before we consider what these are, it might be revealing to look at certain parallels between how things stood in the 1780s and how they stood in the 1980s.

8.2.2

(a) If a revolutionary change takes place in our society over the next few years it will be triggered by a particular piece of equipment, the microprocessor. It will offer both increased capacity and lower costs but it will transform our lives in the process. In the 1780s this was the role of the power spinning frame.

(b) If our lives change it will be to some extent because we are **prepared** to let them change. The eighteenth-century spirit was quite as enquiring and daring as our own.

(c) We have the social infrastructure of an educated population which can adapt to the microprocessor to provide the social energy for the change. The eighteenth century had many displaced people seeking the security of a wage and capable of operating the new equipment.

(d) The economic advantages of the microprocessor mean that it has a ready market in a developed economy. Britain's eighteenth-century expansionism and naval power had created a huge protected market for cheap cotton goods. This made investment in the new spinning machinery too potentially profitable to pass up.

(e) Although the 1780 entrepreneur changed the world when he built mills to house the new technology, he could not have foreseen all the consequences. For his actions started in train a process which gathered its own momentum and thereby wrought a technological, social, economic and political revolution. This process not only changed the physical world to what we know today: it changed the way we see things and the institutions and rules by which we seek to shape that world to conform to our expectations.

8.2.3 This latter idea (that the material world develops its own momentum and is the source of our social institutions and consciousness) is quite Marxist. But the Marxist is so anxious to show that history is the outcome of mechanistic forces that are beyond man's capacity to control that he de-emphasizes the role played by the human spirit. Consequently even when acknowledging the catalytic nature of technology, he cannot bear to think that it is man's creature, for he wishes to maintain intact the concept of history as the mechanistic workings of uncontrollable forces. It would not be enough for him that I would be willing to admit that once such forces are set in train they will have outcomes that go far beyond what we can foresee. Such an admission would satisfy his claim that the process can acquire a quasi-autonomous nature. But it would be far too 'open-ended', too non-directive, for him.

8.2.4 The Marxist believes that he has been vouchsafed a unique vision of the path that history's juggernaut *must* take. This is why he gets a *frisson* of pleasure from contemplating that the bourgeoisie think that they are in the driving seat of this juggernaut, whereas the Marxist is able to savour that *he* knows them to be in the path of the on-coming wheels. The result is, as Burns says (1969; p.11), that 'if we regard the cumulative advance of technology – like population growth, or the expansion of markets – as a circumstance which, though human enough, transcends the purposes and control of any generation of mankind, let alone individual men, then [Marx's explanation]... rests on causes external to man.

8.2.5 So the Marxist is at pains to emphasize man's helplessness to understand, to control or to deflect the mechanistically determined outcomes of technological change. Weber, on the other hand, claims that the mind of the Calvinist Puritan led his fellow Protestants from the earlier 'adventurer's capitalism' to 'rational capitalism'. Those who accept this view have a tendency to discount any specific technological 'trigger' mechanism. Anthony Giddens has pointed out that Weber (who published *The Protestant Ethic and the Spirit of Capitalism* as two long articles in 1904 and

1905) claimed that the switch from the earlier to the later form of capitalism 'often happened without any technological change taking place within the enterprise. Where such enterprises have been restructured, what has occurred is a rational reorganisation of production, directed towards maximizing productive efficiency'. (Giddens, 1971; p.126.)

8.2.6 Where this happened, the inference is that a particular attitude to life, the 'Protestant work ethic', caused this movement towards modern industrial capitalism. It is a thesis that is more popular with present-day businessmen than with today's historians. My own attitude is to accept it as a constituent element, but not the sole element. Other commentators give it very little credence. Since it denies that we are in the grip of dialectical materialism, most Marxists reject it. *But so too do some non-Marxists who believe that the free acceptance of a simple technological breakthrough was enough to alter the whole of society. The pattern of life changed from people who ordered their own lives within their cottages to one in which they 'clocked on' in factories. Workers operating under the domestic system in England had been free to 'order their own lives' because of two main circumstantial factors. First, they were not called upon to account for their time. The merchant who presented them with the raw material for spinning and weaving would buy it back at a 'piece-work' price. He was therefore not interested in how long it had taken them or what hours they had worked. *I should like the reader to note this point. Many students, I find, believe 'piece-work payment' is a product of the factory system and some believe it originated with Taylor. The reality is that the origins of the system are lost in antiquity. It is not until the rise of the factory system that it was feasible for the entrepreneur even to consider buying an industrial worker's time on an hourly basis, since he couldn't control the arrangement. It is true that some factories*

---

* This *determinist* element in Marx is not without its difficulties for Marxists themselves. It has produced in them an ambivalent response: (1) So-called *Scientific Marxists* are attracted to Marx's *determinism* because it offers them the optimism of certainty. The belief that the course of history is determined is the basis of Marxism's claim to be 'scientific'. The belief that the outcome will be what one wants is, moreover, a great consolation, and never more so than when that likelihood appears most remote. (2) Yet this same determinism is an embarrassment to so-called *Critical Marxists*, whose revolutionary fervour seeks fulfilment in action. That is to say they are looking for a *voluntarist* belief that will allow them, with hope of success, to intervene in the course of history rather than to wait with passive fatalism for the arrival of its slow-moving juggernaut.

It is not a controversy we can pursue here. It is the theme of an excellent book by Alvin Gouldner (1980).

operate piece-work or bonus schemes but these have usually a 'time' element.
The second factor that allowed people to order their lives before the growth
of the factory system was that they might have other means of survival than
the money that they received from the merchant. They might, for example,
have access to a little land for growing food for their families. Yet once they
sold their time in the long factory days of the nineteenth century only to
return to their industrial slum-dwellings, they had neither the energy nor the
access to land that would permit this in most instances. In Marxist
terminology they had become 'wage-slaves'. How then did this technological
invention (the spinning frame) which allegedly caused this revolution issue
in such enormous social changes?

8.2.7 It would not be historically correct to suggest that prior to the
mechanization of spinning all manufacture took place in workers' homes.
Clearly there were exceptions caused by the technical requirements, for
example ship-building, glass and pottery manufacture. But in general it was
so, and it was certainly so in the case of cotton manufacture, and with the
location of the work being in the home, this situation is usually referred to
as 'the domestic system'. However, cotton had one bottleneck operation –
that of spinning. For a weaver could consume yarn as fast as many people
could produce it. (It is interesting to note that those families with too few
women-folk to spin enough thread for the males, who were the weavers,
would arrange to make up the deficit from unattached females or
'spinsters'.)

8.2.8 Not only was the industry output bedevilled by lack of spinning
capacity, but, given the existing technology in spinning, the technically
necessary labour was high, and this fed through in terms of cost into the final
selling price. Solving this technical problem posed by spinning would, by
relieving this bottleneck, make possible such a positive explosion of cotton
commodities at cheap yet profitable prices, for the colonies and the world in
general, that fortunes would be there for the making.

8.2.9 The historian E. J. Hobsbawn has said (1968; p.25), 'It is often
assumed that an economy of private enterprise has an automatic bias
towards innovation, but this is not so. It has a bias only towards profit.' He
is undoubtedly right. But the bias towards profit produced the bias towards
innovation and so the three inventions familiar to every British schoolchild
occurred in rapid succession. There was the 'spinning jenny' of 1760, which
could still be used in a cottage but which allowed the operator to spin several
threads at once. This was followed by the 'water frame' of 1768 and then the
'mule' of the 1780s. This latter was a combination of the other two concepts:

**but it was essentially a 'factory' piece of equipment for it required power to
turn it**. This it was that changed the whole way of life in Britain. The initial
power was from water-wheels. Water was also used in some of the
processing: and for such purposes was the better for being lime-free. The
water for both existed in low-populated areas of Derbyshire, Cheshire and
Lancashire.

8.2.10 Where there was a constant enough flow of water, water-wheels
could provide enough power to run any number of factories. Fast rivers
could use undershot wheels, but even slow rivers, by means of dams and
sluice gates, could feed enough power to run either an undershot or an
overshot wheel. So entrepreneurs built their factories along the banks of the
rivers in the North West of England, and also cottages that would house the
influx of workers: the transformation had begun. The advent of steam as a
source of power led to the possibility of placing factories anywhere, even in
existing towns which were not necessarily adjacent to water power. But the
steam engine (despite its grasp upon the popular imagination as being so)
was not the main technological factor in initiating the Industrial Revolution,
though it certainly was a *catalyst* in what followed. After the 1840s a network
of railways existed which were (except for bulk deliveries and heavy freight)
gradually to kill off by their speed and flexibility the use of the canal system
which had been built 100 years previously. In the same way, and for much
the same reasons, road transport has today eclipsed that of the railways.

8.2.11 Yet even if we perceive the role of the spinning machine as
inaugurating the present factory system, a great many other strands, both
social and economic, needed to be there to get the system to take off. One
of these was undoubtedly the existence of markets which Britain's
freebooting maritime power procured for her. But a major requirement was
also the laissez-faire attitude of government that allowed cotton
manufacturers to flourish and to exploit their workers in the process. It may
be thought that man's inhumanity to man is so universal an aspect of life in
every age that there would be no need to understand it. Yet I believe that
some explanation is called for, and that Kenneth Clark was probably right in
his belief that the Victorians sought for and found a 'justification' in the
concept of an intractable social Darwinism. Clark wrote (1960; p.326):

> This new religion of gain had behind it a body of doctrine without which it
> could never have maintained its authority over the serious-minded Victorians.
> The first of its sacred books – printed in 1798 – was the essay on the Principle
> of Population by a clergyman named Malthus...Malthus's text contained such
> phrases as 'man has no claim of right to the smallest portion of food'... The
> other sacred books were the economic theories of Ricardo...Free enterprise

and the survival of the fittest: one can see how they looked like the laws of nature...

8.2.12 While Thomas Robert Malthus's essay (1798) and David Ricardo's book (1817) may explain the **continued** exploitation of the worker by the Victorians, they do not explain the changes of the previous century, nor why the 'adventurers' capitalism of paragraph 1.2.6 became the 'rational' capitalism of paragraph 1.2.7. The inhumanity of Taylor's creed may find its justification in the legacy of Malthus and Ricardo; but I would maintain that his belief in 'rational capitalism' has its roots in Puritanism. That he came from Quaker rather than Calvinist stock, and that he swore like a trooper, are not fundamental inconsistencies. He used many times to refer to his 'whale of a New England conscience'. As for the swearing, he was prepared to match his language to his workers' language if, in the process, it helped him to gain and to maintain control. The more I have tried to reconcile the paradoxes within Taylor's personality, the more I become convinced that they are the same paradoxes which exist in the worldly/other-worldly image of Weber's Calvinist. To understand Taylor I believe it is necessary to understand the Puritan element in capitalism. Perhaps the most graphic account of the workings of the mind of such a man comes from the historian Richard Henry Tawney. His book was published in 1926 and built upon Weber's thesis of twenty-two years earlier.

8.2.13 Not for Tawney the language of mechanistic metaphors. His imagery urges us to see capitalism as a natural growth, an evolution. He takes up Weber's thesis and infers that it was the Protestant work ethic, stemming from Puritanism, that prepared the ground for capitalism. To this is added the implication that, where Puritanism could not flourish, then neither could capitalism. Tawney contrasts England and Ireland in this respect. In England

> Puritanism worked like the yeast which sets the whole mass fermenting... The effect was [both] an irritant and a tonic. Sapping [the surviving elements of feudalism] by its influence and overthrowing [the authoritarian state's ideal of an ordered and graded society] by direct attack. Puritanism became a potent force in preparing the way for the commercial civilization that finally triumphed. ... Where, as in Ireland, the elements were so alien that assimilation [of Puritan ideology] was out of the question, the result was a wound that festered for three centuries (Tawney, 1926; pp.231–232).

8.2.14 What is this 'Puritanism' and how did it ever come about that the views of a Christian sect should come to be so in tune with an industrial system that seems to contain so many un-Christian features? Tawney explains this paradox in some of the most beautiful prose ever written. It is, however, a long passage. Moreover, it assumes a knowledge of Christian theology that cannot be assumed in today's readership. I shall therefore paraphrase it. Anglicans and Catholics see the hand of God at work in the world in a two-fold way. First that He created it, and secondly that after the sinfulness of mankind had put them beyond hope of rescuing themselves, He sent His own Son to redeem the world through His own death by crucifixion. Therefore, though there is sin in the world, for Anglican and Catholic it is still God's world and the Fatherhood of God makes them acknowledge the brotherhood of man. This is not true of the Puritan. To him the world is an alien and evil place. He therefore does his utmost to keep himself separate both from it and from his fellow-men in order to be nearer his God in individual prayer. A strange starting point from which to become materialistically successful. Let us see why this happens. We had got to the stage where the Puritan has withdrawn into a private dialogue with his Maker. Tawney continues thus:

> Those who seek God in isolation from their fellow men... are apt to find, not God, but a devil whose countenance bears an embarrassing resemblance to their own. The moral self-sufficiency of the Puritan nerved his will, but it corroded his sense of social solidarity... A spiritual aristocrat, who sacrificed fraternity to liberty, he drew from his idealization of personal responsibility a theory of individual rights, which secularised and generalised, was to be among the most potent explosives that the world has known. He drew from it also a scale of ethical values, in which the traditional scheme of Christian virtues was almost exactly reversed... Called by God to labour in his vineyard, he has within himself a principle at once of energy and of order, which makes himself irresistible both in war and in the struggles of commerce. Convinced that character is all and circumstances nothing, he sees in the poverty of those who fall by the way, not a misfortune to be pitied and relieved, but a moral failing to be condemned, and in riches not an object of suspicion – though like other gifts they may be abused – but the blessing which rewards the triumph of energy and will (Tawney, 1926; p.230).

8.2.15 For all that the world is alien, yet the Puritan's energies cannot help but result in its transformation as a 'duty', even though, in the process, he has no regard for the fall of the sparrow. In just such a way was Taylor concerned for the betterment of the lot of the poor, as we have already seen in paragraph 7.1.22. What then about the fall of the sparrow? Taylor's attitude here is well illustrated by the case of the ball-bearing inspectors. One day Taylor heard that scientific tests had shown that the ability of people to identify objects from a quick glimpse at an image varied enormously. (This I can confirm from the ability of myself and other would-be pilots during the Second World War to recognize silhouettes or photographs of Allied and enemy aircraft when projected onto a screen for a second or two.)

8.2.16 At the time that he learnt of this phenomenon, Taylor had working for him a number of girls whose job was to roll ball-bearings down their fingers in order to detect flaws. Taylor reasoned that the ability to recognize such images and the ability to find flaws in ball-bearings would be related. So he tested the girls accordingly. Those that did not pass the test he sacked. This sacking was no reflection upon the diligence of the girl, nor upon her conduct, which could have been exemplary. It was because those whom nature had not endowed with certain characteristics were to be allowed to fall by the wayside: in just such a way did the Puritan discard without compunction those who had not received the gift of 'grace'. As I read Tawney's description of the Puritan's *Weltanschauung* I have little difficulty in conjuring up a morally self-satisfied face to fit this personality. I have only to look at the features of F. W. Taylor, shown in Figure 7.1(a).

8.2.17 The story of the ball-bearing girls will serve to make another point. Taylor regarded unions as being negative and reactionary in character. In the sense that they seek the immediate interests of the work group, it is clear that trade unions will react negatively to changes which they see as detrimental to their members. The reason for Taylor's moral indignation was in part that he regarded it as self-evident that such action would be against the interests of society at large. *(This may sometimes be the case, but it would be a particularly bigoted person who argued that the sum total of trade unionism's impact on the quality of life in society has been adverse. As a pluralist I cannot believe that the quality of life in society would have been enhanced if every employer had been free to negotiate with each individual on the basis of that individual's disproportionately lower bargaining power.)* The second reason for Taylor's moral indignation reflected his belief that the worker too would be better off without a union. Scientific management had established what was a 'fair-day's work'. The corresponding wages could have no possible scientific base, but the evidence of the Bethlehem Steel plant suggested that workers who performed to those standards would be paid 160 per cent of average industry rates. So (for Taylor) union opposition to a system which could supply these benefits showed clearly that unions operated against the worker's *own* interests.

8.2.18 This brings us back to two questions I should like to pose about the ball-bearing girls, which should help the reader to decide whether Taylor's views (as expressed above) were justified or not. In answering it the reader will also be brought face to face with his own *Weltanschauung.*

Question 1   *In this specific case, what right did Taylor have to sack the ball-bearing girls and what right would a union have to resist such sackings?*

Question 2   *To what general conclusions does that lead about management's right to manage and a union's right to stand in opposition?*

8.2.19 To see the mind of man putting its stamp upon circumstance (Weber) as well as seeing circumstance putting its mark upon the mind of man (Marx) (a 'both…and' approach) makes such basic sense that it seems to me that to insist upon either the one or the other as an interpretation of history says much more about the historian's ideology than it does about reality. Moreover, among the differences exhibited by Marx and Weber there are certain remarkable similarities. We should note, for example, that both Marx and Weber regarded the following conditions as prerequisites of modern industrial capitalism, and we have noted that each of these conditions was fulfilled in the England of the 1780s.

(1) The existence of a large number of wage labourers who are not only free to sell their labour but who need to do so to survive.
(2) A relatively free market in which neither the producers nor the consumers have a monopoly.
(3) Some form of rational technology (e.g. mechanization).
(4) The detachment of the place of production from the home.

8.2.20 There is, however, a significant omission from that list. Nowhere does anyone claim that there is any need for a cadre of managers. Such management as was necessary was minimal. This was fortunate, because it all had to be supplied by the entrepreneur. I find the situation analogous to the way in which the early aircraft pioneers had not only to build their own aircraft, they also had to teach themselves to fly. It is therefore just as well that the first aircraft were as primitive as they were. It would have been an impossible task to teach oneself to fly if the first aircraft had been as complex as (say) Concorde. Similarly, these first 'mechanized' factories were organizationally primitive in the extreme. After all, all they housed was one simple operation, spinning. They didn't even include weaving since the weaving could still take place in the worker's own home. Indeed, until weaving also became a bottleneck, which was not for another 30 years or so, and certainly not prior to the Napoleonic Wars, there was no economic need for weaving 'sheds' (as the factories for that operation came to be called).

8.3 The era of Taylor and the need for a quantum-leap' in management skills

8.3.1 My thesis is that the man and the need coincided. The fascination of historians with the impact of industrialization, and their natural lack of knowledge of industrial detail, has disguised from them the fact that virtually no operational management skills were required before the late nineteenth century. Then the development of standardized engineering products led to batch production taking place on general-purpose machines. The vast variety of these products led in turn to the need for 'process layouts'; process layouts led to a quantum jump in management skills; and this requirement produced Taylorism. All of which I shall explain presently.

8.3.2 My interest at the moment is to illustrate that prior to the intricacies created by this development there was almost no need at all for anything other than the most elementary operational management skills.

8.3.3 It was one of Taylor's axioms that, if management did not gain control of an industry, then clearly 'management' of that industry rested with labour. Managerial control was therefore something that had to be 'wrested' from the worker. That such control has lain with the worker in many industries, even until the present day, is undoubtedly true. The general pattern of development seems to have been that managements have only interfered with the autonomy of skilled workers as and when economic threats or opportunities have been seen by management as critical. When this happens management tries to change the work pattern, often de-skilling but always limiting the previous autonomy of the craft. The result is, naturally enough, conflict.

8.3.4 In the mining industry, the 'hand-got' method of coal mining went on until the middle of this century (and doubtless even beyond in certain instances). I have already mentioned (paragraph 4.2.12) the effect of mechanization upon this culture. What I now wish to emphasize is how **little** management there was in 'hand-got' mining. Here are the words of E. L. Trist and K. W. Bamforth on the work organization associated with earlier mining practice, namely the 'hand-got' method: [Pugh, 1971; pp.345–346).

> A primary work-organization of this type has the advantage of placing responsibility for the complete coal-getting task squarely on the shoulders of a single, small, face-to-face group which experiences the entire cycle of operations within the compass of its membership. For each participant the task has total significance and dynamic closure. Though the contract may have been in the name of the hewer, it was regarded as a joint undertaking. Leadership and 'supervision' were internal to the group, which had a quality of responsible autonomy. The capacity of these groups for self-regulation was

a function of the wholeness of their work task, this connection being represented in their contractual status. A whole has power as an independent detachment, but a part requires external control.

(The reader will note how these last words echo the functions of an autonomous cell as described by Koestler in paragraph 3.1.20, *a cell which, although triggered by the hierarchy, is able to operate independently of that hierarchy.*)

8.3.5 Similar worker autonomy had existed in most industries for centuries. Nelson's famous flagship at Trafalgar, HMS *Victory* had been made of wood. It therefore required only one basic trade to manufacture the hull and superstructure: that of the shipwright. He used his skills as he had for centuries. He was not unlike his fellow craftsman, the stonemason. We do not regard the building of St Paul's Cathedral as an exercise in management. Small autonomous groups of craftsmen took Sir Christopher Wren's designs and translated them into stone. The shipwright had done the same in timber from the design of the naval architect. The building of the railway network of Britain was similarly designed and surveyed by such people as Isambard Kingdom Brunel. But it was 'managed' by the gang-bosses of the construction teams.

8.3.6 As the nineteenth century wore on, the technical complications of such unique large-scale projects (which we will henceforth refer to as 'large-scale jobbing') increased in magnitude. Largely this was caused by the specializations that a developing technology required. Shipwrights had built the fleet that fought at Trafalgar in 1805: yet what a vast number of different skilled trades had been required to build the fleet that fought at Jutland in 1916. Clearly management of our shipyards, if they were to remain efficient, should have developed means of integrating the work of all these various trades. They did not. Nor did the builders of the Empire State Building of 1930–31. We have to wait until 1958, until a dissatisfied and powerful customer dragged such firms into the twentieth century.

8.3.7 It is a matter of history that large-scale jobbing was able to bumble on in this way. It is a matter of speculation as to why the management of such businesses allowed such a mess to continue. That speculation is part of the next section. The focal point of this section is the reverse. *Why was batch engineering **not** permitted to bumble on in an equally ineffective way?* Why was Taylorism adopted by that sector of industry long before it was adopted elsewhere? It could be argued that the techniques required to control large-scale jobbing were late in developing because of their complexity. It is an argument which loses a great deal of its strength when we see how far from complex the concepts PERT (performance evaluation and review technique) and CPA (critical path analysis) prove to be. My own belief is that the social, technological, economic and political pressures were such that batch-engineering managements were shepherded into adopting Taylorism. By contrast there were similar pressures at work in large-scale 'jobbing' that perpetuated inefficiency, as I shall later attempt to show.

8.3.8 However, let us return to batch production to show why it created a need for Taylorism. Wedgwood had made 'standardized' products in the eighteenth century by setting up a 'product layout', that is to say a line of machines through which each unit travels, and (as we saw in paragraph 4.2.3 to 4.2.5) this worked efficiently and with little management or paperwork. Moreover, by 1913 Ford had taken the product layout to the ultimate with the conveyor-belt system. Why should not the engineering industry as a whole have gone over to 'Fordism', as Merkle refers to it? Why get tied up with paperwork and control problems when there is apparently this easy option?

8.3.9 Well, of course the answer is that it is is **not** an easy option, or even an option at all. In most 'batch engineering' situations the approach would prove a technical and economic nightmare and quite impossible. I doubt whether Merkle recognizes this, for certainly she does not convey that message to us. She recognizes that a product layout of the sort used in a car line could be (Merkle, 1980; p.95) 'adapted only under tremendous external pressure and with great internal disruption' (though she and I may not mean the same thing by those words. The reason I say this is that she seems to see in Taylorism **not** the means of controlling many batches on a day-to-day basis, but some sort of **evolutionary aid**. In contrast with 'Fordism' she alleges that Taylorism has an 'immense advantage in its ability to absorb new technologies over time.')

8.3.10 It is my intention to show that 'Fordism', 'flowlines', 'conveyor belts', or indeed any variant of what I would term a 'product layout', will not work for most batch production, and that Taylorism becomes essential to meet the economic and technical needs of batch production.

8.3.11 The conveyor belt system, and indeed any product layout in which the machinery is laid out in the logical sequence for the product in question, can only be used in certain circumstances.

(1) The product must be required in sufficient volume in order to justify setting all the machinery in that position in the first place.
(2) The product must be more or less standard. (Slight variations can be accommodated. My factory made blazer jackets on the same product

line as ordinary suit jackets. This was possible because the girls who put the 'patch' pockets for the blazers were flexible enough to make 'jetted' pockets for the suits. However, variation is a nuisance and readers will remember Henry Ford's own dictum concerning variations to his early cars, 'They can be any colour you like so long as they're black!'

8.3.12 Product lines suffer from other technical problems which we shall consider in paragraph 15.10.3. It is not necessary here to do more than to point out that most batch-engineering concerns could not satisfy either of the above two requisites. They could not do so in Taylor's day, and they cannot do so now.

8.3.13 The numbers that I have inserted in the following imaginary example are not critical to the argument. They could vary enormously and would still substantiate the point that I am making. Let us assume the case of an engineering works with a few drills, a few lathes, a few milling machines, etc. Let us also assume that they have (say) 100 customers and that each customer buys from them about 40 simple piece-parts. Let us also assume that each customer orders about 4 months' supply of each of these piece-part products at a time. This means that 4000 different products need to be made every 4 months. If we were to consider setting up product lines to make each of these products we should need to set up 12,000 product lines per year. Assuming that there are 240 working days in the year we should be moving machinery about to set up such a product line and then moving it all yet again to set up a different product line at an average rate of 50 times a day. That's roughly once every 10 minutes. The question would be, when would we ever find time to actually do the manufacture? The situation would be quite impossible. Ford-type product layouts would be a total nonsense for such a firm: that is not a matter of opinion, it is not something that one management would accept and another reject, it is the nearest thing to a brute fact that I can imagine. For such a firm 'Fordism', as Merkle chooses to call it, is definitely out and, if it is to be efficient, 'Taylorism' is in.

8.3.14 Since such firms cannot lay out their machines in a 'product layout' the question arises, 'How should they then lay them out?' Quite definitely the answer to this question is 'In a process layout.' By this is meant that machines which perform the same process are grouped together in 'banks'; here a bank of drills, there a bank of lathes, etc. There are several reasons why the grouping of machines in this way is useful. First, each bank of machines can have next to it a 'marshalling area' in which work requiring that process can be stored. All the work in the marshalling area next to the 'drilling machine bank' will require drilling as the next operation. Secondly, if an operative who tends to specialize in one type of operation, e.g. milling, needs to move to another machine, he won't have far to go. Thirdly, the foreman can be a specialist in that particular operation. Fourthly, all the spares and tools and any jigs and fixtures relative to that operation can be stored nearby. Fifthly, since the machines are of the same type, the foreman can control the priority sequence of the work as it is issued, making certain that the most urgent work gets loaded on to the first machine to become available. There are other subsidiary reasons, but I have said enough to illustrate the basic logic behind 'process layout'.

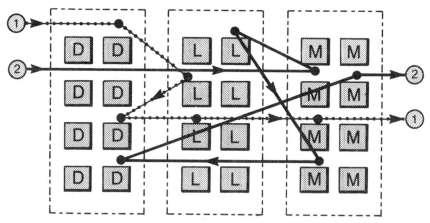

Figure 8.3(a) A 'process layout'

8.3.15 However, if the logic is clear enough, the control problems that such a layout raises are extremely formidable. If the reader refers to Figure 8.3(a) he will see why they are so. There I have sketched a bank of drills, another of lathes and a third of milling machines. They are identified by the respective initials, 'D', 'L' and 'M'. I have also shown the route followed by two products. Product 1 follows the dotted route, 'D:L:D:L:M:...'. Product 2 follows the route of the solid line, 'M:L:M:D:M:...'. Now let the reader imagine trying to control 1000 such batches simultaneously, for we shall see that work-in-progress of this amount is not uncommon, and indeed economically necessary. Moreover, if each of these 1000 batches needed 10 sequential operations to be performed upon them, the management would need to schedule 10,000 currently active possible operations.

8.3.16 This is the type of problem that created a need for a quantum leap in management capability. This is why I have said that if it had not been Taylor who responded to this challenge then somebody else would have done so. Keeping control of the work-in-progress in such an operation is a problem which is of a different order of magnitude from controlling a product line. In the latter case all that the manager has to do is to put raw material on at one end and watch finished goods come out of the other. Of course, there may be some hiccups in production on the way through. But they are hiccups that are immediately visible and the necessary action is entirely obvious. Moreover, the work-in-progress can be very low. In a motor-car factory it is one car per operative. This means that 'floating' workers are required to enable operatives to leave the line in order to go to the toilet, etc., but although such considerations represent an additional cost, they are not problems which require any great managerial ability to handle.

8.3.17 The reader has already seen that in the case of a process layout, work must be done in 'batches' in order to recover set-up costs (paragraph 4.3.4). He has also seen that when any two resources come together, one must wait for the other (paragraph 4.3.8). In a process layout we are bringing one resource, work-in-progress, into conjunction with another resource, the worker who will operate upon that work. One of these will need to queue. Again it is a brute fact that except under the most extreme circumstances, it is cheaper to have work waiting for men than to have men waiting for work.

8.3.18 This means that it is very common in such layouts to have as much as a month's to six weeks' work-in-progress going through the department, all of which needs to be scheduled to ensure that nothing falls behind its delivery promise. If we take our imaginary factory of paragraph 8.3.13, which needed to fulfil 12,000 orders per year, then with an average work-in-progress of six weeks, this would mean that at any one time there would be 1500 batches in circulation and needing managerial control.

8.3.19 Complicated as the issues are that we have considered, they represent any two of the three production control decision areas. These are:

(1) Decide on the size of the batch. (That we have considered.)
(2) Schedule the sequence in which the batches will be made. (That we have considered.)
(3) Make certain that there is enough capacity in every aspect to avoid overloads or underloads. That we have **not** considered.

Yet this the manager of such a department must do. He could even have a situation in which he will fall behind schedule if he doesn't get the milling machines on to overtime this month, whereas only last month he had too much milling capacity. This is because there has been a change in the 'mix' of products that his customers are ordering. Those going through this month require more. But he must not wait until he gets into a mess to know that this is going to happen. He needs to plan ahead to prevent the mess happening.

Otherwise he is no manager. (This, the reader will remember, is the use to which standards based upon work measurement were put; paragraph 7.2.50(d)).

8.3.20 I hope that by now the reader has recognized why I insisted that this technology, which was the essential development of the late nineteenth century, requires a quantum leap in mananagerial expertise. The early engineers had been essentially blacksmiths. If the reader goes to (say) the Transport Museum in York he will be able to sense the crudeness of the early manufacturing techniques. There was no 'batch production'. There was no 'standardization'. The pistons of an early locomotive would be made to match their corresponding particular cylinders. Yet, when we make motor cars in volume we want it to be possible to take **any** carburettor out of stock and fit it to **any** car for which it was intended. Modern life is utterly dependent upon batch production of a huge variety of standard items from a surprisingly limited number of different types of machines. What makes the complexity of the one compatible with the simplicity of the other is management know-how.

8.3.21 This brings us back to Taylor. He was probably the worst propagandist for his own cause that it would have been possible to find. He was so anxious to show to people that a 'scientific' approach to management was necessary that he reduced the whole thing to a manic plea for autocratic control of every simple act. Of course he was correct when he suggested that there was a 'science of shovelling' (Taylor, 1967; p.65). Nobody had worked out how big a shovel a man should have for any given material, or whether he should go into the pile from the bottom, or half-way up, or how he should exert pressure on the handle to push it into the pile, or when he should take rests and so on. Taylor deliberately went in for this *reductio ad absurdum* approach of exposing management's ignorance in the most basic areas. (I do not mean to deny that they were anecdotes from Taylor's own experience: what I mean is that he could equally have chosen other tales.) Yet the net effect of such tales, like the manner of choosing a man of 'ox-brained' mentality called 'Schmidt' and teaching him how to handle pig-iron, is extremely offensive. Nor does it recall truthfully what happened any more than it gives the true name of the name of the man concerned, which (in reality) was Henry Noll. I shall return later to this particular piece of Taylor's poetic licence since what Taylor says, (which would be significant if it were true) is all the more indicative of Taylor's attitudes in that it isn't. It therefore is an important pointer to the situation he would wish for in an ideal world of **his** specification.

8.3.22 Taylor's selection of examples was tragically and unnecessarily to give ammunition to his detractors. For he could have demonstrated managerial ignorance quite as well without references to 'ox-brained' labourers, particularly since most managements would have profited more from examples more relevant to their own fields of interest. We have spoken of the complexities of engineering workshops. Yet we have not even begun to consider some of the problems that Taylor tackled. He came to look at the problems of what design of tool (both in its shape and in its material) should be combined with what lubricants and what rates of tool-feed to produce outputs of a given quality from a variety of metals; and he found that 'not one machine in a hundred is speeded by its makers at anywhere near the correct cutting speed' (Taylor, 1967; p.112). Taylor's point was that it was no use ever expecting the operative to be able to discover the optimum settings because 'before he could use proper speeds the machinist would first have to put new pulleys on the countershaft of his machine and also in most cases change the shapes and treatments of his tools.' In any case, explained Taylor, the operative just would not have the necessary knowledge. He illustrated this by pointing out that there were no less than **twelve** interacting variables. Moreover, he quantified the order of magnitude of the 'spread' of values that could result from each of those interacting variables. For example, the hardness of the steel could affect cutting speeds by a factor of from 1 to 100. Chemical composition can affect the speed by a factor of from 1 to 7; and so on through the other ten variables.

8.3.23 Having identified and isolated all these variables, Taylor still had to develop appropriate formulae to express the interrelationships. These proved to be so complex, that even after he had done so these formulae could not become a day-to-day control tool until he had designed a special slide rule which integrated the variables and then nominated the most 'scientific' answer concerning the machine settings.

8.3.24 The ultimate success of Taylorism is demonstrated by an irony. Anti-Taylor worker unrest in a US defence establishment, Watertown Arsenal, sparked off such concern that it generated the enquiry proceedings of the Special Committee of the US House of Representatives of 1912, to which I referred in paragraph 7.2.4. Yet less than fifty years later it was a US defence contract that stimulated the US Navy (the dissatisfied customer to whom I referred in paragraph 8.3.6) to seek better managerial control. PERT was developed by the combined talents of the Navy Special Projects Office, Lockheed, and Booz, Allen and Hamilton; and PERT is pure Taylor in spirit if not in fact.

8.3.25 The 'before and after' situation at Watertown clearly shows why the men should have been so opposed to the changes. We can also guess from the history of the outcome that they felt confident enough to challenge the new system. They might well have inferred that their customer, the US Ordnance Department, was politically committed to their continuance and not too cost-conscious. Their only competition came from a few similar and equally inefficient establishments. A row in a government establishment could well create political pressure on the management to settle the dispute quietly. If I (as a worker there) had perceived that situation, then I too might have fought to preserve the lovely, comfortable, chaotic mess that was Watertown Arsenal before Taylor.

8.3.26 Although this arsenal 'manufactured a wide variety of articles... its principal product was gun carriages for seacoast and field whose production involved the manufacture and assembly of some 4,500 different components' (Kakar 1970; p.107). So there we have it. The situation is one in which parts will need to be made in batches on a process layout and the sequence in which this happens will be crucial if all the bits are to come together to make a 'network' of sub-subassemblies, subassemblies and final assemblies. We need a quantum jump in management skills. What in fact did they have pre-Taylor?

8.3.27 Sudhir Kakar (1970;pp. 107-109) tells us what went on in great detail; and what a hopeless and inefficient mess it was! All that the foreman received was an order for the quantity of each product. He it was who had to find the drawings of the constituent parts and calculate the raw material requirements. He it was who wrote out the job-cards for the men and ordered the materials. Since there was no pre-planning, material was of course always out of stock. We can infer how little time he could give to supervising the worker.

8.3.28 The worker, on the other hand, having been given the job-card, let his machine stand idle as he hunted to find the drawings and the tools, attempted to locate where the long-awaited material had been dumped, moved it to his machine and finally decided how the job should be done. Since he also had to keep his own machine in repair, we can also infer how low a proportion of the total available time would be his machine's productive time. Moreover, because the right material for urgently needed jobs was frequently out of stock, workers were given non-urgent work simply to keep them busy. This combination of low efficiency and poor sequencing resulted in disgracefully bad delivery performances.

8.3.29 Then F.W. Taylor arrives and puts in his production control procedures. Kakar lists these (1970; pp.111-113). It would be tedious to enumerate them here for they are simply the everyday procedures which are described in every modern production-control handbook and practised in every modern engineering works. The purpose and the result of introducing these procedures was, then as now, not only to enable management to keep the worker actively operating his machine, but to do so with a priority sequence which corresponded to the required delivery dates.

8.3.30 The contrast with the messy, uncontrolled, but convivial and diverting chaos in which the worker had operated could not have been greater; organizationally they had been hit by something akin to a tidal-wave. Kakar says of it, 'The introduction of the new management system thus also meant a change in the social structure of the work groups.' As a comment on a change which, at a stroke, had utterly destroyed the workers' earlier near-autonomy, this goes beyond bland understatement, and suggests that Kakar may possess a streak of sardonic humour. We need no explanation of why these workers fought Taylor tooth and claw to retain their autonomy.

8.3.31 *On the contrary, we need to explain why, within decades, batch engineering workshops throughout the industrial world were all using Taylor's controls to operate process layouts.* It is a question which prompts a further question. *Why was there (by contrast) a time-lag of a further fifty years before similar controls were introduced into shipbuilding and other such work of a large-scale jobbing nature?* I shall now attempt to answer this double riddle.

8.4 Why Taylorism came early to batch engineering and late to jobbing

8.4.1 I shall claim that, whatever the system, workers object to any loss of autonomy and will usually fight to retain it. Whether or not they fight and just how bitter and protracted that fight may become is dependent upon circumstance. For such a conflict to occur at all presupposes that management really **are** trying to take control away from the worker. *I shall claim that historically this is has not always been so.* Management is more likely to attempt to gain control if one of two conditions prevail. The first is when failure to do so would involve the firm in unnecessary opportunity cost. If management were always true to the *mores* of capitalism this would be spur enough. But complacency in management is not unknown. So the real spur for management to take control arises from the second condition. This is when they find that more efficient competitors are a serious threat to the company's survival chances.

8.4.2 By definition, any threat to the degree of autonomy now enjoyed by the worker will come from those who seek to restructure his working practices. To a greater or lesser extent he will be aware that his chances of successfully resisting such a move depend upon how great are the techno-economic pressures on his management. If they are high then management will fight the harder to make the change. Moreover, even if he were to win this struggle with management, it might well be a pyrrhic victory in which the continuing external competitive threat (which he did not allow management to combat) finally costs him his job. We should, in passing, note that fear of job loss from economic competition is one of the many reasons why workers in the 'public sector' resist 'privatization' and explains why unions in the private sector attempt to control technology and working practices industry-wide (as, for example, in printing). Both moves seek to minimize the economic pressures on the individual member's immediate working environment.

8.4.3 The conditions of work which favour employee autonomy are the following:

(1) *He is assigned an area of relatively complex work with the authority to make certain discretionary decisions.*
(2) *During long periods of activity, he has no cause to refer to persons other (possibly) than members of his work group operating on the same project. That is to say, he has no need to seek instruction or to subordinate how or when he performs his work to some other project with which it must be co-ordinated.*

The conditions of work which are unfavourable to employee autonomy are the opposite. *They require him to perform short-cycle work in which he has frequent need to interface with a superior or a colleague on a separate but related assignment.* How, in these latter circumstances would it be possible for him, in any meaningful way, to make a bid for autonomy?

8.4.4 Where economic and physical pressures have combined to dictate a technological solution in which this latter state of affairs **must** prevail it would be a nonsense for the worker to fight for (or for anyone else to suggest that he should be offered) more autonomy. In practice the worker has shown more realism in this matter than have some commentators. To suggest that he should be given more autonomy is to imply that the factors which brought about this state of affairs were unreal. It infers that someone, presumably management, was not only responsible for denying the worker more autonomy *but had done so arbitrarily and for questionable motives*. But the interface requirements I have just described are *not* arbitrary. They grow naturally out of the nature of the hierarchy and its specialisms. They create (to use Mary Parker Follet's words in a way she did not intend, but which is nevertheless appropriate), 'the authority of the situation'.

8.4.5 If a worker in such circumstances were to make a bid for autonomy, what would that imply? Presumably it would mean that he was seeking to operate without instruction or consultation. On what basis would he make the requisite decisions? How would he come into the possession of enough relevant knowledge? By what means would he acquire the perspective? And finally, what would be the basis of his authority? This is not merely a practical question (though it is also that), but one also of the moral basis of his claim to autonomy. This is because his autonomy will impinge on the autonomy of others and the clash of interests raises the question of who has the right to exert the hierarchical authority which will save them both from chaos. In many cases therefore, autonomy is something denied him by the situation **and quite beyond management's power to return to him**. If, consciously or unconsciously, he recognizes this then he will be unlikely to continue to fight for it.

8.4.6 Something else needs to be said before we turn to look at the historical development. The evidence that workers will often fight for continued autonomy seems to me to be irrefutable. However, deciding upon *why* they do so would be far less certain. Those who support the neo-human relations school of thought seem to feel the reason is self-evident. According to that school, the worker will seek psychological growth in his work situation (self-actualization), and to do so would need an adequately autonomous existence. Now I will accept that if this desire for self-actualization could be proved it would be *a priori* evidence of a need for autonomy. What is not necessarily true, however, is that proving a need for autonomy is evidence of a desire for 'self-actualization'. Any autonomy he achieved would be equally capable of serving other ends. (We discussed the philosophic problem this represents in 2.1.8. To cap it all there is the question of why 'self-actualization' will make him company-orientated anyway.)

8.4.7 The resistance of the worker to Taylorism during Taylor's lifetime shows quite clearly that the worker was not then prepared to regard the manner in which he was organized and controlled as being a matter of indifference. Indeed, he demonstrated that as long as there were alternative viable means other than Taylorism by which he might make a living, then he would take such alternatives. To this extent Taylor's vision of 'economic man' would seem to be wrong. The worker did not, *given a choice*, conspire with management in the destruction of his own psychological and sociological aspirations. We do not necessarily know what his aspirations were. *(I use 'aspiration' neutrally to cover all goals.)* What we do know is what his aspirations were **not**. *(Popper's insights into the asymmetry between proving and falsifying we considered in paragraph 2.1.12.)* They were **not** the exclusively 'economic man' aspirations that Taylor attributed to him. Why should we expect them to be? It was Taylor who 'projected' a personal attachment to himself from the very men with whom he was, in his own words, 'at war'. He was wrong twice.

8.4.8 Yet there is another side to this coin. For, as I have said, Taylorism is now virtually universal. Since Taylor claimed that there was more resistance to his methods from managers than from workers and since Taylorism is now so widespread, we must conclude that something happened to them both which modified their initial rejection of his creed. Are we to believe that there has been a profound change in the inherent personality of workers and managers over the intervening years? Well, I suppose it must be considered a possibility: but surely it is less likely to be true than the alternative explanation. This is that the options which, in Taylor's day, were available to allow the worker to act autonomously, have today disappeared under the pressures of technological and economic change. Such developments have been reflected in the changed *Weltanschauung* of the worker. No longer does he perceive the rejection of Taylorism to be a viable option. So the economic and the technological changes have wrought a sociological change. The same economic and technological changes have amended the *Weltanschauung* of the manager. Those who (from conviction, from indolence, or from ignorance) were prepared previously to grant autonomy to their workers can no longer do so.

8.4.9 This brings us to one of Taylor's aphorisms with which it would be difficult to disagree. This is his claim that unless management wrests power from the worker, *then (by default) such power must remain with the worker*. Now even if we wish to disassociate ourselves from the **coloration** that he gave to that remark, we cannot fault its **logic**. **Power must reside somewhere**. It is not even necessary to regard power as something that both 'sides' fight to possess to recognize the reciprocal relationship. What model, however, are we to use to discuss this reciprocity?

8.4.10 Here the image of Koestler's 'holon' is invaluable. The reader will remember that he ascribed dual Janus-like qualities to the hierarchical 'cells'. Looking up the pyramid they see themselves as parts; looking down the pyramid they see themselves as wholes. *To the extent (paragraph 3.1.21) that they see themselves as parts of a larger structure they are integrative.* Simultaneously, however, *to the extent that the group or individual … see themselves as forming a quasi-autonomous whole they are self-assertive.* If we link such a concept to the second concept of political options we would surely infer that the worker's attitude to those same options, and also management's attitude to its corresponding options, would be conditioned to a significant extent by where they perceive themselves upon the dependence/autonomy continuum of Figure 8.4(a). There I suggest that batch engineering workers have little autonomy in their situation, 'hand-got' miners have a great deal and ship-building workers come in between.

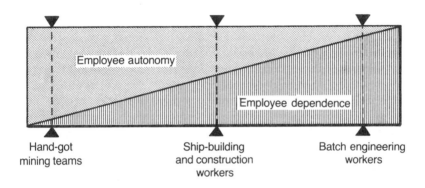

Employee autonomy

Employee dependence

Hand-got
mining teams

Ship-building
and construction
workers

Batch engineering
workers

Figure 8.4(a) Dependence/autonomy/ continuum

8.4.11 This figure assumes that there is a natural degree of employee autonomy, or conversely of employee dependence, that is technologically determined. Of course no employee has complete autonomy nor does he have complete dependence. To this extent each end of the continuum suggested by Figure 8.4(a) must be a theoretical abstraction and **not** the diagrammatic representation of a practical possibility.

8.4.12 Nevertheless, the most autonomous jobs are **extremely** autonomous. Even this is a situation which is largely technologically determined. This is because management is based upon control, and the best control is based upon an extremely rapid 'negative feedback'. Here I need to digress to explain these terms before continuing.

CONTROL CHARACTERISTICS

8.4.13 First of all, what are the characteristics of control? By this I refer to **all** control, whether it be driving a motor car or managing a factory. They are three-fold.

(1) I must know the present situation which exists, that is to say the 'actual' situation, e.g.
    (a) I am driving along 3 metres from the kerb, or
    (b) I am manufacturing 600 items per day
(2) I must know what 'ought' to be the situation, that is to say the 'Standard' situation, e.g.
    (a) I should be 1 metre from the kerb, or
    (b) I should be manufacturing 800 items per day.
(3) I must have the power to change, e.g.
    (a) I will turn *towards* the kerb, or
    (b) I will *increase* production by 200 items.

The reader should notice that the action, if it is to correct the error, must be in a direction **opposite** *to that of the error.* This is why it is 'negative' feedback which maintains control: it is negative to the direction of the existing error. *Positive feedback* in each case would only make the situation worse and therefore completely unstable and unmanageable.

8.4.14 What has this to do with the model in Figure 8.4(a)? Simply this: if any of those three requirements of control are absent, then effective management is impossible. So, in the light of this, let us consider the technological determinants in the three cases shown in Figure 8.4(a), starting with that of the 'hand-got' mining teams.

8.4.15 Now there are certain very strong reasons why management should have left such teams in their ancient autonomous state. Firstly, it is highly probable that such teams will perceive that they have the politically available option of continuing in that autonomy, and would thus be correspondingly more likely to fight for it. Management would therefore be more tentative about imposing control than might otherwise be the case. Secondly, we have already seen that control needs rapid negative feedback. But to give this in response to the minute-to-minute exigencies of mining requires that the manager of the team must also be at the coal-face. Yet with a team of from two to eight men this would give an enormous overhead burden. In any case the 'management' that was required was precisely the sort of *ad hoc* organizing that a first-class artisan does out of practical necessity, born of the technical requirements that have arisen. Such decisions would be entirely within the competence of the more experienced colliers. Moreover, the team had no need to integrate their work with others. There were therefore no management problems of the sort that occur when different specialist activities need to be co-ordinated with each other. We should not be surprised to learn that these groups were left to their own devices until the introduction of mechanized coal-cutters and mechanical conveyors led to 40-strong teams with specialist functions of borer, cutter, gummer, belt-breaker, belt builder, ripper, filler, etc.

8.4.16 We have already seen that the converse is true of batch engineering workers. The very technicalities of getting to grips with the control of such production (described in paragraph 8.3.13 to 8.3.19 inclusive) demand a degree of co-ordination that the worker cannot aspire to organize. His situation is therefore almost the reverse of the miner's. He cannot perceive what 'autonomy' would even mean in the context in which he finds himself, let alone fight for it. True, his grandfathers did so, but that was in the days when the pre-Taylor shambles that we saw at Watertown was economically viable. He knows, as does his manager, that such an option, thanks to the ratchet effect of Taylorism, is not a political reality. It is indeed no option at all. So the manager has an intense pressure upon him to take control, and the man has no 'reasonable' justification for resisting that pressure.

8.4.17 We should not be surprised therefore that batch engineering was the activity that first became the subject of widespread Taylorite control, nor that mining (and other such activities that demand decision-making on the part of small bands of geographically isolated men whose work does not impinge critically upon that of others) should have tended to escape such control.

8.4.18 Lastly, we should neither be surprised that large-scale engineering projects of a unique nature should have resisted Taylorism for half a century, nor that they finally capitulated. It would be anachronistic to ascribe the techniques of PERT and of critical path analysis to Taylor; but it is not incorrect to ascribe them to Taylorism. Yet the development of Taylorism in large-scale jobbing was fraught with problems. In part this was because managements had reasons for **not** seeking control, in part it was the difficulty of measurement in this area, and in part it was that even the changes proposed could not erode all reliance on 'craft' skills which remained a strong political weapon for the worker. It was these features, I am convinced, that delayed the introduction of these techniques for, as I said in paragraph 8.3.7, the techniques themselves would demand no great intellectual effort to have developed. It is their **application** that would have proved disproportionately troublesome to management. Let us see why, by reference to what I witnessed in ship-building during the early 1950s and before the introduction of such techniques.

8.4.19 A carpenter came to the newly constructed and empty steel compartment of a ship, which would ultimately be the cabin of a crew-man, and measured it for the berth and wardrobe that he was going to fit. (He had not, it will be noted, attempted to prepare the work in parallel with the building of the cabin, even though the two jobs (had they all worked precisely to drawing) could have been performed independently and in parallel with each other.) He then went away to his workshop to fabricate the assembly. A week later he came back. He had no problem with the bunk, but the wardrobe could not be fitted because, during the intervening week, one of the other tradesmen had run some huge pipes across the cabin at head-height right where the wardrobe was intended to be fitted. He cursed roundly and went away to spend many hours of labour cost as well as further material cost in converting it.

8.4.20 This shambles was repeated all over the ship wherever different trades came into contact. Yet this problem had existed for over a hundred years. The technique for controlling it is almost self-evident. It is obvious that some sort of logic network needs to be drawn. By that I mean that the sequence in which jobs should be done, whether they are dependent or independent of each other, needs to be spelled out diagrammatically. Then if we are to use this information we must ensure that each activity is given a feasible time scale. Otherwise, although the sequence will be correct, the disproportionate times taken by the various activities may mean some resources standing idle while they wait for the other resource to catch up. Now all this is so very basic that it may seem astonishing that PERT should not have been devised before 1958.

8.4.21 Yet in much large-scale jobbing there were reasons for management **not** to seek to gain such control. In many cases the different activities to which we refer were the responsibility of sub-contractors who had agreed to do their portion of the job for a fixed price. Alternatively, because of the irregularity of work in such industries, there was a tradition of hiring and firing *between* contracts which sloppy management could use *during* contracts when men were idle because of bad co-ordination. So bad co-ordination meant that the contract would be late, but the manufacturer's costs would not escalate because they were being borne by the worker.

8.4.22 In both these instances taking over control required that management should accept the responsibility for these resources, namely sub-contractor and labour, that is to say, to change a traditional social attitude and to accept a far higher level of responsibility in order to justify making their bid for increased authority. Similarly, the worker and the sub-contractor would have to renounce a corresponding portion of their autonomy. Only then could the technical details be dealt with.

8.4.23 I have said on several occasions that management in rational capitalism will avoid opportunity costs where they can. Such costs include those of possible disturbance to the business from strikes induced by management policies as well as those of gratuitously incurred business liability from accepting unnecessary contractual obligations. Attempting to get managerial control in the large-scale jobbing industry would have been perceived, in the first half of this century, as entering into risky and unnecessary obligations. True, the job was extended by lack of co-ordination; true, there were unnecessary costs. But these were borne either by the employee, or by the sub-contractor, or by the customer. The customer bore the costs in terms of any late delivery; and he paid more because the sub-contractor had to put enough 'fat' into the contract price to cover the maladministration. The customer however was trapped. If he went elsewhere he would meet the same fate. So the combination of social and technological factors conspired against Taylorism. However, by the mid-twentieth century these factors had changed.

8.4.24 They had changed in two ways. First and foremost the nature of the long-term jobbing activities that were being undertaken changed. PERT was introduced for the production of probably the most complex and technologically advanced jobbing-project that had ever been attempted to date – 'Polaris'.

8.4.25 The firms who produced Polaris were not employing labour that could be hired and fired. If the growth of union pressure and perhaps of a stronger social conscience towards these workers had not convinced management that they needed to accept responsibility towards their workforce, then their self-interest would. Many of these employees had high skills as well as knowing a great deal about the company's technical practices. Obtaining such people on a casual basis is not feasible; letting his competitor absorb them (and their knowledge) is enough to make a chief executive weep. But if they are to be a well-paid fixed expense upon the company then they must be kept constantly active: their workload must be estimated in advance and scheduled.

8.4.26 Similarly, the sub-contractor faces the same problem. The net result is that, for reasons of resource allocation, neither can afford **not** to schedule. This would have been true anyway: but by 1958 there was another catalytic reason for change. The customer, who until now had been so docile, was becoming very critical indeed. Not only was he critical of the cost, he was critical of the time taken. It is not simply that time is money, but that lost time is a period of lost defence capability: for the customer was the US Navy in the midst of a 'cold war'. So PERT was born.

8.4.27 Once this Taylor-like technique arrives it cannot be ignored by anyone in 'large-scale jobbing'. **The Taylor ratchet makes it imperative to match the new-found efficiency of the competition or die.** Perhaps it would be fair to say that the speed at which other countries adopted PERT compared with the UK is as much a factor as any other in the relative decline of the UK's shipbuilding market. Once again, therefore, slowly but inevitably, Taylor triumphs. Managements gain more control, and the workers lose more autonomy. Both parties have mixed feelings about the change: both accept it.

8.4.28 So, in the sense that the worker would rather come to terms with a high degree of managerial control than suffer the collapse of his firm and the loss of his livelihood, the worker proves to be an 'economic man' after all. But this is only in terms of the overall framework within which he operates. It certainly cannot be assumed that because the worker has accepted this framework that he does not resent his loss of autonomy and the various purposes to which he could put such autonomy. Nor is he completely certain that his firm's success will not be a two-edged sword. Taylor insisted that the workman's belief was fallacious that higher productivity might work against his interest (whether from redundancy or from such other causes as, for example, low selling prices from oversupply). If it **is** a fallacy, there are many capitalists who share it. The bumper crop for the French champagne harvest of 1982 was seen by the growers and merchants as constituting a threat to their profits. The whole trade agreed, in the face of this 'threat', to limit production of the wine. No one, as I recall, said that such thinking was a 'fallacy'.

8.4.29 *Moreover, there was nothing in early Taylorism to convince the worker that he did not need to protect himself against the very **logic** of Taylorism.* I would remind the reader of the plight of the ball-bearing inspectors. It was Taylor's case that the worker would welcome an end to 'arbitrary' management. In some respects he was right. But a worker that gets the sack does not particularly console himself with the thought that it was for good scientific reasons rather than for bad arbitrary ones. Taylorism did nothing to lessen the attitude of the worker to seek, by concerted action with his fellow workers, to bring as much concerted pressure to bear upon management as he felt would prove to be in his interest. Under the paternalism of Taylor the worker was being made an offer he couldn't refuse. It is in keeping with our view of 'political holon man' that he should enter into mutual aid pacts with his fellows. He did. This is an aspect we will consider when we turn to 'social man'.

8.5 The manager and Taylorism

8.5.1 Over the years, managers have subtly modified their stance on Taylorism. Ever since Taylor's day every management has to some degree adopted Taylorism. This is because it is a technical and administrative system which the firm **must** adopt if it is to remain sufficiently competitive to survive. Yet, even in Taylor's own day, with the exception of a few followers whose critical ability was clearly no match for their enthusiasms, I would doubt just how many 'scientific' managers swallowed the whole of Taylor's message. They perceived that Taylor was right in his beliefs concerning the economic need for the firm to adopt Taylorism, and the material advantages that it would bring to society as a whole. But I believe that very few managers, even then, would have accepted his belief that his system was a sovereign remedy against the evils of worker/management conflict. However, I hope to show that for reasons of expediency it was sometimes advantageous for managers in earlier times to act as though they did indeed share this latter belief. This is not so today.

8.5.2 This change in the situation has not occurred because Taylorism is dead. On the contrary, it is flourishing. The fact that the literature does not speak of Taylorism or scientific management except in historic terms does not mean the concept has been renounced. Rather is it because the concept has become so much a part of our lives as not to need stating.

8.5.3 When I was a small boy a nearby Derbyshire village boasted a converted hut with the proud title 'The *Electric* Cinema'. Only a decade or so ago, we spoke proudly of 'EDP' which stood for '*electronic* data processing'. Today we speak of 'DP'. To do otherwise (and thereby emphasize its electronic nature) would be to imply that the abacus and the quill pen were viable options, Nowadays, we just assume that data processing will be 'electronic', so we assume that management will be 'scientific'.

8.5.4 In saying this I do not withdraw my previous objection to the manner in which the use of this word imparts a spurious objectivity to Taylorism. Nevertheless, despite the inappropriate name he used, the actual coloration of the meaning which Taylor attempted to impart to the title 'scientific management' is precisely the coloration that the word 'management' has acquired today. Taylor was desperately anxious that it should not be seen as a mere 'bag of tricks' (my terminology), but a whole new attitude. In this too he succeeded, for today the word 'management' is used by us to describe the whole philosophy that assumes that no unnecessary opportunity cost should ever be accepted.

8.5.5 The scores of modern-day techniques that management use, including those that on the face of it are anti-Taylor, are no more than a means, whose end is to enable us to identify and eliminate those same unacceptable opportunity costs. If Taylor could return, he would doubtless be gratified to see the quality of some of our modern-day techniques. But I can imagine that what would delight him more would be that when we speak of 'management', we are assuming the adoption of a whole philosophy that he chose to call 'scientific'. Perhaps a better description would be to refer to this approach as that of 'rational' management. If we were to do so, we would need to put the word 'rational' in inverted commas to highlight that its so-called rationality implies that it is correct to prize above all things the ability to perform activities with minimum resources. There are occasions on which all of us think otherwise. Life which was wholly functional would be very grey. But, over and above that, there are many areas of life in which the attitudes of Taylorism are being questioned. There could be nothing more rational than producing eggs and poultry by the methods of 'battery' farming. *So those who challenge it as a system do not do so within the framework of economic rationality.* They demand that we use another frame of reference, based upon respect for animals and ecology. Indeed, the lack of a common frame of reference (not made easier by the hen's 'dumb-cluck' image) has meant that no dialogue can take place between the two sides.

8.5.6 We saw that Taylorism was adopted by Lenin in Russia, so that there is no literal sense in which it is possible to claim that Taylorism is uniquely associated with the capitalist system. Yet, in a different and more profound sense, there **does** exist a unique affinity in the relationship between Taylorism and capitalism.

8.5.7 Indeed, it is this very affinity which is the reason why Taylorism was bound to fail as the mediating influence between the capitalist firm and the worker. The 'rationality' of capitalism works from the general 'ends' of avoiding opportunity cost, but it is less specific about how it is to be done. By coming together, Taylorism and capitalism support each other like a pair of matching book-ends. Taylorism assumes that the 'means' which the manager will use will be 'rational': that is to say, they will be governed not by sentiment, but by logic and efficiency. However, Taylorism cannot **of itself** justify the 'ends' which its 'means' of logic and efficiency are serving. That justification comes from capitalism.

8.5.8 Supporters of capitalism justify the system on the following grounds:

(1) By the separation of economic and political power, it promotes pluralism.
(2) By and large, the invisible hand of market forces is the best means of distributing resources, even if many of us want that hand to be given a bit of a push from time to time in the interests of social justice.

So it is a philosophy admirably suited to Taylorism. For the concept of the 'invisible hand' is that society will benefit providing the fittest survive. By an inversion of this concept the Taylorite is able to assume that the ability to survive is not only proof of the company's physical fitness, but (since only firms which benefit society survive) of its moral fitness also. That being so, the Taylorite needs only to get an affirmative answer to the question 'Will this action enhance the company's survival chances?' to give that proposed action an aura of moral justification, which would override any appeal to emotion, sentiment or any such human value.

8.5.9 So, although Taylor thought that the 'fairness' which he was introducing into management would gratify and therefore win over the worker, it was a vain hope from the start. For the 'light of reason' (by which Taylor's justice was to be dispensed) is that same light which MacRae (1974; p.86), in another context, described as illuminating 'all being with a shadowless and clinical light before which fly poetry, faith and myth'. Not the thing to reassure the insecure worker, who, like the ball-bearing girls, would henceforth be even more likely to be sacked for good scientific reasons than he had been for bad unscientific ones.

8.5.10 It follows that the worker could look for human consideration only as the by-product of enlightened self-interest in the firm, or from the social or political constraints that government or unions might impose upon management, or, in the last resort, from the constraints of conscience to which the manager is subject when he takes off his 'managerial-capitalist' hat and puts on his 'member-of-the-human-race' hat.

8.5.11 So, for all that Taylorism enjoyed almost universal application, no significant body of managers could ever have believed in the alleged conflict-reducing properties of Taylorism. The nearest that any of them could have considered that it came near to satisfying the worker's aspirations was when its use enabled the competitively pressured firm, by means of payment-by-results (PBR) systems, to maintain or reduce its unit costs even as it paid higher take-home sums per operative. Yet managers are quite aware that such incentive schemes, even when circumstances make them the lesser of all the envisaged evils, are likely in themselves to be a source of constant friction.

8.5.12 So the continued use and expansion of Taylorism does not lie in its power to reduce conflict, nor is it because managers are blind to the many adverse social reactions that it generates. Its continued use lies in its ability, for all its shortcomings, to enhance the firm's chances of survival. This piece of stark realism is not only part of management thinking, but part of the worker's also, together with that of his union. Despite their antipathy to both the socially divisive aspects of PBR and its implications about human nature, workers and their unions have regularly accepted payment-by-results systems.

8.5.13 Indeed, the intervention of government into pay negotiations during the 1960s was to bring both sides of industry to commend themselves to the government and the nation in that they had 'correctly' applied PBR. The government of the time was so convinced that 'wage drift' was not only affecting incomes but also prices, that in 1968 it commissioned the then existing National Board for Prices and Incomes to study PBR (HMSO, 1968). The government implication was that managements had a national duty to avert inflation. Past PBR negotiations at the workplace had failed to secure the increases in productivity which would have off-set the inflationary effect. In future, managements should see this did not recur. The effect of this accusation was to make temporary allies of the unions and management: management because it made them out to be easy prey, unions because it cast them in the role of predator. Neither approved of this imagery. Not surprisingly, both denied the imputation and both declared that their every waking thought was to care for the national interest. Indeed, neither would dream of subverting that interest by allowing PBR to be less than effective.

8.5.14 But time passed, governments and their boards went, unemployment came, the Department of Employment and Productivity' became (significantly) 'The Department of Employment'. Left-wing economists challenged the right-wing view that wage rises cause inflation, and substituted for it the view that inflation causes wage rises. At a stroke this took the unions from being the predators in the scenario to being the prey. This was immediately picked up as the official union stance, for, unlike managers, the role of innocent victim gives to the unionist considerable political leverage, for it is evidence of a grievance in need of rectification. More significantly, the reversal of roles meant that neither side had any further political interest in furthering their strangely based alliance. With its death died even the pretence that Taylorism is a formula for peace. In today's world, such a claim would find few adherents. It is the relic of a bygone age, but it has none of the reverence that relics can sometimes attract, for it is not only politically useless, but also embarrassingly silly.

9

The fourth response – 'social man', or Mayo's version of the 'daddy-knows-best' unitary frame of reference

9.1 The myth of Mayo's 'discovery' of group activity

9.1.1 'Taken as a whole, the significance of the Hawthorne investigation was in "discovering" the informal organization which it is now realized exists in all organizations.' So write Pugh, Hickson and Hinings (1971; p.129). It must be said that they put the word 'discovering' in inverted commas, presumably to show that they didn't really mean it. It is also true that they were engaged in writing a short, basic, introductory text. Such a book, which seeks to cover a wide terrain and in the process to make the wood stand out from the trees, must simplify and to that extent will distort. Are we to assume that this explains the distortion present in the above quotation? I think not. For exactly the same sort of distortion pervades most of the writing on Hawthorne and exists in the mythology that surrounds it. Indeed, they have produced a very clear, succinct and undistorted account of the myth as taught to thousands of students.

9.1.2 That having been said, I think we must do something to eliminate the mythology before we can consider the role played by social relationships. Our approach will be to look at what is meant by the 'informal' group or organization, after which we shall trace the attitudes of various people towards it long before Mayo 'discovered' it. By doing so I hope to explain why managers were so predisposed to welcome Elton Mayo's Hawthorne investigation 'findings', to accept them so uncritically, and, further, to invent the myth that he had 'discovered' the informal group. (The Hawthorne investigation is the subject of section 9.2. It started in the late 1920s and continued for most of the 1930s and was carried out at the 'Hawthorne Works' of the Western Electric Company in Chicago.)

9.1.3 Let us consider what would happen in the process of setting up such a factory. We would plan the machines and their layout. We would calculate how many men we would need and what skills they must have: all of which would be formally organized long before we had engaged anyone. Even engaging the men would be a formal activity: we should be taking in individuals to fulfil specific roles. Yet within days the workers would have set up a network of relationships between each other that would have been quite absent from management's plans. Groups of men with certain things in common would have grown informally. Not only that, but, as time went by, each group would develop its own code of conduct. There would be certain things that the group would regard as acceptable and certain things that they would not, that is the group would now have 'norms'. The group would also gradually develop means of enforcing these norms upon the individuals of the group by a system of rewards and punishments.

9.1.4 Now our understanding of this phenomenon and the way that norms operate was greatly enhanced by the Hawthorne investigation, and for this we are greatly indebted to Mayo. Looking at such informal groups some 40 years after Hawthorne, Edgar H. Schein listed five psychological needs that they satisfy for their members. These are (Schein, 1970; p.84):

(a) An outlet for affiliation needs, that is needs for friendship support and love.
(b) A means of developing, enhancing or confirming a sense of identity and maintaining self-esteem. Through group membership a person can develop or confirm some feelings of who he is, can gain some status and thereby enhance his sense of self-esteem.

(c) A means of establishing and testing reality. Through developing consensus among group members, uncertain parts of the social environment can be made 'real' and stable...each person can validate his own perceptions and feelings best by checking them with others.
(d) A means of security and a sense of power in coping with a common enemy or threat...
(e) A means of getting some job done that members need to have done.

9.1.5 Now if we look at this list we shall see that:

(1) Need (e) differs from the other needs; because in an industrial context it is the company that decides which job gets done, when and by whom. Thus (although friends may sometimes arrange to work together), the likelihood is that the group will initially be formally organized by management. Only thereafter will an informal group (or groups) form within the formal group framework in order to satisfy needs (a) to (d).
(2) *The other four needs each relate to an aspect of life which can cause the individual anxiety, but which affiliation relieves. Joining such groups is therefore primarily a search for* **safety**.

9.1.6 Probably the least contentious issue in psychology is the need for individuals to use the informal group to satisfy these four needs. What the individual derives from the group can be restated as follows:

(a) *knowing that there will be support when it is needed,*
(b) *achieving self-esteem,*
(c) *making sense of the world 'out there' (see paragraph 2.1.9), and*
(d) *gaining psychological, physical and economic strength.*

We can point to confirming examples almost minute by minute in our daily lives. We have seen that as early as 1651 (paragraph 2.2.10) Hobbes had come to regard safety as the very trigger that had created human society, and, as I said earlier (paragraph 2.2.11), any attempt to explain trade unions without including some reference to a search for safety would be absurd. Indeed, trade unions will fit neatly into Schein's list as an example of need (d), namely 'coping with a common enemy or threat'.

9.1.7 Two things need to be noted from our discussion so far. The first is the central importance of 'safety' to motivation theory. No other conclusion can be drawn subsequent to Mayo's 1930s work on informal groups. This same general premise holds true whether we accept his, or Hoxie's or Schein's interpretation of the purposes groups serve. Yet by the 1960s, while acknowledging the existence of 'safety' needs, the neo-human relations writers consider them unworthy of attention. If the reader sees a parallel here with the way new communist regimes denounce the 'deviationism' of their predecessors, this is no accident. 'Safety' disappeared as being an **ideologically improper** need in the new regime, and with it disappeared a large slice of realism. I shall try throughout this book to rehabilitate 'safety' and thus put back the realism.

9.1.8 The second thing to note is that, if safety **is** so central to the worker, and if trade-union activity **is** a manifestation of it, we should have expected others to have commented upon group phenomena long before Mayo 'discovered' it in the 1930s. *And indeed that is what we find.* But before we go on to consider some of this evidence, let us consider the basic difference between what Elton Mayo said about groups and what his predecessors had said. Writers prior to Mayo claimed, without any exceptions so far as I am aware, that the *Weltanschauungen* of informal groups led to their operating **against** the wishes of management. F.W.Taylor said so and broke them up. R.F. Hoxie said so, but disagreed with Taylor's response. In 1908 Max Weber said so, and claimed that underperforming or braking ('*bremsen*') would occur even in the absence of trade unions and that (Kakar, 1970; p.89) 'conscious and intentional [braking] will occur...wherever the workforce or even some considerable fraction of it, feels some measure of solidarity'. That is to say, wherever an informal group exists.

9.1.9 What a depressing message for managers! It is not very difficult to understand why Mayo should have become for them the hero of the hour. In place of this depressing news he brought a new gospel. Managers, it would seem, could smile again. Contrary to the story that Hoxie and the others had spread, managers could hope to manipulate the informal group. Moreover, Mayo had the required formula. *That was the real message of the Hawthorne investigation,* **that** *was the reason for the excitement it generated, and* **that** *was the reason for wiping the historic slate clean of all previous 'group' references.* Groups were 'discovered' anew without any of the nasty debris of past 'group' experience. The reception of Mayo's message is as much an interesting psychological and sociological study as ever Hawthorne itself was. For it showed that workers were not the only ones seeking safety: managers too were more than ready to welcome the psychological safety of a comforting myth.

9.1.10 Let us now consider how the role of the informal group was described by R.F.Hoxie, as early as 1917. We should notice in particular his unerring instinct that the group creates its own vision of the world, and also that, when a trade union is true to its purpose, its goal is to guard the rights of this primary group.

9.1.11 Here is Hoxie virtually saying what Schein said, but 50 years previously and over 10 years before Mayo (quoted in McCarthy, 1972; pp.34–35):

> The trade union program...rests on the broad foundation of conceptions of right, of rights, and of general theory peculiar to the workers, and it fans out to include or reflect all the economic, ethical, juridical and social hopes and fears, aims, aspirations and attitudes **of the group**. It expresses the workers' social theory and the rules of the game to which they are committed, not

only in industry but in social affairs generally. It is the organized workers' conceptual world. (My emphasis.)

I pointed out that Taylorism was suited to utilitarianism. It follows naturally that most of the Taylorite arguments emphasized the good that Taylorism would do for society at large. That may be true, countered Hoxie, but for the group it is irrelevant. Here are his words (McCarthy, 1972; p.37): 'Much of the misunderstanding and controversy between scientific management and unionism, for example, results from the fact that scientific management argues in terms of the individual worker or of society as a whole, while the unions argue primarily in terms of group welfare.'

9.1.12 Hoxie does not argue (as I would) that the interests of the group and the management are ambivalent. He argues that they are permanently and mutually opposed. Here are some extracts from his closely argued case (McCarthy, 1972; pp.38-40):

(1) The interests of the employers and workers of the group are generally opposed; the employer is seeking the greatest possible output at the least possible cost...The union...is seeking the continuous employment of all its members at the highest possible wage rates...All the efforts of the employer...are thus seen to be directly opposed to the interest and welfare of the working group.

(2) ...[T]he workers stand frequently to lose in wage rates or in the amount of wages through increased effort...since the increased output of the group means generally lower prices for the unit of product, rarely or never an increase of the value of group products proportional to increased effort... Moreover, [an] increase in output...where the demand for goods is not extremely elastic tends to weaken the bargaining strength of the workers and so still further to lower wage rates.

(3) ...[T]he wages and conditions...of the...group depend upon the relative bargaining strength of the employers and the workers.

(4) The bargaining strength of the employer is always greater than that of the individual worker.

(5) The full bargaining strength of the employer will always be exerted.

(6) Therefore...competition between individual workers in the group for work and wages will tend to result in lowering wages and conditions to what can be demanded...by the weakest bargainers....

9.1.13 A long section follows in which Hoxie argues that the union develops a logical two-pronged response which flows from this analysis. *(1) Individuals in the group must not compete against each other and their output must therefore be restricted to that of the weakest member.* That is the conclusion that they reach to prevent management picking off individuals. But they must also strive to improve the bargaining strength of the group. To do this,

(2) the union must control the personnel within the group. This is an argument that leads on to the 'closed shop' (i.e. an agreement with management that they will only employ union labour). However, it goes further, because, even **within** a closed shop, management can differentiate between workers because of differences in skill. The union response is to demand apprenticeship training to defeat such specialization.

9.1.14 It is important to recognize that there is a difference between the bureaucratic union structure and the work group; a difference that led to the marked increase in the power of shop stewards during the 1960s and 1970s. But this does not diminish Hoxie's claim that when the unions are true to their goals they serve the primary group. Rather it shows that, when the primary group feels neglected by the union, it throws up its own representatives. The other thing that I would ask the reader to note is that when we come to look at the bank wiring room situation in the Hawthorne investigation, we shall find (1) output restriction by the group, and (2) group members performing work that was supposed not to be done by them. Yet, if union policy is formulated to protect the group, then it is not surprising that the group should adopt it. Everything that Mayo found in the bank wiring room was predictable from Hoxie's analysis (given above) over a decade beforehand.

9.1.15 Taylor knew about informal groups. He saw them, particularly when backed by trade unions, as being highly restrictive, and he wanted nothing to do with either. Here is Taylor on the setting of group norms of low output (Kakar, 1970; pp.95–96): 'It evidently becomes for each man's interest then to see that no job is done faster that it has been in the past. The younger and less experienced men are taught this by their elders, and all possible persuasion and social pressure is brought to bear on the greedy and selfish men to keep them from making new records.'

9.1.16 The reader will remember that I equated Taylor with Tawney's Puritan who was convinced that 'character was all' (paragraph 8.2.14). Here is Taylor's comment on the situation that he has just described and to which he referred as 'systematic soldiering': 'Unfortunately for the character of the workman, soldiering involves a deliberate attempt to mislead and deceive his employer, and thus upright and straight-forward men are compelled to become more or less hypocritical.' (Kakar, 1970; p.96.)

9.1.17 Taylor thought that such 'soldiering' was a natural response to the employers' practice of cutting the cash associated with each item produced whenever it aggregated to a high wage. They did this because they were ignorant of the true work content. Taylor claimed that, since he **did** know that content, and since he paid the man what he earned and without quibble, he had obtained the answer to systematic soldiering.

9.1.18 There are three things to note about this. The first is that Taylor knew all about group norms being restrictive. The second is that he was inviting the individual to make a personal deal with him and break the power of the group. The third is that, although he spoke of 'greedy and selfish men' breaking group norms, yet these were the ones that he was looking to to achieve his ends. That is why his account of the engagement of 'Schmidt' in his experiments is so interesting, and the more so for being, as Merkle tells us, (1980; p.28) untrue. *For it illustrates thereby what* **would** *have been Taylor's approved recruitment technique if it had proved possible.*

9.1.19 What he would have done was to have chosen a greedy 'loner'.

> 'Finally we selected a little Pennsylvania Dutchman who had been observed to trot back home for a mile or so every evening about as fresh as he was when he came trotting down to work in the morning. We found that on wages of $1.15 a day he had succeeded in buying a small plot of ground and that he was engaged in putting up the walls of a little house for himself in the morning before starting to work and at night after leaving. He also had the reputation…of placing a very high value on a dollar. As one man said, 'A penny looks about the size of a cart-wheel to him'. (Taylor, 1967; p.43.)

9.1.20 We should also note that, according to Hoxie's analysis, the 'fairness' that Taylor had brought into rate-setting would not have made the slightest scrap of difference to the tendency of workers to go on 'soldiering'. Without the group the worker would feel exposed. Nor should we overlook the incident of the ball-bearing girls who were sacked by Taylor (paragraph 8.2.16). However, as it happens, Taylor too would have expected the men in the Hawthorne bank wiring room group to have been engaged in 'soldiering' because they had never been work-studied and no one in management knew what a 'fair day's work' measured. Management's only yardstick was what the men had traditionally produced.

9.1.21 Having disposed of the myths concerning the situation before the Hawthorne investigations, let us look at the actual investigations and some of the claims made about them.

9.2 The Hawthorne studies: relay assembly and interview stages

9.2.1 The studies take their name from the plant in which they were carried out, the Hawthorne works of the Western Electric Company in Chicago.

They started out as pure Taylorism. Many years before, Taylor had discovered that a shovel must be a certain size to obtain maximum efficiency: too small it didn't hold enough, too big it was unwieldy. The ideal shovel, he found held 21 lbs. For this reason, when an operator went from shovelling one material to shovelling another, he changed shovels to maintain this figure. We can see the same sort of thinking in the experiments on illumination that started at Hawthorne back in 1924 and before the arrival of Mayo. The assumption obviously was that there would be an 'ideal' level of illumination, not too dim and not too bright. But there was no correlation between the lighting and the output. Indeed, although output rose as illumination increased yet it continued to rise as illumination was later decreased.

9.2.2 This lack of correlation was a disappointing result. The researchers assumed that too many variables were at work and started again in the Relay Assembly section. This operation was chosen because it corresponded to certain criteria that the researchers had developed.

(1) It was repetitive (*and so relevant to the many repetitive jobs in industry*).
(2) All members of the group would be doing identical work (*for ease of comparison*).
(3) It was short-cycle (*so facilitating a large statistical sample*).
(4) It was not machine-paced (*so allowing the operators flexibility of behaviour*).

Relays consisted of about 35 parts and took about a minute to assemble.

9.2.3 The researchers wanted to keep the experiment pure, but they were breaking new ground and uncertain of their methodology. It is ironic that, for the very purpose of keeping the experiment 'pure', they should have explained to the girls what it was all about. Since previous management had **never** confided in the girls, the researchers came to see, with hindsight, that this act created an extraneous psychological impurity. I shall recount a few details from the study with the purpose of explaining and of commenting upon the reasons for Mayo's optimistic message. A full account is to be found in a book by Roethlisberger and Dickson (1970), who were engaged in the study. My data is drawn from their book unless otherwise stated.

9.2.4 For a continuous period of two years (April 1927 to June 1929) a group of 6 girls (5 assembling and 1 servicing the others' needs) were monitored over 13 periods (though 2 of the girls were changed after period 7). During period 1 they were in their original department. During period 2 they moved into a separate room with almost identical equipment. During period 3 and thereafter they no longer had their bonus payments made on the basis of the average output of the main department of 100 girls, but on the average output of their small group. From periods 4 to 7 there were changes in their rest periods. From periods 8 to 13 there were changes to the length of the working week. However, periods 7, 10 and 13 were identical. Throughout, output rose.

9.2.5 The lack of correlation between output and conditions is highly significant and mirrors the illumination study findings. Roethlisberger and Dickson maintained that over the period the relationship between the supervisor and the girls improved. The verbatim exchanges they report substantiate this. The researchers attributed the improvement in output to one or more of five hypotheses (pp.87,88):

(1) ...improved material conditions and methods of work...
(2) ...rest pauses and shorter working hours had provided a relief from cumulative fatigue.
(3) ...rest pauses and shorter working hours...reducing the monotony of the work.
(4) ...wage incentive had become an important factor. The girls were given an opportunity to earn more directly in proportion to effort expended...
(5) ...gaining the operators' confidence and establishing effective working relations between operators and supervisors.

9.2.6 Others who have worked on the data agree with the researchers that hypothesis (1) is insignificant. Hypotheses (2) and (3) are considered by Roethlisberger and Dickson (pp. 90-127). They conclude that the 'rest from fatigue hypothesis' should be abandoned and that the 'rest from monotony hypothesis' is inconclusive, and in any case relates to hypothesis (5). From the text I find their conclusions reasonable. Clearly the running is between (4) and (5).

9.2.7 Clearly also, I conclude from the treatment of the evidence, they would prefer (5) to be the winner. How conscious they were of bias is impossible to know. I suspect they were not. Yet when they found evidence to support hypothesis (4) they de-emphasized its significance considerably. Hypothesis (4) was checked by them in two ways:

(a) by taking another group with unchanged conditions but changed pay;
(b) by taking a further group with unchanged pay but changed conditions.

9.2.8 They made the first check by leaving a second group of five girls in the main department, *but with a separately calculated bonus*, for a period of 9 weeks. I find the results impressive. Output rose by 12.6 per cent but dropped back by 16.4 per cent on reverting to the original situation (p.132). Astonishingly, the researchers find this result is not significant. First they claim (p.158) that the increase was really a form of competitive imitation of the original group. Then they claim it was plateau-like. This is not interpreted by them as a **sustained** effect; on the contrary they claim (p.159) it had 'worked itself out rapidly'. Such treatment of the evidence I find incredibly specious.

9.2.9 Nevertheless, it is as nothing when compared to the knots that they get into when interpreting the evidence from the second check. This involved girls whose job it was to split mica (an electrical insulator). With **no** changes in their bonus payment system they were put into another room.

9.2.10 It is interesting to note that, when the second group of relay girls were put on to a separate bonus and showed an immediate 12 per cent increase in output, the investigators cut the experiment short with uncharacteristic impatience after only 9 weeks. When the mica girls showed no great increase, they nevertheless kept the experiment going for 14 months until the increase had got to 15 per cent.

9.2.11 Yet 15 per cent was still disappointing for those who would like to down-grade the significance of incentive payments, for it fell a long way short of the 30 per cent increase achieved by the original relay assembly group. It is at this point that the researchers' conscious or unconscious bias against incentives and in favour of psychological factors becomes quite comic. For in one of the most unbelievable pieces of logic they manage, as Americans would say, to 'shoot themselves in the foot'.

9.2.12 Let us remember that the question is 'Do incentive payments make a significant difference to output, and if not, why did the mica girls only increase their output by 15 per cent whereas the relay girls, whose scheme was changed, increased their output by 30 per cent?' Roethlisberger and Dickson's hypothesis is that the mica girls had less 'slack' available. They argue that the mica girls were previously on an individual piecework scheme under which (p.159) 'operators would tend to work closer to their maximum capacity than under group piece-work'. By their own assessment it seems that the lack of increase is caused **by the effectiveness of a previously operating strong incentive scheme!**

9.2.13 But this is only one example of a number of 'colorations' that entered the study. However, it did raise the legitimate issue of the difference which 'operator morale' may make to output. The researchers had no doubt at all. But although they tried to stress its importance to supervisors, they soon found that there were conflicting opinions and no facts about what **influences** morale. The outcome of this was the enormous interview programme, which spread over three years and involved 21,126 interviews.

9.2.14 Here again, the interpretation is interesting. I would have no great opposition to the diagram that they use to support their interpretation (Figure 9.2(a)).

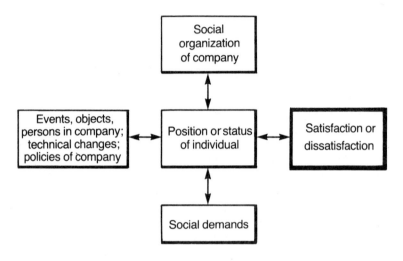

Figure 9.2(a) (Reprinted by permission: Roethlisberger & Dickson, *Management and the Worker*, Harvard University Press (1970; p.375))

9.2.15 Their text states that (pp.374–375):

This figure attempts to show in terms of their relations to one another those factors which have to be taken into account when considering employee content or discontent. According to this interpretation, it is not possible to treat, as in the more abstract social sciences, material goods, physical events, wages, and hours of work as things in themselves, subject to their own laws. Instead they must be interpreted as carriers of social value. For the employee in industry, the whole working environment must be looked upon as being permeated with social significance. Apart from the social values inherent in his environment the meaning to the employee of certain objects or events cannot be understood. To understand the meaning of an employee's complaints or grievances, it is necessary to take account of his position in the status of the company. This position is determined by the social organization of the company: that system of practices and beliefs by means of which the human values of the organization are expressed, and the symbols around which they are organized – efficiency, service, etc. In these terms it is then possible to understand the effect upon the individual of – or the meanings assigned by the individual to – the events, objects, and features of his environment, such as hours of work, wages, etc. Only then is it possible to see what effect changes in working environment have upon the social organization to which the employee has become accustomed, or upon that ideal type of social equilibrium which he desires. In terms of his relative position in the social organization it can be seen what values such changes overemphasize or under-emphasize.

Then follows a statement that is surprisingly modern, indeed, anachronistic to someone who, like myself, regarded 'systems thinking' as essentially post-Second World War; for let us not forget that this was written in 1939. In paragraph 15.2.3 we shall consider the difference between 'open' and 'closed' systems in an organizational context.

9.2.16

But the relation of the individual employee to the company is not a closed system. All the values of the individual cannot be accounted for by the social organization of the company. The meaning a person assigns to his position depends upon whether or not that position is allowing him to fulfill the social demands he is making of his work. The ultimate significance of his work is not defined so much by his relation to the company as by his relation to the wider social reality.

9.2.17 Now, as it is expressed here I have only one criticism to make of the model given in Figure 9.2(a) and the above statement. This is that, although technical changes appears in the left-hand box of the model, it is quite clear that the writers are only thinking in terms of the social impact of a period of technical **change**. There is no evidence that they shared Trist's perception of the firm as a socio-technical system. That being so, neither did they consider the significance of the way the technical element of the socio-technical system **constantly** impinges upon, and acts as a modifier of, the social part of that system.

9.2.18 It would also be easy to read too much into the researchers' claim that it is against 'the wider social reality' that the employee's work gains 'ultimate significance'. It seems to be making an appeal to values which transcend those of the firm, and therefore of management. This appeal to 'society's' values is, however, not to be taken as illustrating Mayo's pluralist sympathies. *Management, for Mayo, are the agents of society and can claim to have the moral approval of society.* (The way such an attitude is justified I explained in paragraph 7.2.35). The Mayoite reference to the 'external social reality' of the worker is simply to explain why there are so many and such strong anti-management 'illusions' held by the worker. They come from this 'reality'; a place to which management does not stretch and for which management cannot be held responsible. However, if anti-management propaganda is emerging from this place, (this 'external social reality'), it makes it proper for Mayo to set up 'counsellors' within the firm, to work on the worker's *Weltanschauung* and counteract the harm done. The assumption of this right by the Mayoites illustrates one particular example of an attitude which some managements apply to their dealings with their workers and which Rose refers to as 'corporate fascism'. As such it is quite the opposite of pluralist. Let us consider the pointers which allow us to infer this of Mayo's ideology.

9.3 Inferring Mayo's ideology

9.3.1 The work of Mayo is so often presented as being anti-Taylor that readers either do not realize, or else lose sight of the fact, that Mayo was Taylorite enough to have written two articles for the *Taylor Society Bulletin*, one in December 1924, and another in December 1925. It is from the former that we learn what this 'wider social reality' meant to Mayo. As I have said, it turns out to be no more than that circumstances that affect the worker outside the plant can have an adverse effect upon their output within the plant. Mayo's writings allow us to infer four concepts that underlie his attitude to the worker:

(1) His major concern is not primarily the psychological well-being of the worker, but simply reflects his theory that a worker who is happy will be a high producer. (In the cruder form of management jargon shorthand this is sometimes expressed as the 'contented cows give more milk' concept.)

(2) That any dissatisfaction that the worker may feel with his job arises from a lack of true understanding and that it is important that he should be shown the error of his ways.

(3) The monotonous work that many employees are engaged in induces, says Mayo, a low-grade reverie, in which molehills become mountains as a result of obsessive thinking.

(4) The sociological aspects of the worker's life seem to be regarded by Mayo as little more than fuel for these obsessions. The impact of family and friends is acknowledged, but they are simply in the wings, a self-appointed 'Greek-chorus' whose comments upon the scenario do little to help management and who need to be countered by counselling the worker.

9.3.2 The one thing that Mayo does not do is to suggest that the worker's standpoint is rational and valid. At one time I believed that he had consciously chosen to **deny** the rationality of the worker's belief-system *as a deliberate stratagem to avoid the implication of Hoxie's model, in which conflict **stems** from the very rationality of the worker*. Mayo's claim that the worker is non-rational I now find to be less calculated to serve this end than I did previously. The **effect** is the same but the **cause** I see as different. In this I have been influenced by Rose.

9.3.3 Rose (1978; p.115) tells us that Mayo started to study psychology in 1905, but that he 'had virtually no knowledge of sociology until 1926 when the biochemist Lawrence J. Henderson introduced him to Pareto's theories.' (Vilfredo Pareto (1848–1923) was an Italian economist/ sociologist.) Rose comments (p.117) 'Pareto's ideas are complex but what impressed Mayo was his notion of non-logical action. This allegedly predominates in social life and springs from "sentiments" (a largely unconscious predisposition or state of mind). People impelled to act...by a "sentiment" can only offer a **rationalization** for their behaviour, not a genuine scientific explanation or theory'. Rose goes on to say that 'Pareto also believed élite rule was inevitable' and that Mayo too 'concluded that pervasive sentiments disqualify the majority from rule'. Why is this? Rose's explanation is a little vague. He says it is because these 'sentiments': 'function mainly to sustain stability in face-to-face relations'. What I take this to mean is that those who rule should base their judgements upon something more long-term and rational than that of framing policy simply on the basis that it is in line with the prevailing sentiment and thus serves, however irrationally, the cause of short-term harmony.

9.3.4 Yet if Rose is right about Pareto's influence, Pareto had certainly found a predisposed disciple in Mayo. Two whole years before the time when Rose claims that Mayo was introduced to Pareto's thought, Mayo had expressed very similar views in the article that he wrote for the *Taylor Society Bulletin* of December 1924. In it (Del Mar and Collons, 1976; p.269) Mayo claimed that a patient, and so, by extension, a worker, would make 'the incidents of his upbringing and education, [and] his adaptation to his surroundings, his dominant trends of revery or day dream in moods of mental relaxation'. Such reveries thus begin 'to bear an important relation to his total attitude to life at any present time...' Later he contrasts the impact of such reveries upon the 'normal' as opposed to the 'abnormal' person.

9.3.5 'In the normal person revery illuminates concentration, concentration supplies the material of observation and brings the inspiration of revery to the test of empirical fact. In the abnormal person, concentration and revery are pointed in different directions; the result is that mental condition which is described as divided or alternating personality', (p.269). It should already be clear where Mayo is going. He is preparing the ground for a pro-management 'Catch 22' situation. (*The original 'Catch 22', of the satirical novel of that name, trapped the bomber crews of the Second World War into flying missions thus: (1) Only if those same missions had sent you mad could you claim to be released; (2) yet, if you were rational enough to make such a claim, you clearly must still be sane. Mayo's 'Catch 22' is similar.*)

9.3.6 Mayo's 'Catch 22' is as follows: (1) The work situation contains no elements to dismay the worker when its true reality is understood. (2) Since there is no disparity between the real world and the reverie of a 'normal' person, it follows that those who are dissatisfied with their situation must be the victims of their own obsessions. This is *a priori* evidence that the complainant is 'abnormal'. That is to say, by the act of complaining the worker has disenfranchised himself and cannot be taken seriously.

9.3.7 If this sounds too outrageous to be true, I believe that this is a result of the Mayo myth which has made him one of the management 'saints'. Here is one of many statements that, in their aggregate make it impossible for me to reach any other conclusion that that expressed in the preceding paragraph. It should be remembered that this is still from the 1924 article, before Pareto had confirmed Mayo in his prejudices and long before Hawthorne.

> ...modern methods of industrial organization tend to impose on the average individual long periods of revery thinking. Machine operation, once the worker is habituated to it, does not demand a high degree of concentrated thought. On the other hand, it is impossible for him to concentrate upon anything else. One finds in actual practice, therefore, that the mental mood which accompanies work is very frequently a low-grade revery of a pessimistic order...Now the danger of this general condition of things both to the individual worker and to industry is obvious to anyone acquainted with psychopathological work...[W]hy psychological investigation is necessary to industry is that these **pessimistic reveries which culminate in disorder and unrest (absenteeism, high labor turnover, strikes) are relatively easily controlled** provided that the management has a means of discovering the nature of the cause. (Del Mar and Collons, 1976; pp.272–273.)

On that evidence alone I should expect some of my readers to begin to suspect that my claim in paragraph 9.3.6 is one to be taken seriously.

9.3.8 For Mayo has dismissed without a second thought the possibility that absenteeism, high labour turnover and strikes, can be caused by anything other than the sick imaginings of the worker. Never once does it seem to occur to him that the worker's response might be a rational reaction to unfair management treatment. Yet Mayo was far from unintelligent. I find that we must conclude that his ideology vitiated his work as a scientist. This is a conclusion that also casts light upon certain other features of the Hawthorne studies. It is often claimed that the two assembly-room girls who were dropped from the experiment were dropped from ignorance of methodology. Thus Roethlisberger and Dickson say (1939; p.54), 'Had the investigators possessed at that time the technique developed later', then the situation might have been different. Yet Mayo exhibited very disturbing signs of questionable research in far more basic experiments, and **always with a pro-management bias**. Are we really to believe that it was as a result of methodological ignorance that they removed these two relay girls as they did? 'The first step was to call Operator 2A into a conference with the test room authorities. She was told of her offenses, [*sic*] of being moody, inattentive and not co-operative…Operator 1A was clearly her ally.' (p.55.)

9.3.9 Let us go back to another experiment that Mayo reported in his 1924 article (Del Mar and Collons, 1976). For it seems to me that, if we are truly to believe that Mayo did not see the methodological bias it contained, then (even given the state of the investigative art at that time) he would have needed to have been singularly obtuse. That being the case, we must choose between labelling him as having been as obtuse as this or else as having been strongly ideologically motivated to serve management rather than science.

9.3.10 In the winding department of a textile mill, women had been absenting themselves because, they claimed, they were suffering from menstrual 'cramps'. Mayo conceived these absences otherwise, and as 'largely due to a **tradition of incapacitation** by menstrual "cramps"'. Mayo is anxious that we should fully perceive that, although the steps taken had the effect of completely removing absenteeism from this cause, yet those steps contained little physical relief. He obviously only knows the facts at second-hand as we can infer from such phrases as 'I am expertly informed'. Yet this does not prevent Mayo from drawing two absurd morals. The first of these is that **the illness was no more than the product of their reveries**. The second was that **when this had been clarified the problem disappeared**. Here are his very words (Del Mar and Collons, 1976; p.275): 'the individual attack [*sic*] upon the reverie and traditional expectation by the nurse in charge has had the effect of almost entirely removing this cause of absenteeism. In one period of four months, for example, there was no time lost by reason of this ill.'

9.3.11 What an incredible position for an intelligent investigator to adopt, even in 1924! Previously up to 50 per cent of the girls had absented themselves for one or more days per month because of this problem. Why this illness should not have been entirely legitimate rather than the result of an obsession generated by low-grade reverie, he doesn't explain. Yet among the pressures which will affect a girl when she feels ill from menstrual pain will clearly be the degree of sympathy that she gets from her employer. The employer, via his agent, the 'nurse in charge' (we should note her title), tells the girl that no longer will he take seriously the claim that she can be incapacitated by menstrual 'cramps' because it is all in her mind. The threat is obvious. No matter how ill she feels she now crawls to work. But for Mayo it is proof that the original problem was reverie-induced; for, following this 'counselling' it has disappeared. He thus reinforces his belief in the non-rational behaviour of the worker. Moreover, nowhere does he give us any figures to show what happened to absenteeism in total. We cannot judge, for example, whether the unacceptable reason, **menstrual pain**, became the acceptable reason, **migraine**.

9.3.12 This then is the *Weltanschauung* of the guiding light in the Hawthorne experiments. Rose (1978; p.113) claims that 'Mayo never conducted these studies', adding moreover that the human relations movement was 'diffuse, and Mayo never led it except in a symbolic sense – and largely from the grave'. Well, I should need something more than the arguments that Rose advances to disassociate Mayo from his traditional role of being the Hawthorne studies' mentor; and particularly when those same studies are pervaded by Mayo's *Weltanschauung* so completely as to share his contempt for the rationality of the group and his obsessive preoccupation with reverie-induced obsessions. Let us then look at the findings in the bank wiring observation room study, for we are now in a position to understand the cavalier treatment of the evidence by the researchers.

9.4 The Hawthorne studies: the bank wiring observation room

9.4.1 As I mentioned earlier, both Taylor and Hoxie would have expected to find the men in this room to be, in Taylor's terminology, 'systematically soldiering': Taylor because there had been no attempt by management at work measurement, Hoxie because (following the rationale of paragraph 9.1.12) it 'made sense' for them to act so. For Hoxie this would have been the case **whether or not** there had been work measurement. Indeed, the reported comments of the workers support Hoxie's thesis. To support Mayo's thesis these comments have to be explained away. But that is no problem for a student of Pareto with the innate leanings of Mayo.

9.4.2 However, to understand the points I shall make we shall first need to understand the nature of the bonus system. (The original data appear in Roethlisberger and Dickson, 1970; pp.409–410 and are paraphrased here.) The calculation starts by crediting each operator with his attendance hours during the week multiplied by his guaranteed rate of pay per attendance hour. The better operators are on a better rate of pay, so that in any one week their guaranteed wage for any given number of hours is proportionately higher.

9.4.3 A further calculation is done at the end of the week. A physical count of the units manufactured during the week is made and multiplied by a piece-work price per unit. If this value is higher than the total wages of the department, then the excess will be distributed pro rata with the guaranteed pay which the worker is already due. Here is a hypothetical example to make this clear. Assume Joe Dough has worked for 50 hours at a guaranteed rate of $0.40 per hour. His guaranteed wage would be $20. Let us assume that when all the men's guaranteed wages are totalled they come to $240. Let us also assume that the piece-work value of their joint output is $300. Each man's wages will be inflated in the ratio of 240:300, and Joe Dough will actually receive $25.

9.4.4 There are two further points to note, though neither of them affect the actual earnings of the workers. The first is that a worker who had difficulty with a job could claim a 'daywork allowance'. It did not affect the wages in any way but it was an alibi to justify that, from causes beyond his control, his output was low. The second is the idea of 'bogey. Ostensibly this was no more than a target concept of what output the worker should get per hour. It formed no part of the payment calculation as such. **I shall claim that the researchers used this fact speciously.** *They tried to maintain that, because it would not change any of the calculations in the existing scheme, the workers' preoccupation with the 'bogey' figure was non-rational.* If I had been one of those workers I should have seen all the other calculations as having been grounded in the concept of 'bogey'. The fact that it formed no part of the current calculation system would have been to me an irrelevancy.

9.4.5 So if I had been one of the Hawthorne study investigators I should have considered that workers who feared the raising of the 'bogey' were acting entirely rationally.

9.4.6 The bogey was 914 connections per hour and the men worked an eight-hour day. The daily bogey was therefore 7,312. I invite the reader to listen to the words of Wireman 3 to the interviewer. This man, by the researchers' own showing, was the key member of one of the two cliques which formed within the informal group. Indeed, his status is shown by the face that (p.506) he 'was helped more than anyone else in the observation room, even though he did not need it... They liked to work with him.' Wireman 3 is therefore a man of considerable influence, and I suggest, nobody's fool (p.417).

> W3: No one can turn out the bogey consistently. Well occasionally some of them do. Now since the layoff started there's been a few fellows down there who have been turning out around 7,300 a day. They've been work-ing like hell. I think it is foolishness to do it because I don't think it will do them any good, and it is likely to do the rest of us a lot of harm.'
>
> Int.: 'Just how do you figure that?'
>
> W3: 'Well, you see if they start turning out around 7,300 a day over a period of weeks and if three of them do it, then they can lay one of the men off, because three men working at that speed can do as much as four men working at the present rate.'
>
> Int.: 'And you think that is likely to happen?'
>
> W3: 'Yes, I think it would. At present we are only scheduled for 40 sets ahead. In normal times we were scheduled for over 100. If they find that fewer men can do the work, they're going to lay off more of us. When things pick up they will expect us to do as much as we are now. That means they will raise the bogey on us. You see how it works?'

9.4.7 The researchers would have us believe that this intelligent, observant man wasn't capable of realizing that the current 'bogey' figure was not used in bonus calculation at that time. Otherwise, they claim, he would recognize that 'they will raise the bogey on us' (even if it were to happen), would **not** affect earnings. They insist that (p.410) '...[r]aising a bogey had none of the effects of reducing a piece rate or hourly rate'.

9.4.8 We are left with the impression that the researchers were either extremely naïve or extremely disingenuous. Throughout they use their 'Catch-22' argument that, since the workers distrusted management, and since this was plainly an absurd thing to do, the workers were being less than rational. In this instance I see Wireman 3's statement as a form of shorthand. For him, the significance of 'raising the bogey' was self-evident. In default of measurement (and they had not been work-studied), Wireman 3 would have been very stupid indeed if he had not perceived that the only way in which the bogey had been set was by adopting some figure which was related to, but in excess of, **actual** performance. He would equally have been extremely stupid if he had not concluded that the payment scheme was designed with the 'bogey' figure in mind. Consequently he would have every reason to fear that a raising of actual performance might well herald a new and higher bogey. The result, he feared, would be a redesign of the payment scheme related to this higher bogey. Put simply, higher output would result in a wage cut per unit produced.

9.4.9 Let me confess that this is speculation. It nevertheless raises two very interesting questions. Were these researchers so inept that they didn't recognize the above interpretation? If they were, it explains a great deal. However, if they were **not** so inept, why did they not go further with Wireman 3 to establish how, in his view, 'raising the bogey' would be disadvantageous to him? Could it be that they feared that he might put forward the rational economic argument that I have just advanced and thereby spoil the evidence for Mayo's thesis that worker's are non-rational?

9.4.10 This brings us to the motivational conclusions of the Hawthorne studies. It is that people operate within two logic systems. One is the 'logic of reason' and the other is 'the logic of sentiment'. Now it must already be clear that, correctly applied, I have nothing against this proposition. On the contrary, I have consistently maintained that we need to oscillate between different frames of reference if we are to form a balanced judgement. This applies to managers no less than workers. Indeed, what shocks us about the 'Pinto' car court case (a cautionary tale we will consider in Section 16.3) is the inhuman commitment of certain Ford executives to the 'logic of reason'. We do not deplore, of itself, their adherence to the premises inherent within the capitalist frame of reference. Nor do we deplore that, in keeping with these, that they should have sought to minimize opportunity cost. What we deplore is their single-mindedness in doing so. The result of that single-mindedness was as inevitable as it was tragic. Having ignored all alternative frames of reference, including those whose 'logic of sentiment' would have placed a premium on human life, they discovered it was more cost-effective to let people die than to modify a car.

9.4.11 Even the Hawthorne researchers could not bring themselves to suggest that only workers are motivated by sentiment and the managers by logic. No. They were at pains to point to the way in which (p.565)'...'[a]ll groups within industry participate in these different logics', but then they add (with the overtones of Orwell's *Animal Farm*) 'although some participate to a greater or lesser extent than others'.

9.4.12 The Hawthorne researchers therefore claim to ascribe both sets of sentiments to managers and workers alike: but they betray their real belief-system in the examples they give. These depict the worker as moved by non-rational fears which management quell, by being long-sufferingly and

OM-H

paternalistically rational. Typical is the case of hypothetical 'Mary Jones' (p.599), who 'has for some weeks past been displaying symptoms of discontent and unrest. Her efficiency has decreased somewhat, her attendance has become irregular, and she seems fretful and moody.' They are keen to stress the wholly non-rational nature of Mary's problem; for it is not only Mary's supervisor who has noticed it but also her friends. Then the expert 'counselor' is brought in to deal with it. Had the problem originated outside the plant 'no direct action could be taken'. That in itself is revealing. The researchers go on to imagine that the problem is within the plant. Needless to say the whole issue turns out to be a misunderstanding and eventually the counsellor 'calls Mary up to his desk and gives her a more adequate understanding of the situation. As a result of this process she goes back to her work in better spirits. She is restored to her normal effectiveness and her efficiency may rise.'

9.4.13 If Mayo had set out to undermine Hoxie's claims he could not have done a neater job. Hoxie's thesis (paragraphs 9.1.12 and 13) was that workers were acting rationally so as to manipulate the labour market in their own favour. Not only did they engage in restrictive practices, but it made sense for them to do so. This seems to imply that the 'logic of reason' will always place the worker and management at loggerheads.

9.4.14 I differ from Hoxie in that I maintain that this is only one of two poses which the worker adopts. I claim that, dependent on circumstance, he will oscillate between restrictive and non-restrictive practices (see also Roy's comments in paragraph 9.4.25). Nor, given the basic ambiguity of his position in relation to the capitalist firm (paragraph 1.2.15), should we expect him to act other than with ambivalence.

9.4.15 But given Mayo's unitary pro-management attitudes, he would have found my pluralist views unacceptable and those of Hoxie impossible to contemplate. The Hawthorne researchers could not deny the many restrictive practices which they had observed in the bank wiring room. However, by a number of disingenuous statements they could, and did, argue that there was no rationale behind these restrictions. They accomplished this in two steps. First they claimed that such restrictive practices could only be understood if they were seen as loyalty to the *mores* of the informal group. So far so good: even Hoxie was saying that. But then they go on to claim that these group *mores* are rooted only in emotion, (the 'logic of sentiment') and not in rationality (the 'logic of reason'). The effect (and the purpose) of this was to suggest that only the view of management was valid because only the view of management was 'rational'.

9.4.16 Even after we have made allowance for Mayo's all-pervading Mosaic-myth ideology we are left to wonder that they could do this: for Wireman 3's statement and what happened in the bank wiring room matched exactly Hoxie's published account of how economically rational groups of workers would react when safeguarding their interests. It is difficult to see how the researchers could, with honesty, have denied that the 'logic of reason' applied to the workers' position quite as much as to management's. The differences between management and worker did not stem from their having different frames of reference, but from the workers' recognition (within that situation) that they and management shared the same frame of reference but did not share common interests. We must also consider why Roethlisberger's and Dickson's distorted interpretation of the evidence was so readily accepted.

9.4.17 I think that there are two related reasons for this acceptance.

(1) We have seen how few commentators have recognized that the employer/ employee economic relationship incorporates a fundamental ambivalence because the worker is both potential asset and potential liability. So they fail to see that the worker's most rational response is to be equally ambivalent, namely to adopt contradictory 'both...and' postures to match each aspect of the original ambivalence. Having totally failed to see the duality in management's position, such an observer argues
   (a) that it is the worker alone who is inconsistent, and
   (b) that inconsistency equals non-rationality.
   The result is that the contradictory signals in the study, (positive from the relay assembly girls, negative from the bank wiring room men) are misunderstood.
(2) The same 'either...or' attitude which made them fail to see that the workers' 'both...and' response was appropriate affected their vision of what room they had to manoeuvre as managers. Failing to see a 'both...and' policy was possible, they applied an 'either...or' approach to
   (i) Hoxie's total-conflict pluralist frame of reference, and
   (ii) Mayo's 'daddy-knows-best' unitary frame of reference.

It really was no contest...Hoxie had to go!

9.4.18 Moreover, they were also aware that if the conflict of interests really were total, that is to say, if the worker saw no practical advantage in the relationship, it would not continue, nor would the trade-union movement itself continue in its symbiotic if ambiguous relationship with capitalism. So with no models to handle the reality of this ambiguous 'love-hate' relationship they went for the more positive approach of Mayo. Interestingly enough, the Marxist's refusal to validate the worker's love-hate relationship with capitalist managements is essentially the same as Mayo's. The Marxist claims it stems from the worker's faulty perception, his 'embourgeoisement', which has created in him a 'false consciousness'. Had it not been so he would be totally **anti**-management. Mayo's claim differed only in that if the workers saw things aright they would be **pro**-management. But for him, as for the Marxist, the problem stems from the worker's 'false consciousness': for how else can we describe a 'logic of sentiment' which contrasts with, but does not inform, the 'logic of rationality'?

9.4.19 Mayo had no doubt of his moral right to 'counsel' the worker into a true consciousness, and any future Western Marxist industrialized society will surely do the same. Marxism's abhorrence of unorthodoxy suggests any future Western Marxist society will be as totalitarian as the Eastern bloc. In such a society, complaining workers will surely receive the same short shrift they got from Lenin (paragraph 7.2.18). *Not least because in their society conflict is theoretically not **supposed** to occur, we can be sure that it will not be **allowed** to occur.*

9.4.20 Marxists and Mayoites are equally arrogant in their denial that the ambivalent worker's viewpoint corresponds to reality, and that this gives them the right and duty to correct him. But at least in the Marxist's case this position is in accord with his belief in a unitary society...an appropriate enough belief for one who has encapsulated 'Truth'. The Mayoite, by contrast actually does violence to the 'natural' belief system of capitalism (namely pluralism) when he adopts **his** position.

9.4.21 Marx was indeed correct when he claimed that (Marx and Engels, 1970; Vol. 2, p.503), 'the economic structure of society' is 'the real foundation on which rises a legal and political superstructure and to which correspond definite forms of social consciousness'. Which is why, although capitalist economies have not always avoided dictatorships, yet the type of society capitalism naturally generates is that of parliamentary democracy. It is all of a piece with capitalism's respect for free markets, coupled with its inherent pluralism, that it leads to the recognition that the worker too has the right to exert market pressure. What Mayo's contempt for the worker's rationality does is to undermine that right.

9.4.22 It is scarcely surprising that one writer, commenting on Mayo's 1932 book *Human Problems*, should find that Mayo's 'political observations... degenerate into radically right-wing ideology: in effect a plea for corporate

Fascism, albeit with a human face' (Rose, 1975; p.121). Another commentator (Coser, 1972; p.20) says

All of Mayo's research was carried out with the permission and collaboration of management. It was conducted to help management solve its problems. To Mayo, management embodied the central purposes of society, and with this initial orientation he never considered the possibility that an industrial system might contain conflicting interests, as distinct from different attitudes or 'logics'

9.4.23 Put another way, any other view than management's was inadmissible to Mayo. How could such a totalitarian attitude become so popular at a time when America was to become embroiled in war with the totalitarianism of fascism? I have already suggested one philosophic blind spot. Additional to this is the American preoccupation with 'togetherness' which disposes many Americans, like the highly influential sociologist Talcott Parsons, to treat conflict as a social sickness (Coser, 1972; p.21): 'Focusing on normative structures which maintain and guarantee social order, Parsons was led to view conflict as having primarily disruptive, dissociating and dysfunctional consequences. Parsons considers conflict primarily a "disease".'

9.4.24 I should not have spent so much time on such ancient history if it were still not being taught with Mayo's interpretation applied to it. To regard the workers as non-rational creatures of sentiment is dangerous nonsense. It is the more so because those managers to whom this patronizing rubbish appealed were precisely the ones who were likely to be already practising what Rose calls 'corporate fascism'. By reinforcing such prejudices, Mayo did them and all associated with them a great disservice. Nothing could have been more calculated to discourage the self-critical study that every good manager should engage in than to be told that disquiet among his workforce, though requiring attention, needs propaganda rather than redress.

9.4.25 Furthermore, it is probably fair to say that the balance of the evidence since Hawthorne has done little to substantiate Mayo's thesis. Discontent may lower output, but there is remarkably little evidence that the reverse is true: 'contented cows' do not necessarily produce more 'milk'. More significantly, however, there is a lot of evidence for considering workers as 'economic men' who use social alliances in the manner that D. Roy has so graphically recounted (Burns, 1969; p.360). On occasion, says Roy, output could be high. This was because

machine operators characteristically evinced no reluctance to put forth effort when they felt that their group-defined piecework quotas were attainable. It might seem at first glance, that the supporting of operators [by other workers] during intensive application to 'getting the work out' would represent cooperation **with** and not **against** management. However the truth is that operators and their 'allies' joined forces in certain situations in a manner not only unmistakably at variance with the carefully prepared designs of staff experts but even in flagrant violation of strongly held managerial 'moral principles' of shop behaviour. In short, machine operators resorted to 'cheating' to attain quotas; and since this often involved the collusion of other shop groups, not as mere 'accessories after the fact' but as deeply entangled accomplices, any managerial suspicion that swindling and conniving, as well as loafing, were going on all the time was well founded.

9.4.26 As an antidote to Mayo, I should prescribe Roy's article, which is readily available in Burns's anthology. For Roy joined the workforce as an ordinary man. He thus was in a uniquely privileged 'fly-on-the-wall' status. Roy asks (Burns, 1969; p.377) 'Do we see in the situation studied, an economically "rational" management and an economically 'nonrational" work group? Would not a reversal of the labels, if such labels be used, find justification?' I fail to see how those who read the wealth of examples in his article, and who reflect upon his unique position to learn of everything that happened, can fail to agree with him.

9.4.27 Moreover, Roy's evidence is quite in line with the events reported by Mayo's team. Those who take the trouble to go back to Roethlisberger and Dickson's account will find nothing in the evidence in the bank wiring room which is not completely in keeping with what Roy was to find two decades later in another place. In the bank wiring room the men did each other's work. They 'cooked' their figures. They claimed difficulties that they never had. They brought other members of the group into line, sometimes by punching ('binging') them. Those who underproduced were cheating them of their bonuses and were labelled 'chisellers'. Those who overproduced, by the standards of the group, threatened their security and were labelled 'slave', 'speed-king' or called 'Phar Lap' after a race-horse. Only in their interpretation of what all this meant did Mayo's team differ from that which a less ideologically motivated observer might have given. For the men used social means to achieve economic ends and in the process, like Roy's work-mates, they engaged in 'swindling and conniving, as well as loafing'.

9.4.28 It is unfortunately true that management theory is full of historical debris which other disciplines seem able to dump, but which our writers regurgitate. My hope is that Mayo will one day be dumped. The irony is that by writing about him I am feeding him back into the system and revivifying him. Yet not to do so allows the myth to be perpetuated. The same is true

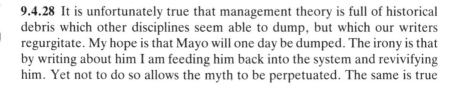

of the mathematical mumbo-jumbo of V.A. Graicunus who we meet later (paragraph 12.6.7). It is another classic 'Catch-22' situation: for if I wish to kill them off I have to write about them. In Mayo's case we are indebted to him for publicizing the concept of group norms. I hope that one day we shall be able to acknowledge that debt without also needing to drag around the Hawthorne detritus in perpetual payment.

9.5 The manager and Mayoism – is the role of 'totally impersonal bureaucrat' the capitalist manager's only honest stance?

9.5.1 Mayo's suggestion that the manager should adopt a form of *fatherly* relationship with his workers would seem questionable on two grounds:
(1) The first is that in today's society the word 'paternalism' (which describes such a role) carries socially offensive overtones.
(2) The second (and more serious charge) is that the contractual employer/ employee relationship would appear to make this stance basically dishonest and fundamentally immoral.

9.5.2 Yet before we are too dismissive of this role for the manager, we had better consider the reverse side of the coin.
(1) We object to 'paternalism' because the love it implies is coloured by the overtones of parental control and condescension. Would we be quite so dismissive if the word used were 'avuncularism'? This conjures up an image of a supportive love which does not dominate. In effect, it is an image of human warmth.
(2) Because one day the employer/employee contract may be revoked, does the honest manager continually remind the employee of that possibility by maintaining an impersonal legalistic aloofness at all times? For all its honesty and consistency, would not this role of 'totally impersonal bureaucrat' be insufferable for all parties?

9.5.3 To deal with these questions we need some models to describe the nature of authority and the types of relationship which different authority systems can engender. For these we can turn to one aspect of the work of the German sociologist Max Weber (1864–1920). (This is the same Max Weber who suggested (paragraph 8.2.5) that the rise of capitalism was fostered by the spirit of Protestantism. Earlier I referred to the manager as being able to adopt the role of 'bureaucrat' and earlier still (paragraph 2.3.1) I alluded to 'bureaucracy' as an authority system. It is, however not the **only** type of authority system.

9.5.4 Weber claimed that there were three basic kinds of authority: charismatic, traditional and bureaucratic. Although many critiques question whether the characteristics of each type are quite what Weber claimed, I know of no challenge to his choice of these three basic subdivisions, nor indeed can I imagine any. So I shall assume that these three types are the basic elements of all authority, even if in practice, every situation is likely to contain constituents of all three.

9.5.5 Charismatic authority stems from the personality of the leader. The impact of certain individuals upon their followers, and so upon the course of history, is undeniable. But such authority is unstable. The leader may be capricious and in any case his death will create the problem of succession. Moreover, his charisma is no guarantee that he will devise the best solutions to his regime's problems. Having so dismissed the issue, most textbooks move on to other matters. I do not know one that then asks 'But how far is organizational success the result of charismatic authority, even when that element is not officially acknowledged?' We shall come back to this question later in this section.

9.5.6 Weber's second authority type is 'traditional'. Traditional authority, though typified by feudalism, is not exclusive to it. It is perhaps useful to think of traditional authority as an institutionalized form of charismatic authority, of which the monarchy is a good example. It is a form of authority which does not suffer from the whims of the charismatic leader; nor does it die with the person, but passes to his successor. Yet these are not unqualified gains. At least the whims of the charismatic leader might have broken the mould and it is quite possible for his actions to have been governed by reason. Traditional authority, for all its similarities to charismatic authority (and these include its emotional appeal) is, by contrast, *essentially* non-rational. Its response to how things should be done comes not from logical analysis, but from appeal to custom and practice. So it is a static thing. Here again the textbooks usually just note this and move on dismissively. This is a strange response when it is demonstrable that the appeal of tradition is exceptionally strong and that its strength lies in its ability to supply people with some kind of tribal identity. That being so, surely it warrants the question 'Does that mean that tribal identity is something that the firm must supply if it is to satisfy its employees' needs for identification?' I think that it does, but this again is something to which we shall return.

9.5.7 This brings us to bureaucracy, sometimes referred to as 'rational–legal' authority. It is rational because the nature of the organization and its operations are held to be the logical way by which to achieve the desired ends. It is legal because the system of rules and procedures and the hierarchy of posts within the organization are perceived to be legitimate by those involved. These aspects are what give the organization its impersonal nature, for the rules which govern situations are determined in advance and people are dealt with according to these rules and dependent upon the role that they fill in the hierarchy. This impersonality serves to maintain fairness and consistency. Promotion is by merit, so that, unlike the feudal aspects of traditional authority, such a society should eventually lead to 'social movement' based upon meritocracy. To help to ensure that meritocracy is achieved, office holders are expected to acquire formal qualifications for their posts. All of this makes it sound a great deal better in many respects that the other two systems. Moreover, it has the advantage that it is a system which can handle scale very much better (which is why it has affinities with classical organization). We can also see why it should have meshed so well with the 'rational' nature of capitalism and the latter's acceptance of impersonal market forces. Lastly, we can see why they all came into mesh with Taylorism. (This is not an anachronism on my part, for although Weber's analysis of bureaucracy was not popularized until long after his death in 1920 – some 5 years after Taylor himself had died - the **fact** of bureaucracy, and its impersonal implications, were clearly appreciated intuitively during the earlier Taylor period.)

9.5.8 Yet there is another side to this coin which makes it essential for a healthy organization to adopt some aspects of the other two types of authority. For even Weber (who had eulogized the advantages of bureaucracy) saw that there was another side to its impersonal rationality that has a devastating effect upon the human spirit: it is cold. In the words of MacRae (1974;p.86), it involves

> the displacement from life of the emotional and the traditional modes of legitimate behaviour as socially unacceptable. As a result the world loses its savour. The spontaneous affections of the heart, the hatreds of the moment, the comely and honourable ways of tradition, are all forbidden. Reason illuminates all being with a shadowless and clinical light before which fly poetry, faith and myth. One does not even find in the merciless light of reason the consolation of injustice: reason is its own justification, the legitimator of its own necessities. Weber took from the poet Schiller a phrase that is usually translated as 'the disenchantment of the world'. The German in fact means something more precise: the driving out of magic from things.

9.5.9 As I have already pointed out (paragraph 8.5.9) prior to Mayo the manager had been presented by Taylor with a system which could never have been expected to satisfy the security needs of the workforce precisely *because* it fitted so well the rational impersonality of capitalist classical

organization theory and of bureaucracy. Consequently only someone with
Taylor's capacity for self-delusion could have dreamt that his system would
drive out conflict. The average manager would have had no such illusions.
*He used Taylorism because it improved productivity, but it had done so by an
impersonal specialization which had **also** driven out the magic from things.* So
we come back to the question with which we started this section. Given the
contractual nature of the capitalist employer/employee relationship, is the
coldness of the impersonal bureaucratic/Taylorite/classical organizational
stance the only honest attitude that the manager can adopt?

9.5.10 To my mind no manager who is able consistently to behave like a
bureaucratic cipher has any place in management: indeed I would suggest
that he is in need of psychiatric help. Nor does a manager need to be
inhuman to remain honest: he only needs to keep the employee aware of
which 'hat' he is wearing at any given time. This may sound difficult: in fact
it is not. Indeed, far from being confused by these changes of 'hats', the
worker understands completely what is going on. So clear is the worker
about the rules of this game that if the manager attempts to cheat and to blur
the distinction between his role when he is wearing one hat and his role when
wearing another the worker knows immediately *and resents the action.* This
is why 'works councils' failed. They were attempts by Mayo-type
managements to create a platform for management/worker discussion. The
aim was to demonstrate 'family-like' solidarity within the firm. The workers
were not fooled. They did not (as many managements hoped they would)
see them as a substitute for trade unionism. Yet that same worker would not
resent or see as manipulative a manager who advised him as a friend, or who
agreed to join the worker in a friendly drink in the pub one evening and
reverted to 'business-as-usual' the next day.

9.5.11 I should like for a moment to digress from the context of the capitalist
firm to illustrate how the armed forces succeed, without cheating, to
introduce charismatic and traditional elements. The armed forces are
fundamentally bureaucratic (and must be so), but the average sailor, soldier
or airman does not see his branch of the forces as being subject to the 'clinical
light [of bureaucracy] before which fly poetry faith and myth'. For the armed
forces are at great pains to put back some of the 'spontaneous affections of
the heart' as well as the 'comely and honourable ways of tradition'. Yet
neither does the average serviceman fail to recognize the essentially
bureaucratic nature of his arm of the services.

9.5.12 Let me give a specific example of this. It is the custom in many ships
of the Royal Navy for the officers to wait on the men at table on Christmas

Day. This tradition doubtless started from a genuine wish to commemorate that God became a carpenter who was born in a stable: there is no deception and certainly no intention to cheat, because everyone knows and understands the ground-rules. Nobody is in any doubt that hours from now, the Navy will be as bureaucratic as ever. Elsewhere on the ship where normal duties prevail; any action which was found to have been 'prejudicial to good order and Naval discipline' would be punished.

9.5.13 I suggested earlier (paragraph 9.5.6) that 'tribal identity' identity was something that the firm must somehow supply if it is to satisfy its employees' expectations. To some extent the Navy's inversion of roles at Christmas has that effect. In the army, so does the concept of taking pride in the regimental battle-honours or in the regimental mascot. As if deliberately to underline that it is not the mascot itself which is being fêted (but the regimental tradition of which it is an embodiment), mascots are usually inherently absurd. I do not wish to say anything offensive about goats in general, or in particular about those which are regimental mascots, but some observers might find such a choice of mascot odd. However, that is a highly normative judgement. Marching along behind a goat may seem entirely proper to those who hold regimental parades every St David's day, for the express purpose of formally presenting every man in the regiment with a vegetable, namely a leek, to put in his hat. Yet, even as I joke about it I feel convinced that organization and management could learn a great deal from the role of traditional institutions in the British army.

9.5.14 In each of the cases we have considered there has been no blurring of the distinction between the type of authority. Weber suggested that his three types of authority were 'ideal' types: useful for analysis purposes but seldom if ever found in their pure form in practice. I disagree. I believe that they are never met as a mixture but always as pure types. The fact that within one and the same business organization it is possible to find simultaneous expressions of all three does not mean that when they are found they exist in a murky blend, as when red and yellow and blue mix to give a brown. Rather do they co-exist like the various colours in the 'pointillism' style of painting of Georges Seurat, in which 'any one patch of uniform colour...[is] a whirling swarm of little dots which contain all the elements out of which the relevant colour tone is composed...Set out on the canvas in very close proximity but separately, these colours mix on the retina.' (Keller, 1980; p.221.)

9.5.15 In my opinion it is not only that each type of authority has a different **basis** for its legitimacy which makes blending impossible, but blending is also made impossible because each type of authority demands a different form of **reciprocity**. The whole question of reciprocity in management/worker relationships would be a highly rewarding area of study. Charles B. Handy (1976; p.391) points out that 'the principle of reciprocity has been around in sociology for a very long time', and so it has. But in management terms it has been peripheral to the main teaching. Handy believes that Harry Levinson was the first to describe this reciprocity in the management sphere by the term 'psychological contract'. Yet when Handy looks around for literature to make the point I have been making, he has himself to inject the phrase 'psychological contract' to imply the need for reciprocity, because the authors from whom he wants to quote did not speak of it so. It is certainly **implicit** in Etzioni's claim that there is an innate appropriateness between the type of involvement that the members have with an organization and the nature of that organization. For example, a church member has a moral involvement with his church, whereas a prisoner's involvement with his prison reflects its coercion. But Hardy still had to alter Etzioni's use of language to make explicit the implications, namely the psychological need for reciprocity. Moreover, Etzioni reduces the nature of the organization and the nature of the response to a single pair of factors. It is therefore over-simplistic. I do not disagree when Etzioni claims that the appropriate involvement of a worker with his business is that he should be 'calculative'. But it is a statement which is impoverished almost to the point of being meaningless. It conveys none of the richness of tapestry that would underlie these calculations nor their emotional aspects. So my criticism stands: it is an area in need of urgent and serious study.

9.5.16 Although Mayo's paternalism was offensive, it was really in his failure to offer adequate reciprocity that he came to grief: to put it bluntly, he cheated. He attempted to get the worker to regard the firm as family when he knew very well the firm could not reciprocate by regarding the **worker** as family. Yet it isn't necessary to cheat. In the example I gave in paragraph 9.5.12, the manager (in this case a Royal Naval Officer) was able, possibly unconsciously and certainly without cheating, to introduce a charismatic element into his future bureaucratic relationship. The worker (in this case the Naval Rating) recognizes the difference between bureaucracy (how it is legitimized and what reciprocity is appropriate) and charismatic authority (how it is legitimized and what reciprocity is appropriate). At no time did the manager (officer) communicate the notion that on behalf of the firm (The Royal Navy) he was entering into a hybrid relationship. Maintaining separation between actions performed in one context and those performed in another is vital if a quite disastrous confusion of psychological contracts is to be avoided.

9.5.17 I should like to add one last word concerning authority. It is usual to stress that authority comes from the governed. I get my students to discover this for themselves by asking them what prevents them from walking out of my seminars. However, although most of them conclude that any authority I have comes from them, the more intelligent also recognize that this is rather disingenuous. The standard textbook distinction between authority (which is the free acceptance by the governed of those who govern), and power (which is the imposed will of those who govern), is just a little too neat. So the cleverer students invariably see that my authority, while stemming from them, is related to my power (stemming from the rules of the bureaucratic system) to withhold something they want – namely their qualifications. A colleague of mine questions whether Weber himself ever made so clear-cut a distinction between power and authority and thinks that the claim that he did so came into the literature from a secondary source. I am not sure that in this he is correct because of the way in which Weber speaks of all three types of authority as 'resting on a belief in a system' or 'resting on devotion to a person'. Both these descriptions seem to imply that it **is** the governed who grant the authority. But whatever Weber's intentions, I can think of no real-life situation in which authority is devoid of power. The eagerness to show that authority comes from the governed (with the implication that it is therefore not power-related) is intended to support the myth that hierarchies are unnecessary.

S. M – clear
H – R – cheated .

10

The fifth response – 'self-actualizing man', or McGregor's version of the 'all-pals-together' unitary frame of reference

*'I can't believe **that**!' said Alice. 'Can't you?' the Queen said in a pitying tone. 'Try again: draw a long breath, and shut your eyes.' Alice laughed. 'There's no use trying,' she said: 'one **can't** believe impossible things.' 'I daresay you haven't had much practice,' said the Queen. 'When I was your age, I always did it for half-an-hour a day. Why, sometimes I've believed as many as six impossible things before breakfast.'*

Lewis Carrol (1832–98)

10.1 All 'content' theories – of which 'self-actualizing man' is one – assume that the worker is obsessed

10.1.1 Table 6.3(a) on page 118 identified six responses to the question 'How are managers to motivate their workers?' Table 10.1(a) opposite re-lists these responses and adds further descriptive features in columns 3 and 4.

Table 10.1(a)

Column 1	Column 2	Column 3	Column 4
Response	*Vision of man*	*Source of pro-management – goal motivation*	*Category of theory*
first	Marxist man	none	none
second	Hoxie man	none	
third	economic man	money	'content' theories
fourth	social man	comradeship	
fifth	self-actualizing man	psychological growth	
sixth	political holon man	multiple reasons which shift with circumstance	'process' theory

10.1.2 We have discussed 'Marxist man' and 'Hoxie man'. Neither of these concepts accepts that the manager can bring the worker to adopt management's goals. Thus, by definition, neither accepts the 'motivation' is possible. We have also discussed 'economic man' and 'social man'. It will be seen in column 4 of Table 10.1(a) that these are both classified as 'content' theories. They each assume that the management/worker relationship will contain a certain commodity, (i.e. its 'content') which will bind the worker to management. From column 3 we can see that in the case of 'economic man' the commodity is assumed to be money and in the case of 'social man' to be comradeship.

10.1.3 The present chapter deals with the fifth response, which is that of 'self-actualizing man'. It will be seen from Table 10.1(a) that this is also a 'content' theory; though now the commodity which allegedly prompts the worker to fulfil management's goals is that of his own psychological growth.

10.1.4 There are so many inherent absurdities in the suggestion that any single commodity can have the effect of binding the worker to the firm that I find it difficult to know where to start my criticism. In practical terms the assumption that there exists such a possibility implies that the firm has some monopoly of supply. If this monopoly is not total then it assumes

(a) that the organization can hold its employees in ignorance of other sources, or
(b) that its position is secure because (among the alternative sources known to the employee) the organization represents the best source around.

Further practical difficulties stem from the fact that the organisation is socially, technologically, economically and politically constrained. Yet these constraints must neither

(c) prevent the commodity from being offered, nor
(d) impinge on the employee's perception of the commodity as an all-consuming need.

If they do, the content theory will not succeed in its purpose.

10.1.5 This brings us to the psychological difficulty which lies at the heart of every 'content' theory, irrespective of the commodity. *This is the obsessional attitude it ascribes to those who seek the commodity.* I maintain that anyone who was so obsessive would be very sick indeed. It is a view with which Mary Midgley would agree. She writes as follows (Midgley, 1984; p.146): '[O]bsession is a possibility for all of us, and a danger to many, because the balance of motives which we normally maintain is incomplete and insecure. But that it should not be a danger – that it should be a normal condition – is unimaginable in such a creature as man...the capacity to balance one's life, to relate one's aims, is essential to sanity and maturity'. And indeed, if we reflect on the matter, we can see that it was because Taylor attributed a money-obsessed nature to the employee that Michael Rose made the tart comment he did. For if the worker's obsessive desire for money really could cause him (without regret) to forego both his own creativity and all sense of social solidarity with his fellow workers, then he would indeed be (paragraph 4.1.11) 'a monstrosity: a greedy machine indifferent to its own pain and loneliness once given the power to maim and isolate itself'.

10.1.6 Nor was it because Mayo attributed social needs to the worker that Rose considered that these proposals reflected Mayo's 'corporate fascism'. No. What makes Mayo's ideas appear so is that he attributes to the worker a need to belong which is so obsessive that the worker's emotions will lead him to espouse the cause of any group which has exhibited social concern for him. In Mayo's assessment, the worker is therefore entirely vulnerable to capture. Mayo's aim is to create a social system which has the nesting properties of Russian dolls, Figure 10.1(a). The informal group captures the individual, and the firm captures the informal group. Subsequently, by its power to absorb totally the successively smaller dolls of the informal group and the individual, the firm eventually creates a closed system in which it is allegedly able to shape the perception of the worker to its own ends. It would do so by making the employee believe that there existed a paternalistic relationship towards him on the part of the firm.

Figure 10.1(a)

10.1.7 In fact, of course, Mayoism was never able to succeed in this, because the employee realized that no capitalist firm would ever go beyond a contractual relationship with him. Nor was he so overwhelmed by this 'paternalism' that he failed to see that trade union power was more likely to gain him better conditions than a policy of 'filial' piety to the management. This was why after a decade (roughly 1945 to 1955) the heyday of Mayoist 'togetherness' passed. Fewer company social clubs and works councils were formed and many of those which had previously existed now died. In the main they were unmourned by either side.

10.1.8 Even allowing for the ethos of that decade I find it surprising that so many intelligent managers should have failed to see what nonsense was contained in the unitarist concepts of Mayoism. For example, Wilfred Brown, although he was later to correct this, actually then thought that when managers dealt with grievances, they were not engaged in an 'executive role' but were assuming a 'judicial role' (Brown, 1965; p.270). Hidden within that belief was the presumption that the firm's policies were as impartial as the law is supposed to be, that the manager is as impartial as the judge, and that the 'appellant' (worker) would accept that impartiality as his means of obtaining justice: none of which is so. In practice the manager is committed to executing company policy, and (although policy which made no concessions whatever to the worker's sense of justice would be very silly) neither that policy, nor the manager's implementation of it is at all impartial.

10.1.9 So instead of making the assumption contained in all three 'content theories' of motivation, namely that it should be possible to win over the worker by granting him some commodity, let us try to see if there is any *a priori* reality which we must acknowledge and which any valid theory of motivation must be able to accommodate.

10.1.10 *The employee's position.* Every employee comes to a firm by means of a series of chance happenings and purposive acts. Like all of us, he is multi-faceted. He also comes with the influences of his genetic inheritance and the historical influences of his socialization to date. He has certain aspirations which may or may not be reasonable, and certain physical and psychological needs, the satisfaction of which may or may not be possible. If he is normal he is aware of international, national and local issues, and of the conflicts and alliances of the various factions in all three. He is aware of opportunities offered by other employers in similar or different occupations to his own. He is aware of the unemployed. He is aware of union activity and of politics and religion. He is, in short, aware of options, of factional interests (including his own), and he is aware that his interests and those of his firm are not identical. However, the fact that he is currently employed by the firm suggests that, for the moment, to a lesser or greater degree their different interests share some commonality. That is the status quo from which both sides must consider their position and from which management can begin to consider how to motivate the worker.

10.1.11 *The position of any manager who is not sole owner.* Each manager has a responsibility to his own conscience. This gives him the absolute right to resign from his firm if need be. It does not, in my opinion, give him the right to remain in the post and (with no mandate from the shareholders to do so) satisfy that conscience at the firm's expense. The essence of capitalism is (1) its contractual nature and (2) its *mores* (i.e. avoiding all unnecessary opportunity cost). **Put those two things together and it is clear that capitalist managers have a stewardship responsibility to review all relationships continually and dispassionately.** They do so to ensure that in fulfilling the firm's purposes they are using the least resources. With that as a constraint they have to decide whether (among the options open to them) it continues to be advantageous to offer employment to someone. In calculating this they have to consider the cost versus what they get for it. That are in effect asking:

(a) 'what are the minimal cost-effective inducements which will get the employee to stay with the firm?'
(b) 'will what he is expected to do (in terms of both his role and his performance of that role) be worth (a)?'.

In performing the calculations which result in this decision, the manager may first have entered into discussion with the worker or his representative, or he may have hypothesized the worker's reaction. *(In either case, whenever the social obligations of the firm towards its employees have become an issue, it can only be because they involve a greater opportunity cost than is believed by management to be the minimum. This does not mean that the management will not pay the difference. It does mean that the excess cost must be small or the dangers of social unrest high if the manager is to avoid the charge of misusing the shareholders' money.)*

10.1.12 *The interplay of these two positions.* The worker may accept the firm's offer, either because it is the best one around, or because he finds he has formed a social attachment to the company, or because he lacks the initiative to move. Alternatively he can try to improve the terms of the offer. Individuals whose skills are in short supply may demand better conditions under threat of leaving. The less-skilled or more socially minded may bring union pressure to bear to improve the offer. Whether he is gratified or disappointed by the offer, the worker is aware that the potential economic pressure he can apply to the firm is less than that which the firm can apply to him.

10.1.13 Within the reality of this background management cannot reasonably expect to get the employee to believe that his identity of interest with the firm is total. To attempt it would be both a forlorn hope and an act of questionable morality. Nevertheless, this is what all 'content theorists' sought to do...and to do by means of a single factor only (i.e. pay, social concern or psychological growth).

10.1.14 Let us consider pay as such a means. Pay may well induce workers to join the company and later to stay with it. Indeed (despite Herzberg's claims to the contrary), incentive payment schemes may motivate the worker to higher output. Nevertheless, it would be absurd to believe that a normal human being could become so obsessed with such payments that he would lose sight of all differences of interest between himself and his employer.

10.1.15 Indeed, the higher his pay, the higher must his output be if the cost per unit is to be kept competitive: so, the higher his pay, the more he increases his inherent risk and induces managerial pressure for work intensity. This threat may mean that (like the bank wiring room men) he will instead choose to join with his colleagues in restrictive practices. But to feel really secure, he needs some reassurance that similar restrictive practices will also occur in the other companies of the industry with which his firm operates (so reducing their competitiveness to the level of his own firm). It is this logic which creates the spread of industry-wide unions, such as the print union SOGAT. It also explains the frustration, anger and mass-picketing directed by such unions towards small, emergent non-unionized firms; a fury which seems, to the uninitiated, disproportionate. Yet, the importance of maintaining industry-wide control to reduce productivity is vital if the restrictive worker's company is to remain **relatively** competitive. The purpose of this pay example is not to comment upon the respective moralities of managements and their workers. It seeks only to illustrate how naïve it was of the Taylorites to suggest that large pay-cheques would cause the worker to discover an identity of interest between himself and the employer.

10.1.16 Yet what is true of pay is true of all such commodities. Management 'content' theorists have attempted to find an obsessive factor which will bind such a man to the company, either because the employer pays well, or expresses social concern, or offers room for growth. My argument has been that, irrespective of the factor chosen, these aims are doomed to failure.

10.1.17 Clearly this criticism applies to the neo-human relations school as much as any other. Yet so influential is that school that this basic flaw will not be sufficient to damn it. That will require the 'overkill' contained in the rest of this chapter and the Appendix. Even then there will be many who will remain caught in the emotional/intellectual log-jam which the ideas of that school have created in management theory and which are unfortunately well set to do the same in political and economic theory.

10.2 Maslow's 'hierarchy of needs' – the foundation of the 'neo-human relations' school

10.2.1 Among the many things that the worker brings to the firm with him, as I said in paragraph 10.1.10, are 'certain physical and psychological needs, the satisfaction of which may or may not be possible'. In 1954 a psychologist named Abraham H. Maslow published a book called *Motivation and Personality* which unintentionally, indirectly and on balance regrettably, left a more significant mark on management thought than any work since Taylor's. Maslow claimed that human needs fall into five basic categories. But the really significant point of his theory was his claim that they form a hierarchy in which the so-called 'lower needs' must be met before the so-called 'higher needs' become active. Maslow's book has no diagrammatic representation of this concept. Many management textbooks show the concept as a set of steps. My own preference is for the way it is shown in many other books (Figure 10.2(a)).

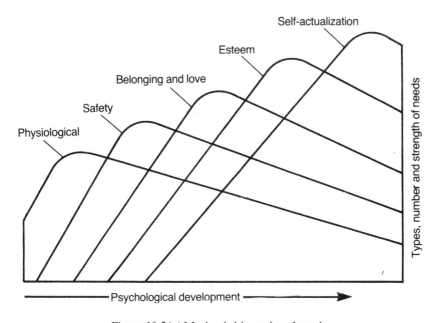

Figure 10.2(a) Maslow's hierarchy of needs

10.2.2 The diagram is read from left to right in which sequence it indicates the growth of the individual's psychological development. It is this view of 'growth' as essential to the human psyche and prepotent in the worker which is the essence of neo-human relations writers who base themselves upon Maslow. As we move from left to right we see that the first need sought by the developing personality is physiological, that is to say the basic requirements, from the air we breathe to the food we eat. I find it unlikely that anyone would disagree with this premise: deprivation of these needs would so concentrate the mind that all other needs would surely recede.

10.2.3 This highlights another point made by Maslow. Living in a relatively affluent Western society, I am able to eat regularly. Eating therefore is a pleasurable habit which is made the more so by the genius of a good cook. Yet I confess it is little more than a background to my life: between meals I seldom give food a thought. This is because we have no need to strive for what we have. Since my **physiological** needs are met, they are no longer motivators. The consequence is, according to Maslow, that I would become preoccupied with the next category in his 'hierarchy', namely the need for **safety**. When once that was secured I would move on to **belonging and love** then to **esteem** and finally to **self-actualization**, this need being to become what it lies within my capacity to become, i.e. self-fulfilment.

10.2.4 Could this theory ever be tested? I doubt it. If it can I certainly could not imagine by what means. Nor can Hunt and Hill (Dalton and Lawrence, 1971; p.338) for they point out that

> ...[Maslow's] original papers present very little empirical evidence in support of the theory and no research at all that tests the model in its entirety. Indeed Maslow argues that the theory is primarily a framework for future research. He also discusses at length some of the limitations of the model and readily admits that these needs may be unconscious rather than conscious. While Maslow discusses his model and its limitations in detail...McGregor [the writer who thought that he understood Maslow's ideas and who was the first to attempt to apply that vision to industrial management theory] gives the impression that the model can be accepted without question and also that it is fairly easy to apply. In truth the model is difficult to test, which is why there are so few empirical studies to either prove or refute the theory.

10.2.5 Is that sufficient to damn the theory? I think not. We must allow some latitude to our intuitive feelings about our own motivation and that of our fellow men. So, just as I accepted the primacy of physiological needs, I find the subsequent search for 'safety' and then for 'love' to be intuitively 'right'. I do so mainly because (a) safety, and (b) love are (a) the physical and (b) the emotional aspects of 'security'. It therefore makes sense that if we start with the physiological needs and move towards the 'spiritual' needs we should do so via first the physical and later the emotional aspects of security. Beyond this point I find Maslow far less convincing.

10.2.6 Maslow is correct when he says (1970; p.6) 'Science is based on human values and is itself a value system'. It is a sentiment which Bronowski echoed when he wrote (1973; p.436) 'Knowledge is not a loose-leaf notebook of facts. Above all, it is a responsibility for the integrity of what we are, primarily of what we are as ethical creatures.' It is a sentiment with which I concur. But it also raises problems, which Maslow acknowledges in the remainder of the above quotation, for he adds: 'However the only way we know of preventing contamination of our perception of nature, of society, or of ourselves, by human values, is to be very conscious of these values at all times, to understand their influence on our perception, and with the aid of such understanding to make the necessary corrections.'

10.2.7 Unfortunately, Maslow did not heed his own advice. To avoid cluttering the main text of this book with evidence of Maslow's ideology I have put it in the Appendix. There I claim that, for Maslow, this 'hierarchy of needs' was not just, nor even primarily, the sequence in which the human psyche developed. It was a concept which also placed the needs in a hierarchy of moral worth. The physical needs are the lowest. They are essential to life and were accepted by Maslow as basic. The next-to-lowest needs are those of 'safety'. These Maslow regards as unhealthy because they tend to inhibit self-actualization. As I explain in the Appendix, his ideal society is clearly élitist in character, and indeed echoes the morality of Nietzsche. The highest virtue is possessed by those whose will-to-achieve is so great that nothing (not even compassion and consideration for others) can deflect them from their purpose. **In such a world, there can only be peace if sufficient 'space' has been left to the achiever by the non-achiever**. So the last thing that such a creed can be is democratic. It is therefore not only ironic that a thorough-going democrat, Douglas McGregor, should have found in Maslow's propositions the raw materials of 'industrial democracy': it is a monument to tunnel vision.

10.3 A pyramid of fallacies: the work of Douglas McGregor

10.3.1 Douglas McGregor would never have seen Maslow's connection with Nietzschean concepts. To do so one would have to worry about Maslow's inconsistencies. Yet McGregor gave no indication of having noticed these. McGregor thought that he was interpreting Maslow. He was only interpreting Douglas McGregor. What they said sounded the same: what they meant was worlds apart. Without McGregor the management world would never have heard of Maslow. But Maslow gave McGregor intellectual credibility: and, in management circles, McGregor gave Maslow fame. Despite McGregor's message being backed by no research, and a philosophy he had failed to understand, the world was waiting to hear the message he offered. Taylorism had been too authoritarian for most tastes, and Mayo's promise that management could manipulate the norms of non-rational workers had foundered upon the inherent rationality of the informal group's self-interest. A new initiative was required, and McGregor supplied it. Although I shall attempt to show that McGregor's neo-human relations concepts were used for devious purposes, this was never his intention.

10.3.2 Far from being intentionally devious, the neo-human relations theme seems to me to be based upon no more than the fear of conflict inherent in the work of the sociologist Talcott Parsons and to be essentially an extension of it. Both Parsons and McGregor saw conflict as socially undesirable. The fact that this attitude also tends to legitimize the existing system (in that solutions are thereafter only sought from **within** the framework of the existing system) is sheer accident. The fact that it tends also to make revolt against the existing system illegitimate is also accidental. In the light of this naïvety it would be beyond the neo-human relations writers to be as cold-bloodedly devious as is the model that I shall next present. In any case it is just not possible to read either Maslow or McGregor without forming the opinion that they are basically good men and well-intentioned. I find it difficult to imagine that either they, or the many people who have adopted their ideas, would be as consciously manipulative as the next passage might suggest. No. it is **their** idealism that blinds them to the following implications. It is **my** idealism, after having **seen** the following implications, that makes me have reservations about the neo-human relations school's position.

10.3.3 My one regret in attacking the neo-human relations position is that I did not do so sooner. I had long seen the Machiavellian possibilities for exploitation that it contained, and which I shall explain. I earlier felt that it would do more harm than good to illuminate these aspects and thereby encourage their cynical use. The position that I now adopt is that publication will only inhibit such exploitation. Moreover there were two other considerations. Firstly, the inherently unitary concept that the neo-human relations model contains **has warped and largely halted the growth of genuine ethical concepts of organization and of motivation based upon pluralism.** Secondly, there are many people, particularly since the *Bullock Report*, whose instinct has been to oppose the unitary concept of McGregor: but having done so they are left with a vague sense of guilt. They should not reproach themselves. **Challenging the neo-human relations approach is not the same as spitting in Church.**

10.3.4 The first devious element that most people sense is that the neo-human relations approach seems to question the right of the informal group to **resist**, on occasion, the aims of management. Most people seek to safeguard this right. By contrast, Taylor did not, for he regarded the restrictive practices of such groups as plainly dishonest. Such conduct cheated the employer, but more significantly, it cheated society also, and not least it cheated the poor (paragraph 7.1.22). In Taylor's view 'scientific' managers were crusaders against ignorance, acting in the service of mankind. Yet that has never been the most persuasive of viewpoints, whatever truth it might contain. A more popular interpretation saw workers as an economically disadvantaged class who were attempting to redress the balance of a society in which the depredations of technocratic exploitive managements served the interests of the wealthy. Against such attacks the group was **morally justified in standing firm and the Schmidts of this world were traitors who sold out their own kind**. One didn't have to be a Marxist to sense that there was enough truth in this imagery to make many people question Taylorism.

10.3.5 The first thing that the neo-human relations approach does is to disorientate the worker completely. For years he has been protesting about instrumental repetitive, 'alienative' work. Now along comes a group of managers agreeing that he was right so to object, and that he should be allowed to 'self-actualize' by accepting more responsibility for his own actions.

10.3.6 This creates an emphasis upon the rights of the individual to develop to the best of his ability, and thereby makes it immoral for anyone, *manager or fellow-worker*, to interfere with that growth. At a stroke management has placed itself in the position of being 'in' the group, and has placed moral limits upon the rights of the group to impose its norms on its members.

10.3.7 The next stage is to propose that **active participation** should be engaged in by both worker and management. This is because, since both sides are in the same boat, no legitimate cause for conflict remains: for the success of the company is vital to both parties. Differences that arise cannot therefore be real, but must be the result of misunderstanding. This throws the worker completely, for two reasons. Firstly, he is thrown because it is an appeal to co-operation rather than confrontation. He may be suspicious of the fact that such an appeal has come from the other 'side' of industry, but he cannot gainsay the sentiment. Even those who, like myself, see in the aspirations of the various Utopias an implicit guarantee of future tyranny, can nevertheless be moved deeply as Beethoven's music thunders out Schiller's words, *'Aller Menschen werden Brüder'* ('All men will be brother'). The worker also longs for this universal brotherhood.

10.3.8 Secondly, it has within it a large element of truth. There is, for example, a symbiotic relationship between trade unions and capitalism; a symbiosis which is the despair of those who would prefer **revolution** to **evolution**. Notwithstanding these two concessions the worker feels that, in accepting this apparently 'reasonable' approach, he is in some way selling his birthright. On the other hand, to refuse the proffered hand seems downright churlish. It is no wonder then that 'participation' has become a perplexing business for him.

10.3.9 Yet academics did not have the same right to be perplexed. As long ago as 1951, H.A. Clegg made abundantly clear the reason why, however amenable the individual worker might be in his dealings with management, his trade union should protect his interest by refusing 'active participation'. This is a full nine years before McGregor. Clegg said (McCarthy, 1972; pp.84–85):

> ...'active participation' slips so easily into the assumption of a common purpose and thence to some mystical 'general will'. Then those whose actions and ideas seem contrary to the 'general will' are regarded as evil and soon suppressed as disrupters of the common purpose. So that the last state of the democracy of participation is indistinguishable from totalitarianism...we cannot for these reasons, accept 'active participation' based as it must be, if anarchism is avoided, on managerial leadership, as a full and adequate definition of industrial democracy. We must also include the trade union as an **opposition** body which, **however beneficent the employer**, however eager he may be to carry his workers along with him in everything that affects them, **can never be absorbed into an organic industrial order: for if it is absorbed, where is the guarantee for democracy?** (My emphasis.)

10.3.10 Clegg's argument, which gives trade unions the moral right to stand in perpetual opposition to management, is irrefutable to my mind. In parliament there is a need of, and consequently there should be respect for, the views of the Opposition. 'Her Majesty's Loyal Opposition' is a most happy turn of phrase for that parliamentary institution. The institution of the trade union deserves as much respect, and for precisely the same reason.

10.3.11 Allan Flanders claims that the political Right Wing look upon trade unions as being... 'there to act as a kind of social police force – to keep the chaps in order and the wheels of industry turning', and he quotes Michael Shanks's amusingly ironic image of the trade union leader's main responsibility, [which], to judge from the sort of comment one reads in the press and hears from middle-class lips, is to 'keep his chaps in line' or 'knock some sense into them'...In practical terms, the main function of a union leader according to this view is to deter his members from putting in ambitious wage claims, stop them going on strike and behaving in other anti-social ways, and encourage them to work harder and increase their productivity... Having done all that, he can gracefully retire with a peerage. (McCarthy, 1972; p.19).

10.3.12 Shank's imagery, claims Flanders, 'has amusingly characterized, and only slightly caricatured, this view'. In this assessment I believe that Flanders is right. However, a corresponding attitude from the trade-union side also exists. It is moreover, as amusing a characterization, is not in the least a caricature, and is very frequently seen on television. 'We', says the trade unionist, 'are always prepared to negotiate. We would stop our strike action today if the management say they are also prepared to negotiate.' 'But' says the interviewer 'the management also say that the are prepared to negotiate.' 'No, they are not!', says the trade unionist, 'If they really were prepared to negotiate they would agree to our just demands.'

10.3.13 In Shanks's imagery and in mine, both parties are engaging in pompous moralizing. I do not mean by this that they are being consciously hypocritical, nor that their proposals may not seem to them to be eminently 'fair'. But there is surely an element of oily self-righteousness in seeking to portray your opponent as morally reprehensible because (in the process of resisting **your** coercion) he has caused inconvenience to third parties. Morality, it would seem, consists of giving in to your coercion and accepting your terms for the good of all.

10.3.14 The conclusion I draw, and which I invite the reader to share with me, is that justice is a two-edged sword. The 'right' that guarantees the legitimacy of the union position when they oppose management is the same right that legitimizes the management when they resist the coercion of trade unions.

10.3.15 But having said this and having agreed that both parties have the right to reserve their position, a life of internecine conflict between management and labour would be hell on Earth. It would also be a severe handicap to the commercial prosperity of the firm and its chances of survival. So the impulse towards a life of industrial accord cannot be bad in its intent, nor would it be in practice, providing that

(a) the ensuing philosophy did not, either by statement or inference, deny the right of both parties to disagree; and

(b) the philosophy did not use morality as a weapon, by suggesting that the motivation of the other in the disagreement was essentially base. For this too would be a subtle means of arguing that the right of the party in question to his position had been vitiated.

In his search for industrial peace, Douglas McGregor came to violate both these provisions. He did so by implication from the position that he adopted, a position which, moreover, was based upon fundamental fallacies.

10.3.16 I doubt whether he was aware of many of these fallacies. Why should he have been? Nobody else appeared to be so. They were not apparently noticed when in 1960 he published *The Human Side of Enterprise*. Neither were they noticed some seventeen years later, even though the rejection then in Britain of the *Bullock Report* was a rejection of the ultimate implications of McGregor. But that rejection was made with an air of sullen guilt. Still no one had seen the fallacies in McGregor. They did not even see the modelling in the word 'participation' under which the fallacies were buried. This was why they were guilt-laden. But they were also angry: for they could **sense that they had somehow been put in the false position described in paragraph 2.3.20**.

10.3.17 Even stronger than any sense of guilt was the sense of outrage. For McGregor's fallacies were **felt**. **That** is basically why the *Bullock Report* was rejected by pluralists on both sides of industry. Peace may be difficult or impossible to obtain when the parties are honest about their differences. Yet the situation can surely only be made worse by the introduction of falsehood into the proceedings. To my mind, this is true irrespective of whether that falsehood is introduced inadvertently, or deliberately (even with the best of intentions).

10.3.18 The fallacies in McGregor (1960) start in earnest with the introduction to his third chapter. In that chapter he depicts the assumptions which he claims are held by 'traditional' managers. These have since become renowned as the 'Theory X' assumptions and they are listed in paragraph 10.3.25. 'Traditional' is not a completely neutral word. When it is used about culinary dishes or folk-dancing it is positively loaded: these are things that have stood the test of time. When it is used about managers it implies 'out-of-date' and is therefore derogatory in tone. So it will be noticed that already an insidious element of blackmail has crept in. If a manager wants to maintain such a position he is aware of a certain stigma associated with doing so. To be fair to McGregor he does not complete the inference by calling the 'Theory Y' assumptions 'modern'. That is left to be done by others. They do not disappoint him.

10.3.19 Caplan, for example, contrasts 'behavioural assumptions of **"Traditional"** Management Accounting Model of the firm' (Bruns and DeCoster, 1969; p.118), which are based upon 'Theory X', with 'some behavioural assumptions from **Modern** Organization Theory' (p.122) which are based upon 'Theory Y'. Moreover, although Caplan puts 'Traditional' in inverted commas, the word 'Modern' has none: a very subtle endorsement.

10.3.20 But let us return to McGregor and his most major fallacy. It starts by taking a potential truism and distorting it. This is the truism contained in the ideas expressed in paragraph 1.3.4, namely that *in the very act of managing, the manager demonstrates that he is a theorist who holds certain beliefs about how-the-world-is.* Let us see what McGregor does with this truism.

10.3.21 He says (McGregor, 1960; p.33) 'Beyond every managerial decision or action are assumptions about human nature and human behaviour.' Now this is clearly untrue. Many management decisions are based solely upon assumptions about inanimate material. However, let us not carp. Although this is a false statement, its only real significance is that it warns us of further possible lapses to come.

10.3.22 Clearly many management decisions **are** based upon assumptions about human nature and behaviour. During a year when the kapok harvest seemed likely to be poor, I bought a large tonnage at current prices for much later delivery to my firm. My actions were not based simply upon fear of scarcity but fear of the price rise that I assumed that scarcity would bring. I had made certain assumptions about the market which were based upon human nature. Is this McGregor's point? Not a bit.

10.3.23 What he is referring to is Maslow's preoccupation with the 'good' and 'evil' in human nature. Here again we meet a lapse in the rigour of his argument but this time it is not a negligible aberration: it is a lapse at the very core of the position that he adopted. Nietzsche's thought had been centred on the **individual**. He didn't really care whether society worked or not. He didn't even care whether people suffered or not. Russell imagined Nietzsche and Buddha in argument: 'Why go about snivelling because trivial people suffer?' Nietzsche asks, '...trivial people suffer trivially, great men suffer greatly, and great sufferings are not to be regretted because they are noble.' (Russell, 1979; p.738.) Maslow cared, but he also dreamed of an élitist society with a natural 'Taoistic' symbiosis between the 1 per cent who were striving and the 99 percent who weren't: utopian nonsense, it is true, but theoretically possible, providing both sides could bear to leave the other in peace.

10.3.24 McGregor, on the other hand, was essentially a democratic liberal. He took Maslow's neo-Nietzschian, tentative and élitist view of a utopian future and recognized it for what it wasn't: a firm blueprint for the nuts and bolts of democratic/liberal organizations in the here and now. Maslow's theory became McGregor's dogma. In McGregor's case the 'perfectability' model was not a symbiosis between strivers and non-strivers. Even if he had seen Maslow's model in this light, his democratic concepts would have not permitted him to accept such a Utopia. No: for McGregor **everyone** was a striver (as the democratic principle demanded), but they all strove in happy accord. This was because the worker and the manager had identical goals. It was true that not all enterprises showed these characteristics, but **that was the fault of the management**. Their low expectation of the worker generated in the worker the response it deserved.

10.3.25 These 'traditional' managers by their decisions and actions had demonstrated certain negative assumptions about human nature to which McGregor gave the name of 'Theory X'. These assumptions McGregor claimed are also evident

> in most of the literature of organization and in much current managerial policy and practice, [namely that]:
> 1. The average human being has an inherent dislike of work and will avoid it if he can...
> 2. Because of this human characteristic of dislike of work, most people must be coerced, controlled, directed, threatened with punishment to get them to put forth adequate effort toward the achievement of organizational objectives...
> 3. The average human being prefers to be directed, wishes to avoid responsibility, has relatively little ambition, wants security above all. (McGregor, 1960; pp.33–34).

10.3.26 Moreover, says McGregor, it isn't only motivational theory concepts that illustrate these assumptions: '...the principles of organization which comprise the bulk of the literature of management could only have been derived from assumptions such as those of theory X.' (McGregor, 1960; p.35).

10.3.27 This dreadful nonsense, this claim that hierarchical structures, co-ordination and control are not really necessary, but are simply the reflection of pathological attitudes within management, has been the inspiration for a tremendous amount of similar naïve literature. For example, the common belief now is that 'centralization' is paternalistic and bad, 'decentralization' is democratic and good. As Luthans says (1981; p.524) 'management writers and practitioners generally favour decentralization. It is one of the "in" concepts and identifies the advocate as a modern thinking theorist or practitioner. Centralization has taken on the connotation of being traditional and even authoritarian.' However, the appeal of McGregor goes beyond the opportunity it affords to show others that one is 'modern'. Koestler (1975a; p.307) has pointed out that watching the illusions on a stage or cinema screen has a cathartic effect. It enables the watcher to free himself from his personal anxieties and by identification with the *personae* in the play or film to achieve a certain self-transcendence which is very peaceful. Yet, as Koestler points out, the **stimuli of the illusions are all we buy** when we buy a ticket at the box office. **It is we ourselves that supply everything else.** I tend to think that the appeal of McGregor is similar. Those who buy a ticket to his illusion of a possible world without conflict come to experience freedom from their past perceptions. They thereby enter into a self-transcendent state in which they identify with the images that he has projected. The cinema is safer, however. Having aroused our dormant self-transcendent potentials and having provided them with an outlet, they can die away and we can return to reality. If we use McGregor's images for the same purpose we are likely not to recognize where reality ends and illusion begins. Let us consider some of his illusions.

10.3.28 '[T]he trends in some companies toward recentralization after the postwar wave of decentralization [is an assertion] that people will only work under extreme coercion and control.' (McGregor, 1960; p.34.) Of the many things wrong with this statement, I'll offer just two. Firstly, it isn't true. There has been a tendency for certain functions to become more centralized while others have become more decentralized and both have happened for very good reasons not at all related to 'human nature'. Secondly, the image that it gives – that there is some sort of leverage effect, whereby the strength of the coercion is multiplied by the distance through which that force is applied – is rather silly.

10.3.29 But I am beginning to fall into the same trap which McGregor himself did, namely to talk of such things in the abstract against a set of vague images. I haven't even specified what I mean by 'decentralization' or 'centralization' because that is part of our study of organizational structure. What I wish the reader to do is to register that *McGregor could find no reasons for practising 'centralization' other than that the management in question had a low regard for human nature.* **We shall do rather better than that** (paragraphs 14.2.1 to 14.2.10).

10.3.30 Nevertheless, before we go on to a consideration of organizational structures and their operation, let us look at the reasons why McGregor criticized 'Theory X'. He did so because he felt that organizations should be able to implement another set of assumptions that he called 'Theory Y'. Nor would he have any validity to adopt the moralizing stance that he did against 'Theory X' managers unless he had thought that the 'Theory Y' concepts were capable of widespread application. (We do not take up a moralizing attitude about someone's behaviour unless we believe he had an option which he should have taken.)

10.3.31 In each of the following paragraphs I shall list McGregor's 'Theory Y' assumptions and consider how universally applicable are the preconditions which would make his assumptions a viable basis for organizational theory. (All are taken from McGregor, 1960; pp.47–48).

10.3.32 '**Assumption 1.** The expenditure of physical and mental effort in work is as natural as play or rest. The average human being does not inherently dislike work. Depending upon controllable conditions, work may be a source of satisfaction (and will be voluntarily performed) or a source of punishment (and will be avoided if possible).'

Comment: Let us agree with the sentiment. What does the word 'controllable' mean? Does it mean that management **could** enrich all work if only they **chose** to do so? But there are a myriad reasons why this is not true. The things that I said about the difficulty of enriching work on special-purpose machines (Section 4.2) and general purpose machines (Section 4.3) will do to disprove the point. If such 'enrichment' is not achievable, then how can the situation be 'controllable'? Yet if it is not 'controllable', why should we **not** expect some work to be a 'source of punishment'?

10.3.33 '**Assumption 2.** External control and threat of punishment are not the only means for bringing about effort toward organizational objectives. Man will exercise self-direction and self-control in the service of objectives to which he is committed.'

Comment: Agreed. But this is **not** the same as saying everyone in the organization will share the management goals, or that management should adopt the workers' goals (assuming that these are homogeneous and **not** those of one worker versus those of another), or that compromise goals are always there to be found by men of good will. Why does McGregor make the point negatively? Is it because its hollow nature would be perceived if he said it positively? Let's say it for him. 'No organization need in any circumstances apply either external control or coercion to achieve its goals.' Does the reader believe this? Does McGregor believe this? In the large print he answers 'Yes': in the small print 'No': 'In terms of existing views...individuals seeking their own goals...would lead to anarchy, chaos, irreconcilable conflicts of self-interest, lack of responsibility, inability to make decisions, and failure to carry out those that were made.' (1960; p.53). So McGregor cannot be said to have misunderstood the problem. By the wording of his caveat, 'in terms of existing views', he tries to imply that it is primarily **a lack of management will** that stands in the way of finding common ground between management and employee. This implication parallels the assumptions of Sirota and Wolfson that the lack of management will is all that prevents the successful implementation of job-enrichment (paragraph 4.1.22). I trust that Sections 4.2 and 4.3, (which are not the entire argument against their views) were sufficient to convince the reader that Sirota and Wolfson's assumptions are wrong. So is McGregor's implication: and he knows it. The organization, via its management, has the right to seek its legitimate goals. If the workforce will co-operate, fine. If the workforce requires those goals to be modified in order to match their own goals, that may also be possible. But the time may come when the management can go no further without renouncing their stewardship duties. This sticking point is something that McGregor's intellectual honesty eventually forces him to admit is legitimate. In a key sentence (1960; p.56) he says this: '**Nevertheless, it is clear that authority is an appropriate means for control under certain circumstances – particularly where genuine commitment cannot be achieved.**' It is not much of a disclaimer in a book which is wholly devoted to another emphasis. However, I suppose the more questionable feature of his presentation is that although he is prepared to tell his readers that coercion is a sure sign that the manager holds 'Theory X' assumptions, yet he does not choose to spell out with equal emphasis that coercion is also sometimes necessary for 'Theory Y' managers. Had he done so, his simplistic message would have been watered down, but he would have been also nearer the truth.

10.3.34 'Assumption 3. Commitment to objectives is a function of the rewards associated with the achievement. The most significant of such rewards, e.g. the satisfaction of ego and self-actualization needs, can be direct products of effort directed toward organizational objectives.'

Comment: This statement as it stands is true. My son's comment that he would pay them to let him do the job he is doing is evidence of this. But is that **all** McGregor is saying? No it is not. He clearly wants us to believe, from the rest of his text, that such efforts **would** be directed towards the organization's goals if the chance were given. Moreover, if we had any doubt of this, McGregor's next assumption is worded in such a way as to support this latter interpretation. Here it is.

10.3.35 'Assumption 4. The average human being learns, under proper conditions, not only to accept, but to seek responsibility. Avoidance of responsibility, lack of ambition, and emphasis on security are generally consequences of experience, not inherent human characteristics.'

Comment: The modelling is extremely confused here. In some respects I think McGregor has deliberately made it so. In others I think he cannot correct the errors because he does not see them. I think he sees, but disguises, the 'unitary' assumptions it contains. If someone dislikes my policies, and so refuses to carry them through, I do not take that to be a sign of 'irresponsibility'. What else can he do than attempt to frustrate me if he is to be 'responsible' and true to his beliefs. So if I am unconvinced that he shares my goals it is common prudence for me to limit his power to frustrate my achievement of them. *It does not constitute a judgement by me upon his sense of 'responsibility' in general, nor when he is serving another cause.* McGregor (1960; p.56) admits as much. Yet this does not deter him from presenting the issues in this distorted way. So why does he persist in this travesty? The answer is, I think, because he has adopted two linked 'liberal' fallacies which are very widespread. The first is that people are fundamentally 'good'. (This is the humanist reaction to the ambivalence of Christianity which sees us as both 'built in the image of God'... yet 'flawed'.) However it is the second fallacy which makes him so dangerous. This is that all men of goodwill have an identity of interest. **McGregor never legitimizes conflict.** The other modelling his thought contains is Maslow's neo-Nietzschean ideas. He tends therefore to imply that not to strive is **improper** since it is a denial of the will. Maslow put needs for 'status' (esteem) and 'self-actualization' above the 'love' needs. As I said earlier, it seems clear that this is not simply Maslow's view of the **sequence** in which these needs emerge, but also a comment upon their **worth** in Maslow's eyes. Well, from a neo-Nietzschean, although this is a highly subjective judgement, it is also a logically consistent one. But it is a very strange judgement indeed for a democrat like McGregor to make. Clearly some people will resist promotion because they feel that the acquisition of 'status' over their fellows will cut them off from 'love'. Maslow would find this a sign of poor psychological health: nothing should inhibit the Will. *But should McGregor see it in the same way, given his attitude to people?* I conclude that McGregor just hasn't recognized the implicit selfish élitism in Maslow. Of course it is arguable that McGregor thought that the best democracy is universal élitism: but the egocentric dynamism of neo-Nietzcheans is not conducive to democratic society. I think McGregor just didn't see any of these implications.'

10.3.36 'Assumption 5. The capacity to exercise a relatively high degree of imagination, ingenuity, and creativity in the solution of organizational problems is widely, not narrowly, distributed in the population.'

Comment: Agreed, and it is just as well that it is so in the case of such companies as the one described by Kidder and discussed earlier (paragraphs 3.1.25 to 3.1.32). But the above statement implies that the main problem of management is to find enough creative people. This is quite true in some cases. **But the big problem of most managements is how to achieve economic viability without boring the employees to death. Nobody would guess this from McGregor's wording.** He invites us to see managements as hoarding the interesting bits, or deliberately and wantonly making the employee's job boring. He invites us to conclude that they only do so from their improper perceptions of humanity. This is another fallacy. It is this fallacy that breeds a further one, namely, that given sufficient management will to act, 'job-enrichment' is possible on a widespread scale.

10.4 The manager and McGregorism

10.4.1 Although the concept of 'self-actualizing man' resulted from the accidental interaction of Maslow's and McGregor's respective visions, American and European managements were already predisposed to welcome the development. It had become clear to them that the informal group was no more manipulable than it had been in Taylor's time. Taylor's answer had been to refuse to acknowledge the group, and, in effect, to bribe the individual into accepting a social split. But the crudeness of these methods and the baseness in their purpose were undeniable. Neither the crudeness nor the baseness were erased even if the net result **did** benefit society in general and give material prosperity to the worker in question. Both these gains had been at the cost of the worker's autonomy and, many claimed, of his humanity.

10.4.2 Managers who had turned from Taylorism to Mayoism found Mayoism failed them. The group had not proved to be the malleable, emotive, non-rational creature of Mayo's imaginings. Perhaps this was only to be expected, for to be honest, neither had they, as employers, been able to fulfil the social obligations that the firm would need to adopt if it were to be as feudal as it would need to be in order to play Mayo's role for it; namely that of extended family.

10.4.3 So if, at that stage, managers had been able to specify the general requirements of what the next attempt at motivation theory should provide, I suggest that they would have prescribed the following characteristics:

(1) It should allow a return to dealing with the individual, rather than the group, but in a manner that appeared noble and to which the group could not make any legitimate objection.

(2) It should be an amalgam which preserved for the firm the most advantageous properties of Taylorism and Mayoism while limiting their disadvantageous elements. So, on the one hand the theory should call upon the employee to return to self-reliance and the protestant work ethic, yet this self-reliance should not make him so independent that the firm lost him. Logically, the result of making this a condition would be to seek some assurance that the employee would not be able to develop this new-found self-reliance except through his work in the company. Lastly, since the company could not enter into a feudal relationship with the employee, the employee ought not to expect that it would, nor should his commitment to the company be diminished by this lack of reciprocity.

Whether this specification had been written by a 'liberal-democratic' manager, or by a so-called 'hard-nosed' manager would have changed the emphasis of the specification from idealism to cynicism. but it would not have changed the basic demands. Although it would always have been absurd to expect any theory to satisfy such an unrealistically demanding specification, the neo-human relations approach seemed to do exactly that. *(Of course, my whole point is that it did not – nor could it do – any such thing. But it does go a long way to explain why experienced managers, from every sector of capitalism's political spectrum, should have welcomed it with open arms.)*

10.4.4 So, valid or not, the 'hard-nosed' manager could find the strongly élitist tendencies of Maslow and thereby confirm his own conviction that old-fashioned 'get-up-and-go' was the highest virtue that anyone could possess...even if it were now called 'self-actualization'. Similarly, valid or not, the liberal democrat could find McGregor's democratic concepts, which confirmed what he had always known, which was that anyone who behaves 'immaturely' or 'irresponsibly' does not do so because of any inherent shortcoming but because of adverse social conditioning.

10.4.5 Both had separate reasons for agreeing that, if 'self actualization' were to occur at all, then it must occur at the workplace. The hard-nosed manager agreed because to do otherwise would be to infer that people could self-actualize anywhere they chose: in which case, what would be left to bind them to the company? Besides, 'get-up-and-go' meant the Protestant work ethic. It didn't mean pursuing some sort of pastime, however pleasant. The liberal democrat had different reasons for agreeing. If the worker had it in his power to self-actualize elsewhere, then what became of his liberal theory that worker indifference and hostility found their origins in society's conditioning and not in him? Apart from which, even if managements could not assume their social obligations to the worker in a Mayoite way, that was no reason for denying the worker more autonomy. So both ends of the management spectrum could agree that the workplace was essentially where self-actualization must occur, and both declared (either from conviction or from cynicism) *impoverished work creates impoverished leisure.*

10.4.6 The neo-human relations link between 'achievement' and psychological health could also be used cynically or in good faith. In either case, a great deal was expected of the worker. This situation satisfied the hard-nosed manager's need for high performance levels by which to improve the company's efficiency. It also satisfied the liberal democrat's wish to enrich the worker's psychological development.

10.4.7 I am not suggesting for one moment that the neo-human relations writers recognized at the beginning that their theories encouraged 'hard' or 'soft' usage, and certainly I do not imagine they recognized that their claims were false. Partly, this was because those few experiments which they had performed (mostly in the area of 'job-enrichment') encouraged them to think that they were on the right track, for they often achieved a very positive reaction from the workforce. Nevertheless, this optimism resulted from their not having thought the problem through. For, by attaching the significance that they did to these results they illustrate their fallacious assumption that 'gradualism' would get them to where they wanted to go. By that I mean that they hoped, by the patient building of one stone of trust upon another, to make a sequence of evolutionary changes, which would be revolutionary in their aggregate impact. So each small gain in achieving worker co-operation seemed a step nearer that goal. The only remaining problem was that they had not yet travelled far enough along this road.

10.4.8 *Thus their very achievements hid from them the realization that the worker could not join a fully integrated worker/management team unless he made at some stage a 'quantum leap' on to management's plane of perception. Not only that, for the worker to make this 'quantum leap' required him to be blind to all the social and technological constraints upon the individual which are inherent in all hierarchies, and also to ignore the fact that a capitalist management's attachment to him was contractual and ambivalent.*

10.4.9 How could the neo-human relations writers have adopted all these errors? Largely it resulted from their ideology, but other factors also intervened. We have already seen how language ensnared them, so that they did not recognize the semantic trap contained in their favourite word – 'participation'. Nor did they recognize how false were their assumptions about 'hierarchy'. They assumed that it meant only an organization imbued with a particular right-wing ethos: an ethos, moreover, which was in two senses arbitrary. They thought it was (1) arbitrary in the sense that it produced inappropriate decisions, and (2) arbitrary because it was unnecessary. *They were wrong on both counts.* As if this were not enough, their academic discipline failed to make them aware of the technical and economic problems that stood between them and the achievement of a harmony of interests. I do not mean by that to imply that I believe that all conflict is primarily linked to technological or even economic factors. Nevertheless, one does not need to be a Marxist to admit that such considerations do add a further dimension to the problem.

10.4.10 So, I would argue that the neo-human relations school's hopes of 'gradualism' were doomed before they started, and their limited successes served only to whet an appetite which they had no hope of satisfying. For if we consider their ultimate claims and aspirations, they demanded the complete transformation of human nature: a transformation which, if it were **indeed** to satisfy full-blown McGregorism, would (and still will) need to be as total as that for which the Marxist yearns.

10.4.11 It has been the inherent impossibility of ever achieving full-blown McGregorism that has caused the neo-human relations movement to separate into two streams with lesser objectives. Possibly because both streams still use a common vocabulary, the fact that the movement **has** streamed seems to have gone unnoticed in the literature. Yet despite their common vocabulary it is the manner in which each stream emphasizes one aspect and de-emphasizes another which enables us to identify that streaming **has** occurred. So we have the irony that at the very time when the whole McGregorist movement has proved its inadequacy, it has never been so influential, nor does this influence show any sign of abating.

10.4.12 It is useful to regard full-blown McGregorism as a mainstream which has come to a delta. Here it has split into two main branches. These branches represent the different emphases of two distinct groups:

(1) Those that accept that the capitalist firm cannot make neo-feudal long-term commitments to its workers and that 'participation' only means some degree of involvement (such as job-enrichment) which is contained within a framework that accepts capitalist *mores* as paramount.

(2) Those who assume that 'participation' means that the present workforce, having invested their lives in the firm, have a right to information about the future. Further, they should have the institutional power to block any move in which the long-term commercial interests of the firm appear to be taking precedence over their workers' short-term interests.

10.4.13 Clearly the main emphasis of (1) has been in the USA, while the main emphasis of (2) has been in Europe. Indeed, I sometimes think that the European tendency of referring to American unions, somewhat disparagingly, as 'business unions' is meant to deny that they have the same social conscience as European unions. *The truth of the matter is, I think, that American unions are more inhibited by the sheer logic of operating within capitalism than are their European counterparts, who are still trailing completely impossible dreams of a capitalism that is nevertheless neo-feudal in character.* Indeed, it is clear that this is precisely why British trade unions don't know what their position is. For if management are placed in an ambivalent position by capitalism, it is nothing to the ambivalence felt by the unions. It is small wonder therefore that each successive Trades Union Congress secretary should have

> 'developed some sense of irony and resignation which goes with the job, as they sit up on the dais at the annual conference, listening to the demagogues and wondering where their movement is going. "What are we here for?" asked Woodcock in 1962. "When we know, then we can talk about the kind of structure that will enable us to do what we are here for." ' (Sampson, 1982; pp.59–60).

10.4.14 Let us return to the aftermath of McGregorism in America. It is interesting to see the subtle ways in which the literature uses the hidden modelling of language to sweep under the carpet and so out of our consciousness the fact that the firm cannot be socially committed to the worker.

10.4.15 One of the cleverest subterfuges in doing this is to talk about the firm as a 'team'. In my experience this is particularly a device used by 'hard-nosed' management, though it slips almost unbidden into the everyday usage of all managements. Its effect is to make it appear reasonable to expect more loyalty from the employee than the firm will reciprocate.

10.4.16 We have seen many times throughout this book the hidden modelling of language, but this use of the word 'team' is one of the most interesting. A sports arena is rather like a stage: it is a separate world, a closed system with its own norms. It is not a place for you to bring your personal problems. The team player is expected to forget, for the time that he is on the field, all the worries about money and his wife's health that kept him awake all night. But that is a negative requirement. The positive requirement is that while the player is 'on the team' he adopts unquestioningly the rules of the game. The rules are not there to be challenged, but to challenge the player. Consequently he doesn't ask why a seemingly rational person should attempt to get a certain ball over a certain line, but accepts a set of arbitrary rules which make the act more difficult, just as he also accepts the assumption that 'teamwork' means total internal co-operation.

10.4.17 Consciously or not, an American colleague who slapped me on the back, pumped my hand and welcomed me 'aboard' and 'on to the team' was conveying all of these nuances. Being 'on the team' means that you play by the rules. Being 'on the team' means that the speaker is paying you the compliment of assuming that you see things the way that the rest of 'the team' does. But being 'on the team' is not the same as being 'one of the family'. The family, while respecting the bread-winners, does not value its members in terms of their respective usefulness. Indeed, loving families tend to show even greater than normal care for the member whose usefulness has been diminished by circumstance. By contrast, team members who do not perform get axed.

10.4.18 We can therefore see that it is entirely possible for the hard-nosed manager to apply the 'participative' vocabulary of the neo-human relations writers to describe practices which are as uncompromisingly harsh as Taylor's. While being as careless about the fall of the sparrow as Taylor ever was, they use a sporting metaphor to hide this fact. I find this attempt to hide behind the clichés of the sports-field a particularly distasteful piece of evasion.

10.4.19 Another set of curious neo-human relations language images are those of Frederick Herzberg. I have not said much about Herzberg's job-enrichment theories, because one can only agree that if a manager can (without loss) improve the quality of life for an employee, he should do so. However, if it cannot be done without opportunity cost, then that creates for the manager a problem of stewardship: for the cost could put at risk the firm's competitive position and adversely affect both workers and shareholders. In discussing Herzberg we need to distinguish between what he said, and the popular misinterpretations of what he said. Herzberg claims that two sets of factors influence the worker. Those which have to do with the avoidance of physical and social deprivation he terms 'hygiene factors', and those which have to do with psychological growth he terms 'motivators'. At no time does he suggest that the hygiene factors are less important than the motivators. Nevertheless, his message is that the only way to motivate someone is to present him with the means of psychological growth, and this, from the evidence of essays from students over the years, appears to have caused them to interpret him in this way. Not only do many of them attribute to him a tendency to regard 'motivators' as more significant than 'hygiene factors', but they clearly also find the concept appealing.

10.4.20 Herzberg cannot avoid, I think, some responsibility for a state of affairs which arises primarily out of his choice of labels. There is a tendency to regard hygiene as no more than good housekeeping. In the context of industrial relations it sounds like the sort of thing we could reasonably expect any competent personnel department to handle; just as we assume that a good cook (whose main satisfaction lies in the creation of an appetizing dish) will, as a matter of course, first ensure that the kitchen table is clean. Yet the essential problems of the employer/employee relationship stem from the fact that market forces make the employee both a potential asset and a liability. Against that reality, to give 'pay' as passive a role as is implied by the imagery which lies within the concept of a 'hygiene factor' seems to be very unrealistic.

10.4.21 Moreover his emphasis upon 'job-enrichment' leads naturally to the assumption that this is the most important bit. He even gives the impression, intentionally or otherwise, that he is getting just a little impatient with managers who do not seem able to solve such a simple problem. As I mentioned in paragraph 4.1.19, the title of one of his articles seems to me to encapsulate exactly this didactic, rather exasperated stance. It reads, 'One more time: How do you motivate employees?' (Herzberg, 1968). Whatever the individual parts of his message say, the whole of it conveys this attitude and the implication that industrial peace can come from what is essentially a technique applied within the existing framework. When we add to that questionable proposition the economic and technical problems which constrain job-enrichment (discussed in Chapter 4), we can perhaps see why the technique has done little to revolutionize industrial relations.

10.4.22 Consequently, if I have not chosen to comment upon the dubious methodology which brought Herzberg to his 'two factor' theory, it is not only that this criticism appears in much of the other literature, but because I believe that to discuss his methodology at all is to give to his basic thesis a validity which it does not warrant. Where job-enrichment is possible, it is almost certainly advantageous. Far more has been done for the cause of job-enrichment by the autonomy which complexity, novelty and change have demanded (and which has flowed naturally from technological development) than has ever been done by exhortation. Where technical and economic considerations make job-enrichment impossible, it will remain impossible whatever the exhortation. Where it has been introduced it may have increased job-satisfaction, but it has not diminished the problems of job security and the other issues related to that problem.

10.4.23 However, what Herzberg did was to encourage McGregorism in the United States to stream into the narrow channel he had dug. By this act any discussion of the real problem (namely dealing with the present conflict of interest between society, commercial organizations and the employee) was effectively by-passed. Let me not be misunderstood. Job-enrichment is important. But it is another example of taking a problem with many ambiguities (namely 'How does one motivate employees in a capitalist context?') and then divesting it of all reality by ignoring the major part of the problem. It is another example of using an 'either...or' viewpoint when a 'both...and' viewpoint was needed.

10.4.24 So with the aid of job-enrichment the neo-human relations concept in America subtly degenerated into a unitary view which, if it did not deny the existence of social problems in capitalism, assumed they had little importance, or assumed they could not be solved at the workplace, or did both. In Europe the reverse was true. Not only unions, but also those politicians who like to be thought of as 'caring' and academics who like to be considered 'progressive' came to realize that they could use the language of McGregorism to deny capitalism's contractual economic basis and to claim that the capitalist firm had a neo-feudal responsibility towards its workforce. *So, in Europe, 'obtaining participation' did **not** mean harnessing the worker to the goals of management as it did in America. In Europe the same phrase meant ensuring that the worker got into a position from where he could deny management the right to independent action.*

10.4.25 In both America and Europe it was in large part the self-congratulatory moralizing stance of the neo-human relations school which made it so attractive to many of its supporters. Being in favour of McGregor's ideology was quite as sure a sign that a person was a 'progressive' as being against McGregorism was that he was a 'reactionary'.

10.4.26 In Europe the significance of linking this moralizing attitude to a politicised version of McGregorism caused the greatest dismay among managers. Yet though they saw that the dice had been loaded against them, it clearly escaped most of them quite who had done it, and quite how it had been done. Certainly the letters that they wrote to the Press at the time of the *Bullock Report* made no attempt to challenge the hidden neo-human relations' assumptions that 'participation' was good and 'hierarchy' was bad.

10.4.27 Yet the rejected Bullock proposals have since been followed by the draft proposals for worker democracy known as the '*Vredeling*' and 'Fifth' Directives of the European Economic Community. To counter this subtle denial of the right of firms to adapt and change, I believe that managers had recognized by the late 1980s (possibly for the first time this century) that they needed a **pluralist** management theory with which to add moral conviction to their instinctive objections.

10.4.28 So it is that we come to the last of the six responses. It is the most difficult of the responses to handle because it demands the maturity which can acknowledge the incongruities in organizational relationships, and yet the doggedness to continue to attempt to resolve the irresolvable. Those who tread this path know that their most earnest endeavours are bound to have only partial success. They recognize that there are incongruities in every social system and that those present in capitalism have a particularly chilling effect upon human relationships because of the extreme impersonality which is the inevitable accompaniment to its 'rationality'. It is therefore scarcely surprising that very little of the management literature has had the courage to acknowledge this aspect of the situation, nor that, when it did so, it was previously decidedly unpopular. I believe that this must change.

11

The sixth response – 'political holon man', or my version of the love-hate pluralist frame of reference

11.1 Some antagonistic responses to the constraints of hierarchy, both in society and the firm

11.1.1 We have seen that every ordered society forms a hierarchy of systems and subsystems which need to be managed. So it is no accident that in all societies there is a basic conflict between the individual's claims to freedom and the demands and constraints with which society's institutions burden him. On the other hand, he also has certain expectations of those institutions, which if unfulfilled may create in him a sense of intense grievance.

11.1.2 This sense of grievance is not simply a problem for the individual. For centuries it has been a core issue for the many social commentators who seek a better world. I maintain that the hierarchical nature of society means that there are only three options which can answer this need. They are:

feudalism (which is a hierarchy based on kinship),
bureaucratic centralism (which is a hierarchy based on a structure of posts to be filled by individuals performing a role), and
capitalist pluralism (which employs a legal hierarchical framework in which contractual exchanges are made based on mutual advantage).

Moreover, even from the earliest time they have co-existed. In so-called 'feudal' society the Catholic Church could not be based on kinship because of the celibacy of its priests. It was based upon bureaucratic centralism. Co-existent with both were the people in the towns whose hierarchy was essentially capitalist pluralism. Both the Church and the townspeople were a means of facilitating the existence of feudalism by taking some of the stress out of the system (even though capitalist pluralism was eventually to take over completely). It is because these are the only available systems that Russia was bound to become bureaucratic centralist in character even though that outcome was also encouraged by her geography, her history and the personalities of the Revolution.

11.1.3 Yet none of the possible frameworks (feudalism, bureaucratic centralism, or capitalist pluralism) are happily accepted. Western Marxists with their eyes on 'permanent revolution' try to avoid giving any specifics to their future system and can only be said to be against the above three options. Nevertheless, we shall consider them together with the others who would challenge or modify capitalist pluralism. These objectors are those who favour

(1)   anarchism,
(2)   Marxism,
(3)   syndicalism,
(4)   co-operativism (or collectivism).

ANARCHISM

11.1.4 The first we shall consider is that of the anarchist who correctly identifies that antagonisms between the individual and his society will always exist. He also correctly sees that changing the political complexion of the society will not help. His response is as logical as it is startling: namely to renounce all forms of organized society. Perhaps anarchy deserves better than that one should be totally dismissive about it. But there are few who would contemplate this 'solution' with any enthusiasm, and I confess to being grateful for that. It means that, the prospect is very remote of waking up one morning to find that eight million people, in an area the size of Greater London, were busy putting anarchic theory into practice.

MARXISM

11.1.5 The second response is that of Western Marxists, who are in no doubt that they have the answer to society's problems. Marxists acknowledge the tensions in present society. Indeed they make the point that such tensions have existed throughout history. Today's society is different only because of the manner in which the present class struggle will end. Other societies ended when a minority created a revolution for the benefit of that minority. The next revolution will be brought about by the majority, the proletariat, and will be for the benefit of all. The resulting society, consisting of the 'dictatorship of the proletariat', will be without tensions. This famous Marxist expression does not appear in the *Communist Manifesto*, although the thought does. It is a very convenient catch-phrase. It has the double value of being resonant and vague. It is therefore a useful smoke-screen to disguise the reality, namely that no society can overcome its basic antagonisms with the individual. In their hearts the Marxists realize this, and their complete failure to produce any practical and detailed blueprint for the new society which they expect to emerge bears witness to that.

11.1.6 Marxists usually claim that they have not done so because such an act would be 'utopian'. I suggest that the opposite is the case. Only by consistently refusing to explain the mechanisms of their new society have they been able to continue their utopian claims. If they were ever to get down to the practicalities of how that society would function, it would become apparent to them that many of the hierarchical problems they now associate with capitalism would still be there. All societies have a hierarchical structure to ensure that individuals and institutions obey certain rules which correspond to rights and obligations. In capitalism however, most of the lesser hierarchies which produce the goods and services and allocate the resources are independent of the State. The capitalist State makes certain obligatory demands upon the people in it. Beyond that its principal concern is to ensure that people and institutions honour (or are punished for failing to honour) the contracts which they enter into and which collectively run the economy by means of the 'invisible hand'. The Marxist State, having got rid of these market forces, has to involve itself fully in every aspect of economic activity and will need to plan centrally. Thus, whether the Marxist likes it or not, the introduction of Marxism into a developed industrial society requires a centralized and highly directive bureaucratic machine to perform the task which in capitalist states is done by the 'invisible hand'. Moreover, a Marxist regime is bound to destroy that economic independence which permits pluralist government to flourish in capitalism. If, as one suspects, it will prove quite as inefficient a system as that in Russia, it will prove also to be quite as lacking in the means of redress as theirs has proved. For never was Marx more right than when he claimed (Marx and Engels, 1970; Vol.2, p.503) that the 'relations of production [are]... the foundation on which rises a legal and political superstructure'. I shall come back to this because some Western Marxists, when pressed, express hopes for some form of syndicalist society. These I shall claim are vain.

11.1.7 In accordance with their principles, neither the Marxist nor the anarchist have the slightest interest in supporting the existing system. Indeed, since there is general agreement that the majority of trade unionists, far from seeking to overthrow capitalism, are primarily seeking the best deal for themselves that they can within the system, it makes no sense at all for trade unionists to elect Marxist officials. By their *own* standards Marxists are not seeking what the trade unionist wants and are using the office as a power-base for other ends. For them to act so makes good tactical sense even if they have no affinity with the aspirations of those who put them there. For trade unionists to elect them, on the other hand, is illogical. That they do so appears to result from a combination of three factors:

(1) apathy;
(2) a misunderstanding of Marxist aims and, in particular, a tendency to believe that they differ from the traditional members of the British Labour Party only to the extent that they are seen as being more actively committed;
(3) a belief among those who **do** know the above difference that they can use the militancy of the Marxist, but still hold him in check.

Some readers may doubt if reaction (2) above can be very widespread. I believe it is the most common. I am sure that despite all the trauma of decades of strife within the Labour Party which culminated in the break-away of the 'Gang of Four' to form the Social Democratic Party, the average British voter most commonly thinks of the two wings of the Labour Party simply as the respective ends of a continuum. The reality, of course, is that they stand either side of a great gulf between those who are seeking a modified capitalism (which they choose to call 'Socialism') and those who want to destroy the system completely.

11.1.8 Both anarchists and Marxists have directed their attacks against the capitalist productive enterprise. The anarchist tends to focus on that area because it is in the relationships of the production system that we see most blatantly the instrumental way with which society harnesses the individual to its purposes. The Marxist tends to focus on it because, in the words of Marx (Marx and Engels, 1970; Vol.2, p.503), 'the sum total of these relations of production constitutes the economic structure of society – the real foundation on which rises a legal and political superstructure'. In other words, the Marxist sees the antagonisms of the social system as flowing from the production system.

11.1.9 One of the reasons why the Marxist makes such a good analysis of the faults of capitalism and such a poor showing when it comes to his own future system comes from the legacy of Marx's teacher, the philosopher Hegel. Hegel claimed that every idea produced a reaction; a sort of 'counter-idea'. What then happened was that these two concepts worked on each other to give birth to a new idea which contained elements of both the original idea and the counter-idea. But this new 'mixed' idea produced in turn a new counter-idea...and so on. Life therefore progressed, according to Hegel, in a series of triangular steps. He called the idea the 'thesis', the counter-idea the 'antithesis', and the result of them working on each other gave birth to a 'synthesis'. (Figure 11.1(a) shows the concept diagramatically.)

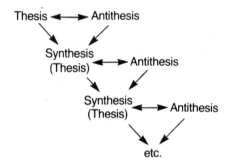

Figure 11.1(a)

11.1.10 This Hegelian view of history implies that **ideas move the world along**. Marx took the machinery of the Hegelian dialectic, but (following Feuerbach) he insisted that it was **the world which moved ideas along in the inexorable progression we encountered in paragraph 8.2.4.** In Marx's own words, 'The mode of production of material life conditions the social, political, and intellectual life process in general. It is not the consiousness of men that determines their being but, on the contrary, their social being that determines their consciousness.'

11.1.11 History for Marx, therefore, went forward like the triangles of Hegelian thought, but the triangles were not composed of thoughts but of economic actualities...until with socialism the process literally stopped. For as A. J. P. Taylor says (1982; p.9), 'The social conflicts which were the basis of his system would finally produce a synthesis where no conflicts were left, and history would come to an end...an ideal society or Utopia where everyone would be happy without conflict for ever more...according to [Marx's] own account...There was no need to postulate some impossible change of heart. Dialectic materialism would compel men to live in Utopia whatever the promptings of their hearts.' Of course, as A. J. P. Taylor says, '[Marx's] theory was also implicitly a judgement in psychology...ultimately the inhabitants of Utopia would always behave in a Utopian way.' That is to say, Marxists refuse to admit perfectability, but their future won't work without it.

11.1.12 Nevertheless, in language that disguises those claims, they still make their perfectability assumptions. Let me add my explanatory gloss to the muted language of the American Marxian economists Baran and Sweezy (1968; p.53). 'The character of the system determines the psychology of its members, not vice versa' is their way of saying that capitalism has made us rotten; '...one corollary of this analysis requires particular emphasis. "At the dawn of capitalist production", Marx wrote, "avarice and the desire to get rich are the ruling passions...Accumulate! Accumulate! That is Moses and the prophets!" But he was careful to point out that this ruling passion was not an emanation of human nature but rather was the product of the system in which it played so crucial a role.' This is their way of saying that after the revolution we shall all be beautiful.

11.1.13 So the problem with the whole approach is that it has no positive coherent and cohesive propositions which one can visualize will work. Based as it is on the above Hegelian-like mechanism of contrast which is known as _dialectical materialism,_ it starts with a devastatingly detailed, analytical and accurate analysis of the problems associated with capitalism. Marxist theory assumes that their social antithesis to capitalism is where further historical development ceases. Thus the logic of their dialectical materialism leaves us with their proposed socialism expressed as the antithesis of capitalism, rather like the concept of a universe of 'anti-matter' which mirrors the universe of 'matter'. But that is the **only** way it is expressed; they offer us only the vaguest of concepts of how this socialist world will appear and only then in terms of its polarity with capitalism, and no concepts at all as to how it will work.

11.1.14 Yet whether we are speaking of 'mirroring opposing universes' or 'mirroring opposing socio-economic systems', we cannot assume that opposing everything in the original system will produce a counter-system which works simply **because** it is an act of contrary nature. Indeed, if we are to believe Koestler's claim (paragraph 3.1.10) that hierarchical structures are necessary to _all_ systems, then neither an anti-matter universe nor a Marxist society can do without hierarchy. I believe that the Marxists know it too: otherwise they would have produced something a little more convincing than their empty catch-phrase of 'the dictatorship of the proletariat'. To most Westerners therefore the obligation is on Marxists to show how their hierarchical forms will be less offensive to the individual than those of capitalism. So far the indications are that they will be **more** offensive. In part this is because individualism, a strong feature of capitalism, is, *ipso facto*, ideologically questionable to the Marxist. But the greatest reason is because the cement of capitalist hierarchies, namely market forces, will need to be replaced by the cement of dictatorship.

11.1.15 Nor, in default of any theoretically worked out systems, are Western Marxists very happy if we attempt to infer a theory by analysing what has happened in countries which claim to have espoused some form of Marxist practice. Since Stalin's day the Russian model's brutal totalitarianism, coupled with its inefficiency, has led most Western Marxists, who in any case are largely Trotskyite, to renounce it as a model. As for the Cuban model, it is inappropriate to an industrial economy and needs constant external Eastern bloc subsidy. Cuba's problems may in part be a result of that island's geographic and historic legacy; but that is to excuse, not to recommend, the system there. Possibly the Jugoslav model is the most convincing, but (as in China) it flirts with capitalism, is still largely peasant, and is no model for a comparable British economy.

11.1.16 As early as 1913 that left-wing commentator G. D. H. Cole (McCarthy, 1972) saw that there were 'two opposing alternatives to capitalism, which we may call roughly syndicalism and collectivism [i.e. co-operativism]' (p.68). Co-operativism I shall deal with later, because it is not really a Marxist solution, being in Cole's words 'more a business proposition and less an aspiring ideal' (p.72). Syndicalism was essentially a French movement aimed at transferring the means of production and distribution to the workers. Cole recognized that, so conceived, it wouldn't work. Its purpose was to secure the position of the producer. Yet as Cole remarks, 'obviously the consumer, the person **for** whom the goods are made, and not the person **by** whom they are made, must decide what is to be produced, when it is to be produced, and in what quantities' (p.62).

11.1.17 Cole's solution was to have the State reconcile the producers' and consumers' interests. This, of course, is a system which will work, but, as we have seen in the Eastern bloc, it is inefficient and becomes totalitarian. This is why, most Western Marxists of my acquaintance (despite Trotsky's anti-syndicalist attitude) yearn for small independent administrative syndicates in which the consumers and producers are one and the same people...in effect, the country would allegedly go back to medieval economy without the hierarchy of feudalism. There is an irony here, for in the Spanish Civil

War such syndicates were indeed set up. They were created by the anarchists and destroyed by the communists.

SYNDICALISM

11.1.18 Historically, syndicalism has occurred when there has been a breakdown of authority. Normally the chaos of anarchy is a price no one will pay. *However, if order has **already** broken down and chaos **already** reigns, then to decentralize decision-making into the smallest feasible geographical unit makes sense.* The chaos created by the start of the Spanish Civil War, coupled with the ideals of anarchists in the Barcelona area, led naturally to the setting up there of small syndicates. Moreover, if one ignores the excesses perpetrated by the anarchistic leaders of such syndicates, they did get around the problem of 'who calls the tune?' This they managed by their small size, by which means producer **and** consumer were reduced to being the same person or group.

11.1.19 It would not be possible to sustain a principally urban population of fifty million in Britain under such a system, even in brute conditions. Moreover, if such syndicates remained independent of each other they would suffer from shortages and excesses which trade might have eliminated. They would also suffer from tremendous diseconomies of scale.

11.1.20 It follows that a wider economic canvas is necessary than that of the medieval town: indeed, the nation is the smallest reasonable economic entity, and for some purposes even that is not large enough, as is evidenced by the existence of international trade. However, at the national level this can be organized. Nor should we dismiss the concept of the society being large enough to maintain its sovereignty. Even with their scale, nations find that to ensure their sovereignty they need to make alliances. The Spanish syndicalists were, in a sense, unable to defend their 'sovereignty'.

11.1.21 Having been born of the chaos which occurred at the start of the Civil War, they had achieved what they wanted. They had therefore no further interest in prosecuting the war. Indeed the war was for the control of the State; an institution that no longer had any meaning for these separate anarchistic units. This eminently logical position was, not surprisingly, anathema to other socialists who were still fighting the war, and who believed that these syndicalists had no right to opt out of the struggle. So the dream of one set of 'socialists' was smashed by the dream of another, for the syndicates were too small to avoid defeat and *were dragooned into the* *struggle for the Spanish State, precisely because they were too weak to defend their own sovereignty.*

11.1.22 So for a whole spectrum of reasons the power shifts from the syndicate to the State. And since, by destroying capitalism, syndicalism has destroyed the 'natural' market forces of capitalist society, the State now has to specify what is to be produced. Nor will such a State tolerate the pluralist claims of trade unionism, as the Polish 'Solidarity' trade unionists have found to their cost. The cycle is now complete and the pluralism for which many Western Marxists hope has been shipwrecked.

CO-OPERATIVISM (OR COLLECTIVISM)

11.1.23 I said that both the anarchist and the Marxist have seen fit to concentrate upon the production enterprise. The anarchist does so because it is the means of production that most clearly illustrates the instrumental way with which society harnesses the individual to its purposes. The Marxist does so because he sees the antagonisms of the social system as flowing from the production system.

11.1.24 If we now turn to capitalism we find that the crucial role of production, and the fact that it has been the focus of anti-capitalist criticism, make it similarly important there. The very warts of capitalism require pro-capitalist writers to show that it has the social, technological, economic and political ability, materially and morally to out-perform every other system, such as Marxism, or any non-system (anarchy). This they can only do by taking upon themselves the issues raised by the productive enterprise.

11.1.25 Yet few Organization and Management writers have made any attempt to show that the capitalist productive enterprise is materially and morally able to out-perform rival systems. Organization and Management writers in America have indeed concentrated upon the productive enterprise but they have not seen any need to defend its assumed superiority. Nor have they bothered to justify two more assumptions which they have adopted. The first of these is:

(a) that the basic capitalist *mores* are shared by management and worker alike. This might often be the case. Many a worker dreams of becoming a future capitalist: but it is by no means universal.

Yet any error this first assumption may contain is as nothing compared with that contained within the second assumption. This is:

(b) that the roles of the various participants within the *mores* of capitalism will not be such as to create any significant differences of interest.

The three approaches we considered which contained these erroneous assumptions were the so-called 'content' theories, namely:

(1) 'economic man', which I labelled a form of the 'daddy-knows-best' school of unitary thought, and which is typified by Taylor;
(2) 'social man', which is also a version of the 'daddy-knows-best' unitary school of thought, but is based on the ideas of Mayo;
(3) 'self-actualizing man', which I have characterized as the 'all-pals-together' unitary school of thought of McGregor.

I have given reasons in each case why managers had reason to embrace these three theories despite the ridiculous assumptions being made. Nevertheless, it does show how little thought has gone into alternative productive frameworks that no one seems to have bothered to ask the question, 'if the concepts contained in social man and self-actualizing man lead to better performance, why are not the most successful firms in capitalism those run as worker's co-operatives?' **For this they most certainly are not**. Such co-operatives have an abysmal record in the retail area, and an even worse one in the production area. Only when individual farmers have got together collectively to market their separately produced merchandise has it worked well. In other words, they have set up an independently operated marketing subsidiary in the capitalist mould to take the middle-man's profit. During the late 1960s it was claimed that the socialist politician Tony Benn had a 'hit-list' of fifty large firms he wanted to nationalize, one of which was said to be the highly successful Marks and Spencer's retail chain. The joke at the time was that his object was to make them as efficient as the Co-op.

11.1.26 It had not been the inefficiency of co-operative ventures which led Cole and other socialists to express displeasure with such 'collectivism', but the fact that they did not represent thorough-going socialism. *There is no logical reason why co-operative enterprises should not flourish within the capitalist system. I shall suggest that why those that exist tend not to flourish is largely psychological.* Indeed, it is the logical ability of co-operatives to operate within the capitalist system that caused Cole to see 'collectivism' as (paragraph 11.1.16) 'more a business proposition and less an inspiring ideal'. All of which explains why I maintain that, if Mayo and McGregor are right, it would indeed be logical to expect that the most successful capitalist organizations would be those of workers' co-operatives. They are after all a form of organization which is designed specifically to offer what Mayo and McGregor saw as their respective keys to success: (a) worker social solidarity, and (b) worker autonomy. In the event, however, they fail because they do not have a strong enough hierarchy either to discipline the workforce or to take such action as is required for the continued health of the company **if that action is seen by individual members or groups as being against their sectional interests.**

11.1.27 In 1981 Tony Eccles published a sympathetic account of the story of Britain's largest worker co-operative, KME. Eccles was himself a Labour parliamentary candidate in the 1974 elections. He came up the hard way from the shop floor to being, at the time of writing his book, Professor of Business Administration at the London Business School. I strongly advise anyone who doubts the need of a management caucus with the power to exert its will, to read that book. These are the words of Jack Spriggs, a director of KME and also convenor of shop stewards for the Amalgamated Union of Engineering Workers (AUEW) to a mass meeting in 1977 (Eccles, 1981; p.192–193): '...I was naïve to believe that in 1974/5 the workers alone would create the self-discipline, the productivity, to move forward without the need of supervisors being necessary to discipline people. Yet we find sunbathing and card schools, a little intimidation where people have done extra work. These are not mythical situations – they are fact...We don't need stop-watches in here. We barely need a sun dial. It is obvious what could be done if people had a mind to do it.' He had earlier pointed out that their problems did not stem from any shortage of orders. Indeed, they had turned away business contracts 'because we couldn't get them through the place even though all the budgets said it was possible'.

11.1.28 Throughout the whole book the insights of Eccles are as unblinkered as it is possible to be and unclouded by his obvious compassion. His conclusion is equally revealing. He says (p.404), 'The key conclusion is stark. Unless KME is an aberration, industrial democracy and sizeable worker cooperatives will not work in Britain whilst worker attitudes and trade union policies remain as they are. The gap between socialist rhetoric and the likelihood of effective action remains depressingly wide.' Yet he cannot finish on such a note. He says (p.405), 'I would like to feel that KME's story will not be used as evidence of the stupidity of encouraging cooperatives, for, despite its oddities [sic], that should not be the lesson.'

11.1.29 I agree that co-operatives **need** not fail. It is not the basic concept of co-operative enterprise that causes such ventures to fail, **but their total inability to accept that they must give power to a management caucus.** For a while some co-operatives may well fare better than when they were in private ownership. This is particularly likely if the unions are more ready to accept the *mores* of capitalism, as occurs in the USA. Yet even here the real crunch question arises when part of the organization has to be sacrificed for the economic well-being of the rest.

11.1.30 An organization will fail unless there is a management caucus which is able to make its will prevail **even when its policies do not gain universal acceptance from the rest of the members of the organization and even when some of those members are seriously disadvantaged by the policy.** The issue is therefore not one of whether the workers will respond to the challenge of production when times are good: the issue is, 'How they will respond to deprivation and redundancy when times are bad?' Firms which have no strong hierarchical authority will not flourish within a market economy.

CAPITALIST PLURALISM

11.1.31 This being so, the ability of management to manage must be maintained. We must concede that Taylorite writers were a little too ready to identify the 'will of management' with 'the good of society'. But if in this matter they were glib, it would be even more glib to suggest that there is **no** such relationship. Indeed, any government which has hitched its country's economy to the engine of capitalism (and this includes most Western states and covers an extraordinarily wide range of political complexions) had better look to it that their policies do not undermine management's right to manage. Otherwise the engine will run out of steam.

11.1.32 Of course those pluralists like myself who believe that unfettered power leads to tyranny, would also maintain that that same government must ensure that the worker is not prevented from setting up some degree of countervailing power by means of a trade union. So the issue is not one of whether management **or** worker should have power, but how that power is to be kept in balance. This is where the image of 'political holon man' becomes so vital and where we must accept that most areas of life contain ambiguity, and not least the area of industrial relations. For if we were naïve enough to swallow the unitary views of the various 'content' theorists we would not, in the case of the third and fourth response, pay sufficient attention to the rights of the worker to oppose management. On the other hand, in the case of the fifth response, we should fail for the opposite reason (and as I write this is a much more urgent threat). European governments are becoming so enamoured of the idea of 'participation' that they are legislating its enforcement to the point where the workforce or their unions can put grave obstacles in the way of unpopular mangerial decisions. Such governments are steering their countries towards general economic and social disaster.

11.1.33 If capitalist society is not to suffer, Western governments must steer between Scylla and Charybdis. Too much favour in one direction will harm management: too much in the other will damage the unions. Either way, that country's society would be the loser. It is against this background that we must discuss the matter of motivation theory. Moreover, it is a nonsense to attempt to discuss motivation theory at the microeconomic level without regard to the macroeconomic background. This brings us to the role of government in times of unemployment. Unfortunately the promise of a new dawn is past in which Keynesian economics would solve unemployment – that thorn in the side of capitalism. Many would say that following Keynes's death his mantle fell on Joan Robinson. At one time (Robinson, 1962; p.95) she was able to claim that Keynesian policies enabled the Conservative Party in Britain to say to socialists 'You used to complain, we now admit with justification, that a capitalist system that permits heavy and chronic unemployment is indefensible. Now we offer you capitalism with a high and stable level of employment. You have nothing to complain of.' At that time she also felt able to claim that Baran was wrong to suggest that 'government expenditure causes inflation'. She has long since amended her ideas. Government intervention to stimulate capitalist economies does appear to be inflationary, and capitalism's failure to deal with unemployment remains its biggest failing.

11.1.34 Whether this problem is beyond solution is a matter for speculation. If Marxian economists like Baran are right in their claim that the problem is inherent in capitalism, and represents merely a symptom of the inevitable destruction of capitalism by the process of dialectical materialism, then such destruction **will** be inevitable. But *if they are correct in this I believe a very sad day will have dawned.* Happily I doubt their premises. I find the popularity of the Marxist premise that Hegelian triangles have forced the juggernaut of history on to a predetermined path is as psychologically interesting as it is improbable.

11.1.35 The whole paraphernalia of Marxism seems to me to be only one of many manifestations of a particularly strong yearning in the human psyche, namely to reject responsibility for our own destinies, and to look to either someone or something to take over. This role is often filled by mechanistic concepts; moreover, such concepts seem to be able to fulfil that function, even when the concept in question is one of gloom and doom. Anything, it would seem, is better to some people than uncertainty (which is of course why ambiguous models are so unpopular). Clark (1969; p.4) tells us of 'a poem by the modern Greek poet, Cavafy, in which he imagines the people of an antique town like Alexandria waiting every day for the barbarians to come and sack the city. Finally the barbarians move off somewhere else and the city is saved; but the people are disappointed – it would have been better than nothing.' Yet it was not 'nothing' that they had. It was 'everything', including control of their own destinies: surely that was what really frightened them more than the barbarians?

11.1.36 By the seventeenth and eighteenth century the Deists, fascinated by clockwork mechanisms, saw the universe as a gigantic piece of clockwork, with God as the clock-maker. This gave to life a predetermined element which (psychologically) they clearly needed. But it was in the nineteenth century that man's real love affair with machinery reached a climax and the imagery of a predestined universe in which man was only a puppet reached its greatest heights, or depths (depending on one's viewpoint). Marx's juggernaut was just one of many such which were built in that age and were all designed to show that because man had no free will he had no responsibility for his actions and was caught in the grip of impersonal forces.

11.1.37 Thomas Robert Malthus, writing in 1798, built a juggernaut called the *Principle of Population* which held that (Galbraith, 1977; p.32) '...“given the passion between the sexes”...population would always increase in geometric ratio 2, 4, 8, 16 and so on. Meanwhile at best the food supply would increase only arithmetically 2, 3, 4, 5,...from this came the inevitable result. In the likely absence of “moral restraint” population would be subject only to the recurrent and ghastly checks imposed by famine or by war or natural catastrophe.' In 1817 David Ricardo took Malthus's rural juggernaut and converted it into a 'Mark II' industrial version. According to Ricardo, similar impersonal forces not only justified the employer in paying starvation wages, but would, by inference make it immoral of him to pay more (Galbraith, 1977; p.35):

> In the Ricardian world workers would receive the minimum necessary for life, never more. This was the iron law of wages. It led amongst other things to the conclusion that not only was compassion wasted on the working man, but it was damaging. It might raise hopes and income in the short run, but it accelerated the population increase by which both were brought down. And any effort by government or trade unions to raise wages and rescue people from poverty would similarly be a conflict with economic law, be simply frustrated by the resulting increase in numbers.

11.1.38 Not only has history made both these premises questionable, but the belief that we are trapped by fate is often the justification for man's worst inhumanity to man. When Ireland, then part of the United Kingdom, was in the grip of the potato famine of 1845–47, the Treasury used the Malthusian and Ricardian juggernauts to hide behind (Galbraith, 1977; p.38). 'The custodian of the Ricardian tablets was Charles Edward Trevelyan...Permanent Head of the Treasury. Trade, he advised would be "paralysed" if the government by giving away food interfered with the legitimate profit of private enterprise.' Having done nothing to avert the heavy death toll which followed the famine, Trevelyan used those very deaths to justify himself: 'in 1846 he wrote that the problem of Ireland "being altogether beyond the powers of men, the cure has been applied by the direct stroke of an all-wise Providence in a manner as unexpected and as unthought of as it is likely to be effectual".' (Galbraith, 1977; p.38.)

11.1.39 Although there must be limits to the Keynesian activities of governments, and limits to the social welfare programmes which can ride on the back of capitalism, yet capitalism still seems the most powerful system for producing the surpluses which make such relief possible. It is clear that there is a limit to the resources that even capitalism can dedicate to those socially desirable schemes which cannot be funded by the normal interplay of market forces. Nevertheless, in my view, capitalist governments have an interest in, as well as a duty towards, alleviating the social problems caused by managers responding to free market forces. By so doing they will help to maintain a system which in every other way has demonstrated to me (and hopefully to the reader) its practical and moral superiority to any known alternative.

11.1.40 It follows that Western governments would be wise to keep continually under review the country's social 'safety nets' and to use their powers at the macroeconomic level to alleviate as much as possible the distress caused at the microeconomic level when managements react to adverse market forces. This is not only a moral responsibility towards the unemployed but a practical step in the preservation of parliamentary democracy, which Marx was right to see as the product of the capitalist system. That being so, champions of laissez-faire policies would do well to consider the political impracticality of their position even if they cannot be brought to change it for its moral shortcomings.

11.1.41 Yet if the more laissez-faire persons in society need a lesson in humanity, the more liberal persons need to consider more carefully than they have their continuing demands of 'more-cake-for-everyone'. It is only because capitalist managers are permitted to exercise their criterion of minimizing economic opportunity cost that our societies have resources above subsistence level with which to support altruistic and socially desirable ends. Given the general drift of liberal sympathies, we cannot wonder that, on occasion, at the micro-level they challenge the rights of managers to take harsh decisions; nor that at the macro-level they should advocate widespread Keynesianism. *But some of us do wonder at the* **frequency** *with which they wander down* **both** *those particular primrose paths...and then come back.* In the early 1980s such policies by the Socialist French President, Mitterand, took his country into an economic morass. It surprised few observers when by the mid-1980s in an effort to retrieve the situation he had made a U-turn and started to follow policies identical to Thatcherism in the UK.

11.1.42 *That having been said, the real liberal danger arises when they allow their sympathies to ally them with the Marxists in calling into question either the concept of the role played by market forces in capitalism, or the managerial criterion of minimizing economic opportunity cost.* In the autumn of 1984, when the leader of the National Union of Mineworkers, Arthur Scargill, was asked to denounce picket-line violence, he reacted instead by denouncing the 'violence' that was done to mining communities when the uneconomic pits on which they depended were closed. His turn of phrase has some merit, and it is no mere metaphor. It certainly poses the question as to whether successive governments have taken sufficiently active measures to create a 'spread' of alternative employment in such areas. It also underlines how badly we in Britain have handled the problem of pit closures. Anita van de Vliet (1984; p.21) points out that 'In North Rhine-Westphalia, which still produces 85 per cent of German coal...the number of miners has shrunk over the years by the startling figure of 300,000, from 450,000 to 150,000. Equally arresting is that all those laid off were found jobs in other industries.' But the Germans, as she points out, had the foresight to do this during the post-war boom of the 1950s and 1960s. So there is room for criticism about both the manner and timing of pit closures in Britain. But this cannot be allowed to be turned on its head to support a demand that no pit may be closed, nor to infer that the act of doing so justifies physical industrial violence. For Marxists to claim that such industrial violence is justified if plants close is logical, for they wish neither the capitalist system nor the parliamentary system it produced to survive. But for liberals to aid and abet them in this is another matter. Yet they often come very close to doing so.

11.1.43 In the autumn of 1984 liberals from all walks of life, including bishops and clergy, began to echo the NUM leader's claims that if management were to close unprofitable pits, then this would be a 'form of violence' against their associated mining communities. Though few of these commentators went on to suggest that this justified the violence of the pickets, many were prepared to say that it made that violence '**understandable**'. They thereby not only denied the role of market forces (and the freedom and relative prosperity which stem from that role), but (irrespective of their intentions) *they appeared to be condoning violence and thereby justifying it.* What part such sympathy plays in causing violence to escalate is a matter for conjecture, but it was following such pronouncements that violence became worse during the 1984 miners' strike. Starting with thousands of mass-pickets who sought physically to prevent miners from working, it then moved to arson against vehicles used to move coal and working miners; it then moved to picketing the homes of working miners; it then moved to attacking working miners within their homes and to burning down their homes after the families had fled; and finally, with an inevitability against which police had warned if the violence were not checked, it moved to the killing of a taxi-driver taking a working miner to work.

11.1.44 Capitalist parliamentary democracy can only survive if people in general admit the right of managements to manage and unions the right to take industrial action. But industrial violence cannot be allowed to become a standard feature of industrial disputes, it has to be outlawed **by everyone who supports parliamentary institutions**. Only so will it be seen as counterproductive to the interests of those who perform such acts. Interestingly enough, the same violence which was 'understandable' to many of Britain's leaders was sickening to some striking miners. Many gave it as their main reason for thereafter returning to work. *Those who have to live with the reality of violence clearly do not treat it with the indulgence afforded to it by high-minded (but well-distanced) commentators.*

11.1.45 This history emphasizes the basic nonsense of the aim of the three schools of 'content' theorists to get us to believe in a unitary proposition. But neither do

(a) the lengths to which miners would go to fight pit closures, and
(b) the risks that other miners took, in the face of such violence, to go to work,

support the Marxist proposition that the worker identifies with his fellows in a 'class' struggle, and that he is alienated from the capitalist system. Rather does the worker's position appear to be one of **ambivalence**.

11.1.46 Indeed, if one considers the total psychological switch that a working miner goes through when he goes on strike or that a striking miner goes through when he chooses to go back to work (particularly when he has colleagues in both camps), it will be seen that the size of the switch is immense. He may take days or weeks to struggle with the **greys** of the issues, but when he chooses he is (temporarily) committed to the **black** or the **white** of one of two polarized standpoints. *Any theory of motivation must recognize not only the reality of this capacity to switch: it must also grant his right to do so.* **By that I mean that the company should not attempt to load him with so much psychological indebtedness that it pre-empts his right, short of calling into question his personal integrity, to make a future switch.** This limitation applies to **all** employees, management and worker alike: for, as we shall see, managers cannot be expected to be so wedded to the *mores* of capitalism that they are prepared to abandon all other values, and thereby to lose their own souls. In any case (and I know many managers who would echo my sentiments), the fact that I, myself, have always given 150 per cent to every company I ever worked for has not prevented me from resenting those occasions when (a) *the company seemed to expect this as of right, or when* (b) *they assumed that the firm had the right to turn me into 'the organization man' whom W. H. Whyte described in his book of that title (1960).*

11.2 'Political holon man'

11.2.1 In stressing, as I have, the role of the 'content' theories, I have no wish to deny that there is a great body of motivation theory beyond those. Recent interest has shifted from the idea of such 'content' as being central to the worker's motivation, and it now seeks to identify the dynamic interplay of variables which will affect the worker. Because of this shift, the social, technological, economic and political aspects of organizational life take on the nature of a dynamic system: a system of which the worker's motivation forms a part. It is therefore a model which is much less static in concept than the content theories, and has much more affinity with other 'systems' ideas. According to this approach the role of management is to bring the firm into some sort of dynamic equilibrium, so that it may become the vehicle by which the goals which management have set for it are achieved. (My justification for claiming that an organization's goals are those of management is dealt with in Chapter 16.) Clearly there is an interplay here between the means and ends of the firm in shaping the sort of system which the firm becomes. Moreover, if we continue with the metaphors of this approach, the worker (whom I have just described as being a 'part') is more appropriately viewed as being a subsystem. As such, he too needs to be kept in some form of dynamic equilibrium, i.e. 'motivated'.

11.2.2 Such a theory, which visualizes the firm as being not only in dynamic equilibrium but also being the immediate environment of the worker can easily lead to seeing the worker's 'motivation' as solely a response to the dynamics of the firm. Already we can whiff a certain paternalism in the air: a readiness to suggest that the worker's dynamics are insulated from all factors apart from the initiatives of management... though clearly thay are not. Workers are *not* encapsulated in a Mayoite Russian-doll situation (described in paragraph 10.1.16), nor do these later motivation theories (which are known as 'process' theories to distinguish them from the earlier 'content' theories) require them to be so. But it is clearly something for which to be on guard, in case 'process' writers slide into it. Yet if there is a wide body of 'process' writing, why have I spent so much time on the content theories and why am I now going to spend so little time on these process theories?

11.2.3 My answer is two-fold. Firstly, despite these later developments, the earlier content theories continue to dominate the teaching in our institutions. Indeed McGregorism has acquired such dominance that it has, by its assumed validity, subtly become the essential framework within which all aspects of management are taught. Secondly, other than commentaries by writers antipathetic to the capitalist system, the mainstream of process theory writers are still largely regarding the firm from a unitary standpoint; they attempt to use it in a 'Russian doll' manner. Indeed, if the reader considers the description of 'process' theory which I gave in paragraph 11.2.1 and then turns back to look at the diagram on p.194 (which is the work of Roethlisberger and Dickson) he will see that I could have drawn such a diagram as illustrating 'process' theory. Yet, as we saw, the Mayoite philosophy was essentially management orientated.

11.2.4 I have already indicated that there is no inherent reason why process theories should not readily be adapted to take account of pluralist ideas: indeed my hope is that this book will help to induce such an adaptation. But it seems the case that to date most of these writers are American and have followed the American tradition. This tradition allows them to view the organization as an 'open' system when talking about strategy (because competitive forces outside the company are amenable to their culture), but permits them to regard it only as a 'closed' system when considering motivation (because competitive forces within the company are *not* amenable to their culture).

11.2.5 Let us consider, for example, the work of V.H. Vroom (1964) whom I find the most significant of these theorists, Vroom's suggestion is that workers are motivated by a complex set of calculations containing three variables:

(1) There are many things which the worker may want; some he will want more than others. The degree of wanting associated with each thing Vroom calls 'V' for 'valence'.

(2) But what the worker chooses to go for will be modified in the first instance by whether he can perceive any means/end relationships which theoretically should get him what he wants. If he can't he is just baying for the moon. This means/end relationship Vroom calls 'I' for 'instrumentality'.

(3) But even if such a means/end relationship is seen by the worker to exist there still remains the question of what probability he attaches to his being able successfully to harness this means. Vroom calls this 'E' for 'expectancy'.

Since it is the algebraic effect of these three factors which is supposed to motivate the worker, Vroom's model is commonly called 'VIE theory'. If we are to ascribe rationality to the worker, (and my experience has never led me to doubt it), then there is a sense in which Vroom's theory would appear to require no justification in that it is no more than a refined description of human rationality. On the other hand, if one were to deny my claim that this is so and sought to test the theory, it would seem to me that the methodological problems of attempting to verify/falsify it would be enormous. For one thing, any such attempt would bristle with insidious cultural traps. For example, given the cultural appeal of Maslow and the ready acceptance of Maslovian assumptions, even if 'indolence' had a high valence what chance would it have of being so decribed? Would it not be lost and show up only as a lowering in the valence of 'achievement'?

11.2.6 Vroom's theory is amenable to pressures *external to* or *internal to* the firm, and the things wanted could range from seeking the firm's prosperity to seeking its failure as an instrument of capitalism. **It is therefore of itself a neutral concept.** It could for example explain the actions both of the miners who worked during the 1984 strike and those who did not. Its very neutrality means that it can be used equally in a pluralist context and in a unitarist context. But neither Vroom's treatment of his theory nor the treatment afforded it by his critics seems to me to be neutral. Vroom's own tone betrays its management orientation. The mangement orientation of his critics is shown in that they seldom doubt the validity of Vroom's theory. Their attack is to question its usefulness to management as a tool. We shall soon return to consider the staggeringly unitary implications of that criticism.

11.2.7 Why I personally find Vroom's model so convincing is that it reinforced a conclusion I had reached independently. His proposition, it will be remembered, is that the worker's actions will not only be conditional upon what he wants, but also by what he sees as his means and chances of getting those wants. It will also be remembered that I gave a similar explanation as to why workers no longer fight against Taylorism with the same tenacity that they showed in Taylor's day. I suggested (paragraph 8.4.8) it was because 'options which, in Taylor's day, were available to allow the worker to act autonomously have disappeared... No longer does he perceive the rejection of Taylorism to be a viable option'. So what I found both interesting and chastening in Vroom's work was that he had the insight to offer us a concept with *general* application what I, independently of him, had seen only as an aspect of the history of Taylorism. I have called it a 'chastening' experience, for, since the essence of inductive reasoning is to move from the particular to the general, I might reasonably have been expected to have made this obvious step... I confess I did not. I tell the story partly to reinforce the point I made earlier in the book about the problems of modelling, but mainly in the hope that my independent support will add weight to a more general acceptance of Vroom's insight when it is coupled to pluralist concepts.

11.2.8 Let us return to the full implication behind the criticism that Vroom's theory is not of much help to managers. I should like to do so with a quote from Luthans, for his is one of the more even-handed assessments and, as we shall see, he recognizes the insidious element in this particular criticism. '[F]rom a theoretical standpoint the VIE model seems to help appreciate the complexities of motivation, but it does not give managers much practical help in solving their motivational problems' (Luthans, 1981; p.189) Now in one sense this is a valid criticism. A key test of any theory is to demand that it should be predictive. The 1919 eclipse of the Sun could be predicted by Einstein's theory of relativity to occur at a time which would differ from that we would have expected from Newtonian physics. This was because, according to Einstein, as the Sun's rays passed the intervening Moon, gravity would bend them, thus changing the time when an observer on Earth would see the three as being in line. When measurement gave a result which accorded with that prediction it naturally helped to establish the more general acceptance of Einstein's thought and of the implications of his theory.

11.2.9 But this principle cannot be turned on its head so that one declares that if we cannot predict a given outcome by a theory, then that theory cannot be valid. Still less can one say that if a manager feels more comfortable with theory 'A' than with theory 'B', then that is a reason for him to apply 'A'; a point that Luthans also makes. 'The content theories', he says (1981; p.189), 'oversimplified human motivation'. Yet the content theories remain extremely popular with practising managers because the concepts are easy to understand and apply to their own situations'. That may well be, and I have said why I believe each theory would have had its adherents. Nor are these theories particularly wrong or harmful in themselves. Their danger lies, as we have seen, in the unitary attitudes which they induce. I consider there are *a priori* grounds for suggesting that managers could do a lot worse than to adopt the Vroom model, providing always that they couple it with the recognition that it must be treated pluralistically. For given the basic differences which can arise in the respective social, technological, economic and political aspects of management goals and those of the worker, the latter is always capable of a switch into antagonism.

11.2.10 Moreover, when that switch occurs, the natural (and therefore universal) tendency of people to create an internally consistent *Weltanschauung* will cause workers *to suppress or modify many previously held positive perceptions* in order to fit the rationale of the moment. So their whole calculus makes a negative leap. Before the First World War, groups of itinerant German musicians made Germans and things German a source of amused tolerance in Britain. There is an old music-hall song in which the singer invites the audience to come to a famous English pub, 'The Old Bull and Bush'. One of the pleasures they are promised is that they will 'hear the little German band'. The so-called 'rape of Belgium' in August 1914 turned the image of these jolly Germans into 'Huns' *and to this day has left no residue of the original imagery*.

11.2.11 Organizationally this phenomenon is something for which we should be grateful, because the way in which we attempt to create a wholeness of vision in which all the parts of the jig-saw 'fit' makes it the more difficult for people to switch between such extremes. This factor tends to keep people in their existing mode and thereby lends considerable stability to the system. But the ever-present danger of the switch occurring is something of which managers should never lose sight, particularly when the system is under pressure. For, as many a manager can testify, people can switch over some small thing and apparently without warning. Nevertheless, in retrospect the manager can usually see why. He then (too late) recognizes that the issue, small as it was, was the last straw which broke the camel's back.

11.3 How real is 'alienation' as an obstacle to motivation?

11.3.1 'Alienation' is a concept which has markedly different emphases, depending upon who is using the expression. Some words have a positive connotation and invite us to define them by what they resemble. Other words have a negative connotation and invite us to define them in terms of what they are not. 'Alienation' comes in the latter category. But we should beware of such words. When the conjuror waves his left hand we fail to see that the real trick is performed with his right. With such words we are invited to assume that the thing so described is the opposite of an idealized natural state of affairs which has been adversely disturbed. So we forget to ask whether the idealized starting point ever existed. ('Embourgeoisement' is a similar trick-word, for it implies as a starting place a 'natural' state of *holding working-class values* which, by embourgeoisement, gets corrupted.) 'Alienation' is a word which is used to describe the state of affairs which exists when man's nature and that of the world he inhabits are out of harmony. Consequently it infers the thing with which it is contrasted, a lost, undefined 'golden age'. However, let us pretend that this realization has escaped us. Let us even concede that there need be no implied 'golden age' because, whatever reservations we may have about claiming that a primitive savage in his cave was in accord with 'nature', it could be claimed that there is a certain 'rightness' in his relationship to his world. Indeed, Marx himself (always ready to cloak his utopianism in earthy similes) invites us to imagine such a savage. Such a savage, he suggests, is a *fish in water*, whereas someone living in poverty in a Victorian cellar is decidedly a *fish out of water*. There are those among us who would regard this as a case of special pleading: but we will let that go. We will stay with the image to allow this point to be made: namely that *throughout all the different emphases applied to the word 'alienation' runs precisely this common theme...that the alienated person is like a fish out of water.* The differences between the various emphases lies in what is meant by the 'water' of which the 'fish' (man) has been deprived. Consequently, though the emphasis may change, we are always invited to infer that the world of the person who is 'alienated' has become out of tune with human nature; somewhere along the way something has intervened to create a mismatch... an estrangement ...an alienation. Indeed, according to this concept, the world the person inhabits may have become so far removed from any affinity with human values that its effect is to make him lose sight of what his true nature could be, should be, and indeed, had other circumstances prevailed, **would** have been. When this happens his estrangement is complete: unable to know any better, the gulf between what he is and what he could and should be is invisible to him, and therefore impossible to cross... he is alienated in the ultimate.

11.3.2 How can it be possible for a man-made world to become alien to man? This is where the emphases split. According to Hegel's concept, alienation is an inescapable part of the human condition. The very act of living requires us to make and use objects, but those objects actually transform society. In time the external world of man (though man-made) can come to lose all relationship to his inner world. I recently noted what might serve to illustrate this Hegelian concept of 'alienation'. A mother was playing with her little girl. The child was sitting at a toy till in the role of shop assistant and sold her mother a tin of peas. The mother paid for this, and then asked for change. Let us now contrast that image with a peasant society where such a mother might be showing that same child how to sow peas to grow a further crop. We can sense in such a contrast that a tin of peas, although a man-made object, is as alien as the coins for which it was exchanged: not so the sowing of the peas. Throughout this century there has been a growing sense of guilt from the belief that children in inner cities have somehow lost their birthright. 'City-farms' where a few animals are kept so that children can actually see a cow giving milk, are clearly inspired by such a belief.

11.3.3 In Hegel's case such alienation is associated with the making of *all* human objects. For Marx (Gouldner, 1980; p.180) 'it has been narrowed to work products. Unlike Hegel, who stressed one-sidedly the valuable functions that labor performed for humanity, Marx stressed the negative side of labor...no longer [regarding it]...as a universal human phenomenon, but [linking]... it to the mode of production, in general, and to the property system of capitalism in particular'. In the following paragraph I have deliberately chosen to express the Marxist analysis of alienation in the language used throughout this book, rather than to use Marxist terms which might obscure the connection with the other ideas: but I believe few Marxists would find fault with the essential content.

11.3.4 For Marx there are several separate but interacting aspects of alienation, as follows:

(1) Because what the worker produces is taken and exchanged in the market by somebody else, he not only loses all control of it, but he recognizes **himself** as being a commodity to be bought and sold. Moreover, for the transaction to have been valuable to the capitalist, the worker can presume that *he has less worth than the thing he produced.*

(2) The situation just described makes what he produces alien to him. Consequently, whatever the technology used, the worker would be engaged in such activity only for instrumental reasons and not for any intrinsic satisfaction. Division of labour to achieve higher output only makes work even more meaningless and alien. (We have only to recall Charlie Chaplin performing his mindless task on a conveyor belt, paragraph 3.2.17, to understand this latter point.)

(3) The whole capitalist exchange principle means that everything has a

price. This is therefore not only a concept which demeans human relationships, but by making it possible to buy man's very essence, it detaches him from that essence.

(4) Although the working class bear the brunt of this alienation, no one escapes because the rationality of capitalism means that the capitalist too sees the world in terms of exchangeable commodities to which he applies opportunity cost. He is thereby denied his full humanity because he cannot bring to life the wholeness heart that should typify man's appreciation of the world.

11.3.5 For American liberals, points (1), (3) and (4) of the above list are fundamental attacks upon the institution of capitalism. They therefore choose to ignore them. Consequently, for them 'alienation' is merely the result of the division of labour in (2). Even the instrumentality within (2) which flows from (1) is ignored by them. That is to say, they see 'instrumentality' as 'work-which-lacks-any inherent satisfaction'. But providing that the inherent nature of the work is stimulating enough they see no reason why the worker should not get satisfaction from his work, no matter who benefits from it. So, for them instrumentality is a concept which is related to alienation only to the extent that work has been robbed of challenge, usually by specialization flowing from the principle of the division of labour.

11.3.6 Now it will be realized that I have accepted throughout this book the validity of the belief that the employer and the employee are in a contractual relationship and that their interests may diverge. So I have no fundamental disagreement with item (1) in paragraph 11.3.4. Moreover, (3) also flows from it. One of the reasons why we all stand in such need of the love, which (if we are fortunate) we get from family relationships is that the love endows us with worth which does not have a price on it. We are not the subject of opportunity cost. When a close relative underwent an operation for a brain tumour our whole family took turns to sit by her bed to try to talk her out of the subsequent coma. In the later months of her rehabilitation that followed, as each small advance was made towards regaining whatever faculties she might eventually acquire, we all drew from it fresh hope and satisfaction. We alternated between pride and humility at the devotion with which her husband cared for her personal needs. Nor did he count the financial cost. The reader, I feel sure, could supply many such examples from his own experience. But they will not be instances which result from applying the *mores* of the capitalist framework. They occur when the person making the commitment brings to the situation other *mores*. These come from a vision of man as having intrinsic worth. They are the product of a religious or humanist framework which goes beyond the exchange process. Indeed St Luke reports Christ as making precisely that point

(Luke 12: 6, AV): 'Are not five sparrows sold for two farthings, and not one of them is forgotten before God? But even the very hairs on your head are numbered. Fear not therefore: ye are of more value than many sparrows.'

11.3.7 That being so, why do I reject the Marxist conclusions? I do so because they are utopian. By criticizing the rationality of capitalism and claiming that this leads to alienation they invite us to conclude that by adopting their system there will be no such 'trade-off' and no such conflict. This is a children's fable...which is why Marxism has such a strong appeal to the young. If there are limited resources then something must suffer. I spoke just now of the dedication of a loving husband. But there is a twist to the story. He is a capitalist entrepreneur. The moral is two-fold. He was not so 'alienated' by capitalism that he was prevented from bringing other values to the care of his wife. Yet I confess he was not so single-minded that he did not recognize that the time he was spending with her meant that his business to some extent suffered. He consequently felt considerable guilt towards his employees, for his absences lowered the competitive edge of the company, and while this might not have placed their future in jeopardy, it certainly made it that much less secure.

11.3.8 In every aspect of life we meet the conflict of interest which occurs when we attempt to serve the greatest good of the greatest number (utilitarianism) as well as the good of each individual. It is not a product of capitalism. Indeed, agonies of conscience for Catholics the world over at this present time stem from a conflict in this same category. The official position of the Catholic Church towards married couples who practise birth control is to claim that those who do so are treating sex instrumentally. This is seen as debasing humanity in a variety of ways, but among the consequences are the damage such debasement does to them as individuals. (Many people, as I do, would question most, if not all, of the premises behind this viewpoint. But if, like me, the reader believes in the sanctity of human life, he will nevertheless understand how the Catholic Church could come to apply this interpretation.) Yet even those Catholics who would accept the validity of their Church's viewpoint when considering the effect on the individual (the sparrow) are horrified when they contemplate its consequences for the greatest good of the greatest number. When such Catholics lift their eyes from the individual to humanity *en masse*, and particularly to the people of the Third World, they find the Malthusian implications at least disconcerting and frequently insupportable. For the more we succeed in overcoming death from pestilence, the greater is the chance of death from starvation...unless the population is controlled. God forbid that we should ever witness famine, and say with the satisfaction of Trevelyan (paragraph 11.1.38) 'that the problem ...being beyond the powers of men, the cure has been applied by the direct stroke of an all-wise Providence'.

11.3.9 Neither is Marxism free of the contradictions between the good of the individual and the good of all. I have throughout maintained that Taylorism and the division of labour are essential to physical prosperity. Alvin Gouldner (who is better known to management students for his critique of bureaucracy) has written a book which looks at the evolution of Marxism (Gouldner, 1980). Basically he sees it as going through three phases:

(1) a stage when it distinguishes itself from other concepts;
(2) a period when new impulses are constrained by the theoretical commitments of the first stage; and
(3) a third stage as the theory hardens into what is to be handed to posterity. It is at this stage that the theorists have to attempt to cope with the anomalies of the second stage. It is here that Marxism's contradiction between human emancipation and its reliance on a centralized state come into relief.

11.3.10 Of particular interest to this present discussion is that Gouldner draws our attention to an admission of Marx's closest associate, Friedrich Engels (1820–95). Engels argued

> that the division of labor is a need of the society as a whole; it does not result from the class system but from the needs of society; it is not produced by class division but produces it...In short the function of the division of labor and of the class system organized around it is not simply to serve as a framework for the exploitation of one class by another; rather it performs a service to society as a whole. (Gouldner, 1980; pp.182–183). [Then follows a direct quote from Engels.] 'But if, upon this showing, division into classes has a certain historic justification, it has this only for a given period...It was based upon [Gouldner's emphasis] **the insufficiency of production**. It will be swept away by the complete development of modern productive forces. (Gouldner, 1980; p.183.)

11.3.11 Was there ever such a justification for Taylorism – for at what stage are we going to say that we have a sufficiency of production? Life in general will surely mirror what has happened with the National Health Service. There we have found that the need always expands at a faster rate than it can be resourced. Will there ever be a time when this will not be true? Certainly not in the foreseeable future. Yet, as Gouldner says, (1980; p.184), 'wherever there is any institutionalized arrangement allowing one group to exercise control over the means and processes of production , that group constitutes a ruling class. This means that without the total elimination of division of labor, where some direct and others obey, there must always be a ruling class.' Gouldner also points out that this is so irrespective of who the **owners** are.

11.3.12 We have seen that job enrichment is not achievable within the technical and economic constraints which surround most jobs. Does this mean that the worker must lose his humanity by alienation? Much management writing assumes that no worker could operate in a wholly 'instrumental' way and still retain his humanity. There is a great deal of literature that is geared to showing that it turns the worker into a zombie. The result is that it is regarded as quite genuinely surprising when the worker is found to be quite as well-balanced as anyone else.

11.3.13 Sometimes there are quite funny twists in the story. Here is Miklos Haraszti describing his work. Incidentally, it will be noted that he is working in a Marxist-Leninist regime in Hungary and suffering therefore under the yoke of Taylorism in a communist country.

> ... at work, when I have found the rhythm and become one with the machine, thoughts and feelings do not disappear: they change. What disappears is the direct relationship which unites them with me, the identity between me and them. This is very difficult to communicate. The best way I can put it is like this: *I* cease to exist. When the huge side-doors of the workshop are opened and the transporters rattle in loaded with material, I *know* – without having a thought as such, I simply *know* – that I am in a freezing draught, but I do not *feel* that I am cold. My back aches, there is cramp in my fingers, the piece-rate is ridiculous: I don't think or feel any of this. I only know that someone who is me feels them and thinks about them, I don't even feel or think about my work itself; I don't organize it; I only register that I am working. I know that it is I who has stopped the machine at the right time, that it is I who bends down to pick up the next piece, who hurries from one machine to the other, who avoids the crack in the platform. There is no more thought or feeling, or, at least, I'm not bothered by them any more: they have become objects of independent contemplation. In the end exertion itself ceases to exist: there is only a consciousness (or is it a memory?) of my exhaustion. I am aware of how great my tiredness is; I know that when I have finished this run I am going to feel exhaustion right in the marrow of my bones, and I know in advance that it will be hard for me to get the next batch going, and to drop back again into the same state, I am the rhythm of the machine, and this perhaps is why, of all else from the world outside work, it is sex – of the same inert, impersonal character – which finds a place in my consciousness. To make love without loving: the rhythm drives me on; I *know* what I feel and what I will feel, but I do not *feel* it. When a thought materializes against all odds, it cannot break lose. It is snapped up by the rhythm, and turns round, like a caged squirrel in a tread-mill (Haraszti, 1977; pp. 112-113).

11.3.14 Was ever there a greater or more compelling piece of writing to show the allegedly alienative effect of instrumental work? He had previously said that to make his condition tolerable he would put himself into a sort of trance.

> '...The machines themselves help me find ways to do this. Their different rhythms add up to a new rhythm, which I take up, flow with, and try to anticipate: this almost gives me pleasure, because I feel that I am approved of and confirmed by the machines. To become aware of a thought is as much of a hindrance to my work as a fault in the machine, slippage in a spindle, stiffness in the speed controls, or the jamming of the starting button. In the same way, a clear thought emerging in consciousness is also the enemy of relaxation, of that relaxation close to suspended animation into which you plunge when you get home from work. I react to them with the same hostility as in the factory and with the same wish to flee from them as when I am at work. In such moments, I know that I still belong to the machine, that I have not yet regained myself. But if someone lives like this from his childhood on, does he know that there is anything to regain?' (Haraszti; 1977; p. 112.)

11.3.15 He makes us see that the effect of 'alienation' is to prevent anyone from subsequently leaving his place of work and self-actualizing outside the work-place. But now comes the twist. **It is because Haraszti rose above his physical circumstances** and went home to write such a moving explanation of the 'alienative' power of such repetitive, mindless work that we see how **awful** it is. The irony is that, despite all his protestations to the contrary, it still lay within the power of Haraszti to go away from his dehumanizing machinery and write this very human autobiography. He thereby becomes, at one and the same time, a monument to the power of the machine over the human spirit, and the power of the human spirit over the machine. I do not seek to deny the low quality of life when performing so-called 'alienative' work. But I do suggest that (if such work **has** to be performed) mankind has more resilience in handling it than is often assumed to be the case.

11.3.16 Let us turn to the role of 'alienation' in the capitalist liberal's concepts. I have explained that, for him, the concept is the same as 'deprivation in work'. Everyone, in so far as it is **possible** to abolish such deprivation, may genuinely be concerned to do so. But abolition's strongest appeal is to agnostic or atheistic liberals, who believe that abolishing such working conditions will issue in a new era of enlightenment. By contrast Christian, Jewish and other theists who are able to face the duality in human nature are less prone to emphasize the significance of such 'alienation'. This does not mean that they underestimate the effects of monotonous work. Indeed, their religion would make it morally offensive for them to maintain such conditions unnecessarily. However, as 'spiritual' people, they realize also that the human spirit is more resilient than materialistically minded people are inclined to credit. There is also a certain arrogance in regarding another human being as being quite so easy a victim of circumstance. Ordinary people can exhibit enormous spiritual reserves; and in any case, according to Katz and Kahn (1978; p. 381) such people may have three practical reasons for not becoming 'alienated'. These are that:

(i)   '...a better lot for themselves in the future or a better way of life for their children...may be enough to prevent disaffection.'
(ii) 'prevention of alienation may not require the satisfaction of all three types of internal motivation. One type may be enough to keep people involved in their organizations.' [What these three types are the reader can infer from their next comment. 'The worker who does not internalize the values of the company may have fairly interesting work. The worker who lacks that may identify with the immediate work group, with his or her occupational group, or even the organization as a whole.'
(iii) '...workers belong to other system-supportive groupings beside the employing organization... and hence [are] not alienated from the larger system.'

11.3.17 Whether or not we find Katz and Kahn's argument convincing depends upon how we define 'alienation' in the first place. Those who tend towards the Marxist definition of the word will question whether Katz and Kahn's escape routes are really valid. Michael Rose, for example, in commenting upon the lack of self-estrangement felt by some textile workers of whom Blauner had written said the following: 'Far from mitigating their objective alienation, it demonstrates the extent of their genuine alienation... To oversimplify, they are the victims of false consciousness' (Rose, 1978; p.210). Blauner's attempt to equate **'deprivation in work'** with **'alienation'** says Rose (1978; p.211), 'is at best misleading, though it is eloquent of the limitations of the social scientific tradition in which [Blauner] was working'.

11.3.18 Well, we should have been naïve indeed, not to have anticipated this argument from Rose. For clearly no amount of evidence can get past the road-block of 'false-consciousness'. On that basis Rose has a free hand to decide what is, and what is not admissible. We are irresistibly reminded of the way in which Mayo denied the validity of what the worker said because of his lack of reality born of his 'obsessive thinking'. Yet Rose's attack upon the American social scientific tradition is not unjust. Indeed, I have already claimed that a strong case could be made for claiming that the neo-human relations school serves as a devious means to emphasize managerial control. For by making 'alienation' identical to 'work deprivation' *they place the power to eliminate alienation in the hands of managers.*

OM-J*

This monopoly would of course be broken if the worker were able to 'self actualize' **outside** his place of work, which is probably why they are so anxious to deny that anyone can compensate by doing so there.

11.4 The unacceptable claim: 'freedom from conflict'

11.4.1 The attempt to motivate employees means that to a certain extent they must share the goals of management. This has been universally recognized. However, the error that every unitary theorist has made is to attempt to claim for each system the property of being conflict free. This denies the validity of the employee's standpoint in those instances when he challenges the goals of management.

11.4.2 Yet this attitude is basically totalitarian and one that we should shun. Clegg (paragraph 10.3.9) shows that to expect the 'active participation' of a trade union is not a right and proper expectation. Perhaps it would be possible for the employees actively to co-operate while leaving the union job of reserving their position for them. However, this is to suggest that the employee should not interest himself in his own union, but simply regard it as a policeman that he can call upon to guard his interests. Yet this is too undemocratic and political activists will use such apathy to control the union for their own ends unless checked by the rank and file.

11.4.3 Moreover, nearly everything that has been suggested as a unitary motivational system has had strongly manipulative overtones. The imagery is that the system is like an automatic dispenser. If we put the right coins in the slot, out will come the obedient worker. I thank God that this appalling conceit has foundered upon the rock of human cussedness. Long may that live!

11.4.4 Yet if we get rid of this obnoxious imagery, then most of the things that the various theorists have suggested we consider doing have some merit. Mayo is right to suggest that we all need social relationships. He is probably right when he infers that group norms are stronger than other inducements to action in many employees. Where he goes wrong is in his suggestion that these group norms are easily swayed because they have no basis in rationality. In effect the worker is prey to every mountebank who gets his hands upon the levers of the 'group norms', be he manager or agitator.

11.4.5 Yet neither is there any doubt that, on occasion, theses group norms **will** work against management, as they did in the case of the bank wiring room. Roy's experience on the shop floor rings true to me (paragraph 9.4.25). From my own experience I also favour the belief that **when it suits them** (i.e. when in non-threatening and economically bouyant situation under which group norms are relaxed), incentive payment schemes can be very effective. In other situations, where the reverse is true, workers will connive to reduce output. **What else should we expect?**

11.4.6 I shall have something to say about incentive payments schemes after we have considered them technically. Their true significance has less to do with getting high output rates per worker than it does with identifying managerial inefficiency and stabilizing unit costs. This is not generally understood. This same technical ignorance has also meant that the evidence that people frequently **do** usually work harder when on incentive payments has also been ignored.

11.4.7 When departments are work-studied they are frequently also put on incentive schemes. Most frequently the output goes up. Those people who are anxious to show that the donkey will resist running after the carrot usually claim that this increase is principally the result of the method changes. The work-study engineer, however is able to identify the input effort of the people in a department quite independently of the methods used. He refers to it as the 'application' of the employee to the job. He is therefore able to distinguish between increase in output due to *method improvement* and increase in output due to *employee application*. This knowledge is not used in research findings, however. It is a matter for speculation to what extent this glaring omission results from such knowledge being ideologically inconvenient to the researchers and to what extent it is the result of ignorance.

11.4.8 The physical output of the department is measured by the work-study engineer in a unit known as the 'standard minute value' of the work produced. Just as any product has such characteristics as size and weight, so it contains yet another characteristic. This is its 'work content'. By this is meant the length of time it would take to perform that job by a well-trained well-motivated average worker using that technology. When due allowance has been made for appropriate rest and relaxation, the total length of time which results is the *'standard minute value'* of the job. So if product 'A' contains 30 standard minutes of work and I produce 10 of them, then that output is worth *(quite irrespective of how long I happen to spend upon it)* 300 standard minutes, or alternatively, 5 standard hours. Armed with that knowledge, let us look at the claims made for the system known as 'measured day-rates'.

11.4.9 The popularity of neo-human relations concepts in the early 1960's made it fashionable to suggest that work study should be used for measurement of output, but that a high fixed hourly wage should be paid in preference to any known form of incentive payments scheme. The resultant payment system was known as 'measured day-rate'. This meant that factories which had previously used *incentive payments tied to work study* would only be changing the one variable, i.e. *the payment system.* The *methods* would remain unchanged. Moreover, a direct comparison was readily available and to make that comparison involved no extra work. The output in 'standard hours produced' was known both before and after. The attendance hours were known before and after. Dividing **(60 × 'The standard hours produced')** by the **('attendance hours')** would give the operator output of the department in **'standard minutes per attendance hour'** both before and after.

11.4.10 Several consultancy firms of the day were extolling the virtues of 'measured day-rate' and I attended many seminars in which they spoke of their recent successful case studies. Each time I asked the same question, **'what was the standard minute output per attendance hour, (a) before and (b) after dropping incentive payments?'** In no case did they have the figures. Yet if that were really true they were admitting to an unbelieveable piece of technical incompetence. I could only conclude that the results were too embarrassing to publish and would have been commercially damaging to their chances of selling their services as installers of 'measured day-rate' schemes. My own approach is to operate on the basis that incentive schemes are a tool, but should be applied with the greatest discretion, for they can also be inappropriate. They are costly to administer and may reduce quality, and they cannot be used at all where measurement is not possible. Jobs such as those that require much thought do not express effort of a sort that can be measured in the way that physical activity can.

11.4.11 Even if incentive payment schemes based on work study are used, we should not fall into the trap of believing, as Taylor appeared to have done, and certainly as he preached, that this would be a specific remedy for all industrial conflict. The work-study rates themselves can be a cause of resentment, and the belief was silly from the start that the worker would harbour no resentment at being used either intrumentally or individualistically. Yet to imply that Taylorite managers or that Taylor himself **deliberately** created working conditions which fostered these two characteristics is misleading.

11.4.12 He **did** try to stop groups from forming, because he saw their norms as **inimicable** to the interests of management, and (as we saw) Hoxie, Weber and others agreed with that assessment. I am personally less convinced of the permanent hostility of the group to management. I believe that the group's attitude will be **ambivalent.** But a policy of deliberately preventing group formation is more than morally questionable. If we consider such a policy only from the standpoint of managerial expediency, it is arguable that inhibiting such groups from forming would do more harm than good. Managers therefore are stuck with having to deal with problems of group norms in the full knowledge that such norms may be restrictive and also that it will not be as simple as Mayo implied to influence them towards management's goals. This is because, right or wrong, **there is a rationale to restrictive behaviour.** It is no less rational than artificially restricting the champagne harvest in France, or releasing only slowly on to the market all the hundreds of Picasso paintings which that workaholic left behind him when he died in 1973. The tendency to regard restrictive practices as non-rational is based in two associated ideas:

(1) The worker's main preoccupation is to continue to earn his living in that particular environment.
(2) The worker sees a direct connection between his expenditure of effort be his continuance in work in that environment.

Yet neither of these two things is necessarily true. In times of full-employment he may see little to choose between his present job and any other: indeed, the grass on the other side of the fence may look greener. As for the second concept, I suggest that he seldom holds this view, nor is he necessarily wrong in that. In salvaging a company I have sometimes axed a particular department or division. Some of those made redundant were hard-working faithful employees, **but they did not thereby preserve their jobs against the overall economic pressures.** Alternatively, the worker may see his own contribution as doing little to stop the general rot. In any case, my experience has been that few workers, or union officials either, take seriously the economic threats that face a company. They tend to see any warnings as a management ploy. Finally, there is the time-element which militates against high output to safeguard employment. This is that it is **today** that effort must be made, even though the rewards of continued employment are in some hypothetical tomorrow. Let me not be misunderstood. I am not denying that many workers **do** work conscientiously and identify closely with their firms. I am merely emphasizing the reasons why we should not assume that they are 'non-rational' when they do not see themselves as being in the same boat as the management, nor that they are 'rational' when they do. **Groups may very well operate restrictive practices based upon a** *questionable* **rationale, at other times, given their world of 'cost-benefit' trade-offs, it would be difficult**

to fault their logic. Seldom have I met an instance where I felt it could be claimed that their actions were 'non-rational'.

11.4.13 Perhaps we should regard Taylor as being more realistic than most of his critics in his assumption that the worker would be prepared to be used 'instrumentally'. After all, if the technological and economic constraints make jobs intrinsically boring, and if Taylor saw that market- and other forces made it unlikely that those constraints could be relieved, then it would have been logically consistent if Taylor had also seen the worker as being faced with one of three options:

(1) To renounce the work and find alternative work within the system.
(2) To renounce the work and the system equally. (What system will get around the problem and still produce sufficient surplus to raise life above mere subsistence level is another issue. However, it is no new thing for mankind to crusade for the impossible.)
(3) To perform the work in an instrumental way. (Indeed, if the work is boringly repetitive, what other option does the worker have than to insulate himself from it by doing it automatically and living inside his head?)

It seems to me that Taylor's attitude (which was to assume (3) above) was not only logical, but that his payment of high wages in compensation was a moral act. Certainly I find it preferable to the unctious attitude of Mayo.

11.4.14 For it will be remembered that it was exactly the working conditions that are brought about by (3) above that tend to create the 'low-grade reveries' that so much concerned Mayo. He saw these (and not the objective circumstances in the management/worker instrumental relationships) as responsible for (paragraph 9.3.7) 'disorder and unrest (absenteeism, high labor turnover [and] strikes)'. His answer, it will be remembered, was 'counselling'. I find this concept very distasteful. I regret the circumstances that force managements to offer workers employment that they can only perform instrumentally. However, I regard that as forgivable if there is no feasible option. What strikes me as unforgivable hypocrisy is that management should then feel they have the right to 'counsel' the worker involved.

11.4.15 The object of this book is to help the student or manager to understand the existing management theory jungle and to be able to compare and contrast theories. I have used the concept of 'political holon man' to this end. It is not a theory of motivation *per se*. It claims however to be the reality with which any future valid theory of motivation must deal.

The implications of that claim are three-fold. They are:

(1) That pluralist concepts are fundamental to any genuine understanding of (and description of) what motivates the worker.
(2) That capitalist market forces create the survival requirement of co-operation and the potential for a conflict of interests. Whichever mode is prevalent, it will always contain ambiguous echoes from the other.
(3) That the Janus-like quality in all hierarchies creates a further set of ambiguities between part and whole and the need to keep integrative elements in balance.

11.4.16 If I were asked to speculate on where future motivation theory could most fruitfully develop, I would hazard that it would be based on Vroom's model. It should attribute a basic rationality to the worker. It should recognize that his *Weltanschauung* is such that he understands the limitations of the capitalist firm's commitment to him, and has very largely come to terms with this as a fact of life. He also largely accepts the technological and economic constraints associated with his job. So his expectations of his employer are limited by a realistic awareness of the constraints which the capitalist firm operates. To the despair of Marxists, most working men in Britain, even if they call themselves socialist, put their faith in modified capitalism. It is their basic belief in capitalism and the pluralist institution of parliamentary democracy which distinguishes the right-wing of the Labour Party from its Left. The same belief system informs the Social Democratic Party, the Liberal Party, and the Conservative Party. We should not overlook that fact that Conservative governments would never be elected if they did not get a considerable slice of the working-class vote. Yet the worker is vulnerable. So the theory should validate potential and actual conflict and validate trade union activity as a legitimate means for the worker to increase his bargaining position. In short, because the theory is pluralist it must blow hot and cold at the same time, to come up with some sort of calculus which, while acknowledging the validity of conflict, makes long-term co-operation appear preferable.

PART THREE

Organization

In this part I shall seek to show that although classical organization theory is claimed to be outdated and mechanistic, yet it has certain inherent links with capitalism which make it perennially appropriate to the capitalist enterprise. That being so I shall seek to rehabilitate it, for the importance of its role in capitalist firms has been woefully misunderstood.

It is widely realized that classical theory was the earliest attempt to find some way of splitting up a large concern without losing economies of scale. But it is widely maintained that its inadequacies are great, and stem from its mechanistic approach. It is claimed its mechanistic imagery has led classical theorists:

(1) To ignore the human element; (a criticism associated with the human relations approach to organization design); and
(2) To ignore the organic interaction which should exist between the firm and its environment and between its internal specialist sections (a criticism associated with the systems approach).

I accept that classical theory warranted some of this criticism and has profited from the encounter. It is a pity that the encounter taught the human relations and systems theorists so little. I invite them to consider whether they could not, in return, profit from classical concepts. The two things they need most to accept is that hierarchies are a matter of necessity and moreover under the mores *of capitalism, subdivisions must be made in a manner which will*

(a) minimize opportunity costs, and

(b) will be able to demonstrate (by competitive comparison) that they have succeeded in this.

The constraints involved in meeting the above requirements predetermine most organizational design, thereby ridding classical organization theory of March and Simon's criticism. This is that classical theory leaves open too many options to be a useful guide to organizational design. In the abstract it appears to do so... in practice the above constraints almost invariably determine a preferred unique solution. Where they do not, I suggest that the choice of option is then a matter of indifference.

12

How we see the problem shapes our theories

12.1 The importance of asking the right questions

12.1.1 In paragraphs 2.3.2 to 2.3.5 we saw that the question 'What were the causes of the French Revolution?' was, for all its apparent innocence, heavily loaded. By asking it the examiner implanted in the mind of the examinee a readiness to regard human societies as normally stable, and to assume that this stability would resist all but the strongest forces of intervention. Few would be able to see this hidden modelling. Fewer still would be likely to suggest that the question might be inverted so that we asked 'Why was the French Revolution so long delayed, given the iniquitous state of pre-revolutionary society?'

12.1.2 Loaded questions on organizational matters similarly produce loaded organizational theories. Theories are attempts to answer questions about relationships that interest us. 'How can we achieve X?' ... 'Why does A result in B?' ... etc. Yet just as the question concerning the French Revolution was loaded, so too may these be. Perhaps 'X' is not the thing that we **should** be seeking. Perhaps 'B' results in 'A' and we are confusing cause with effect. All this being so, we should expect the theories to reflect the bias contained in the original format of the question they sought to answer.

12.1.3 There have been four fundamentally different ways in which theorists have asked questions about organizations, so four different sets of theories have resulted. These theories have been presented in an 'either ... or' fashion in much of the literature. By now that should not surprise us. Yet if each theory seeks to answer legitimate questions, each may mirror some aspect of truth. If the reader will forgive the lapse in English, reality is better comprehended when we adopt our (by now familiar) *'both ... and'* attitude rather than the more common *'either ... or'* attitude towards all four of them.

12.1.4 With such an attitude the reader will gain a greater insight: but I must warn against any hope that he can ultimately blend all these concepts into a comprehensive, internally consistent whole. For each contains elements antagonistic to the rest. Reality will be found to lie in all and none. We gradually come to glimpse where the truth lies as we oscillate between the *frames of reference* of the various approaches.

12.2. The four organizational models: an overview

12.2.1 I was tempted to write that there were five such models, and to include a school who doubt our very ability to specify organizational goals either with enough rigour or enough awareness of possible consequence ever to deserve the name of 'rational'. Even if we had enough rigour and had been aware enough of consequence, these critics doubt whether management would subsequently try to attain these goals by a process of: (a) finding the best possible means and (b) applying the maximum possible effort. Yet anything less than doing all these things would also be less than 'rational'. March and Simon have drawn attention to this problem and so, from a different standpoint, has Lindblom (Ansoff, 1969; pp.41 – 60). In these critiques all three have performed a great service for everyone concerned with management theory. But, to date, their writings have served only to warn of our inadequacies. They have not provided a positive approach to generating a distinct type of organizational model. I have therefore restricted myself to the other four models, though I shall later question Simon and March's position.

12.2.2 *The 'classical' model.* As its name suggests, this was the earliest approach to organization theory. The problem to which these theorists applied themselves arose from the fact that by the early twentieth century many organizations had grown to such a size that no historic equivalents existed from which to learn (other than the somewhat irrelevant examples of the army or the Catholic Church). In the USA firms were so huge that the Sherman Anti-Trust Act was thought necessary as early as 1890. The Act's effect in slowing organizational growth was minimal. By 1930 United States Steel was a conglomerate owning *'railways connecting its ore and coal properties with the Great Lakes and its manufacturing units, a fleet of vessels on the lakes and a fleet on the high seas to facilitate its foreign business, car, bridge and shipbuilding plants, tin plate, tube and pipe, oil and gas works, cement plants, zinc mines and various other properties...'* (Shields, 1930; p.84) Yet if such size gave the American people a socio-political problem, it gave the managements of such concerns just as much a headache. Size created enormous problems for them; for in any attempt to maintain control, then as now, 'small is beautiful'. On the other hand, their success was related to size, not only because of the oligopolistic markets that size gave to them but also because size brought with it certain economies of scale. This conflict meant that these managers needed concepts that would help them to break these huge concerns into smaller, more controllable sub-units while still hanging on to the economies of scale. Classical organization theory set out to fill this need. It was a child of its age: an age of authoritarianism and an age which had fallen in love with mechanistic concepts of every type. Men everywhere tried to reduce the world to certain fundamental frameworks inside which society could operate, secure in the knowledge that 'natural law' prevailed. Why were such 'natural laws' reassuring? *Firstly, they limited the options open to the administrator and it is reassuring to believe that there are only a limited number of possibilities. Secondly, the 'principles' upon which these laws were supposed to operate absolved the decision-maker of guilt.* Natural law is **not** a matter of *morality*, it is a matter of *fact*. The air was still heavy with the legacy of the late eighteenth and nineteenth centuries. Smith, Malthus, Ricardo and Darwin had all seen the world as a great machine, operating upon certain 'principles'. There had been the 'principle' of the division of labour, of population, of non-intervention in economic affairs, and of natural selection. From the 1890s onward, Taylor had gradually codified the four 'great underlying principles of management' that made up 'scientific management'. Why should not some equally universal 'principles' of organization determine the format and operation of organizations at every level and in every circumstance? It was in this spirit that 'classical' organization theory was born. It has, as we shall see, all the strengths and weaknesses of its parentage.

12.2.3 *The model of the 'contingency theorists'.* These theorists cover a wide spectrum of organizational thought so that their particular areas of interest can be very diverse. What they all have in common is a shared doubt that any 'general' organization theories can exist which have **universal** application. They claim that theories will only be appropriate in specific circumstances and they try to discover what these **contingent** relationships are. In the case of Joan Woodward, (one of the most famous of these) it was the **universal** applicability of certain classical 'principles' that she questioned. *(We should note that not all writers should be classified by the image that they have of themselves. Woodward's research was performed by a 'Human Relations Research Unit' funded by, among others, the Medical Research Council. I make no apology for regarding the whole project as essentially a **modifier** of classical thought, nor for claiming that the outcome was to produce* *'contingency-modified classical principles'. By so doing she reinforced the classical view because, by inference, she implied that their fundamental philosophy was basically right, even if its application were in some respects faulty. Her approach is therefore – to my mind – a variant within classical theory.)*

12.2.4 *The 'human relations' model.* In the area of motivation theory the term 'human relations' refers to the work of Mayo and his followers. When the term is used as an approach to the wider aspects of organization theory it embraces all those concepts which take as their focal point the reciprocal effects that organizations and people have upon each other. As a portmanteau name for this broad approach it includes many 'neo-human relations' precepts in addition to specifically 'human relations' ideas. Its attack is principally against 'classical organization theory'. However, it is probably less concerned with presenting a free-standing and comprehensive approach to organization theory than in seeking to modify 'classical' thought. *It highlights the way in which the mechanistic aspects of classical theory could, precisely because such mechanistic concepts are less than human, prove counterproductive to the very efficiency upon which classical theory so prides itself.*

12.2.5 *The 'systems' model.* Few 'systems' theorists take kindly to their approach being seen as a **reaction** to classical theory. In this they are probably justified. Since the Second World War 'general systems theory' has influenced every walk of life and every academic discipline. It has affected the way we look at everything from weapons to ecology, from economics to medicine, and from mathematics to history. It is arguable that (even if classical thought had never existed) 'systems thinking' would have been applied to management. Yet I cannot avoid the conclusion that the very existence of classical thought has had a channelling, polarizing and detrimental effect upon the emphasis that systems management theory has applied. This is because of classical concepts of organizational structure has absolved systems writers from the need to consider the problems of **authority** relationships. *So although they threw stones at the classical school's hierarchical concepts they were able to duck the issue of creating their own because, in the meanwhile, the world continued to turn, thanks to the continued application of those same classical structures.* This has been a great pity. Systems' antipathy to classical philosophy is fundamental. *The classical authority framework is seen by systems writers as restricting any data-flow **other** than downwards and its rigidity is seen as reducing the organization's ability to adapt.* In systems thought this rigidity is a fundamental sin. The ability of the organism to sense a change in its environment, and then to go through a process of adaptation to accommodate that change, is seen as vital to its survival. Consequently these 'systems' writers think that **the 'classical' manager will fail even in his search for efficiency.** In the first place (they claim) he falsely assumes that making each part of the organization efficient will make the total organization efficient. Moreover, he is so preoccupied with **internal** efficiency that *he neglects to see far more significant changes in the environment to which he should be responding.* In the jargon of the systems approach, the classical manager's tendency is to see the firm as a **'closed'** system, a term that we shall later define.

12.2.6 These then are the fundamentally different issues upon which the various theorists have concentrated. *On a priori grounds we should expect each of these approaches to prove inadequate, precisely* **because** *it does not ask the questions posed by the others.* Of course there are 'systems' theorists who would maintain that if the system has been correctly specified it should cover all four aspects. In a sense they are right. Am I not even now trying to give the reader models which will enable him to build an appropriate organization system when the time comes? Is it not implicit in that aim that we should incorporate all the significant elements of the different approaches in one system?

12.2.7 But there **are** as I already indicated, problems of mutual incompatibility between theories, and in any case systems theorists have to date given us no adequate models of **authority structures** consistent with their position. This is because most systems writers, like Simon, have regarded 'management' as synonymous with 'decision-making'. *This is a serious mistake. Management is much more than that. Not least, 'management' entails ensuring that decisions taken get implemented. This is where classical theory comes into its own.*

12.3 Classical theory's 'loaded' question

12.3.1 A question does not have to be intellectually dishonest to be loaded. Its loading may be such that it directs us towards a half-truth. But most of human knowledge has the quality of half-truth and we find that to be preferable to 'no-truth'. Each of the four approaches to organization theory has produced answers which encapsulate at least a portion of the truth, even if each is incomplete. Classical theory is incomplete because it looks at organizations in a 'mechanistic' way. It is not particularly interested either in creating an adaptive organism or in fostering humanism. Yet it **does** incorporate a strongly held regard for impersonal 'fairness'. This marries the concepts of classical theory to those of bureaucracy, which have the same ethos. Indeed, some of classical theory's search for fairness has made it an object of ridicule. For example, there is a scrupulous attempt in classical theory to ensure that enough authority is given to an executive to ensure that he is able to carry out his responsibilities. I am gratified that most of my students see immediately that such a principle is a **moral requirement.** Their reasoning is based upon their perception that the opposite position would be thoroughly immoral: that is to say, *it would be monstrous to hold somebody responsible for something over which he had no authority.*

12.3.2 Now this may also seem so obvious to the reader that he may wonder why I make the point. I do so because Haire (1962; p.3) is at great pains to deny this relationship.

12.3.3. Classical theory has its shortcomings which I shall not attempt to excuse. But it has also been seen as 'fair game' for anyone who wants to take a pot-shot at it. Had it not been so, I believe that the standard of criticism would have been much higher. I shall therefore attempt to redress the balance. For all its shortcomings, an attempt to give a fair press to classical theory is long overdue, and I shall attempt to show that many of its precepts are less arbitrary than many of the attacks that they have had to endure. Moreover, it asks a vital question: *'How can we subdivide an organization into manageable units without losing the economies associated with scale or losing co-ordination?'* We shall consider its ability to answer this question compared with the ability of other approaches to do the same.

12.3.4 Let us remind ourselves once again of Schein's definition of an organization with which we started Chapter 3: *'An organization is the rational co-ordination of the activities of a number of people for the achievement of some explicit purpose or goal, through division of labour and function, and through a hierarchy of authority and responsibility.'* (Schein, 1970; p.9).

12.3.5 It is, I hope, no longer necessary to argue the need for hierarchies. We dealt with that in Chapter 3. But what we haven't dealt with is *a widespread reluctance on the part of both systems and human relations writers to accept that* **authority** *structures are also part of the hierarchy principle.* This is one of the reasons why so many students of management are led to believe that the authority structures in classical management are there only to satisfy the inherent authoritarianism in classical writers. I shall not deny there **was** gratuitous authoritarianism in some of the classical writers' statements. I shall give an example of this when we deal with Graicunus in Section 12.6. But that does not mean that hierarchy can be thought of simply as a cosy framework for decision-making. Yet this is what some of the writing would lead us to infer.

12.4 Hierarchies are authority structures – we cannot pretend otherwise

12.4.1 Herbert A. Simon's talents and his influence are so great that it is presumptuous to label him. Along with James G. March and C. E. Lindblom, we cited Simon (paragraph 12.2.1) as doubting our ability to specify goals or to create organizations for their achievement with the clarity or rigour that should justify it being regarded as a 'rational' exercise. But, in the widest sense, Simon is a 'systems' writer. Yet even he, who acknowledges the need for hierarchy, seems to shy away from its role as an authority structure. There is no mention, for example, of the need for that role in the following statement. *'I can suggest at least two reasons why complex systems should generally be hierarchical:*
(1) Among possible systems of a given size and complexity, hierarchical systems, composed of subsystems, are the most likely to evolve through evolutionary processes...
(2) Among systems of a given size and complexity, hierarchical systems require much less information transmission among their parts than do other systems.' (Simon, 1960; p.41).

12.4.2 Human relations writers have applied less intellectual rigour to the subject than systems writers, so some of them **may** deny the need for hierarchy. Rensis Likert is not in this category, for he accepts the need, but he attempts to make hierarchy no more than a non-authoritative framework for 'participation'. When the full meaning of 'participation' is understood, however, we shall find that he is ultimately denying the authority role which the hierarchy plays. I shall attempt to show that his search for a non-authoritative hierarchy is a contradiction in terms.

12.4.3 First, however, we must define the terms 'participation' and 'participant'. More confusion has arisen in management literature from the sloppy use of these two slippery words than from any other single cause. Historically the words have implied the concept of 'industrial democracy', and of employees and management negotiating with each other about the running of the enterprise **as equals.** If the recommendations of the *Bullock Report* had been implemented (paragraph 2.3.8), the number of worker-directors on a company's board would have equalled the number of management-directors. This even handed attitude towards their numbers emphasizes the intention that their 'participation' was to be **as equals.**
Argyris uses the word 'participation' with the same implication; indeed he

even coins the phrase 'pseudo-participation' for **unequal** exchanges. (March and Simon (1958; p.101) devalued the word 'participant' to the extent that they used the term to refer to an employee who was bound to the company only by the most negative of ties – a lack of other opportunity. That is certainly not valid in our lexicography.) Our definition of these terms as follows: *'Participation' is the process whereby a group of people of* **equal** *status, known as the 'participants', agree and pursue certain means-ends relationships'.*

12.4.4 But this means that we are unable, by our very definition, to speak about 'participation' between **different** levels of the hierarchy. *(Here the Bullock proposals were at least consistent. The worker-directors would have been at the same level as the manager-directors. The fact that it would have reduced the boardroom to an ideological battlefield is another issue.)* But **between levels** there can only be 'consultation'. For we must face the inescapable fact that there will be times when the higher echelons will impose **their** will on to the lower echelons to ensure the direction of effort is towards **their** view of organizational objectives. This was the experience of both the Microkids and the Hardy Boys (paragraph 3.1.28). West's 'voice from the cave' drowned their protestations and ordered 'Okay, ship it!' This is why I maintain that only 'consultation' is possible between the different levels of the hierarchy. It also prevents us from getting into the tangle that enmeshed Wallace. At the end of an article in which he uses 'participation' as an exchange between equals, he adds the following words. *'In some cases certain goals have to be externally imposed by a higher management level. In these cases the participants can accept them as their goals, in the sense that they participated in the decision to accept them and in deciding how these goals will be achieved'.* (Bruns and DeCoster 1969; p.325). I feel that the study of management theory is difficult enough without this double-talk. Let us call consultation what it is, 'consultation'.

12.4.5 For the same reason I shall deny the validity of the organizational model put forward by the late Rensis Likert (1961). He accepted the basic concept of hierarchy but hoped, by a series of interlocking groups in which the representative of one group was also a member of the next higher group in the hierarchy, (see Figure 12.4(a)), to demonstrate that 'participative' management was possible. By this arrangement Likert hopes to gain the best of two worlds, hierarchy **and** participation.

12.4.6 Likert's model is a sort of conjuring trick to make black appear to be white. He tries to turn the whole pyramid into a debating society of equals. Group 3 are able to 'participate' in the running of the organization because

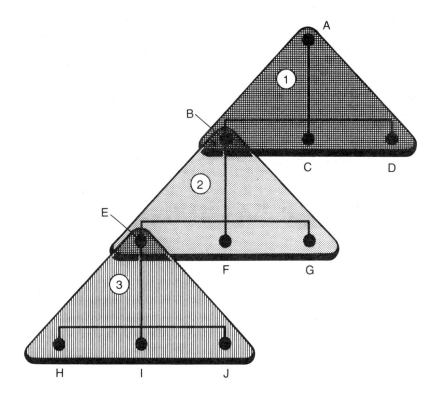

Figure 12.4(a) Likert's 'linking pin' model. (Based upon Likert, 1961; p.105.)

they have a representative, 'E', who is a member of Group 2. A 'linking pin' is Likert's expression for this role. Group 2 is similarly linked to Group 1 by another linking pin, 'B'. But even by such a model Likert cannot disguise the reality of power, nor the duty of the higher echelons to co-ordinate and control the lower ones. These duties include sacrificing the goals of the lower echelons when they run counter to senior management's view of organizational interests. Likert has just not come to terms with what Koestler acknowledged (paragraph 3.1.21), the **duality** of the Janus-like 'holon', which must be given latitude to perform but which must be kept in line by enforced integration.

12.4.7 There is another reason for being suspicious of Likert's model. Frequently we shall find certain management concepts expressed as a continuum between two opposed characteristics. Centralization and decentralization are an example. This continuum is usually portrayed as I have shown it in Figure 12.4(b) We shall find, when we come to consider the centralization/decentralization continuum, that some functions tend to be more centralized and so would tend towards the left hand side of Figure 12.4.(b)., while other functions will tend to be more decentralized and therefore tend towards the right. However, we shall also find that the extreme ends of this spectrum are only theoretical abstractions. Complete centralization or complete decentralization are unrealizable in practice.

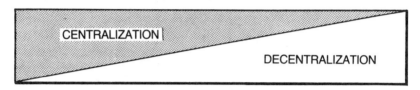

Figure 12.4(b)

12.4.8 Similarly, Likert suggests (1967) that there are four different management systems' which in effect, lie along an authoritarianism/ participation continuum, as shown in Figure 12.4(c) Here again we should doubt the possibility that either end of this continuum can exist. Although economic pressure can enable some organizations to be exploitive and authoritative **to a degree,** in a pluralist society we could question how workable System 1 is. System 4, as I have already argued, is a myth.

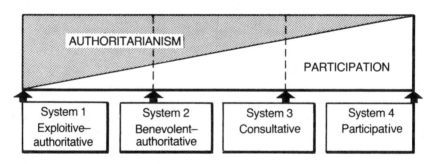

Figure 12.4(c)

12.5 The triangular shape of hierarchies

12.5.1 The characteristic shape of a hierarchy is that of a triangle with the organization coming to an apex of control. What we have already said so far explains why they must come to a central controlling will. Just as the Greeks eventually came to discard pantheism for monotheism, because they argued that order in the universe had to be the result of a single will, so we too can see that there must be some superior will to unify the organization's means with its ends. But although this explains the apex, it doesn't explain the triangle. Why should the arrangement not be that of a single vertical column with a single one-to-one chain of command?

12.5.2 Well one reason is that this would mean that if there were 1000 people in a company, there would be a single vertical chain of command of 1000 levels. Communication either up or down the chain would be a nightmare. Beside which this would be completely crazy from another standpoint. The greatest amount of communication would be likely to be between people in the same function (for example that of production), who should therefore be adjacently located. Let us group people by function within the imaginary column. Then the bottom 300 might be production people, the next 50 research, and so on up to the managing director at the top of the column. In this case, since the column is 1000 people tall, there will be a chain of command of 700 people, of all functions, between the managing director and the first person in the production function. He would presumably be the production director.

12.5.3 Not only would this be a crazy chain of command, with people who had no interest in the production function details getting involved, but there would be the problem of the lowliest worker in one of the other functions giving instruction to the production director. Of course, an alternative would be to arrange the column by status. If there were, say, five functions we could have the top of the column composed of the five functional directors. The next five places in the column could be taken by the next senior person in each function, and so on down the column. Now nobody in the same function is adjacent in the hierarchy to anyone from his own function and an instruction from the production director to the next senior person in the production function would presumably have to pass through the representatives of the other four functions for no purpose.

12.5.4 It wouldn't be very long before they started to cut out the intervening people from different functions. In effect they would have set up five separate parallel columns under the managing director, one for each function. Yet even within the functions this would still seem a silly arrangement. In production we would have a column of 300 people. Yet some of these would be doing identical work and no purpose could possibly be served by putting them above one another in the chain of command even if we could distinguish between them in status. Each needs precisely the same sort of supervision and each must be provided with similar instructions, tools, machinery and raw materials. But none can look to the other to supply these things, for each stands in equal need of them. Surely it would make more sense to have them jointly supervised and to have them fed by others whose specialist duty it is to see that inputs and outputs are co-ordinated? In which case, those performing identical work would be better arranged in a horizontal rather than a vertical grouping. Some teams of people **must** be in such an arrangement. But to go on would be tedious. Such combinations of horizontal and vertical groupings, whose output must be co-ordinated, lead inevitably to the familiar triangle. The only reason why I have bothered to make the point is that there are hints in some of the literature that the arrangement is arbitrary. It is not, though some of the fancy structures that appear in some of the systems writings are, in my opinion, very much so. What **is** negotiable is the way that the various triangles will be formed and interlock within the total triangle of the enterprise, and whether the triangles should be tall and thin or short and fat.

12.5.5 This particular issue has given Simon great scope to pursue his attack upon classical 'principles', which he refers to as 'proverbs'. In the second edition of this book *Administrative Behaviour* (Simon, 1957), he congratulates himself that *'there has been almost no attempt to controvert what is said in these pages* [i.e. his critique of classical 'principles in the first edition] – *indeed they have often been cited with approval. On the other hand'* he bemoans, *'the "proverbs" still occupy the prominent place they have always had in the pages of the elementary textbooks...'* The reason why the question of the shape of the triangle has given him so much ammunition is that classical 'principles' offer conflicting advice in the matter.

12.5.6 To understand the point it is necessary to understand the term 'span of control'. This refers to the number of subordinates reporting directly to any one executive. In figure 12.5(a) the span of control is four. Since the span of control in the above organization is four it can accommodate a total of 21 people in 3 levels. If we wish to increase the size of this organization to approximately 90 people there are two ways that we could do it:

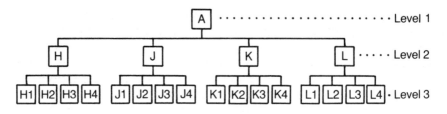

Figure 12.5(a)

1. Giving 4 subordinates to everyone in Level 3 would add 64 people and make a total of 85 at the expense of creating a further layer.
2. Holding the number of levels to 3 but increasing the span of control, say to 9, would give 91 people, as follows:

Level 1	1
Level 2	9
Level 3	81
Total	91

12.5.7 Clearly, as an organization grows in size we cannot indefinitely restrict both the number of levels **and** the span of control. Something has to give. This is why Simon is so ironic in dealing with this issue; for the classical theorists proposed **at one and the same time** that there would be a strict upper limit on the span of control and also the fewest practical number of levels. Such combined restrictions would appear to set the severest limits upon the size to which organizations can grow.

12.5.8 Thus far Simon's logic is impeccable. Yet we need not conclude with him that this conflict shows that the principles are invalid. We often find it necessary to subscribe to two principles that mutually conflict. *Indeed, it is precisely because judges have to hold the balance between two opposite but valid principles that they have such a high degree of discretion when they pass sentence.* For all who break the law must stand trial and, if the case is proven, be found guilty. The greatest good of the greatest number, the principle of utilitarianism, demands this. Yet the Judaeo-Christian principle that the fall of the sparrow is also important makes the individual's circumstances significant. By allowing judicial discretion we reconcile the two opposing principles, sincc no one would dream of suggesting that this conflict makes both or either principle invalid. Why should these two organizational 'principles' receive lesser treatment? In any case common sense dictates that for effective control we must keep both the span **and** the number of levels within limits.

12.5.9 Nor does this create an impossible quandary. If an increase in either is unacceptable, then the two principles have brought home to us that it would be better to duplicate or to divisionalize the organization rather than to go on building a hierarchical monstrosity. The two principles do not in themselves provide us with the criteria by which we may trade off the height versus the width of the triangle. This absence of specific detail concerning how the classical 'principles' are to be applied is also criticized by March and Simon. This is because the most appropriate departmentalization (which is what we are seeking with our triangles of different shapes and natures) will, if achieved, be a product of (1) the ends being sought, and (2) the means available. Yet these are always mutually interactive and other means–end maps may be a possibility. Organizational design could well prove a bog of relativism with no path.

12.5.10 March and Simon (1958; p.31) spell out the dilemma. '[We] will call the organization a "purpose" organization if the separate departments correspond to separate subgraphs of the means–end graph. To distinguish among [the alternative ways of grouping work proposed by Gulick and Urwick, namely by] "process", "clientèle", "place", and "time" departmentalization, we must define what we mean by similarity with respect to these variables. Place and time are relatively simple; perhaps clientele is also. Similarity of process appears to mean similarity with respect to skills employed, knowledge employed, information employed, and equipment employed. Hence to classify activities by process, we need a whole series of propositions with respect to what kinds of "similarities" are relevant. The problem of determining what is in fact the basis of departmentalization becomes more difficult if we are not given in advance a map of the means–ends hierarchy.' [March and Simon mean by this use of the word 'hierarchy' the priority we should apply to the combination of possible means–ends options.] In this case, we first have to construct this map before we can distinguish purpose from process specialization. Moreover unless the map thus constructed is unique, or substantially so, the form of departmentalization will be ambiguous.

12.5.11 Again I find that these two scholars argue with impeccable logic. With equal logic they infer that *the only way out of such a quicksand of relativism would be if the options were so constrained that the way ahead were uniquely signposted.* They do not rule this out, but neither are they very optimistic that we shall find it. However, with their customary intellectual integrity thay admit that certain constraints **might** exist. If they were to exist, these constraints would necessarily fall into the three categories that March and Simon specify, i.e. 'logical', 'physical' and 'psychosociological'. March and Simon have therefore spelled out the problem. *It is incumbent upon anyone following them to show that there **are** constraints strong enough to justify the belief that there is **one** means–end map appropriate to a given organization.* If such constraints **cannot** be found we shall be forced to admit that there is too much ambiguity in the possible means–end maps to advocate any **specific** organizational structure.

12.5.12 To have any hope of success we must make one stipulation. If the value-system that the organization designer adopts is not accepted, the result will be that any and every means–end map that he might possibly draw would be open to infinite challenge. We should then indeed be lost in a quicksand of relativism. Here then is our stipulation. *The ground-rules are that the designer of the organization must specify beforehand the value-system which forms the criteria by which the logic of his means–end map must be judged.* If that value-system is **not** agreeable to his critics then the exercise had better stop right there. *The problem then is not one which relates to* **organizational design.** *It is the far less specific one of* **ideological incompatibility,** for those with different value-systems will certainly design different structures, as I now show.

12.5.13 During the period of British rule in Tanganyika, the medical services which were developed corresponded to a European pattern: a few hospitals in urban centres and the usual hierarchy of medical staff. This was understandable, since it was conditioned by the psychosociological constraints of the administration. Not only would their concept of medical ethics have demanded that certain tasks should only be undertaken by doctors who were qualified to European standards, but they were also catering to a European community of settlers who **expected** such treatment. The organizational pattern therefore reflected these psychosociological constraints.

12.5.14 The country became independent in 1961. By union with Zanzibar in 1964 it became the state of Tanzania. The whole psychosociological framework was now changed. The European priorities were no longer paramount and President Nyerere – a Christian commited to Chinese-aided socialism – espoused utilitarian attitudes. Identifying that a few diseases were responsible for most of the sickness and that this problem could not be dealt with by centralized hospitals, the administration set out to train a corps of medical technicians who would go to the villages, and with the aid of a do-it-yourself medical manual designed for the purpose, prescribe for such prevalent diseases as malaria, tuberculosis and bilharzia. Moreover, improved water resources had to form part of the programme because the latter disease, (which involves the degeneration of the liver and other organs), enters the body via larvae–infected water and is thereafter able to 'camouflage' itself against easy treatment.

12.5.15 Given the different value-systems from which these two sets of organizational concepts started, each was a 'rational' response. Each created a logical means–end map. If either is to be criticized against the other, it must be criticized at the **root** of the respective ideologies, not at the

branch of the organization which grew from each root.

12.5.16 My second example is that of a pottery firm that was in financial difficulty. A client of mine had heard that it was for sale and was interested in acquiring it if I would recommend that (under new management) it was capable of becoming profitable. I discovered that the firm was, in effect, two separate businesses. The ornate stuff they made was sold abroad, while the plain stuff was sold in the home market. The overall company loss, which was in the order of £200,000 was, I calculated, the result of making £200,000 profit on the plain stuff but a £400,000 loss on the fancy.

12.5.17 I advised my client that he had other and better opportunities for investment. I also obtained his permission to offer my findings to the firm, since he had no more interest in acquiring them. My advice was that they close down the part of the factory making ornate merchandise, turn all that stock into cash, and re-invest the money in updating the facilities used in the manufacture of the plain-ware. To give just one example, a new 'intermittent' kiln to replace their 'continuous' kiln would allow a saving in their gas bill of 40 per cent and pay for itself in one year.

12.5.18 The reader will note that I was applying the *mores* of capitalism. I regarded the on-going health of the company as my main criterion, and in the process I was advocating that they should not accept any unnecessary opportunity costs. There was a moral dimension to my proposal. It was true that it would cost the jobs of half the workforce. Yet if it were not followed I visualized that the firm would be in the receiver's hands within two years, and **all** the jobs would be lost. It was not followed. Eighteen months later the firm went into receivership. I phoned the receiver to tell him my findings. He concurred with my conclusions, but in the interim the losses had been so great that the situation was now unsalvageable in the terms that had been possible at the earlier date. It now needed an injection of capital.

12.5.19 Was there anything to be said for the previous management's standpoint? Why, for example, did they reject the advice? They did so because it was a family business which went back for generations and they identified the ornate pottery with their historical tradition. They simply could not **bear** to act as I suggested. Was this absurd? From the standpoint of the capitalist rationality it was quite crazy. It made some sort of weird sense if they had decided upon a sort of kamikaze policy in which the firm and the family would go down intact. But they were not even consistent in this, being prepared to sell out and lose control of the firm's destiny. So presumably they were prepared to have others rationalize their heritage, but not to do it themselves. *However, the important thing for us to note is that, **because of our difference in ideology they kept a structure that I would have abandoned.***

12.5.20 I aim to show that (at least in capitalist firms operating in a free market) there will be constraints of a logical, psychosociological and physical nature which, when linked to the **mores** of capitalism, will produce a means–end map which would meet the near-universal approval of those who share capitalist ideology. The inclusion of classical 'principles' in this means–end mapping will result in an organization with a format that is far less subjective and arbitrary than the unwary reader of March and Simon might suppose.

12.5.21 To support this contention I intend to take an imaginary case-study (section 13.2) and to develop an organization structure based on the logic of the situation within the psychosociological constraints of the capitalist system and the physical options that are open for us to pursue. At each stage I shall explain why I make the organizational decisions that I do, thus identifying my assumptions. Someone wedded to another ideology might well decide on a different means-end map. *I ask only that mine is judged by the criteria that I shall choose at the outset and which I shall now review.* Additionally, I shall incorporate certain 'classical' concepts. Some of these I have already explained. Others I shall apply as they appear relevant in order that the reader becomes aware from the example within the case-study of the purpose and value of the concept or 'principle'.

12.6 A review of the *mores* of capitalism as used in our case-study

12.6.1 I shall, above all, assume that the firm will structure itself to avoid the likelihood of unwittingly incurring an opportunity cost. This might bring us into a moral dilemma. This is what happened with Ford executives, as we shall see when we consider the case of the Pinto car (paragraphs 16.3.4 to 16.3.9). However, if that does happen, one of two outcomes would result. Either we should stay within the capitalist *mores* and minimize economic opportunity cost or we shall switch to some other *mores* based upon 'social concern' and related to a different frame of reference. The discontinuity of thought at that point will become obvious if we do. It will, however, be an example of the psychosociological constraint and will not invalidate my claim that the majority of managers would be equally likely to make a similar switch for the same reasons. Such unanimity would maintain a shared vision of what constitutes a 'reasonable' means–end map.

12.6.2 We shall consider 'opportunity cost' only from the standpoint of the microeconomic system of the immediate company. This not only ties up with the attitudes of managers within capitalism, but it also sharpens up the means–end map that we shall use. For microeconomic means–ends maps are far more easy to design than macroeconomic ones. Let me expand this statement with an example.

12.6.3 If a private railway company wants to improve its profitability it may choose to do so by cutting services. It does not need to concern itself with the rest of the economy. On the other hand, when an economically failing railway system is nationalized (as happened in Britain) its mean–end map should logically become far more complex. *(Although a Socialist government nationalized the railway system out of political ideology, successive Conservative governments with the power to change the situation have not done so. By this omission they signify agreement with a cross-party justification for nationalization. This is the view that the country has economic and social need of the railway system as part of the general national infrastructure, irrespective of any losses it may generate.)* Its performance thereafter should logically be measured *only in terms of its net effect upon the macro-system as a whole.* It is no longer valid to consider the system as if it were the orginal microeconomic system it was when subject to the market. *Despite this, successive governments have forced upon the railways a means–end map applicable to the latter rather than the former situation, if the resultant railway organization and structure really does bring the greatest overall cost-benefit to society, that will be by good luck rather than good management.* **Our** case study means–end map is more simple in being an independent business entity.

12.6.4 In deciding upon the organizational design that will reflect our means–end mapping we shall apply certain fundamental organizational concepts which are to be found in classical theory, but which, I claim, are universal in character. Here are a few. The organization is bound to come to an apex where its purpose will be determined. Below that apex will be a chain of command with successive levels triggering and monitoring the level below. Each level will need a degree of autonomy if it is to operate effectively. Each level will need a degree of co-ordinative control if its efforts are to be channelled and integrated into behaviour that will reflect a rational approach to the attainment of organizational goals. There will be some upper limit to the span of control and to the number of levels beyond which the economies of scale may be offset by diseconomies. When this happens some form of departmentalization or divisionalization which will convert that part of the hierarchy into a semi-autonomous unit of manageable proportions is the requisite move. However, we shall also discover that we shall frequently seek to departmentalize certain aspects of a company's operations long before the criteria of levels and span limitations are reached. Indeed, in my business experience I have never come across a situation in which I have split an organization for span or level considerations where I would not have split it anyway for other reasons. More often than not those other reasons intervene first, as we shall see.

12.6.5 An aspect of departmentalization that is very important, as our case-study will show, has been completely ignored in the literature because it is ideologically out of favour. Yet I hope to demonstrate conclusively that, in the real world, it is probably the most significant feature of organizational design within the capitalist system. The principle requires us to departmentalize any part of the organization that offers or receives a service from any other part. The two departments then negotiate a price for the service. *If the seller can get a higher price from* **an alternative outside buyer** *he is free to take it. If the buyer can get a lower price from* **an alternative outside agency** *he is free to take it.*

12.6.6 It is an essential part of this concept that the service function must:

(a) be able to identify its costs;
(b) have enough autonomy to control its own performance;
(c) be capable of diverting its service to another party without compromising the rest of the organization;
(d) be capable of being closed or sold off or otherwise diposed of without compromising the rest of the organization.

To do all of these things the service **must** be departmentalized. There are some difficulties in the concept for the main board of the concern. These relate to the damage that may result from departmental goals running counter to overall strategy and the problem of overhead allocation and recovery. But these are matters that can be overcome: the principle, from a capitalist standpoint, is basically sound, for it avoids opportunity cost.

12.6.7 Although I do not think that the issue of the span of control has deserved the emphasis that textbooks have placed upon it, I do want to expose some of the classical nonsense that was written about it. For I do not want to give the impression that just because I think that classical thought still has much to offer, we should accept it hook, line and sinker. I'm afraid that I can find nothing good to say about the work of V. A. Graicunus. If I were to ask the reader to list some variables which might limit the span of control, I would not be surprised if he gave a list such as this:

(i) Is the work of the subordinates routine, or simple?

(ii) Are the subordinates competent?
(iii) Does the ethos of the firm encourage initiative in subordinates?
(iv) Does the supervisor have to perform non-supervisory duties?

Such a response would seem legitimate and reasonable. What would really astonish me would be if the reader were to say 'None of those variables is really significant, for a mathematical formula given to us by V. A. Graicunus in 1937 shows we cannot go beyond a span of control of four or five.'

12.6.8 I mentioned earlier (paragraph 9.4.28) that once such rubbish gets into the text books it is well-nigh impossible to get rid of it. John O'Shaughnessy repeated Graicunus's claim thirty years later (O'Shaughnessy, 1969; pp.31, 32) and here I am giving further life to him. Yet perhaps this will be his *coup de grâce*. Moreover, Graicunus does illustrate two general issues:

(1) Mixed up with the *legitimate* authority concepts contained within classical theory, lurk some quite *gratuitously* autocratic concepts.
(2) Many people love mechanistic concepts. In particular, they are ready to attribute scientific objectivity to most things which have sufficient numbers attached, even when (as in the case) we are concerned with **qualitative** relationships and not **quantitative.** Qualitative relationships are just not amenable to this sort of treatment. Using numbers as qualitative indices is sometimes politically necessary. Job evaluation is a case in point. But the hocus-pocus of putting numbers to qualitative concepts, while giving a pseudo-scientific air to the process, is still hocus-pocus, no matter how politically useful it may be.

Both issues arise in the nonsense which Graicunus foisted upon us.

12.6.9 Had he not held certain authoritarian concepts, Graicunus would have never specified the relationships he did. He claimed that when 'A' had two subordinates, 'X' and 'Y', there would be six resultant relationships (see figure 12.6(a).)

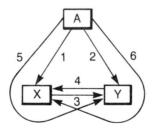

Figure 12.6(a)

These relationships, he claims, are:

(1) A with X
(2) A with Y
(3) X with Y
(4) Y with X
(5) A with Y with X present
(6) A with X with Y present.

It is the rate at which the number of relationships grows when A is given more subordinates that convinces Graicunus that the span of control is severely limited. Why the workload will always be *pro rata* to the number of relationships is a mystery known only to Graicunus. His authoritarianism reveals itself in the way he refuses to acknowledge a relationship other than in terms of the one who initiates it, and it is clear that Graicunus beleives that no subordinate can ever take any initiative at all. For although he allows X to initiate a relationship with Y (relationship 3), and allows Y to initiate a relationship with X (relationship 4), neither X nor Y can initiate a relationship with A. Clearly, like Victorian children, they are to speak only when spoken to.

12.6.10 From such preposterous premises the mathematical formula and its nonsense grow. With N as the number of subordinates, Graicunus expressed the number of relationships as $N\frac{2^N}{2} + N-1$). Because the number of relationships in this arbitrary model increase so enormously as the number of subordinates increase, 5 subordinates was seen as the maximum. Even they gave a relationship count of 100. By 8 the count is 1080, and by 12 it has rocketed to 24,708. All of which is reminiscent of the story that is aerodynamically impossible for the bumble-bee to fly, but, since nobody has explained this to the bumble-bee, it keeps on flying anyway. When Joan Woodward checked on the number of people reporting to the chief executive in a sample of 97 firms, she found that the median was 6 and the highest was 18. In the same sample the number reporting to the first-line supervisors gave a median of 30 and a maximum of 90. So much for Graicunus. Let us now turn to our case-study and real-life bumble-bees.

13

Classical organization: an imaginary case-study in a historical setting

13.1 The American ideology and the British reality

13.1.1 We need strong international management critique if management theory is not to adopt errors which spring from cultural assumptions. In this respect the British have failed the Americans. We have tended slavishly to import their models and to reiterate them – **including their cultural blind spots.** Speaking their language but separated from them culturally, the British were the natural anvil to resist the American hammer and so get the cultural kinks out of the theories. We owed them our minds: instead we lent them only our ears.

13.1.2 Never did we fail them more than in the 1950s and 1960s. Never did we have more to offer. The take-over bids of Isaac Wolfson, Charles Clore, Sir Hugh Fraser, Cecil King, and Roy Thompson had 'transformed whole areas of business: sleepy and comfortable firms [had] been rationalised, combed and costed, their properties sold up, their products standardised, their managers re-valued with unsuspected thrusting men emerging from the undergrowth' (Sampson, 1962; p.495). These thrusting men were too busy putting their theories into practice to become involved in organizational theory. Academics who should have studied what was going on and inferred the theory (as we shall in this case-study) appeared oblivious of a transformation that should have fascinated them. Instead they reiterated the myths which had dominated management teaching in the United States:

myths which had the overriding purpose of ensuring that the corporation should appear to have a human face.

13.1.3 All cultures in the West are at some pains to give a human face to the corporation. In the wake of anti-capitalist propaganda this is a natural and universal response. The human relations and neo-human relations literature tended to make our management schools orientated also towards 'togetherness'. But in the wider arena of the practising British capitalist during the 1950s and 1960s no such concepts dominated organizational design. *On the contrary, the organizational concepts that could have been deduced from the actions of the 'thrusting men' who emerged from the 'undergrowth' were that they were largely departmentalizing their concerns to eliminate opportunity cost in the manner discussed in paragraphs 12.6.5 and 12.6.6.* Meanwhile, not only did American literature show an obsession with 'togetherness', so too in practice did American organizations. Why should they have done this?

13.1.4 I have already suggested that the American attitude to capitalism had developed a form of social schizophrenia. Their response to the social ambiguities of capitalism was to make the boundary of the company the point at which their behaviour 'switched'. Their attachment to laissez-faire beliefs made a fetish of untrammelled market forces, and unlike Europeans they made few attempts to create corners in the economy to shelter the individual from the blast of competition. This left the **inside** of the corporation as the only place left for human warmth. So from Mayo's time onward the organization was cast in the role of 'family'. As Sofer says (1972; p.73) 'Durkheim and others had pointed to dangers of moral breakdown associated with the break-up of small rural communities and the growth of large cities where people did not know each other and where interdependence was not obvious... Mayo's answer was [to create interdependence] (1) through face-to-face colleague work group and (2) through the work group to the management of the enterprise and (3) through them to the wider society.' The result was that American organization theory was quite as preoccupied with internal co-operativeness as it has with external competitiveness.

13.1.5 Such a split is obviously rubbish. Not only will external competitive pressure sometimes drive wedges into such internal cohesion, but we have seen how opportunity cost brings competition into the measurement of internal organizational services. Yet the unconvincing myth persists that competition outside is commendable, and competition inside is reprehensible. Inside, 'togetherness' is the theme.

13.1.6 Against the worst excesses of this philosophy in American firms, W. H. Whyte wrote in 1957 a cry of protest entitled *The Organization Man*. The pretence that an organization seeks an employee's welfare (rather than its own) offends him, as does the way in which the company places a premium upon people who get along with others and get the job done without questioning too deeply why they are doing it. To frustrate the organization's selection procedures to find such people, Whyte tells the mavericks how to cheat in psychological tests, I was reminded of his protest when I received the full 'Welcome aboard: you are now one of the team' treatment from the American manager of whom I wrote in paragraph 10.4.17. A week later when I had need to contact him, I found that he had been sacked on the day following his 'Welcome aboard' speech. It is my fervent hope that he survived the trauma to be more circumspect about 'togetherness'. However, my fear is that he would have seen his dismissal as a need to slap backs a little harder in his next job.

13.1.7 Yet even as we perpetuated American myths in British management schools of the 1950s and 1960s, we needed only to look at the organizational developments about us to see that British industry had taken to heart an old, but neglected fundamental concept of capitalism – the avoidance of opportunity cost. This central concept of capitalist rationalism had lain neglected for years. Now it had become a vital tool in organizational design. Moreover, it was a tool which was not only a measure of the firm's dealings with its environment, but also (as the case-study will make clear) defined how one internal department of the firm was to deal with another.

13.1.8 Yet the reader may think that we shall be paying an impossibly high price for organizational efficiency if the cost is to rob us of a sense of support from the internal 'togetherness' of the company. 'Togetherness' might have been phoney: but at least it was something. If Mayo was right then we seem to have thrown away the only thing between the employee and anomie. First of all, I don't believe that Mayo was right. I believe with Goldthorpe, Lockwood and Bechhofer (1968; p.180) that the conjugal family is the primary group. But in any case the employee can still identify with the sub-unit. Indeed a sub-unit with unambiguous goals is a far more likely object of attachment for the employee. He will be more ready to see himself and his **immediate** management facing the same threats and opportunities, and so identify with the sub-unit's objectives, than ever he would with the more diffuse goals of the organization. Mayo's chain connecting the individual to society: → group → management → society, mirrors Mayo's concern with tying the worker to the firm. Claiming that 'management' is an essential mediating link between 'group' and 'society' is phoney (except to the extent that (incidental to other purposes) management brought the work-group into being). If Mayo's true concern had been the individual's anomie, he would have acknowledged this.

13.1.9 There is always a danger that sub-units may see themselves as being at odds with the main organization. This can result in their following separate goals and only pretending to comply with directives; what Gouldner refers to as 'mock-bureaucracy'. Yet even Gouldner admits that this situation can lead to high morale. The trick would seem to be to ensure that the goals of the sub-unit, real **and** mock, must be in the general interest of the enterprise. Indeed, smart top management may recognize the value of allowing some rules to be broken in the interests of harnessing 'mock-bureaucracy', thereby creating a form of psychological indebtedness on which to draw at some future date.

13.2 A suitable case for treatment

13.2.1 Although this case is fictitious, it assumes as its basis some of the problems which must have presented themselves to Charles Clore and his senior management team when, back in the 1950s, he bought half the British shoe industry when no one was looking. The reason he was able to acquire such plums is evidence of the way that unconscious modelling can be a danger. Those who were in charge of these concerns saw themselves, not as being primarily capitalists who happened incidentally to find themselves in the shoe-trade, but as primarily shoe-traders who happened incidentally to be capitalists. It was a mistake that was to cost them and their shareholders dearly.

13.2.2 Such channelled thinking as they exhibited is largely a question of habit. Charles Clore got moving too early to form such a habit. '[T]he son of a Russian-Jewish refugee who had built up a small textile business, Clore began his property career by buying the Cricklewood Ice-Rink at the age of twenty-two.' (Sampson, 1962; p.494). The era produced a whole crop of such entrepreneurial lateral thinkers who, in that world – which to modern eyes looks not only pathetically innocent, but also appallingly ignorant – could get started with surprisingly little capital and go on to make a fortune. One entrepreneur of my acquaintance took advantage of the fact that legislation had disturbed the free interplay of market forces in order to become very rich. He started by buying two houses in a fashionable area of London. Each had been split into flats. Each contained some empty flats and some with tenants. This is why he had bought the properties so cheaply. Legislation controlled the level of rent that could be demanded and guaranteed the tenants their possession. Had these houses been empty and returned to their former glory they would have been worth a fortune. What he did was to offer the tenants of one house a financial inducement to move into the empty flats in the other house, thereby making a large capital gain. Repeated several times, this process was extremely rewarding since it grew geometrically in size.

13.2.3 Such entrepreneurs might have used property as their base, but as they grew and ventured farther afield they came into the manufacturing arena. Clore not only had shoe interests, but a shipyard, and Sampson claims that it was Clore's attempt in 1958 to buy Watney's brewery interests that caused the old brewers to panic and to begin 'recklessly forming their own mergers in self-defence' (1982; p.309).

13.2.4 It is not really an accident that the impact of such entrepreneurs as Clore has been almost completely excluded from management theory. To the extent that we find this influence at all, we find it in the area of strategic case-studies. There, and there alone, does the use of opportunity cost appear to be regarded as a legitimate tool in selecting one course of action over another. Yet in organizational design, where the use of opportunity cost would be quite as significant, it is virtually ignored by the theorists... though not, thankfully, by the practitioners.

13.2.5 *Indeed, it is strangely reminiscent of our pre-Clore innocence that theorists are* **still** *not prepared to accord to opportunity cost the central position to which it is entitled in organizational design.* In support of this claim I intend to make it abundantly plain over the next few pages that opportunity cost should always have been the main design criterion. *Yet the omission is also, I think, understandable: for it tends to set one part of the organization in conflict with another, and its logic is so devastating that it strips away any pretence of the firm's social obligation to the employee beyond that of enlightened self-interest.* Yet it is arguable that the failure of the shoe industry to incorporate opportunity cost into its internal design procedures was what made it vulnerable to the predatory embrace of Charles Clore. In the outside 'real' world, nothing will be the same following the lessons taught by Clore and his like. Yet even today the textbooks have failed to catch up with this reality. The genie is out of the bottle. Unexploited advantages make boards vulnerable to take-over and *an unexploited advantage* is the same thing as *an accepted opportunity cost.*

13.2.6 Before Clore and the other raiders appeared on the scene, the managements of many companies had, by ignoring opportunity cost, failed

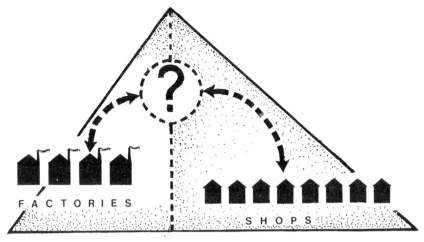

Figure 13.2(a)

to serve the interests of their shareholders. The true worth of the assets that many shoe firms had at their disposal was truly enormous. Not the least of these assets were the retail shoe-shops, situated upon prime high street sites, which had greatly escalated in value in the years immediately following the Second World War.

13.2.7 Yet this real value was not reflected in the balance sheet, perhaps in the false belief that an innate conservatism was prudent. In a cynical sense one could say that that was so, for doubtless the shareholders would have found the profits being generated a relatively poor return upon the capital employed. Under such circumstances they might (had they known the truth) have thought their money better invested in a building society or some other venture. This combination of poor profits and under-valued balance sheets depressed the share price. If some enterprising raider were to buy only 51 per cent of these depressed shares he would have gained the key to Aladdin's cave. Our own case-study starts with the assumption that we have done just that. We have thus acquired a chain of shoe-shops and a number of shoe factories, together with the firm conviction that we will never allow the company henceforth to suffer the opportunity costs that enabled it to fall so easily into our hands. We are not the only sharks in the ocean. In any case, we have no intention, as a matter of principle, of making less profit than we are able.

13.2.8 At this moment we have only the vaguest of ideas of the nature of the final organizational structure that we shall design. Both the factories and the shops exist, so we'll put them in Figure 13.2(a). (Whether they will **continue** to exist is another matter.) Nevertheless, if we do keep them, we recognize on *a priori* grounds that they will be controlled in some sort of hierarchy, and that this same hierarchy will specify how these units are to be related to the whole and to each other.

13.2.9 We shall begin with the shops. This is not an arbitrary choice. We must start somewhere and there are several reasons for starting here. First and foremost, we do so because the shops are a marketing resource, and as Drucker says (1968; p.53),

> 'Marketing is the distinguishing, the unique function of the business. A business is set apart from all other human organizations by the fact that it markets a product or a service. Neither Church, nor Army, nor School, nor State does that. Any organization that fulfils itself through marketing a product or a service, is a business. Any organization in which marketing is either absent or incidental is not a business and should never be run as if it were one.'

In line with this concept the shops should become a key area of interest. Secondly, the shops probably represent the largest single asset that the business possesses in terms of the property value of the buildings they occupy.

13.2.10 If these properties were not occupied by our own retailing section, they would be available for us to lease to another party. We are therefore losing that rental income by allowing our own people to occupy the premises. The only way to ensure that this does not lead us into a hidden opportunity cost is for us to create a separate property company and put all the property that the group owns into its care. Its relationship to our own marketing function is simply expressed. The terms of reference are that the property company should give to the marketing section the right of first refusal of any site. The rental price would be the same as any other would-be lessees would be willing to pay.

13.2.11 This arrangement cuts both ways. If the marketing people find that one of our sites is unattractive to them they may vacate it for another, preferably (but not necessarily) owned by our company. It then becomes the responsibility of our property company to do the best it can with the vacated site.

13.2.12 But what of the actual operation of the shops? First, how autonomous can they be? Can they be completely decentralized? Can all the decisions that affect them be made by the local manager? The answer to this is 'No'. Let us consider some of the reasons why.

13.2.13 First there is the question of 'image'. It is important that the public is able to identify with the image that the chain is seeking to present. Such an image is made up of many things, but the very fact that we are seeking homogeneity of image means that it must be centralized in conception and then imprinted upon all the stores. Yet there are three more fundamental reasons for centralizing the marketing function other than simply presenting the public with a homogeneous image. These are (1) cost spreading, (2) co-ordination, and (3) control.

Cost spreading. A shoe-store serves a certain catchment area, and it does so in competition with other shoe retailers. The resultant market share limits the number of staff a manager can employ long before any other constraining factors arise which could limit the span of control. This limitation in staff numbers means that none can afford to specialize: for there are far too many functions and far to few people to permit this. None of them will be expert in window-dressing, nor in knowing the colours and styles of shoes which will be in style next season. Notwithstanding this, windows will still need to be dressed and shoes ordered long in advance of being able to judge public taste from feedback. So the manager of an independent store has to do the best he can. But such makeshift measures are unnecessary in a store which is part of a chain. Experts can be hired by a central marketing department and that expertise can be used throughout the group at only a nominal cost per store.

Co-ordination. There are advantages in co-ordination irrespective of whether the goods required for the stores are to be ordered from the firm's own factories or from an external supplier. Externally the bulking of orders may enable the firm to obtain discounts. Internally stock may be moved between branches to accommodate better the different sales patterns in each locality. Orders for the factory can be bulked as required and delivery priorities specified to satisfy any urgent shortages. It might even pay the firm to keep a central warehouse in order to limit the depth of stock that each branch needs to keep, and to top-up the branches quickly from that warehouse. For it is statistically demonstrable that stock held in this way can be lower for the same value of service. Advertising needs to be co-ordinated; so does pricing policy relative to the popularity of the different styles. (Pricing by fixed mark-up percentage on cost is rather silly in the fashion business, since it prevents us from making high profits on the 'hot' numbers and leaves us with unsold quantities of the 'dogs'. It therefore would represent an opportunity cost.) During the stock clearance sales that are necessary two or three times a year, the judicious distribution of the stock around the branches and its equally judicious pricing also need to be co-ordinated from the centre. This is necessary for two reasons. Only at the centre can the full picture emerge, and only at the centre can the fashion decision be taken concerning those styles which will be carried forward anyway and therefore should not form part of the sale goods. Personnel policy and records need to be kept centrally to make certain that it is done efficiently and to plan recruitment and promotions as well as holiday rosters. The latter, as well as sickness, need to be covered from a central staff-pool of temporary managers. This centralized personnel department would also be responsible for negotiations with the shop-workers' union to ensure a consistency of approach. Negotiating branch by branch would be time-consuming, would be another area in which the individual managers lacked expertise, and would lay the company wide open to 'leap-frogging', whereby the union negotiates better rates in one store and then demands parity for the rest.

Control. Finally there is the measurement and control of performance in the store to consider. Some assessment of the **relative** performance of a store cannot be made except from a central marketing office which monitors the results of the various stores. The store manager will only have his **absolute** performance, which he may feel is adequate. Yet in relative terms it may be possible to deduce that a change of venue would yield a better return on investment, in which case this should be done to avoid an opportunity loss. There is also a need to ensure that standards of performance are being maintained, and that the morale of the individual store managers is kept high by supportive leadership which trains before it blames, and which only does the latter in relation to specific issues from which the manager can learn.

13.2.14 Of course there will be a tendency for central marketing personnel to want to continue in business even if the whole retail venture is less economic than other commercial propositions. By the time that the shops have paid an economic rent to the property company the net profits may be so eroded that it would be better to liquidate the retailing venture and put the capital which is invested in the stock of goods into some new venture. Alternatively we might sell the retail business as a going concern either with or without the ownership of the properties changing hands. For all such reasons the overall financial control of the business must lie at a level **above** that of the one occupied by central marketing or property management. Our view of the company has therefore now developed to that given on the right-hand side of Figure 13.2(b) where there are now five different entities in three levels: main board, central marketing, wages and personnel, property management, and shops. Yet it will be noted that the reason for creating

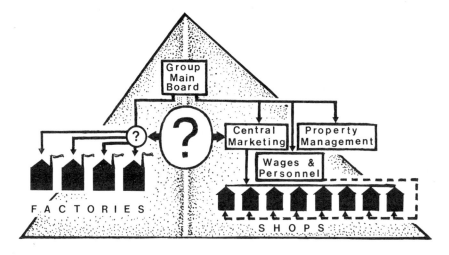

Figure 13.2(b)

these separate departments has in no case been because they would jointly have been too big. On the contrary: the shops were separate entities from geographic necessity. Indeed, the marketing department was created to deal with the problems caused by this fact, and even to create a unit of **large** enough size to justify specialisms. Beyond this the main reason for the separate departments has been deliberately to ensure that departmental goals will be developed which will inhibit the ability of other departments to accept an opportunity cost without senior management becoming aware of it. *We have therefore designed conflicting interests into the organization in order to generate the automatic checks and balances that the organization needs if it is to stay on its toes... and what a long way that is from Douglas McGregor!*

13.2.15 One of the things that needs to be specified is the relationship between the store manager and the rest of the organization. We haven't specified the actual number of stores, for the eight shown in the diagram are merely symbolic. There could as easily be 80 spread all over the country. If we assume that there are 80 and that we wish each to have a visit from a superior at least once a month, then this, and the geographic circumstances, may mean that two sales managers are created: one to operate in the North and one in the South. Each would then have 40 stores to control, and if each visit lasted approximately half a day, including travelling time, then this would meet the frequency requirements and give each a full work-load. (What would Graicunus make of anything so simple as that calculation?)

13.2.16 If the store manager therefore reports to this sales manager, does he also report to the experts that also descend upon him to dress the windows or to review personnel matters? Classical theory would be quite adamant that he did not. For one of the precepts of classical theory is that, although several people may report to one boss (the span of control principle), yet nobody should report to **more** than one boss (the unity of command principle).

13.2.17 We shall find that there are many instances where it is necessary to break the unity of command principle in the interest of more pressing considerations: but this does not mean that the principle itself is not good plain horse sense, nor that breaking it is not something to regret. I said earlier that when classical theory was first proposed there were no organizations, other than the army or the Catholic Church, which were equal in size to the new business empires. Inappropriate as both might appear, it was to the former rather than the latter to which the theorists looked for their models. Armies everywhere believe that a split command is an abomination. Nevertheless, armies, like our shoe-store chain, have need of the services of various experts. To cope with this difficulty armies had developed the line/staff concept, as shown in Figure 13.2(c)

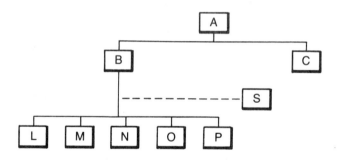

Figure 13.2(c)

13.2.18 The line of command in Figure 13.2(c) goes from A to B and thence to L,M,N,O,P. Yet if we give the expert, S, authority to issue instructions to L,M,N,O,P, then each of these will effectively have two bosses, namely B and S. What would make this an abomination is that B and S might issue countervailing orders. Moreover, their underlings might well use this ambiguous situation in order to confound the wishes of each. It is therefore an invidious situation for both the subordinates and the superordinates, and totally unacceptable on the field of battle. To get around this problem, armies made it quite clear that the line of command was via A and B, and that S had no direct authority over L,M,N,O, and P. He could only advise. But unless they were instructed by B to follow S's advice, such advice did not have the force of an order. S was therefore a 'staff' and not a 'line' officer, and everyone knew where the line of authority was to be drawn. This 'principle' was adopted by the classical theorists, and although, as we shall see, it has to be broken on occasion, I cannot contradict its basic good sense. Indeed, I would go further. If A were to give direct orders to L,M,N,O, and P, then effectively they would again have two bosses, A and B. For this reason A must scrupulously avoid getting into this position. Never in my life have I given an order to anyone who did not report directly to me, except in dire need. If I, as A, saw L doing something damaging to the firm, I might go as far as to ask him to stop until I had had time to speak to B about it: but that would be the extreme limit of my interference, and it is an attitude that I would commend to all managers in such a position. Otherwise B will feel, with considerable justification, that his authority is being undermined. All of which explains why I have shown S connected to the system by a dashed line.

13.2.19 This is also the logical extension of the classical concept that authority and responsibility cannot be separated. If A wishes to hold B responsible for attaining certain goals, then he must not interfere with the resources at B's disposal, namely L,M,N,O, and P. We shall later find instances when the principle of unity of command has to be set aside, but, as I have already indicated, such instances do not invalidate the fundamental morality of attempting to link responsibility and authority. In the case of the shoe-store, the probable arrangement will be that the store manager will take direct orders from the sales manager, and take advice and assistance only from the other experts. For this reason Figure 13.2(b) depicts the line of authority as a solid line running from the main board to central marketing, from whence via the marketing director and the sales manager it runs to the shop managers. By contrast, the link from wages and personnel is dotted to indicate that it is a 'staff', rather than a 'line' relationship. Let us now consider the factories.

13.2.20 From the standpoint of the marketing department the existence of the factories may be an embarrassment. This would be so if their output were dearer or poorer in quality than marketing could obtain elsewhere. This is obviously an area in which there will be a need for some very careful negotiation to decide upon ground rules which do not hamstring either marketing or production, and in the process damage the wider interests of the group. Let us however assume for the moment that some accommodation is likely and look at the factory organization to see whether we wish to change its nature.

13.2.21 The first thing to note about the factories is that they exist. They therefore represent what an accountant would call a 'sunk' cost. It is not as though we were starting from scratch and deciding whether or not to build them. Had that been the case we might have questioned even more fundamentally the value of building factories; given that we could buy shoes from other manufacturers; for we might have had something better to do with our cash than to sink it in shoe factories. Alternatively we might have questioned the wisdom of having four separate factories rather than one large one, for the latter might appear at first sight to offer more economies of scale.

13.2.22 Given that the four existing factories represent 'sunk' costs, they are less likely to be uneconomic when compared with one new factory than if all were yet to be built. For the existing four will make identical goods to the new one, *but the latter would need to cost* **much** *less to operate to justify the cost of sinking the capital which would have to be invested in the new factory.* (The reader will note that the cost of the capital employed is **also** a matter of opportunity cost. When capital is freely available this is the borrowing rate, but when capital is rationed, it is the loss of earnings resulting from abandoning some alternative venture for which capital was also needed.) It should be noted that in making our comparison the totality of all costs, *including all perceived opportunity costs,* must be taken into account. The latter include the value of the alternative uses to which the factories and/or their sites may be put. For example, if one of the old factories stands on a prime site in the middle of a city, then the opportunity costs of keeping it will be higher than if it were out in the country. Similarly, all the incidental costs of start-up and close-down would need to be calculated. Finally, there would be the question of the social costs involved. If there are savings to be made but they prove to be marginal, then it may be that the social cost of making the move would be allowed to override the savings. Yet, given the *mores* of capitalism, it would be hypocritical to suggest that capitalist management would acccept any significant level of financial opportunity cost in order to avoid these social costs.

13.2.23 It is at such a juncture that some managements might be led to abandon the **mores** of capitalism: but if they do, it is quite clear that they have switched frames of reference. They are no longer thinking as capitalists.

13.2.24 As it happens, the savings that can be achieved by building a single shoe factory as opposed to keeping four separate factories will be negligible, and there could even be **losses** instead of **gains**. *Moreover, this could be true* even if we were starting from scratch and were considering the comparative advantages of four **new** *factories as opposed to one large* **new** *factory*. This claim may surprise those readers who have been led to believe that economies of scale are largely a matter of economies **within** the production function. Yet, beyond a certain point, scale can produce losses rather than gains. For as factories grow in size, the incremental economies of the next growth step become progressively smaller, whereas the costs associated with trying to administer the monster plant become progressively greater. Beyond a certain point, 'X' in Figure 13.2(d), the diseconomies of scale overtake the economies and produce a net loss.

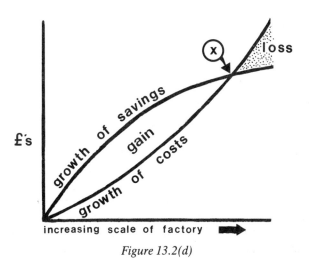

Figure 13.2(d)

13.2.25 Indeed, although in all developed countries there has been a concentration of capital into the hands of a few firms, that concentration has not led those firms in the main to build monster plants, because they are fully aware of this phenomenon. Unilever, for example, duplicate their margarine production in England by having two factories, one in the South in Essex and one in the North in Cheshire. Graham Bannock makes the same point (1973; p.293): '[R]esearch...has found that the share of the 100 largest establishments (i.e. plants, not firms) in UK manufacturing net output remained virtually unchanged at 10 per cent between 1930 and 1963. The share of the 100 largest firms, on the other hand,... increased from 20 to 50 per cent over the same period. It must follow that increasing plant size cannot have been the principal factor favouring concentration.' Economy of scale does not demand us to consider large manufacturing units except in those cases where the cost of the machinery is phenomenal and its capacity equally great, so that duplication would be both costly and unnecessary given the machine's output capacity. Consequently, although we have not yet decided whether or not to keep the factories, we **have** decided that, in the event that we do keep them, we shall do so basically in their present form.

13.2.26 There is another advantage in having four small factories. If at some future date we need to reduce output capacity, we can do so in anything up to four incremental steps, without affecting the rest of our manufacturing units. The only department that we might choose to put under one roof to serve all four factories is that of the bottom-stock room. This is where the leather or synthetic or rubber material used to provide the insoles, soles and heels of shoes is cut out by large presses. In the case of leather it also involves complex grading and selection processes because of the variation in quality and thickness of this natural substance. So amalgamation of all the bottom-stock rooms would help in the more economic use of leather; for in a small unit there is a high likelihood that leather of a superior quality will have to be used for inferior work because of a short-term lack of lower-grade components. Selection from a larger throughput will minimize this.

13.2.27 However, just because we have kept the factories separate does not mean that each should engage in buying its own leather. A centralized buying department would have various advantages, including the ability to demand bigger discounts from the significance of the orders. Moreover, the work of the various factories needs to be co-ordinated, their future kept under review, and the inter-function transfer price of their production has seasonally to be agreed. There is thus a requirement for a higher level in the production hierarchy above that of the factory, which will be presided over by the production director. This arrangement allows the members of that section to negotiate with those of the marketing section as equals, each deriving their authority from their status as agents of their respective directors.

13.2.28 Above the production director too is the authority of the main board, for he too may be tempted to keep the factories in operation even when they represent an opportunity cost. Moreover, the main board will almost certainly need to play 'honest broker' to some extent between the two parties, production and marketing, on the question of inter-function transfer pricing, and/or selling output to competitive retailers.

13.2.29 This brings us to our final organizational diagram. As we have seen, there is no guarantee that this arrangement will be preserved: but although various sections of the organization may be dropped, their initial

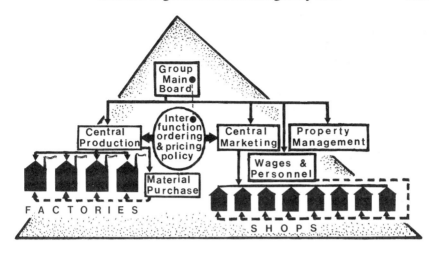

Figure 13.2(e)

relationship will be as shown in Figure 13.2(e) My claim is that, given the *mores* of capitalism, the conclusions that I have reached would have been reached by the vast majority of capitalist managers who were operating from the vantage-point of the main board. It thereby represents an example of a unique means–end relationship precisely because the situation does contain the constraints that Simon said would need to be present to justify that 'uniqueness'.

13.2.30 Above all it has used the concept of opportunity cost, not only as a constraint but as a veritable scalpel with which to carve the organization into shape.

14

Classical organization: how scale is handled

14.1 Some problems of definition: 'departmentalization' and 'divisionalization'

14.1.1 Our case-study has alerted us to a problem of definition. Splitting up organizations into sub-units is sometimes referred to as 'divisionalization' and sometimes as 'departmentalization'. Sometimes the word 'division' is used interchangeably with 'department' and sometimes it has a more specific meaning. We saw how March and Simon spoke of 'departmentalization' when referring to the various organizational 'groupings' which Gulick and Urwick had nominated (paragraph 12.5.10); those of 'purpose', 'process', 'clientèle', 'place', and 'time'.

14.1.2 Luthans (1981; p.533) claims that modern usage is to substitute 'product' for 'purpose', 'functional' for 'process', and 'geographical' for 'place'. Yet a 'product' split is frequently the basis of 'divisionalization', not 'departmentalization'. Imperial Chemical Industries (ICI) for example makes such a split between its products and refers to its 'Paints Division' and its 'Pharmaceutical Division'. In many firms such 'product divisionalization' has resulted from a take-over at some time in the past, when the current 'division', then a separate company, became absorbed. Yet even after the merger the once independent firm is still left as a quasi-autonomous 'division'. Why is this?

14.1.3 *The reason is that to amalgamate the functions of the acquired firm with those existing divisions would be counter-productive.* Let us assume we have merged the functions of the above two ICI divisions, so that we now have a much larger production function making **both** paints and pharmaceuticals which are sold through an integrated sales force whose members **sell both** product ranges. What a monstrous hybrid we should have created: and to what purpose? There would be absolutely no economies of scale to be obtained by such a move.

14.1.4 We have already seen the difficulties which could have been caused in the production function just by extending the size of a shoe factory. It is easy to imagine the problems of attempting to conjoin two completely different technologies. In the shoe factory the scaling-up of the same technology would at least give savings from better machine utilization. In ICI there would be none. Even when positioned on the same site, *the paint machines would need to be adjacent to each other in sequence determined by paint technology*, and so would be **separate** *from the pharmaceutical machines which would be postioned in their own logic-sequence*. To such a constraint could be added the constraints imposed by governmental edicts about what is (and is not) permissible in the practice of manufacturing ethical pharmaceuticals. I think we may safely assume that putting such equipment cheek-by-jowl with paint manufacturing plant would **not** be permissible.

14.1.5 As for the combined sales force, the only advantage that they would gain would be that a salesman who had to call on builders' merchants as well as chemists would, because of the higher density of contacts he could now make in any given area, be assigned a smaller territory and need to travel less. As opposed to that he would need to be technically competent for his job in **both** pharmaceuticals and paints: not, I suggest, easy to achieve.

14.1.6 Maintaining the separate divisions makes a lot of sense, and constitutes an affirmation that the best method of treating the problem is **first to split by product** and only later by function. The alternative of making **a primary split by function,** and of later making separate product splits within the function, would be crazy. *We are therefore in no doubt as to the unique means–end mapping that we should perform.*

14.1.7 Such practical examples are a good antidote to the doubts raised by March and Simon. I will quote again their statement given in paragraph 12.5.10, but will substitute the more recent terminology that Luthans suggested. 'Purpose' therefore becomes 'product' and 'process' becomes 'functional'. Here then is the amended quotation: 'The problem of determining what is in fact the basis of departmentalization becomes more difficult if we are not given in advance a map of the means-end hierarchy. In this case we have to construct this map before we can distinguish product from functional specialization.'

14.1.8 I accept that they are right to suggest that this is a problem which looms large in the **abstract**. Yet in both the **practical** examples that we considered (the shoe company case-study and ICI divisions), *we had not the slightest doubt about the more appropriate means–end mapping that we should adopt.* Instances may exist when goals will be so equivocal and constraints so few that we must agree with March and Simon (1958; p.31) that 'the form of departmentalization will be ambiguous'. *Yet in the realm of capitalist business I would maintain that such ambiguity will be the exception rather than the rule, primarily because of the way in which one option usually offers better hope of obtaining (and maintaining) minimum opportunity cost than any other.*

14.1.9 Moreover, although there are three main splits specified by Luthans (1981; p.533), namely 'product', 'functional' and 'geographic', I can think of no reason to regard 'geographic' as more than a constraining influence upon our choice of 'product' or 'functional' organizational design. As such it **facilitates** rather than **complicates** our means–end mapping. For example, given the spread of shoe-shops, we decided to split our sales function between North and South. Yet I didn't even question the **location** of the factories. This was because the ratio of transport costs to the value of the goods (shoes) is low enough for us to ignore the question of the factory sitings. Besides which, even if we had put factories deliberately in the North and South, then for each to supply only its own area would require duplicating the range of products. By treating the plants as a single resource we can produce one-quarter of all the styles in each of the four factories. Such standardization is usually associated with a cost-saving. For example, different style lasts need not be duplicated, as they would if all products were made in all factories, and production control is much simpler because of the limited styles per factory.

14.1.10 However, if our business were that of producing coal it would make far more sense to relate sales regions to adjacent coal-mines so as to minimize transport costs. (Exceptions would occur when the coal required had to have characteristics not contained by the locally mined product; e.g. anthracite tends to occur in only few localities). We have already seen that diseconomies of scale can make it advantageous to duplicate production facilities. The geographic distribution of customers can only heighten that decision if the product, unlike shoes, comes in a limited range with a low value-to-weight ratio and a limited shelf-life. Thus geography, as well as chauvinism, would make it absurd for Unilever to apply a functional split to margarine manufacture, and to despatch UK-made margarine to Germany where a local company (essentially restricted to the marketing function) would sell it. No: we have no difficulty in seeing that margarine should be manufactured and sold in Germany by a division of Unilever which will be primarily departmentalized by product – margarine – and only within that primary product split will it exhibit functional splits. *Geographical considerations therefore make decision-making* **easier** *rather than* **more difficult** *because they supply physical and, in the case of multinational companies, psychosociological constraints of a chauvinist nature that it would be foolish to ignore.* Whether the salesmen selling Unilever margarine should also sell Unilever soap (on the grounds that they are bought by the same grocery retailers) will also be determined by geographic savings versus the value of specialist selling. *Whichever way we ultimately decide to go, we can see that the geographic constraints are an* **aid** *to decision-making rather than a* **hindrance.**

14.1.11 *What we have not so far done is to identify the difference between a 'division' and a 'department'.* The most commonly assumed difference is that a 'division' is a 'profit-centre', whereas a 'department' is no more than a 'cost-centre'. On these premises we can see why the ICI Paints and Pharmaceutical sub-units are referred to as being 'divisions': they sell to an outside set of customers and can, by that token, be classified as 'profit-centres', which by this definition would also make them 'divisions'.

14.1.12 Yet I would like to refine the crudity of this concept. When we split the shoe company, we did so to avoid 'opportunity cost'. Moreover we did this even when the output of a department was being absorbed by another department within the business. In other words, it was essential for us to compare and contrast *the price which could be obtained by the department that was selling, or which could be obtained by the department that was buying,* to establish whether or not the company was enduring an unjustified 'opportunity cost'. (*It will be noted that in neither case does such external trading need to be taking place. It is only necessary to establish that such trading* **could** *take place.*)

14.1.13 I should therefore like to suggest that we define departmentalization as being *limited to those sub-units in the business which could not reasonably be sub-contracted to an outside party, or which could not reasonably sell their output to an outside party. Under such circumstances it seems to me that these might be referred to as being 'departmental' and should be treated as cost-centres* in default of finding a basis for external valuation of their output. However, some such external valuation should be made *where the output of such a department has independent commercial worth that would make it feasible either to buy such output from the external world or, alternatively, to sell such output to the external world.* Otherwise we could not identify any opportunity cost being endured by either the selling or the buying sub-unit. On this basis, *I should declare any such sub-unit to be a 'division' and treat it as a **profit-centre** for that reason.*

14.1.14 By this device I would ensure that the traditional meanings of 'divisionalization' and 'departmentalization' were essentially maintained, but I would also be giving due warning that 'divisions' will be subject to competitive evaluation of their services: even if currently all outputs are internal transfers. It would also be an indication that (subject to main board approval) they were free to find external customers.

14.1.15 Yet it is only in retrospect, when we know that a sub-unit will be a cost-centre or a profit-centre, that we can know whether it is a 'department' or a 'division'. Until then we cannot say whether we are going through the actions of 'departmentalizing' or 'divisionalizing'. Yet this still leaves us in need of a general term to describe the process **before** the outcome is known. I suggest that this is best described by Luthans' useful Americanism 'departmentation' (1981; p.532–536). This would have several advantages. As yet the word, although not specifically defined by Luthans, has been used by him in this loose way to describe both 'departmentalization' ('functional departmentation') and 'divisionalization' ('product departmentation'). Moreover, it is not a word in general circulation so that it could acquire this usefully vague coloration without doing damage to existing concepts.

14.2 Some problems of definition: 'centralization' and 'decentralization'

14.2.1 I said that McGregor could find no reasons for practising 'centralization' other than that the management in question had a low regard for human nature (paragraph 10.3.29), and I promised that we would do better than that.

14.2.2 However, before we do so we need to define the terms 'centralization' and 'decentralization'. Centralization is the tendency of organizations to keep decision-making power near the top of the hierarchy. Decentralization is the tendency of organizations to allow decisions to be taken at lower levels in the hierarchy. Both are essentially philosophic concepts rather than structural devices. It is therefore not possible to look at an organizational diagram and to discern from it that the organization has either the one or the other tendency.

14.2.3 It is clear from what I have just written why McGregor and others should be so ready to see centralization as no more than a tendency towards authoritarianism, and decentralization as a tendency towards democratic practices. For the very fact that it is **not** possible to infer either 'centralization' or 'decentralization' from organizational structures seems to lend to the concepts an arbitary quality. Whichever practice managements adopt appears to be an issue independent from those which determine the nitty-gritty of organizational design. Seen in this light, both seem a matter of free choice, and this interpretation encourages the belief that centralization is no more than the wilful expression of authoritarian attitudes, while decentralization is the opposite. So the stage is set for the naïve 'good-guys' and 'bad-guys' concepts to which Luthans earlier drew our attention (paragraph 10.3.27).

14.2.4 What is wrong with this naïve position is its implication that no objective good or ill can come to the organization, as a goal-seeking enterprise, from allowing decisions to be made at one, rather than another hierarchy level. *Yet I would strongly maintain that unless some decisions **are** centralized the organization will suffer, and conversely unless others **are** decentralized it will **also** suffer. The trick is therefore to understand why this should be so in order to match each type of decision to be taken to an appropriate level within the hierarchy where each **should** be taken.* It is undoubtedly true that centralization must by definition, limit the freedom of the lower echelons to whom it applies. What is not true is that such limitations are no more than an expression of paranoid tendencies in top management.

14.2.5 We have already seen that, to achieve any scale at all, an organization has to be basically triangular in structure, and that this shape comes from a combination of horizontal groupings (span of control), and vertical groupings (levels). We have also seen that a wide span of control can only exist when the subordinate does not need to monopolize too much of the superior's time. The corollary to this is that those performing the lower duties must be in position to make the majority of moment-to-moment decisions. Such an arrangement is essential if the organization is not to grind to a halt because centralization has overburdened the people at the top.

14.2.6 To avoid such overburdening, control data sent up the organization becomes progressively less detailed. The main board may only get financial totals by which to monitor whether the production function in our shoe company has met its production volume and cost estimates. The production director will have a more detailed analysis for each of the four factories. He may see that there has been an abnormally high incidence of waiting time booked in one of the factories. But it will be the foreman who has data on the reasons for such a result.

14.2.7 This is why, in order to acquaint himself with the circumstances of the occurrence, the production director has to make enquiries down the chain of the hierarchy. Moreover, he does so despite the fact that he is fully aware that on this, as on all occasions when the information has filtered through to him, it will be too late to amend the circumstances of the case. Yet if he is psychologically healthy he does not go to this trouble merely to cry the more knowledgeably over the spilt milk.

(a) The purpose of the enquiry is to discover what adverse pattern of occurrences took place, and whether it was one likely to repeat. If so the pattern must be prevented from recurring or at least be limited in its impact.
(b) He then seeks to identify the warning signals for which the appropriate level of management should watch, and he instructs them in the actions that they should take to pre-empt such a further occurrence.

14.2.8 By these steps he expands the range of situations that become routine for junior management and enhances the quality of their decision-making. Yet we can see that such actions are of the essence of his job. Decentralization of this type is forced upon him by reality. As such it is not subject to whether he is or is not amenable to decentralization as a liberal/democratic practice. This is why I stated that complete centralization was unrealizable in practice (paragraph 12.4.7), although it is naturally somewhat easier to approximate to such a situation the smaller the firm happens to be.

14.2.9 This is a fortunate relationship, for there can be little doubt that the quality of decision-making in the small firm would be poorer if it could not be centralized in large measure. We have seen (paragraph 1.3.5) that there are four steps to goods decision-making:

(a) to create a comprehensive range of theoretical options,
(b) to challenge the assumptions in those option-models,
(c) to develop a set of choice-criteria,
(d) to apply (c) to (a) and choose.

Yet in the small entrepreneurial firm the boss may be the only one who could possibly hope to perform these duties with any degree of sophistication, or with any access to the information required. He would be renouncing his obligations to the firm and its employees if he were to pass the obligation down the hierarchy simply because he felt democratic concepts required it.

14.2.10 Conversely, as a firm grows in scale and complexity it engages specialists in order (a) to cope with the increasing load, and (b) to bring more sophisticated concepts to bear. The result is that the data-base sinks in the organization and the boss no longer has either the physical capacity or the specialist knowledge to make many of the decisions. In such a situation it would be impossible for him adequately to make detailed decisions in enough volume or to a high enough standard to allow the company to prosper.

14.2.11 Even so, we do not need to accept J. K. Galbraith's contention that this phenomenon has made the top management of the mature corporation impotent. He arrives at this conclusion because scale and complexity have led to decentralized experts being asked to prepare data for decisions. This situation allows the data to be filtered and manipulated, Galbraith implies, to correspond to the goals of those same experts. These specialists, who exist in every level of the hierarchy form, in Galbraith's view, 'the guiding intelligence – the brain of the enterprise', to which he gives the name of 'technostructure' (Galbraith, 1974; p.86). Here is his vision of how the technostructure is able to emasculate top management (Galbraith, 1974; p.98): 'Heavy dockets, replete with data [from the technostructure], are submitted to the Board. Recommendations are appended. Discussion is brief, stylized and superficial. Most of the participants are old men. Given the extent and character of the group preparation, rejection would be unthinkable. The Board, nonetheless, is left with the impression that it has made a decision.'

14.2.12 What Galbraith has overlooked is the nature of the constraint that top management can apply to lower management. We met it in the shoe company, and we will meet it again in a further example. The power of this constraint is that it comes from the core of the manager's own being: for, brought up in the *mores* of capitalism *he too accepts the overriding logic of the need to avoid opportunity cost.*

14.2.13 Of course, this does not mean that the marketing director of the shoe company case-study would not be predisposed to keep the retail operations going even when they represented an opportunity cost. He would not be human if he did not try to perpetuate his empire. My contention, however, is that when confronted with evidence of opportunity cost from the main board, he would not be able to resist the logic of their case, simply because he **does** share the same capitalist *mores* as they do. By contrast, worker-directors on a board would be disposed to challenge the legitimacy of the capitalist ideological standpoint when its adoption would throw up unpalatable consequences.

14.2.14 Galbraith would have us believe that the ability of the board of a mature corporation to confront the technostructure in the manner that I have described above is pre-empted by the ability of the technostructure to provide only that information that it has determined top management will be allowed to see. By so doing they have put the board into the position where it can only challenge one committee by setting up yet another committee. Galbraith's claim appears to be that the second committee, being itself part of the technostructure and sharing its interests, will not further the interests of the main board. The only alternative the board has to rubber-stamping the first committee's report, Galbraith infers, is to face an infinite regression of such committees which will always deny power to the main board when such power conflicts with the interests of the technostructure. This leads us to two questions:

(a) Is he right about the central role of such committees?
(b) Is he right about their ability to capture senior management in an infinite regression, thereby enforcing the will of the technostructure upon the organization?

14.2.15 In the next section we shall consider the need for (and the role of) committees, while in Section 14.4 I shall give a case-study to illustrate how top management dealt with the problem of receiving information through the filter of the technostructure.

14.3 The inevitability of committees

14.3.1 The use of specialists and specialist functions may increase efficiency, but it always carries with it the price of having to co-ordinate the activities of the specialisms involved. Commonly in the small firm the boss performs this function in his own person, as shown in Figure 14.3(a).

14.3.2 However, as the orgainization grows in complexity and size, the skills of the functional heads are required in order to be certain that the full impact of functional decisions upon the performance of the firm, and so that the effect of any proposed company decisions upon the operation of functions can be foreseen and any adverse implication dealt with. This creates the committee shown in Figure 14.3(b).

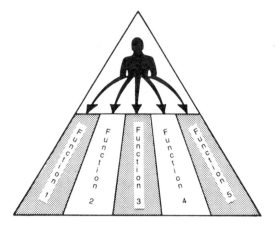

Figure 14.3(a)

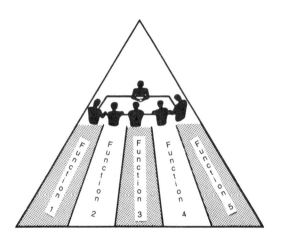

Figure 14.3(b)

14.3.3 As the firm grows yet larger and more complex and the situation gets beyond the capacity of the functional head to handle, sub-committees are formed within his function to make good the deficiency. Gradually Galbraith's technostructure is beginning to emerge.

14.3.4 Galbraith is correct when he states that 'nothing so characterizes the industrial system as the scale of the modern business enterprise' (1974; p.89). It is corroborated by his figures of the USA economy in the late 1960s,

OM-L

and by later figures from other developed countries. If we were to define 'typical' firms as those firms which (in any developed country) (1) produce most products, (2) employ the most people, and (3) own the most resources, then large-scale firms are indeed 'typical'. Consequently, the sort of company which should be of most particular interest to those studying organization theory is a large complex unit that it is far beyond the capacity of even the most talented single individual to control by himself. In such firms committees are not an option: they are a necessity.

14.3.5 That being so, it may be very misleading to draw up lists of activities that committees are good or bad at doing (e.g. Stewart, 1972; p. 67-8; O'Shaughnessy, 1969; p.49). For such lists invite the reader to see committees as being something that may or may not be used, dependent upon taste; rather like deciding whether to have tea or coffee. This is fallacious. *Given a certain level of complexity and scale, high-quality decisions can **only** be taken by the integrative work of a committee which includes representatives of the various specialisms.* Only these representatives can possibly be aware

(a) of the current state of the art in their specialism and the options that are theoretically possible, and
(b) of the resource constraints or capabilities that will make certain options possible and desirable while ruling out others because they are not.

14.3.6 Without doubt there **are** things that committees are bad at doing. Indeed, everything that we have so far discussed about the **implementation** of organizational goals has led us to a *hierarchical authority structure*. It would therefore be very perverse of us to regard a committee, which by its very nature has no hierarchical properties, as being able to **implement** anything well. Of course, the **individuals** on a committee, having reached agreement about the co-ordinated goals which need to be achieved, may well go back to their own functions to implement those decisions. But when they do so they have changed roles from **committee member** to **line manager.** Yet it remains true that committees, because of their ability to co-ordinate the greatest expertise to deal with complexity, are an essential managerial device. The individualist may choose to inflate his own ego with such phrases as 'a camel is a horse designed by a committee'. Yet it was a committee that put a man on the moon, and no other means was possible for so large and complex a programme.

14.3.7 Indeed, there are three things to note about committees which should endear them to the 'classical', the 'human relations' and the 'systems' writers, and yet which seem to have been only recognized partially if at all:

(i) *The 'classical' advantage of committees.* In many texts there is a realization that the classical/bureaucratic model contains a contradiction. For the superior is likely to know far less about specific areas than would one of his junior specialists. Yet the basic model assumes that the superior knows enough to direct the concern, and indeed if the respective 'hierarchical' relationships are not to be undermined, this relationship needs to be preserved. (*I trust by now that the reader will no longer regard such a statement, if he ever did, as indicative of 'classical' paranoia, but of a real problem.*) Yet the expert's opinion **must** be heard. *I do not imply that, **because** he is an expert, it should be **taken**. It may be partial, it may be more concerned with his own (rather than company) goals. There may be ramifications of which the expert, buried in his specialism, is unaware. **Yet it must be at least heard and its implications understood.*** In a committee, such an expert gets a forum in which to make these views known. In such committees it is tacitly understood that everyone can, **without it being seen as a challenge to line-authority,** question the wisdom of certain policies. Moreover, since the chairman of the committee is usually the most senior person present from the normal hierarchy, any proposal accepted, no matter how junior its originator might have been, is seen as having been officially sanctioned and as having the chairman's imprimatur. Committees therefore are a means of circumventing a fundamental problem in authority relationships for the classical theorist.

(ii) *The 'human relations' advantage of committees.* For the reasons that I have just stated, committees are the nearest thing to 'participation' that is possible between the different levels of a hierarchy. (*Of course, since the final outcome is subject to veto, it is still basically 'consultation' but the effect of discussion, of voting, and of sometimes adopting the concepts of junior members of the committee, gives to to the process the aura of 'participation'.*)

(iii) *The 'systems' advantage of committees.* I said (paragraph 12.2.5) that for systems writers 'the ability of the organism to sense a change in its environment, and then to go through a process of adaptation to accommodate that change, is seen as vital to its survival'. It is because the authority structures of classical management allegedly militate against both these goals that systems writers have been so antagonistic towards the classical standpoint. Yet most of the systems writers' objections are met by the use of the committee. Communication is enhanced because every member has his antennae turned to a different aspect of the environment. Co-ordination makes the members realize the impact of their part of the system on the rest, and it frequently happens that it becomes clear that one or more subsystems must sub-optimize if the total system is to optimize. Exposing the integrated needs of the total system means that any department that starts wilfully to defend its own vested interests rather than those of the company is seen to be doing so. In the face of such public critical gaze even the hardiest 'empire builder' has been known to falter and fall into line by adapting his function to accommodate the firm's new real needs.

14.3.8 Galbraith is therefore right about the size of the typical firm and about the role of the technostructure, and the role of committees. What we need to challenge is whether he is right in suggesting that such committees have made top management impotent. To do this we shall consider the real case-study of a firm that we shall give the imaginary name of MultiNat.

14.4 Bringing the 'technostructure' to heel: a case-study

14.4.1 Before we start to consider this case-study, we should recognize that in the majority of large companies the profits of subsidary divisions are usually siphoned off into Head Office, and thereafter controlled centrally. The rationale behind this is not only sound (given the *mores* of capitalism), but imperative if the opportunity cost of **not** doing so are to be avoided.

14.4.2 The rationale is irrefutable. If the group has only limited money to invest, then it should concentrate its use upon whichever division's project will yield the most profitable return to the group. Even if the divisional managements were prepared to move money laterally into another division (which is not inherently very probable), *there would be no* **mechanism** *for the management of each division to become aware of such opportunities.* Nor, just because Division A had a better use for money, should Division B hand it over. For unbeknown to Division B, Division C might have an even **better** use for the same cash.

14.4.3 If on the other hand, the divisions in the group all have **more** cash than they can reasonably employ, there would still be difficulties in leaving it with them. The first is that, because of their smaller scale, they may not have been able to employ the financial expertise which is able to invest it as advantageously as the experts at Head Office could do. The second is that for lack of finding a high enough return for it in the financial market, they may be tempted to invest it internally in projects of questionable financial worth. Either step will result in an opportunity cost to the group.

14.4.4 Divisional managements may resent such centralization (as they did in the following case study). Despite this they also realize that (if their role and that of the main board were reversed) they would do precisely the same thing. The resentment is therefore coupled with a degree of tacit acceptance: and this is yet one more example of ambivalence in capitalism which it would be misleading to ignore. As we shall see, it is upon this attachment to the 'rightness' of the main board's values that the divisions and the technostructures are ultimately tamed (though they may feel resentment even as they acquiesce).

14.4.5 Under such circumstances, it is common for the divisions to have a procedure by which they place bids (in effect) for the money that they need for any capital equipment programme. The main board usually demand that any such bid should show the expected earnings of a project over a period of time, (say) ten years. This the board consider. Their acceptance or rejection of the scheme is based upon their perception of:

(a) the probability of forecast volume being attained, and
(b) the 'net present value' of the revenues that will be generated relative to the size of the necessary investment (a term that I shall explain shortly).

14.4.6 The result of sales levels falling short of the forecast quantities will produce lower gross profits and may, as expenses bite, turn net profits into net losses. The more uncertain the forecast, therefore, the higher is the failure risk. The compensatory rewards from success must be equally great. There is little attraction in accepting high failure risks if the reward for success is mediocre. We need not dwell on this topic here, for the reader will see its relevance. (*Those readers familiar with microeconomic theory will know that, according to that theory, such speculation should ideally use the tools of marginal utility to maximize total utility over time.*)

14.4.7 However, we must say something about the term 'net present value', for it is an important example of the way capitalist theory has instituted a device for measuring the time-value of money with the precise purpose of being able to identify, and thus avoid, opportunity costs.

14.4.8 Whenever revenue is generated, or costs incurred, the further into the future that this happens, the less is its significance in terms of today's money values. This is a feature which is unconnected with inflation and happens in a non-inflationary situation: indeed, inflation tends to oppose this principle. Investment projects are calculated by a technique known as 'discounted cash flow'. This technique is a means of bringing the **time-value** of money into the calculation so that the future value of the project can be expressed in today's money: that is to say in terms of its 'nett present value'.

Let us consider why money has a **time-value**. I would rather someone gave me £1 now than next year. Moreover, this is true even if there is no inflation and even if I could be 100 per cent sure that I really would get the £1 next year. Why is this?

14.4.9 The reason is that if he gave it to me now I could invest it at (say) 10 per cent interest and so by next year I should have not £1 but £1.10: obviously a better deal. Moreover, if the choice were to get £1 now or in two years, the incentive to take the £1 now would be even greater, because in two years, at 10 per cent interest my £1 would have grown to £$(1.1)^2$ or £1.21. Similarly, in three years it would be worth £$(1.1)^3$ or £1.33.

14.4.10 In the technique of 'discounted cash flow' this same principle is applied but it is viewed from a slightly different angle. Instead of asking 'At an interest rate of 10 per cent what would £1 be worth in (say) three years?', and thus obtaining the answer '£1.33', we invert the question and ask 'How much money invested now at 10 per cent would yield £1 in 3 years? This gives us the answer 75 pence: {£1 × 1.00/1.33}.

14.4.11 When any large-scale project is calculated, it is common practice to calculate all the expenses that will be incurred in each year and all the revenues that will be generated in each year, and then *multiply the net difference for each year by the appropiate discount rate for that year as calculated above.* Let us assume that the discount rate was 10 per cent and the *net value of revenue less expenses* for year 3 was £100,000. To find out what that was worth in today's money, we would multiply it by a factor of 0.75; i.e. {$1.0/(1.1)^3$}. Consequently the *net present value* of that third year's trading would be £75,000. When added to the net present value of all the other years in the ten-year life of the calculation, we should have the net present value of the project over the whole decade.

14.4.12 If we are to avoid opportunity costs, therefore, we need to obtain revenues as early as possible, and to put off expenditure for as long as possible. All other things being equal and with an assumed discount rate of 10 per cent, then if we can put off building a plant that would cost £1.0 million now (year 0) until year 5, we could save £380,000, for we need take only £620,000, put it in the bank and let it grow. At 10 per cent compound interest we would have £1.0 million when we needed it, thus:

year 0	year 1	year 2	year 3	year 4	year 5
620	682	750	825	908	1000 (Figures in £000's and rounded)

Expressed another way, the net present value of £1.0 million in year 5 at discount rate of 10 per cent = {£1.0m. × $1.0/(1.1)^5$} = £620,000.

14.4.13 Our case-study concerns the Austrian and Swiss detergent companies of MultiNat. Both had applied to build entirely new plants on entirely new sites. There was no shortage of capital to undertake these projects, and both the projects gave hope of discounted cash-flow projections which would have won approval if they had been applied to a brand-new venture: that is to say if there were no existing facilities already producing. (It is even arguable that the present proposals could be said to have the edge on any new venture, since in the light of the existing strong high-volume market the revenue projections were demonstrably achievable.)

14.4.14 Now according to Galbraith's imagery, we could have expected MultiNat's senior management to rubber-stamp these proposals,

(a) because of the **favourable** cash-flow projections;
(b) because top management were isolated from data which would allow them to challenge these proposals;
(c) because, if they **did** challenge them it would need to be via a committee which would be only first in an infinite regression of committees. All would be intent upon supporting the Austrian and Swiss proposals on the grounds that all members of the technostructure share the same interests.

14.4.15 Only when we bring Galbraith's philosophizing down to hard case-material do we realize what slick assumptions are contained in his claims. Firstly, top management is not devoid of all data. They know very well that *the existing equipment is currently producing goods, and could do so for some time.* Of course it may cost extra maintenance to keep old equipment running, but even if the discounted cash rate is as low as 10 per cent, whatever cost and effort is needed to keep it going for another 5 years will be unlikely to be as great as the alternative. For 38 per cent of rebuild costs could, as we saw, be saved *simply by **delaying** the project for five years.* Such speculation by the main board is beyond the technostructure's power to prevent; moreover, it is inconceivable that such a mode of thought would not be second nature to someone who had been shrewd enough to climb the slippery pole of a multinational company. So however good the discounted cash-flow projections of the Swiss and Austrian companies are in **absolute** terms, in **relative** terms when compared with a **delayed** rebuild they are inherently likely to involve opportunity cost.

14.4.16 Secondly, Galbraith is surely disingenuous to suggest that some sort of brotherhood joins all the technostructure into a cohesive band of musketeers who fight back-to-back, crying, 'All for one, and one for all!' It's a beautiful piece of romantic imagery: but it has absolutely no basis in fact. He is right about the need to form another committee to review the work of the first. But there is no infinite regression. I was a member of the committee set up to look into the situation, yet my stand point, as a representative of the main board, was exactly the same as that of the board, and my yardstick was exactly the same, namely that the group should not incur any unnecessary opportunity cost. No other standpoint would have been acceptable to my professional self-image.

14.4.17 Moreover, I shall show that, through the careful selection of *terms of reference*, the main board put the two subsidiary companies into a position in which **they too**

(a) each had a vested interest in undermining the case of the other, and
(b) each had a vested interest in putting forward alternative proposals which delayed the expenditure of capital by many years.

The main board got what they wanted by the simple expediency of making the two companies competitive with each other, the prize going to the one who incurred the least opportunity costs. Yet, Machiavellian as their moves might appear to be to the reader, they were, in my experience, no more than the sort of moves that any competent top management would use to tame the technostructure. But before I describe these moves, let us look at the nature of the original proposals of the two companies.

14.4.18 There was a remarkable degree of coincidence in each case. At the beginning of the century the entrepreneurial founder of MultiNat had chosen each existing site as the place to build a soap factory. Each was triangular and bounded by railway lines on all three sides. It was this factor that now constrained their growth.

14.4.19 The early soap-making process had been a high user of space, with soap stacked in moulds all over the site as part of the manufacturing process. However, within a short time it became technically possible to make soap as a near-continuous process. In the initial aftermath of this development the sites became far larger than was then required.

14.4.20 But over the years the volume rose, and the products proliferated. They now included not only soaps, but detergents, shampoos, deodorants, after-shaves, shaving soaps and toothpastes. Once again they were constrained for space. Something needed to be done. Here again they coincidentally proposed the same thing. Each suggested that an alternative site should be purchased on which a new manufacturing complex would be built. The old site was to be sold in each case, and, as I have already said, each proposal was supported by a discounted cash-flow assessment that was favourable.

14.4.21 Now let us turn to the main board's reaction. They were complimentary about the existing proposals of the two companies. They began by pointing out that both Austria and Switzerland were in the European Free Trade Area (EFTA) and that the population of both was a mere 12 million (5 million in Switzerland and 7 million in Austria), of which the vast majority were German-speaking. They therefore proposed setting up a committee to look at the possibility of a 'super-factory' to serve both countries. Then the costs of such an arrangement could be compared with the total cost of providing the two separate factories in the current proposals. Of course, they added, if any other idea occurred to anyone in the course of this study, that too could be evaluated, and also form the basis of a proposal.

14.4.22 Membership of the committee was to be two German-speaking consultants from London (of whom I was one), two members of each of the two companies, and any legal, technical or other personnel that the committee chose to co-opt as necessary. (*Incidentally this raises a point made by O'Shaughnessy (1969; p.49), for he claims that committees are poor at fact collection. That is a statement that I cannot understand, for over a broad technical spectrum the various skills of a committee are needed for the evaluation of those facts which are deemed worthy of note. I suggest that the incidence of* **committees of enquiry** *illustrates that in this respect he is mistaken.*)

14.4.23 However, let us return to MultiNat where the top management had just put the cat among the pigeons. Now they had only to wait, quietly confident of the outcome. For, as will be realized, if a larger plant **were** to be more economic, neither company could feel safe: for who was to say that they would be the ones to be chosen to expand? They might well be the unlucky partner in this new variant on Russian roulette. Both companies now felt threatened. It is not always true that a larger plant is cheaper to run when all costs are considered. We saw this in the case of the shoe factory. However, circumstances alter cases. There were a number of reasons to suggest that an increase in the scale of manufacture of detergents and toiletries **would** reduce costs.

14.4.24 Unlike shoe manufacture, detergents and toiletries require less labour per unit value of sale and the dysfunctions of attempting to increase the organization's size are less pressing. Such plants have fewer operations, a lower variety of products, a lot of automatic or semi-automatic equipment, and even some equipment that might well be the cheaper per ton to operate for being enlarged. Detergent powder is made by mixing the ingredients with water to form a sort of porridge and then forcing this porridge through a sprinkler at the top of a high cylindrical 'blowing-tower'. As the drops of porridge fall, they meet a draught of hot air coming up the tower. By the time they reach the bottom of the tower they have been dried into a powder. There was reason to believe that a bigger blowing-tower would use less power for any given tonnage.

14.4.25 Moreover, providing that the range of detergent powders could be common to both countries, the resultant volume increase would permit a super-factory to run bigger batches without incurring higher holding costs. This could result in lower unit cost because the job of cleaning out the blowing-tower between formulations was a major (and so costly) operation. The more packets that were filled from any one set-up, the smaller that cost would be per unit of detergent produced.

14.4.26 My own view is that the super-factory was never really a serious option. There are many other considerations than cost. The Swiss, for example, are very chauvinistic in their shopping habits, and goods made in Switzerland are marked accordingly. Yet if the factory were in Switzerland, it could not be further from the main Austrian population density, which is at the opposite end of Austria around Vienna. Whether the super-factory were built in Austria or Switzerland, it had an inescapable problem. The Arlberg Pass lies between them, and is often blocked in winter to road traffic. Just because both countries were members of EFTA did not mean that there were not various border taxes to 'equalize' what were seen as anomalies, and such products as after-shave contain alcohol which is taxed accordingly. In any case it is dangerous to plan on anything that can be altered by a stroke of the pen: what, for example, if Switzerland were to go into the European Economic Community (EEC) while Austria stayed in EFTA?

14.4.27 Moreover, many of the economies of scale could be nullified because the range of products in the two countries was far from similar. To the casual observer the two countries might appear alike: but Austria was still basically a peasant country while Switzerland was quite sophisticated in its requirements. So batch sizes would not generally be increased following the building of a super-factory.

14.4.28 Real as these objections were, the two companies could not get rid of their unease. Just in case the super-factory became the final choice, the Swiss pointed out to us all the problems that the Austrians would have in operating such a plant, and the Austrians pointed out the difficulties of the Swiss. So much for Galbraith's claim that the technostructure present a united front.

14.4.29 However, their greatest safety lay in moving away from a new-with-new comparison. If they could only make their existing plants last longer then the effect of discounting the cash-flow would make independent national plants in each country more attractive. This is because the basis of comparison would now be between a new super-factory at Year '0' with the two existing plants. True, these would need to be updated; but the following considerations would ensure that these independent plants were cheaper than the super-factory:

(a) **all** existing facilities were sunk costs,
(b) **some** could be kept in use for years to come,
(c) when any **were** replaced it would be in terms of **discounted money**.

14.4.30 Accordingly, it will surprise no one to learn that our joint committee finally agreed on the following proposals:

(a) That the super-factory was a bad idea.
(b) That there was no immediate need for a completely new national plant in each country, for the rebuild could be phased as follows:
   (i)   Buy a large plot of land close to the existing site. (Land was cheap and would doubtless appreciate.)
   (ii) Put on it some general-purpose buildings for packaging detergents and for warehousing finished goods.
   (iii) Transfer the silos that stored powder after manufacture and prior to packing from the old site to the new (for they could be disassembled and reassembled cheaply).
   (iv) Use bulk-tanker lorries to shuttle powder between the old site where it was made and the new site where it was packed.

This would relieve the existing pressure at little cost, and the remaining products would be able to spread themselves on the old site. Then in 'x' years when the greatest single element of cost on the old site, namely the detergent-manufacturing plant, was worn out, it would be possible to replace it at no extra cost than that of replacing it anyway. Indeed. there would be the advantage that during the replacement period the existing plant could remain in use without disruption until building of the new one was complete.

14.4.31 With the acceptance by the main board of these proposals, the committee was disbanded, and the Austrian and Swiss companies were instructed to implement them. (For, as we know, committees are good for complex decisions, but ill-suited to the task of implementation.) Yet there are several morals still to be drawn from this case-study, and a paradox to explain.

14.4.32 The aspect of the situation that I found most remarkable was the ambivalence of the committee members from these two companies. When they learned of the final decision they exhibited both relief and resentment. Relief that their worst fears had not been realized, and resentment that they had lost their pretty new shiny factories as called for in the original proposals.

14.4.33 Yet throughout the whole exercise, for all that they had been self-seeking and in particular had sought to protect their independence, they had done so by using the *mores* of capitalism. They never once questioned the validity of the assumption that when the ultimate decision was made, it would be made on the basis of minimizing opportunity cost. They expected the decision to be made without sentiment, and so when they defended themselves they did so with the weapon of opportunity cost. Other things being equal, they might have made some appeal to social considerations, yet, in their initial approach they made no attempt to bring into the equation the very thing that was, to them, the matter of greatest personal concern; the social implications of making their own plant redundant. **So, in a manner that no trade unionist or worker representative would have conceded for one second, they accepted that the only legitimate criteria for decision-making were those of capitalism. Lack of such *mores* is why 'worker participation' on boards will turn the boardroom into a ideological battlefield.**

14.4.34 But this brings us to the paradox. If these two companies **had** accepted the *mores* of capitalism, *why had they ever made the original expensive proposals and why was their relief, when their subsequent cheaper proposals were accepted, tinged with resentment?* The short answer is that inside every capitalist boss there is a feudal lord-of-the-manor trying to get out. By emphasizing the resultant opportunity costs, the main board check this tendency and also get him to reaffirm his belief in capitalism. The Austrian Managing Director typified this situation. He saw the firm as his own 'baby', a situation that caused his personal and public life to become intertwined in a manner which is not seen as having any legitimacy within the tenets of bureaucracy. There the 'role' that an official performs is supposed to be kept distinct from his private life, and indeed should be performed without passion.

I impute nothing to him of which he should in any sense be ashamed. For him the boundaries of his world were those of his immediate company. For him, 'London' was clearly a parasitic growth. If there were any suggestion of immoral practice, he clearly sensed that it lay there.

14.4.35 Indeed, I found him to be a very fine man and he unburdened his soul to me on the subject. To him **his** firm *was* MultiNat: he acknowledged the existence of the 'group' concept, but, as I listened to his history, I realized that the 'group' was only one more despoiler in a lifetime of vicissitudes. He was an unusual man not least because he was an engineer, and MultiNat was renowned for choosing its managing directors exclusively from the ranks of its marketing men. But his appointment coincided with the outbreak of the Second World War when marketing was no problem, but production was. For rationing meant that sales were controlled at less than their natural demand. On the other hand, the requirement for soap needed to be satisfied, despite improbable raw materials, and a shortage of spare parts. Six years of this was followed by the Russian occupation. The Russians eventually pulled out, but not without exacting a price, and MultiNat was plundered along with the others who paid 'reparations'.

14.4.36 While the War had been in progress there had been no contact with London, and while the Russians were exacting their reparations London kept a very low profile, as might be supposed. Then at long last, with the Russians gone and some semblance of normality having returned, the Austrian company started to make money. 'Suddenly,' said the Austrian M.D., 'London found us interesting and for the next ten years regularly siphoned off our money. Now, when I ask to build a new plant with the money that we've earned, what do they send me? ....Money?' He patted my shoulder and said 'No ...and I don't mean to be offensive, because you're a nice chap...No... They send me **you!**'

14.4.37 This is why all **strategic** planning must be centralized. We can refute McGregor's implications that such policing by the main board or its agents is unnecessary. Yet equally we can see the extent to which **operating** decisions **must** be decentralized. **Administrative** decisions will flow from the other two types and *tend to take the colouring of the issue that sparked off the need*. However, even when administrative decisions have been made centrally, their *implementation* is most frequently a matter for decentralized management to handle, not least because decentralized managements are the only people able to gain the rapid feedback necessary for control, as well as having more detailed data than is available at the centre and being the line-managers of the people who are performing the implementation functions. Hopefully this will kill off some of the more simplistic centralization/decentralization statements.

14.4.38 Lastly, although we concur with Galbraith that most proposals will be the result of the work of the technostructure, and specifically of committees, yet top management is **not** impotent. For even if the report of one committee requires the report of another committee to overturn it, this is something that top management can arrange.

15

Classical organization: the critiques of 'human relations' and 'systems' thinkers

15.1 Systems thinking in management

15.1.1 It is my belief that history will regard the development of general systems theory as watershed in human cognition, the significance of which would be difficult to overestimate. Such criticisms as I might make concerning the systems approach to organizational theory must be seen against that general assessment. Moreover, the reader should by now have recognized that whatever homogeneity of approach this book has, and it was certainly my intention that it should be as holistic as possible, stems from a refusal to discuss issues, so to speak, *in vacuo*. For what is the point of discussing the spots when they are only a symptom of the measles? Even when rival theories vied with each other we sought, as Pears advised us to do (paragraph 2.2.6), to 'ignore the bedlam, and attain some degree of objectivity by tracing the divergent ways in which they have developed from a single starting point'. But the fact that Pears assumes that there **is** a single starting point implies that the problem is systemic in origin.

15.1.2 To identify the interplay of variables in the system we developed the image of the organization, Figure 3.2(b) p.58., whose interactive elements, namely the product, the technology, the work organization, the goals and the constraints, were all being subjected to changing pressures. These pressures were social, technological, economic and political in nature and came not only from within the company but also from the environment.

15.1.3 Moreover, such is the nature of systems that we were brought to realize that few systems are totally good, and even that their worst aspects are frequently the price we pay for insisting that we retain their good aspects. Sometimes these bad aspects are so determined by circumstance that only abandoning the whole purpose of the organization can relieve them. Sometimes they are alterable. But in the act of doing so we shall disturb the original equilibrium and, in effect, create a different system. This was why we had the manager in Figure 3.2(b) choosing from system 1 to system *n*.

15.1.4 If I were to criticise Figure 3.2.(b) it would be that the drawing might imply that the options are there waiting to be picked up: static creations, sitting like different brands of soap-powder on a supermarket shelf. They are not. The apparent static nature of some organizations results from their having achieved a dynamic equilibrium. Attempt to change any of the factors in the equipoise, however, and the whole system might exhibit a dynamism that could be as dramatic as it was unexpected. All this is cloaked by the single word 'choice' in Figure 3.2(b).

15.1.5 On the other hand, changes can occur in the environment which will render the original organization inappropriate; equally the internal organization may develop responses which are inappropriate for the firm's survival. In either case the failure of the management to intervene and to make compensatory changes in the system will cause the organization to atrophy and die. So the systems theorist sees it as vital that an organization should carefully monitor its environment and its own internal activities to ensure that **what is done and the manner in which it is done** are always appropriate. This sounds as though the organization is to be maintained in constant flux, and of course it is. But systems writers also recognize that an organization must maintain its stability. They do not deny that management will seek to make the system grow in size and/or complexity: but throughout it all, they recognize that if stability is lost, the future of the system will be put in jeopardy.

15.1.6 The immediate difference between this and the classical approach that hits the reader is that it has a different 'feel'. In the classical approach we were expressing ourselves in statics. The very vocabulary of classical theory can leave this impression. 'Span of control' does so, for example. 'Span' gives the image of a structural 'bridge'. 'Control', though inevitable in hierarchies and though it is capable of being flexible, is not necessarily or readily **seen** in this light. All too easily we can form the impression that the boss is claiming to be aware of the specific and detailed standards to which the subordinate must perform. *(There is no logical reason why the concept should* *carry this connotation, but it is often assumed that it does because the whole ethos psychologically* **prepares** *us to see it in these terms.)* Yet it is often quite impossible for the boss to control in this way, a fact that was recognized by classical theorists in the concept of decentralization. I doubt the extent to which classical managers, decentralized for the purpose of offering meaningful work to their subordinates. That being so, we can conclude (and classical writings support this conclusion) that decentralization was forced upon them by a technical problem of which they were very much aware.

There were many instances in which, if they did **not** decentralize, they would risk failure of the system through time-lag, overload, lack of data or spatial separation. So in comparing the systems approach with the classical approach we have the problem of deciding whether to concentrate upon the differences that the reader will find are **claimed** to exist in the generality of systems writing, or to deal with somewhat less pronounced differences that must have existed **in reality.** It seemed to me to be more useful to choose the latter.

15.1.7 I need to justify my claim that much systems writing exaggerates the true differences between the two approaches. I shall invoke systems evidence to do so. For the more extreme systems claims about the shortcomings of classical theory are such that if they had been true no classical organization would have had a very long life. What we are to conclude from our knowledge that so many classical organizations survived for many years? Surely it is that they had a capacity for adaptation far beyond that credited to them in systems literature. Nor can classical organizational success be explained away by asserting that it existed and flourished in a by-gone world in which there were insufficient pressures of a social, technological, economic or political nature to expose its inadequacies. The history of the early twentieth century gives no reason to believe this.

15.1.8 What adaptive capabilities must an organization possess to survive changing conditions? Before we deal with that I shall introduce two terms which, in systems language differ slightly from their general meanings, namely, 'import' and 'export'. A system is sometimes regarded as a 'black box'. By this we mean some entity that we do not need to define very specifically for the purpose of discussing the concept. Within this 'black box' some sort of conversion process takes place, by which things going into it, termed 'imports', are modified and result in other things coming out, termed 'exports'.

15.1.9 Schien tells us (1970; p.120) that the adaptive coping cycle has six stages which he identifies as follows:

1. Sensing a change in some part of the internal or external environment.
2. Importing the relevant information about the change into those parts of the organization that can act upon it.
3. Changing production or conversion processes inside the organization according to the information obtained.
4. Stabilizing internal changes while reducing or managing undesired by-products (undesired changes in related systems which have resulted from the desired changes).
5. Exporting new products, services, and so on, which are more in line with the originally perceived changes in the environment.
6. Obtaining feedback on the success of the change through the further sensing of the state of the environment and the degree of integration of the internal environment.

Let us illustrate this process with ...[a ... simple example]... Suppose a manufacturing concern producing electronic equipment learns that the space program is going to increase the demand for this equipment a great deal (stage 1). The information about this change in demand must be imported into the organization in the sense of being taken seriously by those members who are in a position to do something about it. It is not sufficient for the market research department to have the information if it cannot convince the general management (stage 2). If the management becomes convinced, it must change its production processes to enable the company to produce more of the equipment (stage 3). These changes must be accomplished without producing other undesirable internal changes (for example, a strike in response to unreasonable demands for increased production) and they must be stabilized (stage 4). The increased production must be marketed and sold (stage 5). And finally, sales figures and future demand figures must then be analysed to determine whether the organizational change has been 'successful' in terms of increased marketability, and the internal environment must be assessed to determine whether unanticipated costs in the form of lowered morale or intergroup competition have been minimized (stage 6).

15.1.10 This description brings us to the nub of what the systems writers expect of an organization. **They expect it to know what is going on in the environment and then to react.** The capacity to react to fundamental changes in the environment is **crucial** to systems writers. A system with these characteristics is called by them, appropriately enough, an 'open system'. A system which can make no such response to its environment is referred to as a 'closed system'. Within a Second World War torpedo was an inertia guidance system governed by a gyroscope which held the torpedo running straight and true... even when the enemy swerved out of its path! Modern weaponry, such as heat-seeking missiles, are controlled until they are adjacent to the target, but they then react to any avoiding tactics that might be employed by the enemy. (It should be noted that in the early 1980s heat-seeking missiles could still be fooled by firing flares to draw them off: but missiles are getting smarter all the time). Thanks to systems theory, the problem of the Second World War has been turned on its head. **Then** with weapons limited to 'closed' systems, the problem was how could one achieve a hit? **Now** the problem for the Third World War will be what do you do when, thanks to 'open' systems, **nobody** can miss? Who would be a modern-day tank-commander?

15.2 Deciding upon the boundaries of the organizational system

15.2.1 When adopting the systems approach, whether it be in management or in any other sphere of activity, two questions dominate the thinking. The first is, 'Where are the boundaries of the system?'. If we make the boundaries too wide we give ourselves more to worry about with less immediate significance. On the other hand, if we make the boundaries too tight we may exclude areas of vital information. Does the doctor concentrate on the 'heart-patient's' heart alone, or his circulatory system; or is his digestive system included and even his way of life? Conversely, in considering the patient as a 'heart patient' does the doctor need to take into account the patient's ingrowing toe-nail?

15.2.2 It is systems thinking that has brought about the enormous interest in ecology. It is characteristic of a system that when we rattle something in one part of it something jangles in another. When we destroy rain-forests in Brazil something may happen in (say) Egypt. If we make the boundaries of our system too narrow, we shall miss vital information. An English car manufacturer whose system did not include legislation passed in the US Congress could wave goodbye to exporting there if his exhaust emissions did not conform to that legislation. Of course, it is also true that many of us **deliberately** choose to shut out the significant effects that our actions will have elsewhere from sheer self-interest. I enjoy my gas-fired centrally heated home though presumably it is contributing to the amount of carbon dioxide that fossil-fuels are pumping in to the upper atmosphere. So I shall be as responsible as anybody else if the 'greenhouse effect' **does** eventually raise the Earth's temperature by the $2°$ that has been predicted will have catastrophic results. For my personal convenience I treat what goes on in my own home as a 'closed' system and pretend that it has no global significance.

15.2.3 It is the claim of most systems writers that the classical approach to organizations created a 'closed' system. Those managers who based their activities upon classical principles are claimed to have concentrated so much upon internal efficiency that they are said frequently to have ignored what was going on in the environment. To give this some form of concrete expression, it is as though I were making 78 r.p.m. clockwork gramophones, and finding that my profits were slipping I tried to retrieve the situation by making them **more cheaply.** Meanwhile, in the outside world people are turning to electric 33 r.p.m. stereophonic hi-fi and laser discs.

15.2.4 It clearly helps the survival of a company if its management are highly conscious of environmental changes which have to be met. In making the issue so important and by burning it into management consciousness, systems writers have done us a great service. But it is not true that such a realization escaped classical writers. They had as one of their principles 'appropriateness'. Historical studies of companies at a time when classical theory was the dominant element in management thought gave scant evidence of the 'clockwork gramophone' mentality. I accept that the authors of such histories may sometimes be over-sympathetic towards their subject, but the facts and the correspondence of the day show how aware many of these companies were of the threats and opportunities in the environment and their need to respond to these by taking some strategic initiative. Here, for example is one of many similar passages in a history of Unilever. It is speaking of the later years of the nineteenth century and of W. H. Lever, later Lord Leverhulme.

> The nature of the raw materials required by the soap maker made him peculiarly conscious of the importance of foreign supplies. And the quality of Sunlight [soap], depending as it did on imported vegetable oils, made Lever from the beginning alive to the problem of raw materials. Round about the turn of the century, the fear of being 'squeezed' for these materials by the merchants and brokers became almost an obsession with him, and in the projects for winning raw materials that followed there was probably a large element of defensive strategy' (Wilson, 1954; pp.158-159).

There is not much of the 'clockwork gramophone syndrome' in that passage. and we should also note that the passage was written long before 'systems' thinking in management became common currency.

15.2.5 That having been said, I would not seek to deny that our need to monitor what goes on in the environment is made greater than ever by the shortening of the life-cycle of products which has been so striking a feature of this century. This shorter life-cycle has been brought about primarily by the result of technological change, though the life-cycle was also affected by social, political and economic factors.

15.2.6 By contrast, the ridiculous nineteenth century penny-farthing bicycle (Figure 15.2(a) had a life-cycle of 60 years. *Yet the purpose of the big wheel was only to ensure that one turn of the pedals, to which it was directly attached, would move the bike forward by the distance of the wheel's circumference!* It would not **now** take 60 years for someone to think that some form of gearing would make the big wheel unnecessary (Figure 15.2(b)). We should therefore accept the systems emphasis upon the need for the organization to operate an open system, but reject any suggestion that classical organizations did not.

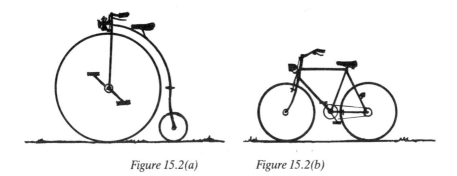

Figure 15.2(a)   *Figure 15.2(b)*

15.3 Deciding upon the boundaries of the subsystems

15.3.1 Having decided upon the boundaries of the system, the second question that dominates systems thinking is the relationship between the subsystems contained within that system. In deciding whether a particular arrangement of subsystems is appropriate or not, one of the main criteria which systems writers apply is *how great the communication burden will be* in any one given arrangement. All other things being equal, the arrangement with the minimum communications burden will be chosen.

15.3.2 Such a position seems to me basically sound. However, that is not the same thing as **assuming that an organization is no more than a communication system.** Nor would systems writers claim that it was. But their emphasis slides easily into **behaving** as though this were the case, and in so doing I believe that they have taken several steps away from reality. They need to retrace them. If my conclusions as to **why** they have wandered are correct, one can only sympathize with what they were trying to do. Having acknowledged that, however, if systems writing on organization and management is to progress, it must first rid itself of this distortion.

15.3.3 The clearest evidence that such distortion has been introduced comes from Simon, (1960; p.1), who admitted that he had found it 'convenient to take mild liberties with the English language by using "decision making" as though it were synonymous with "managing"'. But the two words are **not**

synonymous. It is not only therefore the English language with which he has taken liberties, but the **actualities** behind the language. The reasons for such an uncharacteristic action must, I reasoned, lie in some worthwhile purpose that required the acceptance of this distortion if it were to be achieved. Such a purpose is that of attempting to represent organizational operations, i.e. simulating them, by the use of a computer.

15.3.4 Many systems theorists, Simon included, have been engaged in building such models. Whatever models such theorists build are likely, in the nature of things, to picture the organization as a network along which data flows to and from the decision-maker. This **may** be the operator or it **may** be the computer, but in either case he/it represents the **manager**. Seeking certain goals, yet channelled by various constraints within the model, the 'manager' will examine the latest data and then make a choice from among the perceived means-ends options currently available. This decision will travel as data through the network (with whatever attenuation or distortion that the program has modelled) to the various points in the network that represent either (1) the internal organization or (2) the external environment in which it finds itself. Of course, the decision taken by the 'manager' may trigger many unexpected responses both inside and outside the 'organization'. *Nevertheless, the mere transmission of data is the closest he can get to 'implementation' in such a model.* When he gets back a response to any 'decision' (together with any new data from the environment) he makes yet another decision and the cycle merely repeats. *So in computer modelling 'decision-making' is 'management', and 'implementation'* **is** *no more than successive cycles of data transmission.*

15.3.5 However, the real world is not like this. It is not good enough to regard 'implementation' as being no more than a number of sequential decisions, each represented by a choice from among the possible means–ends options scenarios, and executed by sending data through a network of channels. A practising manager would recognize immediately that this is not what **he** means when he speaks of 'implementation', though he might not be able to say quite what he **does** mean. His vagueness should not surprise us, for 'implementation' leads us to **a consideration of how influence is exerted.** His problem is ours. It is not simply that 'influence' itself eludes us when we try to analyse it; it is also that we are likely to misunderstand it, even in its crudest expression and most obvious form. In its less obvious forms we sometimes catch a glimpse of what it is and how it works before it shimmers into insubstantiality. Yet difficult as it may be to visualize it, and near-impossible as it may be to analyse it, we shall do no service to organizational theory to pretend that 'implementation' is no more than 'the iterative dispersion of data as a result of continuous feedback'. The tail must not wag the dog and the convenience of the computer modeller cannot be allowed to warp our perception of the real world, however laudable may be the ultimate purpose of that distortion.

15.3.6 We must therefore re-examine our approach to systems theory in organizations. Among the requirements of such an approach are:

(1) The hierarchical nature of all organizations should be acknowledged.
(2) The authority structures that this implies should be acknowledged.
(3) The Janus-like nature of the subsystem which makes it a 'holon' should be acknowledged, together with the realization that the system will be impaired if the holon does not achieve an appropriate balance between its self-assertive and its integrative tendencies.
(4) The tendency for organizations to use people instrumentally, and in the case of capitalist organizations to create a contractual relationship with ambivalent implications for both manager and managed, should be acknowledged.

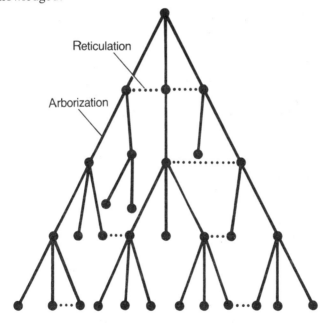

Figure 15.3(a) A hierarchical network.

15.3.7 Moreover, we need to be very careful about the use of words such as 'network' **for they tend to disguise the need for hierarchies.** A hierarchy is rather like an upside-down tree. If we were to take a number of upside-down trees whose branches intertwined, and then were to tie some of those branches together so that each tree were cross-connected at certain levels, we would be approximating to a much more realistic image of relationships within organizations and societies than we would get if we spoke of 'networks'. Koestler talks of the tree-like properties of such a structure as being 'arborization', while the lateral cross-linkages he refers to as 'reticulation' (Koestler, 1975 b; p.345): 'Hierarchies can be regarded as "vertically" arborizing structures whose branches interlock with those of other hierarchies at a multiplicity of levels and form "horizontal" networks: arborization and reticulation are complementary principles in the architecture or organisms and societies.' Figure 15.3.(a) is my graphic interpretation of Koestler's description.

15.3.8 We should also note that only **some** of the branches in that figure are tied together by reticulation. It is one of the faults that follows from speaking of 'networks' that we picture a lattice in which every point of intersection is a receptor–transmitter and every arm a channel of communication to or from that receptor–transmitter. The next error is to begin to imagine that organizations which do not have these network properties are thereby somehow disadvantaged.

15.3.9 This I shall challenge by considering specific types of organization. We shall find throughout from such case-studies that 'arborization' is ever-present, but that the degree of 'reticulation' that is appropriate between the various branches will vary considerably with circumstance. However, before we do that we ought to consider the impact of the human relations approach to organizational theory that our return to the consideration of systems theory can include any ideas that might be picked up on the human aspects of the organizational system.

15.4 The human relations approach to organizational design

15.4.1 The problem of discussing this topic is that, in the main, there is really no such thing. We discussed Likert's ideas (paragraph 12.4.5 to 12.4.8), and that is all that has seriously been proposed in terms of structure. Over and above that, the work of human relations writers has lacked rigour and cohesion. Occasionally they have performed an exercise in job-enrichment, or some such concept, derived from the ideas of human relations or neo-human relations motivational theory, but then they have failed to analyse whether any unique characteristics had made that exercise possible. The result has been that they usually go on to infer that what was possible in that particular case would analogously be applicable in more general circumstances. (This was the inference for example of Sirota and Wolfson which we criticized earlier in paragraphs 4.1.21. and 22.) However, in Sections 15.5 and 15.6 I shall spell out the conditions under which job-enrichment/enlargement which involves machinery is possible.

15.5 'Job-enrichment/enlargement', using 'general purpose' machinery

15.5.1 The work-content of those using general-purpose equipment (whose nature was dealt with in Section 4.3) can be significantly changed only if: *the nature of the work allows the same equipment to be used upon long-duration work-cycles, and only then if there is no costly mid-cycle resetting required by the machine.*

15.5.2 I suggested earlier that the sewing-machine was such a piece of equipment in the garment industry. In the electronics industry the soldering-iron is another. Even then there is no guarantee that enlarging the cycle will lead to lower costs (as we saw in paragraph 4.3.18). On occasion job-enlargement **has** nevertheless led to lower costs. This was apparently the experience at IBM according to Drucker (1968; p.312). So because greater worker satisfaction **may** result from the attempt, when circumstances favour its introduction it is not something to be dismissed lightly.

15.6 'Job-enrichment/enlargement', using 'special purpose' machinery

15.6.1 The work-content of those tending special-purpose equipment whose nature was dealt with in section 4.2) can be significantly changed only if:
(a) the equipment is cheap enough to allow it to be used intermittently without serious economic loss; or
(b) the equipment, though needing to be highly utilized, does not thereby need the constant attention of any particular single operative.

15.7 The affinity between 'systems' and 'human relations' writers

15.7.1 One of the remarkable aspects of the development of management theory over the last twenty years or so has been the gradual coming together of systems and human relations writers.

15.7.2 They make strange bed-fellows if the logic of their basic positions is considered. For the human relations writers have denied the validity of many of the constraints of the organizational system as 'mechanistically' non-human. In this they have been prompted (by their basic ideological standpoint as much as by any other factor) to deny the need for specialization, the need for hierarchies, and the need for coercion. This should have made their position unacceptable to the Systems writers who recognize that complex organisms and organizations must incorporate specialization and hierarchy. *To understand why organisms must do so the reader has only to reach out and pick up a nearby object and then to reflect upon what was involved in the act. What could be more specialized than the cells that form the eye, or those that form the reaching arm, or those of the grasping fingers? Yet how could they have performed their action without the hierarchical control of the brain? Moreover, it was from Simon that Koestler got the idea he elaborated into the story of the two watch-makers, Mekhos and Bios, in paragraphs 3.1.8 to 10.*

15.7.3 Yet if there were **logical** reasons why they should **not** have formed this strange alliance, there were even stronger **psychological** reasons why they should have done so. Systems writers were disturbed that organizations were failing to adapt and change. They had concluded that this was a psychological problem. Managements were using mechanistic concepts which were encouraged by the emphasis in classical thought of functional departments within a hierarchical framework. In making this claim, systems writers tended to lose sight of the affinity that existed between the classical concepts of specialization and hierarchy and their own models. There were two other factors pushing them into the human relations camp.

15.7.4 The first of these as I mentioned in 15.3.4 was computer modelling, now being used in every field of endeavour to simulate what would happen to a system if certain variables were changed. An example is the U.K. Treasury's computer which is used to predict the effects upon the economy of alternative government policies. It was only to be expected that 'systems' researchers would apply similar models to organizations. Yet formulating a program for the computer which represents hierarchical influence would be elusive, and there would be a tendency for what should have been arborization and reticulation to degenerate into a trellis. To justify using this 'network' model the systems would need, consciously or unconsciously, to de-emphasize the importance of the hierarchical control specialisms. For entirely negative reasons, namely the difficulty of the problem, this would put him into the same position as those who were proposing a human relations approach to organizational design and were positively advocating less specialization and less hierarchical control.

15.7.5 At the same time researchers such as Trist were showing that the application of human relations principles to the socio-technical 'system' was having beneficial effects upon productivity. Thus it is scarcely surprising that 'systems' writers should have introduced into their models the assumptions of the 'human relationships' approach. By doing so they gave new authority to the human relations approach which was needed to retain its credibilty. This had been slipping badly. O'Shaughnessy, for example, having assigned a large section of his book *Business Organization* to the human relations approach, made this final comment. 'The human scientists have much to offer. Some however, write more like evangelists than scientists and with aggressive dogmatism that is more a reflection of faith than evidence, (1969; p.124). Thus developed a symbiotic relationship between the two approaches which continues to date.

15.7.6 We saw how sociologists had been using systems language as early as 1939. Roethlisberger and Dickson spoke of firms as 'open' systems (paragraph 9.2.16). This was despite their also having adopted Mayo's assumption that the worker could only be preserved from anomie (and put on the straight and narrow path of social virtue) by listening to counsellors employed by management. Similarly, in 1966, Burns and Stalker, who are sociologists, adopted systems language in their categorization of organizations into either 'mechanistic' or 'organismic' systems of management. Nevertheless, it is clear that Burns is not at all happy with the traditional 'systems' position. He objects that Cyert and March, Simon, and, by implication, Trist and Emery, all see the goals of individuals in the organization as 'residual'. They form, in effect, those frictional elements which cannot be contained within the formally constituted roles as defined in the creation of the formal structure (Burns, 1969; p.239).

15.7.7 We are left in no doubt by Burns that classical organization theory is what epitomises for him 'mechanistic' systems, (Burns, 1969; p.242): 'Mechanistic systems reveal most of the characteristics of the formulation given by Weber to bureaucracy, a formulation curiously, and significantly, similar to that arrived at independently by Fayol and developed by writers on management techniques and by consultants.' *(Quite why it should be 'significant' that the two approaches merge, is something that Burns doesn't elaborate. I find it so because, in studying authority systems and moving towards structures, Weber independently arrives **at the same place** as Fayol, who studied structures and moved towards authority systems. For me that **strengthens** the classical position by offering two paths which lead to the same conclusion. For Burns however, this cannot be its significance, for he uses the word 'significantly' with dark innuendo, and he finds the confluence of*

Weber's and Fayol's ideas to be 'curious'.)

15.7.8 Here are the respective characteristics that Burns and Stalker attribute to mechanistic and organismic systems of management (Burns and Stalker, 1966; pp. 119 – 122):

> A mechanistic management system is appropriate to stable conditions. It is characterised by:
>
> (a) The *specialized differentiation* of functional tasks into which the problems and tasks facing the concern as a whole are broken down.
> (b) The *abstract nature* of each individual task, which is pursued with techniques and purposes more or less distinct from those of the concern as a whole.
> (c) The reconciliation, for each level in the hierarchy, of these distinct performances by the *immediate superiors.*
> (d) The *precise definition* of rights and obligations and technical methods attached to each functional role.
> (e) The *translation of rights* and obligations and methods into the reponsibilities of a functional position.
> (f) *Hierarchic structure* of control, authority and communication.
> (g) A reinforcement of the hierarchic structure by the location of *knowledge* of actualities exclusively *at the top* of the hierarchy.
> (h) A tendency for *vertical interaction* between members of the concern to be i.e., between superior and subordinate
> (i) A tendency for operations and working behaviour to be *governed by superiors.*
> (j) *Insistence on loyalty* to the concern and obedience to superiors as a condition of membership.
> (k) A greater importance and prestige attaching to *internal* (local) than to general (cosmopolitan) knowledge, experience and skill.
>
> The organismic form is appropriate to changing conditions, which give rise constantly to fresh problems and unforeseen requirements for action which cannot be broken down or distributed automatically arising from the functional roles defined within a hierarchic structure. It is characterized by:
>
> (a) The *contributive nature* of special knowledge and experience to the common task of the concern.
> (b) The *realistic* nature of the individual task, which is seen as set by the total situation of the concern.
> (c) The adjustment and *continual redefinition* of individual tasks through interaction with others.
> (d) The *shedding of responsibility* as a limited field of rights, obligations and methods. (Problems may not be posted upwards, downwards or sideways).
> (e) The *spread of commitment* to the concern beyond any technical definition.
> (f) A *network structure* of control, authority, and communication.

(g) Omniscience no longer imputed to the head of concern; *knowledge* may be located anywhere in the network; this location becoming the centre of authority.

(h) A *lateral* rather than vertical direction of communication through the organization.

(i) A content of communication which consists of *information and advice* rather than instructions and decisions.

(j) *Commitment* to the concern's tasks and to the 'technological ethos' of material progress and expansion is more highly valued than loyalty.

(k) Importance and prestige attach to *affiliations and expertise* valid in the industrial and technical and commercial milieux external to the firm.

They then go on to make the usual inference of the human relations approach (which I find erroneous) that because expertise is accepted and harnessed by the hierarchy, it **replaces** 'hierarchy' with 'democratic consensus'. Here are their words:

> One important corollary to be attached to this account is that while organic systems are not hierarchic in the same sense as the mechanistic, they remain stratified. Positions are differentiated according to seniority. – i.e. greater expertise. The lead in joint decisions is frequently taken by seniors, but it is an essential presumption of the organic system that the lead, i.e. 'authority', is taken by whoever shows himself most informed and capable, i.e., the 'best authority'. The location of authority is settled by consensus.

15.7.9 It is difficult to know where to begin to unravel what Burns and Stalker have here run together in a confusion of issues. However, it is important that we mention some of them so that the confusion can be contained. Let us take for example point (k) in the list of characteristics they associate with mechanistic management systems. An accountant in a 'classical' organization would regard his work as

(i) governed by the ethics and *mores* of his profession;
(ii) determined by law;
(iii) inculcated in his training; and
(iv) (in the UK) expressed by the profession's publication of its 'Standard Statements of Accounting Practice' (SSAPs).

Burns and Stalker appear therefore to be in error in suggesting that the **organizational structure** will determine his attitude. Rather it is the **nature of the knowledge held by the participant** in the organization (from training in a particular discipline) that determines the nature of his relationship with the organization. That is independent of the structure though it will doubtless be one of the determinants of the ethos within it. As such it will modify points (g), (h), (i) and (j) in both 'mechanistic' and 'organismic' organizations.

15.7.10 There are further things about Burns and Stalker's modelling which need to be challenged. It is true, for example, that bureaucratic and classical concepts have within them a degree of paradox, in that the senior man in the hierarchy can never know as much about a specialism as someone junior to himself who concentrates upon that specialism. This we mentioned (in paragraph 14.3.7) as an anomaly that the use of committees might resolve, as well as their helping to gain lateral co-ordination. It is interesting that Burns finds the need for lateral communication is dealt with *legitimately* when performed by what amounts to an **informal** committee, yet he sees it as a 'pathological' response the moment the same function is performed by a **formal** committee (Pugh, 1971; p.53).

15.7.11 This is very revealing, for it makes *informality* an absolute rather than relative virtue. Of course there are times when the **urgent and limited nature of the decision** requires an immediate response which is best dealt with informally. However, There are other times when to avoid formal committees for fear of being stigmatized as 'pathological' would be the most pathological thing that one could do. In the 1960s I worked in a vertically integrated textile company that knitted, dyed, printed, cut and sewed its own fashion garments. We would have been quite unable to have supplied our customers on time if we had not been prepared to go into production on **estimated** sales–volumes for every garment by colour and size. We were therefore greedy for information both to correct (before they became irrevocable) any past commitments that we might now regret and also to know what further items we should put into work for which we might now appear to have made insufficient commitment.

15.7.12 In those days computer technology was such that we were restricted to analysing incoming sales by weekly batches. Updates in our knowledge therefore occurred from a computer-run which was made every Wednesday night. It followed that I used to 'chair' a standing committee every Thursday morning at which would be all the departmental managers and their clerks with their respective status reports. We were seeking to recover what **could** be recovered from past overcommitments, and also to issue sufficient work to keep the factory's departments busy over the coming week. The new orders would concentrate upon those fabrics colours, prints and sizes of garment which we needed most urgently if we were to hope for a balanced supply by popularity. *I can think of no other way that we could have achieved the required co-ordination nor have achieved a more rapid response. It would be interesting to know what **precise** aspect of the situation made that committee a 'pathological' means of dealing with the needs of the organization.*

15.7.13 Of course, the situation might well be termed 'pathological' if one deliberately and wilfully put off dealing informally with an issue that could be easily settled and had no ramifications beyond the immediate participants meeting in informal discussion. However, that situation is not something that can be said with any truth to be of the essence of classical theory, since such decisions are by their nature largely decentralized.

15.7.14 It follows that I find Burns's approach less significant than that of Woodward, who pointed out that not all organizations operated as they were alleged to do in classical organization theory. Her conclusion was that 'technology' was a strong determinant of organizations in their practical application of classical theory. However, what is a very interesting question is *whether those organizations saw themselves as **other** than modified classical organizations*. In other words, was there room within the overall **classical** framework to accommodate various versions of 'classical' thought, or are the different versions to be regarded as having gone too far to be contained within that category? To anticipate my conclusions, I believe that just as 'Protestantism' can accommodate the Anglican, the Baptist, the Methodist, the Quaker, etc., so 'classical' theory can accommodate the needs of different 'technologies' (using the word in the Woodwardian sense) as I explain below.

15.8 Technology as a determinant

15.8.1 John Woodward's use of the word 'technology', we should note, differs considerably from the way in which it is normally used. She uses it not to describe the **process** of a specific industry, e.g. 'engineering', or 'furniture manufacture', but to describe the **general nature of the mode of production**. That is to say, although the categories used by Woodward could be refined into ten variations, these were on the theme of three main categories, namely

Group I: Unit and small batch production,
Group II: Large batch and mass production,
Group III: Process production.

15.8.2 When, and only when examined in this way, did any 'pattern' result which reduced the 'spread' of organizational data. For example (Woodward, 1958; p.56), the *size* of the firm did not appreciably affect the spread in the ratio of managers and supervisory staff to personnel. The latter was as depicted in Table 15.8(a).

Table 15.8(a)

Firm size	Spread of ratio of supervisors to personnel
small firm	1 : 22 to 1 : 8
medium firm	1 : 37 to 1 : 7
large firm	1 : 25 to 1 : 7

However, when the firm size was ignored and the figures were instead analysed by the three categories mentioned in paragraph 15.8.1, the results were in a much narrower spread than that given by firm size, as in Table 15.8(b).

Table 15.8(b)

Category	Spread of ratio of supervisors to personnel
production by 'unit' and 'small batch'	1 : 37 to 1 : 22
production by 'large batch' and 'mass'	1 : 18 to 1 : 14
production by 'process'	1 : 8 to 1 : 7

This was only one of several similar analyses which appeared to make 'technology (in the sense of these general modes of production) the determinant of organizational design. We need not dwell upon the topic, for many books give detailed descriptions of Woodward's work. Nor do I specifically wish to deal with her findings.

15.8.3 Rather, I wish to show why there are certain categories of production which are **bound** to affect the structure and ethos of the organization which chooses to use them. My categories differ slightly from those considered by Woodward, but are related to hers.

(1) The first thing that I wish to point out about these differences is that I have ignored what she chooses to call 'process production' In her classification 'process production' was characterized by (though not restricted to) batch or continuous production of chemicals, liquids and gases. Within the scope of this book this is too specialized an area for us usefully to enter. *Nevertheless, to avoid any possible confusion in the mind of the reader I must point out that her use of the word 'process' has imparted to it a quite different meaning from the use of the word in connection with 'process layouts'. Such layouts refer to the system of production which I described in paragraphs 8.3.14 to 20.*

(2) The second thing is this. Her suggestion that 'unit production' is a useful classification seems to be grounded in the fact that

    (a) such a title is vague enough to cover both large- and small-scale jobbing, and/or

(b) because both proved to have certain ratios (e.g. supervisor to worker) which are similar.

I would claim that any similarities between building the Kariba Dam and making a made-to-measure suit are tenuous and largely coincidental.

(3) Finally, I find it very strange of her to have lumped together large-scale batches (*produced by process layouts*) with near-continuous manufacture (*produced by product layouts*). These are treated by me as two separate categories.

15.8.4 It follows that in my analysis of those production categories which affect the structure and ethos of firms, we shall largely abandon Joan Woodward's categories for ones which I believe are better grounded. They are:

(i)   *Continuous production by product layout.* Product layouts were described in paragraphs 8.3.11 to 12 and their impact on organizational ethos and structure will be considered in 'continuous production' (paragraphs 15.10.3 and 4).

(ii) *Intermittent batch production by process layout.* Process layouts were described in paragraphs 8.3.14 to 20 and their impact on organizational ethos and structure will be considered in 'intermittent batch production' (paragraphs 15.10.5 to 7).

(iii) *Large-scale jobbing* and its organizational implications will be considered in Section 15.12.

15.8.5 Yet before we go on to consider these issues we should first consider whether a particularly well orchestrated joint attack on classical theory made by 'human relations approach' and 'systems approach' critics is entirely justified. This attack concentrates upon the issue of 'communication'.

15.9 The attack upon 'classical' organizations' ability to communicate

15.9.1 Commentaries on 'communication' practices which occur within classical organizations are apt to suggest that there is a great deal of communication downward, with little of it going upward or sideways. In the main, such commentaries carry the implication that this is a situation to be deplored. Systems people deplore it because it indicates that full use is not being made of all the available knowledge within the company in the act of decision-making. Human relations writers deplore it because it smacks of authoritarianism and they see a more democratic regime as being more socially acceptable and (they infer), more efficient. There is therefore a considerable amount of emotive content in such writing, no matter how prosaically it is expressed. Few commentators have asked:

(a) Is the criticism borne out by the facts?
(b) If it is true can such practices be justified?

15.9.2 *Upward communication.* There would seem to be little doubt that upward communication **is** strongly filtered. Several researchers have found this to be so and have generally attributed this filtering to an awareness on the part of the subordinate that something less than the truth would be more politically acceptable to the superior, and therefore (by implication) less damaging to himself. Now this sounds psychologically convincing and should not be dismissed too lightly. The implication that the subordinate would not create this filter (which is always assumed to be adverse in its effects upon the organization) unless senior management had gratuitously inhibited upward communication, is implicit in the range of books which invite management to do various things to reverse this. I have already suggested that the contrary vision of a 'participative', non-coercive organization owes more to ideology than to reality, and we need not restate that argument. Neither do we need to restate the argument (given in Section 3.1) that hierarchical structures are essential to organizations. However, we do need to reassert that they **are** so. There is a further claim to be made. **This is that all hierarchies (and by extension this means all purposive organizations) are dependent upon some filtering of upward information to preserve their efficient functioning**. Here are some generalizations from Koestler on the topic (1976; p.344):

> Output hierarchies generally operate on the trigger release principle, where a relatively simple, implicit or coded signal releases complex, pre-set mechanisms...A holon on the *n* level of an output-hierarchy is represented on the $(n+1)$ level as a unit and triggered into action as a unit. A holon, in other words, is a system of relata which is represented on the next higher level as a relatum. In social hierarchies (military, administrative), the same principles apply. Input hierarchies operate on the reverse principle; instead of triggers, they are equipped with 'filter'-type devices (scanners, 'resonators', classifiers) which strip the input noise, abstract and digest its relevant contents, according to that particular hierarchy's criteria of relevance. 'Filters' operate on every echelon through which the flow of information must pass on its ascent from periphery to centre, in social hierarchies and in the nervous system...Output hierarchies spell, concretise, particularise. Input hierarchies digest, abstract, generalise.

15.9.3 What Koestler has expressed in this unequivocal generalized statement is something that we know in our bones, as a result of practical experience.

15.9.4 If a manager is not competent to handle **most** of the issues that trouble his subordinates without reference upward, then we must conclude that **something is seriously wrong with that organization**. We have seen that organizations are only physically capable of achieving size and maintaining integration providing that the concept of the 'span of control' is applied. It follows that every manager must handle most things himself, for he is only one of several reporting to his superior. Only those things that he or his colleagues are **not** competent to handle, should therefore be passed upward. Failure to filter in this way would create an impossible overload upon senior management. Yet we should not be surprised to find that so many critics of classical management have overlooked or minimized the significance of this basic truth. This is because those critics who have implied that decentralization is only withheld because of the somewhat paranoid tendencies of senior management do so precisely **because** they have not recognized the need for hierarchy. They are therefore equally unable to acknowledge that the upward transmission of more than a small proportion of data would create a managerial overload.

15.9.5 The attitude of the human relations writers in proposing that managers who filter data do so to the **detriment** of the firm is not without its comic overtones. For those same writers are the apostles of decentralization. This being so, what possible harm can this filtration do? We are left to infer the following reasons for concern:

(a) That senior management is thereby deprived of data which they need for the successful direction of the business. (This is a strange position to be adopted by those who condemn centralized control.)

(b) That the workers' grievances go unheard and thus unrectified. (This too, with its implication that some policing of junior management is required, sits very badly on those who preach the trusting relationships of Theory 'Y'.)

15.9.6 Burns agrees with Koestler about the different characteristics of output and input hierarchies, but we do not form the opinion that it is a situation of which he approves: 'with information flowing upwards through a succession of filters, and decisions and instructions flowing downwards through a succession of amplifiers' (Pugh, 1971; p.47). Nor does Burns seem to acknowledge one of the basic characteristics of hierarchies stressed by Koestler. It will be remembered that Koestler said that downward communications 'generally operate on the trigger release principle, where a relatively simple, implicit or coded signal releases complex, pre-set mechanisms'. Burns seems to deny the ability of the lower levels of the hierarchy to perform 'complex, pre-set mechanisms', for he makes the following claim: 'as one descends through the levels of management...one...finds [that]...beyond a certain point...[a person] has insufficient authority, insufficient information and usually insufficient technical ability to make decisions. He is informed quite clearly when this limit occurs; beyond it, he has one course open – to report to his superior.' (Pugh, 1971; p.50.)

15.9.7 Here again there seems to be a confusion of ideas. Burns leads us to believe that there **are** options open to the operative but he doesn't know which one to take and so must have recourse to management. To a certain extent this would be true in a process layout, when the *sequence* of work that he is required to perform on the available batches must be nominated by someone with a wider perspective than that which the worker possesses. In a product layout the sequence is known by everyone. But in neither instance does the worker require close supervision. It is not by the **absence** of information or technical ability that the worker loses operational choice, but by the **surfeit** of technological and economic constraints under which he performs the 'complex, pre-set mechanisms' of Koestler's description. If it were not so, the lower echelons of the organizations would be associated with a very narrow span of control to cope with all the instruction that Burns implies is necessary. In fact the reverse is true. The span of control of first-line supervisors in such a situation can afford to be extremely wide *because workers know **precisely** what is expected of them, and recognize that technical and economic determinants limit any freedom of choice.*

15.9.8 *Lateral communication.* There is a tendency for both human relations and systems writers to deny that much lateral communication takes place in classical organizations. We have seen that this is true of Burns, for we have only to contrast item (h) in the lists of characteristics he and Stalker assign to 'mechanistic' and 'organismic' systems (paragraph 15.7.8). I shall try to show that the claim is wrong in two respects. Firstly, it is not true that there is very little lateral communication in classical organization. Secondly, it is not necessarily true that the performance of an organization would be more effective for the existence of more lateral contacts in each case, though this tends to be the inference.

15.9.9 There are three basically different ways in which discrete products can be manufactured. These are:

(a) Continuous production on a product layout of the type described in paragraphs 8.3.8 to 8.3.11.

(b) Intermittent batch production on a process layout of the type described in paragraphs 8.3.14 to 8.3.16.
(c) Large-scale 'jobbing' production of the type described in paragraphs 8.3.5 to 8.3.7.

All three can be accommodated within classical theory, yet all three induce different communication patterns (as Table 15.9(a) illustrates).

Table 15.9(a) Relative strength of organizational communication by technology

Direction of Communication				
Technology	Upward	Downward	Lateral within function	Lateral across more than one function
Product layout (continuous)	low	low	high	mixed: some high, some low.
Process layout (batch)	low	high	high	mixed: some high, some low
Jobbing (large-scale unit)	high	high	high	high

15.9.10 Similarly, all three induce a different pattern of behaviour from the participants which is largely determined by the nature of the technology rather than by management's wishes. Why the communication patterns should be those shown above and why the social behaviour should be modified by the technology used is the subject of the next section.

15.10 Some technical determinants of communication practice and of social ethos which all approaches should acknowledge, (1): 'continuous production' and 'intermittent batch production'

15.10.1 To my mind Trist's view that organizations are socio-technical systems in which both elements interact is demonstrated very clearly by a consideration of product, process and jobbing as categories of production. Yet, if we are to appreciate **why** they produce such radically different organizations we have to perceive the way in which one operation is linked with another. I should like us therefore to adopt the smallest significant 'building block' of each system that we can consider, namely one which comprises two sequential operations and the interface between them. (Such a 'building block' is more useful as an instrument of analysis than a single operation; but I would agree with anyone who suggested that it is not adequate to be fully representative of the interplay of the true network of relationships in each of these types of manufacture. Yet that is not the purpose it serves, which is simply to expose the validity of certain observations concerning these three categories of production.) Figure 15.10(a) shows the suggested 'building block'.

Specification of operation 'A'	Specification of interface	Specification of operation 'B'
(characteristics of a functional or aesthetic nature and the means and time needed for their achievement)	(where, when, who, what, and how)	(characteristics of a functional or aesthetic nature and the means and time needed for their achievement)

Figure 15.10(a)

15.10.2 What makes this particularly useful as a concept is that it leads us to see that the nature and quality of the relationship between worker and management is largely determined by how the particular production system supplies the information needed to specify the three elements of the block. This will decide the communication system that is appropriate to, and/or determined by, the technological arrangement. We shall start with the implications of continuous production on a product line.

15.10.3 *Continuous production.* When continuous production is envisaged on a product layout the production 'line' must be carefully pre-planned. We have seen that such layouts are easy to supervise, can operate with very little work-in-progress, and, because a clear sequence determines the flow of work, are easily understood by everyone. Technically they have many disadvantages. The absence of an operative or the breakdown of a machine will bring the whole system to a halt unless there is some sort of back-up. They have little output flexibility other than running the line for longer or shorter periods. For example, if each operation on a conveyor-belt takes 3 minutes, then the output will be 20 per hour. If the factory normally works an 8-hour day, then it is to be hoped that marketing can sell 160 per day. If they can only sell 120 we have problems. Balancing the conveyor can also be a headache. In Figure 15.10(b) the output of the conveyor is governed by the longest operational cycle. This is the 2 minutes taken by operator D. Consequently the output of that conveyor cannot be more than 30 per hour from 5 operatives. Yet the actual work content of the product is only 8.4 minutes. Therefore in an hour the work content produced will be 30×8.4 minutes = 252 minutes. But the total attendance time for the hour for

5 operatives = 300 minutes. In other words, the layout efficiency, for reasons outside the operator's control, is only 252/300 × 100/1 = 84 per cent.

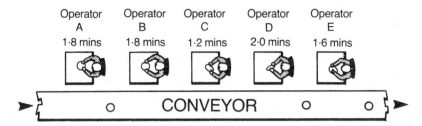

Figure 15.10(b)

15.10.4 It follows that a product layout requires a very high degree of pre-planning on the part of management to decide the precise specification of the jobs to be done, the times that they should take, and the facilities required. It also requires them to ensure that the individual operations are well fed with the correct materials. But that too is part of a pre-planned procedure. From the operative's standpoint the system appears to run itself in a deterministic fashion. Once shown the routine, an operator knows exactly what to do. He knows exactly from where the work is to come (the previous operative), and he knows exactly where it is to go (the next operative). Moreover, the time available to him is also determined. He must perform the task in the interval between the previous operative passing him the work, and the succeeding operative becoming unoccupied for want of work. It is not a recommendation to point out that such a system means that the operative will be left alone by management, precisely **because** management has nothing to offer (beyond praise or blame). Nor can we conclude that he is relatively unsupervised. *The system provides its own inanimate controls which are all the more soul-destroying for being impersonal.* This was Chaplin's message to us (paragraphs 3.2.16 and 17). It does, however, explain why the ratio of supervisors to workers is so low in such systems. When I reorganized suit production in a large multiple tailors, there were technical reasons for keeping the existing conveyors, despite their shortcomings. Each jacket conveyor had 80 operatives and was controlled by only 2 supervisors. This ties up with Woodward's experience, for the median span of control for first-line supervisors she found to be 40 in this sort of production system.

15.10.5 *Intermittent batch production.* I explained in paragraphs 8.3.14 to 8.3.19 why process layouts are required, and in paragraphs 4.3.4 to 4.3.6 I explained why the work is handled in batches in such layouts. With such an arrangement the departmental foreman is frequently limited in the number of men he can control, not because of the degree of contact with him that each requires, but because of the amount of ancillary work that is required to ensure

(a) that the capacity available, in terms of plant and labour, is adequate to meet the forward demands of the firm,
(b) that the sequence in which work should be issued is known and used,
(c) that general administrative problems are dealt with (e.g. losses from spoilage, mislaid work, queries on payment), and that those with the greater skills are assigned the more complex work, etc.

It was part of F. W. Taylor's thesis that because these duties required different skills, they should be performed by each man having several specialist bosses. Taylor's ideas could not prevail, however, against the power of the 'unity-of-command principle' of one-man, one-boss. This aspect of his theory of management never appealed to either theorists or managers, which is why, in most companies, production control still takes up far too much of the production foreman's working day.

15.10.6 This is an area where over the next few years I can visualize a revolution from the use of computers to take some of the weight off his shoulders without proliferating the number of bosses. It is common to recognize that critical-path analysis is a tool essential to large-scale jobbing. It is less commonly realized that (since most products result from a network of operations) the same idea can be applied to **process** layouts. By correct coding, the computer will recognize the logic of such a network, the work content of each operation, and the specific type of machine upon which it is to be done. If the due date of each product batch is fed into the computer, together with decision rules concerning priorities relating to the 'lead-times' necessary to meet such deadlines, and these requirements are matched by the computer against the available hours on each facility, the computer can designate in what priority to issue work to the department. As work is completed, the fact can be registered in the computer so that the computer now knows that the next operation in the sequence is available to work upon as and when required, relative to other priorities.

15.10.7 Yet none of these developments are likely to make any significant change in the position of the worker in a process layout. For the reasons given in paragraph 8.4.8, while the technology stays as it is he is unlikely to be able to visualize, let alone to attain, freedom from the instrumental way in which he is currently being used. Conversely, for the reasons given in paragraph 4.3.14, the advance of technology that might have produced more interesting work for the operative is far more likely to produce his redundancy in favour of robotics. No amelioration in the working conditions of process layout workers are therefore to be expected before their jobs disappear by the advance of technology.

15.11 Do 'classical' attitudes to lateral communication warrant the criticisms applied to them by 'systems' writers?

15.11.1 The previous section makes it clear that in practice continuous production of discrete articles requires little to be communicated either up or down, though it may need a lot of lateral communication to ensure a free flow. Batch production needs the foreman to issue instructions largely on the matter of the sequence in which operations should be done, and again the free flow of work will require considerable lateral communication to ensure the progression of the work. Seldom is there any need, however, for any **inter-function lateral communication** to occur (other than in material acquisition, or in quality control matters), since designs are usually standardized and sales requirements are known.

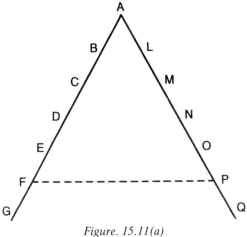

Figure. 15.11(a)

15.11.2 Lateral communication **was** permitted under classical 'principles'. One of the earliest and most renowned classical theorists, Henri Fayol, advocated lateral direct communication on the grounds that to go up the chain and down again could (Pugh, 1971; p.117) 'pass through twenty transmissions, inconvenience many people, involve masses of paper, lose weeks or months [in order] to get a conclusion less satisfactory generally than the one which could have been obtained via direct contact...' (see

Figure 15.11(a)). He therefore maintained that, rather than go from F to A and down again to P, which the literal interpretation of the scalar chain of command would have entailed, F and P could deal direct via a 'gang-plank' providing 'F and P remain in agreement, and so long as their actions are approved by their immediate superiors...but from the instant that agreement ceases, or there is no approval from the superiors direct contact comes to an end, and the scalar chain is straightaway resumed.' (Pugh, 1971; pp. 116–117).

15.11.3 Those who have held managerial jobs in the production area know that most production functions would grind to a halt if the foremen did not enter into an enormous amount of lateral communication both with their peers and with work-study and production control staff. Luthans (1983; p.361) refers to studies which support this view.

> One observation study found that 17 percent of the total communications of a line-production manager in one plant were sent horizontally and 22 percent were received from a horizontal source. In another plant in the same study 41 percent of the production manager's communications were sent horizontally and 40 percent were received from a horizontal source. Obviously, the exact amount of horizontal communication is highly contingent upon the situation. One significant research finding is that the nature of the productive or technological process will influence the type of communication that occurs. For example, the researcher found that communications of first-line supervisors were mainly horizontal because of the mechanized, assembly line nature of their work.

I have already noted that the assembly-line supervisor has little need to approach the worker except to praise or blame. Luthans says something similar and then adds (p.362) 'but there is a necessity to communicate along the line to get the job done'.

15.11.4 The evidence points to there being a great deal of lateral communication **within** the production function of a classical organization, and no prima-facie reason to believe that the same is not true of any other function. Claims to the contrary are either mistaken, or alternatively must refer to the subject of lateral communication **between different functions**. That being so, we must next look at the issue of whether there **is** a lack of lateral communications between the functions in classical management, and if so whether this is or is not a disadvantage.

15.11.5 For the moment I should like to look at this question in respect of the two production methods that we have already considered, namely the continuous production (product layout) and the intermittent batch production (process layout) of discrete goods. Moreover, I would claim that in their relationship with other functions, these two methods of production can be considered as effectively having no significant difference. It is true that a product layout is likely to place different pressures upon a sales force in that its output is likely to consist of less variety and to be delivered with a regularity which could be embarrassing. But this is a minor issue compared with the similarity of the two methods of production. For **both** are likely to produce a range of products in high volume as a result of considerable separate pre-planning, research and development. **Both** are likely after an initial running-in period to have achieved a degree of familiarity with the product, and to have found it advantageous to bureaucratize the manner in which such output will be made.

15.11.6 Because of this similarity, it would not be out of place to refer the cross-functional relationships of the case-study of the shoe manufacturing and retailing company (which we justified by the logic of Section 13.2) to **both** these production methods. Because of the way we arrived at the final organizational form shown in Figure 13.2(e) p.320 I would maintain that where that form has resulted in lateral relationships they are appropriate, but that where it does not they are equally inappropriate.

15.11.7 Now we find that there is a very strong lateral relationship between the production and marketing function at the level of the **directorate** of each function. Indeed, because the organization was set up to avoid opportunity cost there is a very fine balance to be maintained between their mutual dependence and their mutual independence. This will certainly make for an interesting and high interactive relationship. Moreover, what is true there, is also true of the relationship of both these directorates with that of the property company.

15.11.8 It is evident from this case-study (which is nothing if not classical in its treatment) that the suggestion that there is **no** lateral communication between the functions at the higher echelons of the hierarchy, is frankly untrue. There **has** to be considerable reticulation to integrate the internal activities of each function with those of any other function with which it shares any degree of interdependence. *Such reticulation occurs near the top of the arborizational divides which form the respective functions.*

15.11.9 We are left to presume that critics of classical theory are claiming that because the lower strata of the functions fail to interact, the theory is, in some sense, inadequate. Yet what communication, which would have significance for the company, could occur if the foreman of (say) the lasting room were to be in close contact with (say) the manager of one of the shops?

I can imagine that quality-control complaints might be the subject of some of their exchanges. Yet it would still not be helpful for them to have such an exchange without sharing it with the respective bosses; for the problem might be isolated or widespread, related to the one factory, or to all four, etc. Moreover, given the ambiguous relationship which the avoidance of opportunity cost has created between the two functions, such communications would not be the frank co-operative exchanges that they are pictured as being in the idyllic models of the human relations approach or the systems approach. Yet we can't have it both ways. Either we encourage the competitive element that minimizes the fostering of opportunity cost, or we don't. If we **don't**, we tend to breed the complacency that allowed Clore to make his fortune from the errors of the previous management (paragraph 13.2.2). If we **do**, we tend to breed a guarded attitude between the functions and between each function and the main board. Capitalism itself fosters the latter outcome.

15.11.10 My conclusion is that, in so far as we are dealing with these two types of manufacturing concern, there is little low-level contact between functions, **nor should there be.** Yet there is very strong lateral communication between functions at the higher levels, which is precisely where it is needed.

15.11.11 This whole issue is not without a certain irony. It will be remembered that one of the principal aims of the systems approach was so to arrange the subsystems that the communication burden was minimized. As a result of creating **subsystems** by means of **functional splits**, classical organization makes it possible for those people who need to interact strongly to be together, while separating those who do not. It succeeds in reducing the communications burden to such good effect that its very success is used to denounce it *for **not** needing a higher degree of interaction between functions*!

15.11.12 Let us now turn to the third of the possible methods of manufacture that we sought to analyse in its communications effects and social ethos, namely large-scale jobbing.

15.12 Some technical determinants of communication practice and of social ethos which all approaches should acknowledge, (2): 'large-scale jobbing'

15.12.1 There are two features about large-scale jobbing which are highly significant. The first is that its control should be planned by either PERT or critical path analysis, for reasons that we examined in paragraphs 8.4.1 to 8.4.27. The second is that the most appropriate design for the organization is so-called 'matrix' structure. The former we shall not concern ourselves with, since it is covered more than adequately with in so many textbooks, the latter needs more interpretation than it has usually received. To this we now turn.

15.12.2 It will now be remembered that in paragraph 14.3.2 I said that 'as organization grows in complexity and size the skills of the functional heads are required in order to be certain that the full impact of functional decisions upon the performance of the firm, and so that the effect of any proposed company decisions upon the operation of the functions can be forseen and adverse implication dealt with. This creates the committee shown in Figure 14.3(b).' This figure is reproduced here as Figure 15.12(a).

15.12.3 However, even the lateral communication of the higher echelons in committee is not adequate to handle the volume, depth or urgency of cross-

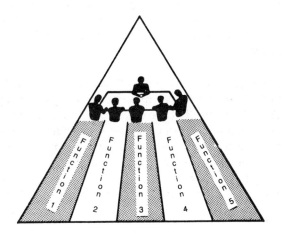

Figure 15.12(a)

functional communication which is necessary to solve the problems that arise minute by minute in the design and production of a large-scale jobbing venture. It is therefore usual to assign a project boss to each of the projects currently in work, as shown in Figure 15.12(b). The name 'matrix organization' comes from this fact, for, as can be seen, the organization does now form a 'matrix' with the functional bosses on one axis, and the project bosses on the other.

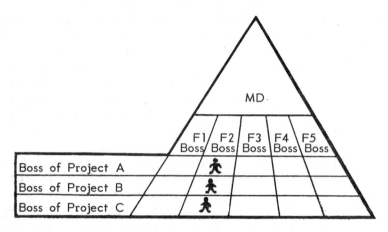

Figure 15.12(b) A matrix organization.

15.12.4 Most texts assume this organizational format to be the outcome of 'systems' influence. I do not believe this to be so, but I can imagine two reasons for others concluding that it is.

(1) *The first is that the matrix forms a 'network' which seems to accord with 'systems' thinking.* The error in this is that, as we have seen, a matrix organization is not applicable in all cases, and it would be a very unscientific 'systems' writer who suggested it as a panacea for organizational ills.

(2) *The second is that the matrix network breaks the cardinal 'classical' principle of one-man, one-boss: it is therefore thought of as a recent 'systems' idea.* Certainly it does break the 'classical' one-man, one-boss principle, for as can be seen in Figure (15.12(b)) each of the little figures who come under functional boss F2 also report to project bosses A,B, and C respectively. But it is certainly not a new idea, and it was for many years adopted by organizations who were aware of classical principles, but not yet aware of 'systems' thinking. In 1960 I worked as a consultant to help bring back on target three large-scale jobbing projects that were being built concurrently by the same firm:

(a) the installation of the telemetering of the Kariba Dam,
(b) an automatic signalling system for the Eastern Region of British Rail's Shenfield Line, and
(c) the monitoring and controlling panel for a power station operated by the UK Central Electricity Generating Board.

Each had a *project boss* and each was designed and built by employees who reported to a *functional boss,* but whereas this was acknowledged by everyone to be in breach of the classical 'unity of command' principle, they felt that the circumstances warranted it. They never doubted the fundamental validity of the principle, nor did they see the matrix as anything other than a classical variant. No one, for example, regarded it as justified by 'systems' theory, any more than Joan Woodward did during her work in the mid-1950s. Indeed, although they were essentially 'systems' engineers, the term was never applied by them to the matter of organizational design or operation. In common with many other firms of the time who had adopted matrix structures for large-scale jobbing, 'systems' thinking had not penetrated their consciousness in the area of organizational design. Should this surprise us? I think not. As late as 1960, in an article in *The RAND Corporation* (Optner, 1973; p.61), Jordan stressed that a 'system' does not only depend upon its existence 'out there' but also upon our internal cognition of it as **being** a 'system' because *we see it as a perceptual or conceptual figure.* For years senior production managements had employed 'progress chasers' to help to bring pressure to bear upon manufacturing departments, and so get priority for those parts of an order that were urgently required. Such 'progress chasers' had 'staff' rather than 'line' status and as such were allegedly 'advisory' in their actions. Nevertheless, the realities of the situation were that they could certainly appeal to higher authorities if they did not receive adequate co-operation, so that they had acquired at least some overtones of 'supervisory' status. With this status the principle of 'one- man one-boss' had already been breached. If we were to give more formal 'teeth' to such a person, together with the recognition that he should attempt to head off troubles by anticipation, rather than to react to them after the event, we arrive gradually at the position held by the project boss in a matrix organization.

15.12.5 Is this a fair representation of the situation: that is to say, is it more honest to see matrix organizations as *a mutative form of classical theory* than it is to see them as a *systems rebellion against classical thought?* I believe so. Although Roethlisberger and Dickson in 1939 had inferred that organizations are 'open systems' (paragraph 9.2.16), and although Burns and Stalker applied systems ideas to organizational thought in 1961, yet for decades before that, companies such as the one I instanced earlier had used matrix structures with no 'systems' influence. Systems thinking had been preoccupied with matters **other** than organizational design problems. Particularly active had been the RAND Corporation, but their approach was directed towards the use of such concepts in the design and operation of sophisticated weaponry.

15.12.6 Reviewing the papers from the RAND Corporation, Optner (1973;

p.17) points out that 'the writing of the 1950s and early 1960s illustrates a preoccupation with **uncertainty**, a new use of the term, which was coined to identify the part of the problem least susceptible to precise solution'. It was not until Optner reviewed the papers of the 1960s that he found (1973; p.18) 'the introduction of new subjects such as **self-organizing systems, perception** and **cognition** in a systems context [which] constituted a step away from exclusively military applications, and a step toward the use of systems analysis in a variety of social and industrial problems'.

15.12.7 Indeeed it is high time, since I have been critical of some of their modelling, that I acknowledged the seminal quality of the work of Burns and Stalker. Although the way in which they have tried to apply blanket categories of 'mechanistic systems' and 'organismic systems' (to which certain characteristics are attached) seems to me to be unhelpful, yet as late as 1961, when they first published '*The Management of Innovation*', the application of systems thought to organization had previously made little impact.

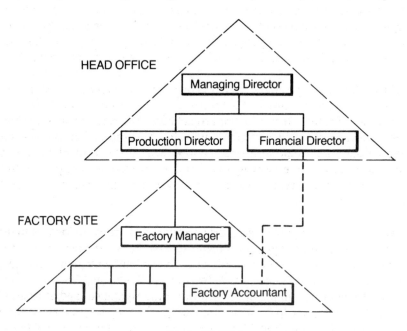

Figure 15.12(c)

15.12.8 It should also be noted that a matrix organization would not be the first time that classical organization had had to break the 'one-man, one-boss' principle. Nor does a matrix structure cause too much difficulty thereby, for reasons which I shall shortly explain. A far worse example is that of the accountant in Figure 15.12(c). Here I have assumed that he operates in a factory which is geographically separate from Head Office. To all intents and purposes he reports to the Factory Manager, who reports in his turn to the Production Director. There is therefore a 'line' of command from the Production Director to the Accountant. However, he also owes technical allegience to the Financial Director and sends him reports.

15.12.9 Now let us assume that there is a degree of rivalry between the Production and the Financial Directors and that the Finacial Director makes use of adverse cost data (obtained from the Factory Accountant) to embarrass the Production Director. Clearly the poor Factory Accountant would be the unlucky pawn in a political game which he cannot control or escape, short of leaving the company. Yet no one would take this unfortunate failure to maintain the one-man, one-boss principle as evidence of 'systems' thinking. Neither is the failure to maintain the principle in the far-less-damaging circumstances of the matrix organization (associated with large-scale jobbing) to be taken as being any more a 'systems' concept **per se,** even if systems writers are prepared to espouse the latter in a way that they would never seek to do in the case of the unfortunate Factory Accountant.

15.12.10 It would repay our consideration to see how much more benign the case of the matrix structure is. First the worker is allocated by the Functional boss to cater for the interests of the Project boss. The role of functional boss is to allocate the staff who come within his function and to provide the technical and moral support that his people need. This is very different from the concept of a worker serving two different masters who require of him two completely different services, and which is so unsatisfactory to both managers and worker.

15.12.11 In the case of the matrix organization, all parties are looking to the worker to perform an agreed task. Let us assume we are referring to the young design engineer who is working on one of the units that will jointly make up the telemetering system for the Kariba Dam. Because of the novelty element he will possibly need technical assistance, and at times of overload he can get help from other people in the function who are lent for the purpose by his functional boss. He therefore sees the functional ties as reassuring. They will become especially so as the project comes to an end, for then the function is his 'home' where he can feel some security from the knowledge that his boss (who is technically qualified to know his worth) will find *something* to do until the next project materializes. On the other hand, from the organization's standpoint, the arrangement allows the allocation of the effort within the function to whichever project is in need of the greatest support. This arrangement offers the most flexible use of labour from the economy of scale which the functional organization provides and which would be lost if the functional organization were destroyed.

15.12.12 For this reason, although I perceive the problems of the matrix structure, it has not been my experience that 'firms may move on to project managements where the specialists are allocated to a project for the duration of its life and are answerable only to the project co-ordinator until the project is finished (O' Shaughnessy, 1969; p.153). Nor is O'Shaughnessy himself happy about this proposal since it is gained at the price of:

(i)   Under-utilization of resources in order to achieve self containment of projects.
(ii) Failure to achieve some economies of scale.
(iii) Failure to achieve co-ordination of functions company wide. There is difficulty in maintaining standards of proficiency and uniformity of practice among specialists who are no longer controlled by a common head.
(iv) Insecurity among project members since project teams are disbanded on completion of a project (O'Shaughnessy; 1969; pp.153-4)

15.12.13 If we acknowledge that matrix organizations are a classical variant (rather than a systems backlash) we see that again the claim is correct that there is little lateral communication in classical theory. Moreover, this time the *lateral communication is across functions and at relatively low levels in the hierarchy*. If we take any of the projects that I mentioned in paragraph 15.12.4, we see immediately how not only must each of these orders go through each of the various functions, but equally any decision in some area must affect, and therefore needs to be accommodated by, all the other functions. Even in the act of obtaining the order we see this:

(1) Marketing must arrange to tender.
(2) Engineering Design must make preliminary designs of the necessary circuitry and of what that will require in 'hardware'.
(3) Costing must estimate the price.
(4) Production Control must estimate the delivery, relative to what the order entails and all other outstanding commitments.

But since each decision affects every other, there is an essentially intricate exchange of ideas even before Marketing are in a position to quote. If following that quote, they get an order, it all starts again.

PART FOUR

Organizational Goals, Strategy and Tactics

I claim that cultural pressures have led to myths replacing the reality of the situation. The reality is that the goals of the organization are essentially those of management, while the goals of all other parties form the constraints within which management operates. This tends to focus (rather than diffuse) management goals. The myths, which have understandably (but mistakenly) been fostered by today's anti-élitist/ pro-democratic ethos, are of three general types. Their respective claims are that:

(a) Organizations have a transcendent life of their own (which includes goal-setting).

(b) Organizational goals are a matter of consensus between interested parties.

(c) The typical organization is so big that top management are impotent. Experts of every status and buried deep within the firm (the technostructure) have the real power.

These myths have just a large enough element of truth to be accepted. They are, however, almost wholly false.

The need for strategic planning and the manner in which existing organizational structures predispose the outcomes are also considered.

16

Goals, strategy and tactics

16.1 Organizational goals: fact or fiction?

16.1.1 'When we speak of organizational goals... we must restrict our reference to certain leaders or subgroups and not regard the organization as a person. If we do not we will oversimplify organizational behaviour...[for] there is no organizational equivalent of the single unitary nervous system of the individual.' So write Katz and Kahn (1978; pp.480–481). The clear truth of this statement has, as we shall see, not prevented some writers from choosing to support the fiction of 'organizational' goals.

16.1.2 I agree with Katz and Kahn's claim that only people can have goals. But by making that affirmation we present ourselves with two associated problems. We now need to answer the questions (i) 'What goals, and (ii) whose goals are legitimate?' Ansoff claims that the answer we arrive at needs to replace 'the public outrages of the "smash n'-grab imperialism" of the nineteenth century ...[by]... a sense of social responsibility to society in general and participants in the firm in particular. Thus Frank Abrams speaks of the firm's responsibility to "maintain an equitable and working balance among the claims of the various directly interested groups – stockholders, employees, customers, and the public at large".' (Ansoff, 1968; p.39). Ansoff points out that this 'stakeholder theory' of the firm makes 'responsibilities' and 'objectives' one and the same: *though he and I maintain that clearly they are not.* Nevertheless, in the stakeholder model there is little doubt that **managers** are the 'stakeholders': **theirs** is the right to decide how to balance the trade-offs that **they** will make between the various interests. While not confusing the difference between responsibilities and objectives, this is basically the model that I shall adopt and which finds its expression in the model of the organizational system given on p.58 in Figure 3.2(b).

16.1.3 Yet this basic model has been attacked on two fronts, and despite its fundamental validity, it has never quite overcome these combined attacks.

16.1.4 The first of these is that of Cyert and March (1963). They pick up the 'stakeholder' model, but in line with the neo-human relations ethos of 'participation' they attempt to rob the 'stakeholder' of its hierarchical imagery. They do this by claiming that the stakeholder's powers are subject to limitations which other will impose. This is clearly so. Management, like politics, is the art of the possible. Yet even as Cyert and March paint this picture for us, they proceed in that same instant to blur the imagery by adopting language that is inappropriate to the very claims that they are making.

16.1.5 At first sight their attitude appears to be grounded in the same pluralist stance that I have maintained throughout this book. They admit there may be a diversity of interests between the various parties. They also acknowledge the power element in the struggle. They even acknowledge that, as the position of the various combatants changes the situation will become unstable and need 'renegotiation'. But in the end they cannot live with their own analysis and they seek (by the language they use) to disguise the very reality that we have just described.

16.1.6 It is clear that any business which continues to exist does so because *the constraints which others have imposed upon its management do not make the opportunity cost of continuing to run the business greater than the cost of closing it down.* Conversely, it equally means that *whatever constraints management have imposed upon the other parties have not been so great as to have them refuse to continue to operate.* To that extent they have accepted whatever politico-economic muscle that management has brought to bear upon them. Yet in neither case could the continued operation of the company be honestly described as evidence that the parties have reached a 'consensus'. Indeed, if anyone did so it might be viewed as exhibiting a certain cynicism about human affairs. Yet 'consensus' is what Cyert and March call it.

16.1.7 For reasons that will become clear shortly, I am convinced that Cyert and March intend no such cynicism and are most probably completely unaware of the cynical overtones contained in referring to the outcome of a power-backed bargaining process as 'consensus'. I do not imply that the process itself is in any way questionable. (*A case can be made for governmental interference in the process in certain circumstances in the public interest and a case can be made out that any such intervention by government* *is a step towards centralized control and the slippery path to totalitarianism. But, generally speaking, I regard the autonomy of management and other interested parties to bargain together without interference from others as being desirable.)* So I am not questioning the morality of the **means** by which some equilibrium is achieved in this power struggle. What I most certainly do question is the morality of describing the **outcome** of this bargaining process as being a 'consensus'. Let us consider what this travesty of the use of the English language implies. *It implies that those who have not had the political will or the economic muscle to resist the terms of any opposing party can be assumed, from their inadequate resistance, to have concurred with what was being done.*

16.1.8 To sharpen up the point I am making, let us not consider it in institutional terms until we have considered it in a personal context. By Cyert and March's logic, the fact that Bob Cratchit, a poor clerk with no bargaining power in Dickens's London, accepted the starvation wages offered by the unregenerate Ebenezer Scrooge would be proof of 'consensus' between them.

16.1.9 In institutional terms the imagery is less emotive but the issue is the same. It is less emotive because 'exploitation' has proved to be as much a trade-union characteristic as ever it was of hard-nosed employers. Accordingly, there is a great gulf between the image of Bob Cratchit and that of the miners' union pulling down of the Heath Government of 1974. (*That crash has reverberated through the consciousness of the British people, and future historians may well see it as the trigger that has cost unions the goodwill of much of the general public and ultimately may bring into question the extent to which trade-union extra-parliamentary power of such magnitude can ever be legitimate. In just such a manner has the British consciousness, since the time of Cromwell, regarded any degree of political involvement by the armed forces as unthinkable.*)

16.1.10 Nevertheless, if the mutual confrontations of managements and unions are less emotive than those of Scrooge and Cratchit, it still remains monstrous to suggest that the continuance of a commercial institution is evidence of 'consensus' between the various parties. Cyert and March's language demonstrates how complete and how unconscious is the denial of the validity of conflict in American management literature. Taylor, Mayo and McGregor never really legitimized the worker's viewpoint. But Cyert and March tried to do so, and fell at the last fence. When the final trial came they could not bring themselves to call 'imposed conditions' anything other than 'consensus'. Moreover, we must ask ourselves why it is that their fellow writers and critics found nothing in the least disturbing about claiming that Scrooge and Cratchit must have negotiated a 'consensus'. The only acceptable solution is that American social conditioning has created a perceptual blind-spot.

16.1.11 Cyert and March present a model in which, presumably, the goals of Scrooge and those of Cratchit (together with the goals of any others who impinge upon the firm of Scrooge and Marley) form a Venn diagram. Only the area of common interest can be regarded as representing the goals of the organization (as shown in Figure 16.1(a)).

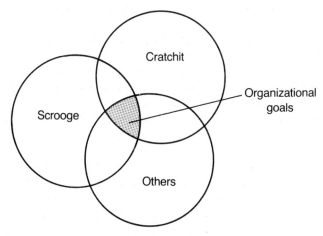

Figure 16.1(a)

16.1.12 It will still not deal with all the difficulties raised by the Cyert and March model even if we were to set aside the earlier moral objections that I had to their use of the word 'consensus', and treat the above Venn diagram as a serious proposition in which the common area were seen as representing the goals of the company. Ansoff, who does not question whether they were justified in creating such a model, nevertheless goes on to show it is flawed in practice. Such a concept fails to account for strategic plans for, says Ansoff (1968; p.41), it cannot account for why the firm should have chosen the specific objectives that it did nor how the participants would ever rise above 'operating' considerations in order to get to 'strategic' matters.

16.1.13 Yet there is in Ansoff a strange duality. He does not deny that it is management who set the company's strategic goals; indeed the preface of his book (1968; p.9) states that his very purpose is 'to develop a particularly useful series of concepts and procedures which managers can use to manage'.

Nevertheless, he is strangely ambivalent about his position. He sees (p.41) 'the choice of philosophy' as resulting from a consensus of 'the board, the corporate management and the key operating managers... within the present power structure of the firm'. But he appears to do so only to establish 'a basis for a practical system of objectives'. At certain points in the text, he makes clear his opinion (in which he is correct) that management's objectives are normative. At other points he appears to be suggesting *that his own view that the management are in control may **also** be normative. This is not the case. Management **are** in control.* Nevertheless, Ansoff leaves us with the distinct impression that emotionally he would rather believe that they were not so – even while his intellect tells him that they are.

16.1.14 This sense of unease builds until eventually he tries to resolve the tension in a quite astonishing turn-around. Having previously operated upon the assumption that management are in charge, he quite gratuitously goes back on this position and claims that, despite Cyert and March, a company **is** capable of possessing a collective mind. Such a mind enables it to have 'objectives which are different and distinct from the individual objective of the participants [and that these] can be inferred from its relationship to the environment, from its internal structure, from the functions it performs, and from its past history'. (Ansoff, 1968; pp.43–44.) I said there had been two attacks on the 'stakeholder' approach. The first was Cyert and March's refusal to acknowledge managerial power and to insist that 'consensus' rules. The second is this reversion, by others as well as Ansoff, to the view that an organization possesses a collective 'mind' which **transcends** the minds of individuals in the company, including the minds of the managers.

16.1.15 It doesn't require any great insight to see that both these attacks (neither of which will stand up to any logical analysis) are attempts to serve a common psychological need. *They both seek to reassure the theorist and his audience that the powers of management are severely limited.*

16.1.16 The 'consensus' view of Cyert and March and the 'transcendent' view of Ansoff and others both spring from a common root: the fear of what any individuals who have been given sufficient power might do with it. This is the fear that I have already admitted makes me shun the idea of any centralized state control of whatever complexion. This is the fear that led the Founding Fathers of the USA to build the 'separation of powers' into that country's constitution, and this is the fear that Lord Acton encapsulated in his dictum that 'power tends to corrupt and absolute power corrupts absolutely'.

16.1.17 To what safeguards can we turn from such tyranny? Well, perhaps in the final analysis there are **no** safeguards, yet two possible illusions can be adopted, represented by the attitudes of Cyert and March and Ansoff respectively. One sets faith in the efficacy of countervailing power groups to oppose any decision other than one supported by all parties ('consensus'). The other seeks to convince us that the system has a life of its own and has now become far too complex for anyone to get his arbitrary hands anywhere near the levers of power ('transcendence').

16.1.18 **Now** at last we can see why Cyert and March claim that Scrooge and Cratchit are in 'consensus'. They are **not** being cynical about poor Cratchit's plight. On the contrary, they are trying to spare us (and doubtless themselves) from the need to face up to the fact that the exercise of power **is** often both untrammelled and arbitrary. The form that their reassurance takes is to claim that Scrooge could only use his power *to the extent that Cratchit allowed him to do*. We can applaud their motive even as we consign the concept to the realm of mythology.

16.1.19 Similarly, we now can understand Ansoff's unease and see why he had had no sooner given the levers of power into management's hands than he tried to tell us that the organization was possessed of a mind of its own, a sort of mystical inertia guidance system, that would limit the power of the individual. Galbraith (though he substitutes the concept of 'the technostructure' for 'the firm') treats that **too** as if it had a corporate and transcendent mind of its own.

16.1.20 Bannock, who has not made the connection that I have just made, nevertheless puts his finger accurately upon the sense of comfort that Galbraith clearly derives from the impersonal and transcendent qualities of the technostructure. He notes that Galbraith 'seems to think that on economic matters the technostructure is beneficent, infallible and indispensable, although he clearly has doubts about the equity and aesthetics of the system' (Bannock, 1973; p.12). To satisfy his need to take the arbitrariness out of managerial power, Galbraith is at great pains to claim that the individuals who make up the technostructure are quite prepared to sink their separate wills for the sake of the community of interest that they enjoy as a group. So strong is this community of interest that the group can be thought of as being an inanimate device, an 'apparatus'. *Moreover, it is an apparatus on which we can safely rely. For, like us, the one thing that the technostructure can be guaranteed to fear, and therefore to oppose, is arbitrary activity. It is, as I have already indicated, an inertia guidance system.* 'This, **not management**, is the guiding intelligence – the brain – of the enterprise', (Galbraith, 1974; p.86). (My emphasis.)

16.1.21 We have already seen that this claim is completely fallacious. The 'MultiNat' case-study in Section 14.4 showed that Galbraith was wrong on all counts. *Top management was **not** impotent, the 'technostructure' did **not** provide a united front, and in its actions it can be quite as arbitrary as any other human institution.* But what we did **not** consider earlier was **why** Galbraith should have been under such psychological pressure to sell this myth, nor why so many people have been happy to buy it. Now we can see why. He and others who have adopted the concept of the 'technostructure' have done so because they see it as a benevolent machine that is unlikely to go off the rails. Here is Galbraith's own ill-concealed adulation for the machine that will protect us from our own human failings (Galbraith, 1974; p.91):

> The corporation...accommodates itself admirably to the needs of the technostructure. This we have seen, is an apparatus for group decision – for pooling and testing the information provided by numerous individuals to reach decisions that are beyond the knowledge of any one. It requires, we have also seen, a high measure of autonomy. It is vulnerable to any intervention by external authority for, given the nature of the group decision-making and the problems being solved, such external authority will always be incompletely informed and hence arbitrary. If problems were susceptible to decision by individuals, no group would be involved.

16.1.22 Well, it is time for the fairy-tales to stop. The goals of the organization are essentially those of management. Dependent upon how prepared we are to find this fact reassuring, we shall welcome or regret their ability to implement these goals. Certainly they will not be able to do so without facing constraints of a social, technological, economic and political nature. These will modify the **original** social, technological, economic, and political aims that the management **might** have sought to embrace if those constraints could have been relaxed.

16.1.23 Yet, even before we start to consider the constraints that **others** may place upon management, we must consider *the constraints that will be placed upon management by the fact that some goals may be mutually antagonistic.* We may well find that long-term considerations mean that we have to forgo short-term advantages. We do this because the overall effect of our choice minimizes our perceived opportunity cost. I shall come back to why I find it more legitimate to regard the minimizing of opportunity cost as the key management goal. Microeconomists use profit-maximization as a basic assumption to explain what motivates managements. It follows that they are committed to a policy of projecting the goal of 'profit-maximization' on to all company strategists willy-nilly. I am not. But let us first turn to the problem of how the manager deals with those goals which he finds desirable, but which mutually have a greater or lesser degree of incompatibility. For clearly this dilemma must force the abandonment of certain goals, or alternatively the acceptance of some compromise.

16.2 Organizational goals: a vector of objectives?

16.2.1 As an analysis of what strategic planning demands, Ansoff's findings appear to me to be irrefutable.

The method must:
1.   Include all four...steps of the generalized problem solving sequence.
     [(i) Perception of need or opportunity.
     (ii) Formulation of alternative courses of action.
     (iii) Evaluation of the alternatives.
     (iv) Choice of one or more alternatives for implementation.]
     Emphasis should be on the first two steps.
2.   Handle allocation of the firm's resources between opportunities in hand and probable future opportunities under conditions of partial ignorance.
3.   Evaluate joint effects (synergy) resulting from addition of new product markets to the firm.
4.   Single out opportunities with outstanding competitive advantages.
5.   Handle a vector of potentially antagonistic objectives.
6.   Evaluate the long-term potential of projects even though cash-flow projections are unreliable. (Ansoff, 1968, p.28.)

16.2.2 This is, as Ansoff dryly remarks, an 'imposing list of requirements'. Not least among these is the question of how one handles a 'vector of potentially antagonistic objectives'. Now although I agree that certain management goals will be antagonistic, I find singularly unhelpful Ansoff's use of the word 'vector' to describe this problem. It invites us to conjure up imagery of aims which are so divergent that management are effectively rendered impotent. Pulled in different directions, they would appear to be about to suffer the fate of Pavlov's dogs under conflicting stimuli and finish up in hysteria.

16.2.3 This imagery of a 'vector' of forces is taken from physics. When, for example, two forces are applied in order to move an object, they will produce a resultant force whose strength can be calculated by the principle known as the 'parallelogram of forces'. In figures 16.2(a) and 16.2(b) the respective forces (goals) are identical in magnitude. $G1$ has a strength of 40 units and $G2$ has a strength of 36 units. However, because these two forces (goals) are more opposed in Figure 16.2(b) than they are in Figure 16.2(a), the resultant force (*R*) which is represented by the diagonal, has been reduced from the 50 units that it would have in Figure 16.2(a) to only 20 units in Figure 16.2(b). Moreover, if the angle of the vector were opened even more, so that *G*1 were now diametrically opposed to *G*2, the resultant force would only be 4 units (40 − 36), or in managerial terms a state of near-impotence.

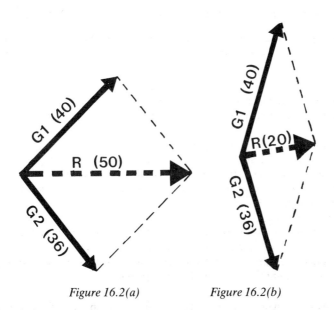

Figure 16.2(a)   *Figure 16.2(b)*

16.2.4 Yet this imagery does not represent managerial reality. Let us take an example. Generally speaking, as Ansoff himself has demonstrated, it is less risky, and probably more rewarding in the short-term to invest in the same product-market in which the firm is currently engaged than it is to venture into an entirely new product-market. This is because there is usually some potential in the system which can be realized by merely unblocking some small constraint. Consequently money spent in unblocking this constraint is likely to yield a much higher return than money invested in an entirely different venture. This disproportionate advantage is usually referred to as 'synergy' and its more than average yield is often highlighted by the equation '2 + 2 = 5'.

16.2.5 Yet this concentration on an **existing** product-market may carry with it the danger of holding all our eggs in one basket. The effect of moving into **another** product-market might cause us to forgo the short-term advantages of synergy but might gain us the advantage of long-term stability. This is the sort of problem with which managers deal almost every day. What happens in practice is that they weigh up the relative risks and then take action in respect of some sort of hierarchy of objectives. I do not mean to imply that such decisions do not require courage nor that the manager does not have to agonize over which way he should jump. My point is that finally he does jump and does not dither in a state of impotence between the two forces.

16.2.6 Let me give an example from my own experience. When I was party to the setting up in the UK of a subsidiary of an American firm which made photograph frames, our first priority was to become the supplier of a large retailer who bought his supplies centrally. This way we could get high volume quickly to generate a good gross profit which would not be eroded by the expenses created by a sales force. However, as soon as that base was secure we would immediately try also to start selling through other outlets, namely photographers, etc., who would want bigger margins and whom, in any case, it would cost us more to service. We must therefore seek in that sector of our business to present a more 'up-market' image so as to justify the higher selling-prices that would be inevitable, and to differentiate the product from those in the original large retailer's range. Consequently, although we desperately wanted to obtain that first large retailer's order, we nevertheless showed him only our **poorer** quality frames, and would only offer to supply him with them if we could use 'face-papers' which displayed **his** company logo and name and not **ours**.

16.2.7 Such a decision requires considerable courage when a firm is hungry for business, and it has always struck me as a serious shortcoming that the element of courage that management requires is not more strongly expressed in management literature. Yet, having made the decision, we agreed that there was no point in agonizing about it: **that** was the way we were going to play it. Consequently the long-term flexibility of our company was given priority above the aspect of getting that initial major customer at all costs. In this way the 'vector' of opposing goals did not reduce us to impotence.

16.2.8 Ansoff, in a footnote (Ansoff, 1968; p.68), seems to disagree with this **serial** approach to problem solving. He says '...it should be pointed out that some writers assert that firms do not pursue more than one major objective at a time, shifting their attention in time from one objective to another. See for example Cyert and March. To us this appears to be a convenient but an oversimplified assumption.' Ansoff himself acknowledges that there **is** such a thing as a 'hierarchy of objectives', but he uses the term only in respect of those things which might be classified under the headings of 'economic objectives', 'non-economic objectives' and 'reponsibilities and constraints'. He makes no attempt to give decision-rules for trading off the conflicting claims of such a situation as I have just described. True, he acknowledges that our aim of increasing the number of independent customers represents an objective which he would label **defensive flexibility**. But he gives no explanation of how we could have implemented our decision **other** than serially. My own view is that **strategic decisions have to 'nest' inside a 'hierarchical cascade of importance'** and by this means the apparent conflicting pull of the various elements in the vector is eliminated.

16.2.9 As to the question of 'responsibilities and constraints' it seems to me that these are dealt with by managers in one of three ways, *dependent upon which of the following categories the responsibility or constraint falls into:*

(1) *Responsibilities and constraints which are*
  (a) not currently being actively enforced by others
  (b) not of moral concern to the manager, but
  (c) are perceived as being detrimental in the long-term unless attention is paid to them.

These, if ignored, would represent a possible opportunity cost. They are therefore treated as 'goals' and given whatever priority in the nesting hierarchy seems appropriate (relative to all the other pressures).

(2) *Responsibilities and constraints that*
  (a) create a moral dilemma for the manager. (The situation with the Ford Pinto car in the following section (16.3) would be such a dilemma.)

These he can try to 'sell' to the directors of the company as issues which go beyond the *mores* of capitalism and which should be made paramount in the goal-nesting hierarchy since they are grounded in humanitarianism. (*He can try to use the additional lever of showing that public knowledge of the matter would damage the 'corporate image'; but that of course is only to threaten those who have too little conscience for a direct appeal.*) If he succeeds, fine; if he fails he has to decide whether he can stay with the company and look himself in the eye thereafter.

(3) *Responsibilities and constraints which*
  (a) are currently being enforced by others,
  (b) are not of moral concern to the manager, but
  (c) on the contrary are seen by him as claims which threaten the company's future and need therefore to be de-fused with the minimum of adverse reaction.

These do not create any tension for the manager, they are not part of his own 'vector' of goals, but they **do** require judgement in their handling to minimize the damage that they may do to the company. Far more problems lie in this category than is usually realized and it is helpful, as I shall now do, to give to them their own appropriate imagery.

16.2.10 Nearly all these third types of constraint have to be resisted, *because they represent demands which, if fulfilled, would remove* **one** *pressure only to substitute* **another**. In such circumstances the job of the manager is the same as that of Odysseus: deciding how to steer a course that will avoid the monster Scylla on the one hand without being swallowed by the whirlpool of Charybdis on the other. This need (to trade one danger off against another) is at the heart of the majority of management decision-making and, though it may be irritating to be so constrained, it makes the options open to the manager in such cases crystal-clear. We need only to consider two examples to illustrate this.

| Factor 1. | If we pay our workers more we shall run into economic difficulty |
| Factor 2. | If we don't pay them more we'll risk a strike |

| Factor 1. | If we don't have more work-in-progress we'll risk more costs from idle time |
| Factor 2. | If we do have more work-in-progress we'll not only extend cycle times but also tie up more capital with resultant interest costs |

16.2.11 Such opposing pressures have a funnelling effect which limits the manager's range of options. They therefore create what I have chosen to call a **goal window**. (In space launches the objective of the mission can only be achieved by the craft following certain trajectories. These constrain the launch-time options. But launch-times are also constrained by adverse weather. In bad weather, they can only launch if a break in the weather coincides with the launch time of a possible trajectory. This relief from impossible constraint is appropriately termed a **launch window**.)

16.2.12 When the self-generated goals of the manager come into mutual conflict, he has a problem. He resolves this by subjecting these goals to the filter of hierarchical 'nesting'. No such problem results from his having to deal with external constraints imposed upon him by others or by technology: indeed, such constraints actually sharpen up his vision. In Figure 16.2(c) we can see that the goal window between the opposing factors is quite wide. It is as a result of increasing the externally applied pressure (as illustrated in

Figure 16.2(d)) that the goal window is narrowed. This narrowing only serves to confirm the manager in his view of what actions he must adopt to cope with the threats. His choice becomes progressively easier to make as the opposing threats increase. Not until the encroachment of the two opposing factors destroys completely his goal window (as in Figure 16.2(e). will he meet a situation of real, as well as psychological, 'goal crisis'. The effect of such a crisis is clearly catastrophic and can turn managers into blatant gamblers. Such a situation occurred with the Rolls Royce aero-engine company. Desperate to pick up business they signed a contract to produce the RB211 engine which was so large in magnitude and so tightly costed (considering that the company was operating at the limits of technical knowledge) that the chances of bankrupting the company (which is what the contract did) were very high. Yet clearly they considered the risk preferable to the manner in which the company would bleed to death if the contract had not been signed. It was not, however, a 'management decision': it was a pure 'gamble'. There was no goal window open to them. We can therefore sympathize with their situation even if we might question the ethical basis of their decision.

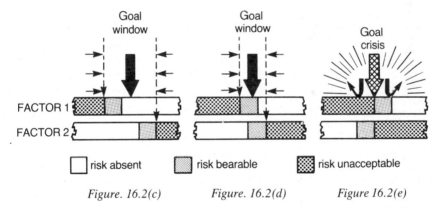

Figure. 16.2(c)   *Figure. 16.2(d)*   *Figure 16.2(e)*

16.2.13 The practising manager will recognize the validity of this 'window' model and will realize how many of his decisions are taken within such constraints. Yet, to my knowledge, it is not a model that has been previously proposed. Nor could we expect the 'goal window' model to develop in a culture in which the predominant ideology of recent years has been neo-human relations, (and I include there not only the USA where the ideology developed, but also the UK management schools where it was treated with the reverence due to holy writ). True, the 'goal window' concept explains why most managers see the actions that they take as having a degree of inevitability. True, it explains why conflicting goals do not create widespread managerial schizophrenia, in that there is no onus upon the manager to accept the conflicting goals of others. He need only agonize between those conflicting goals that he himself sees as valid. (Even then he can handle them by 'nesting' them in some sort of hierarchy.) *But this 'goal window' imagery is predicated on the belief that conflict can and does exist within organizations, that it is legitimate for others to oppose management, and that it is equally legitimate for management to resist that opposition.*

16.2.14 All of this is anathema to neo-human relations ideology. We have already seen how their 'participation' claims have led them to criticize 'mechanistic efficiency' and to refuse to give students the knowledge of work-study that they will need as managers.

16.2.15 Now we can see how that same ideology can emasculate the teaching of strategic planning, by bringing to the topic its assumption that all conflict is to be treated as a disease and that hierarchical structures are illustrative only of managerial paranoia. No truth can emerge if the validity of anything that does not conform to this ideological strait-jacket is treated as heresy. Moreover, the final irony is that, though it achieves its impetus from moral self-righteousness, it can lead to such enormities as giving the title of 'consensus' to any exploitive situation that can maintain sufficient stability to endure for any period of time. If my imagery of 'goal windows' does anything to undermine unitarism, then I should regard that alone as justification enough for the time and effort which this book has required.

16.3 Morality in goal-setting

16.3.1 It will be remembered that part of the reason that Marxists see capitalism as 'alienative' is that its exchange system encourages the belief that everything can be traded in terms of everything else (paragraph 11.3.4, point (3)). Thus capitalism leads to the belief that everything has a common basis of comparison; money. But it is a belief which implies that everything (not only material objects but also beauty, love, honour, whatever) has a price; a conclusion which demeans humanity. Nor, from our own analysis of capitalism can we fault them in this. Clearly if we use the concept of 'opportunity cost' as the means of deciding between alternatives, and we have consistently maintained that the *mores* of capitalism demand this, we are implying that the alternatives are of the same order, and amenable to comparison by a common (economic) yardstick.

16.3.2 Yet I have also claimed, (paragraph 11.3.6), that the *mores* of capitalism do not make the capitalist incapable of wholehearted love or compassion even though he habitually applies the concept of opportunity cost to his everyday business decisions. We need to recognize, however, that when he acts in the latter vein he has abandoned the *role* of capitalist, and has switched to some other frame of reference. The Marxist would like to claim that the capitalist is 'alienated' and beyond any such humanity. If the Marxist were to accept the possibility that a capitalist could act so, it would only reinforce his Marxist critique of capitalism, for it would have demonstrated that true humanity is possible only after abandoning a capitalist framework. By contrast, the Marxist believes his brave new world will contain no such problems. I, on the other hand, would claim that every frame of reference will ultimately prove inadequate if pushed too far. For example, whatever the political system there will need to be a trade-off between

(a) actions predicated on values which express concern for the individual, and
(b) actions predicated on concern for the many.

This will lead to conflict and require some degree of trade-off between the values inherent in the 'fall-of-the-sparrow-frame' versus those in utilitarianism's 'greatest-good-of-the-greatest-number-frame'.

16.3.3 My claim is that it is quite utopian to expect that we might one day develop some frame of reference whose logic system we can follow consistently to the bitter end without results which are either tragic or absurd. This is so because there will always be value-laden concepts which, although they were originally dropped (because of their lack of affinity for the other values in the system) need nevertheless to be re-introduced if we are to achieve a sensible and/or civilized balance. Without their restraining influence, a nightmare quality can begin to creep in. If my use of such words as 'civilized' or 'nightmare quality' sound exaggerated, we should consider the case of the Pinto car. It is a cautionary tale.

16.3.4 When Robert McNamara became US Secretary of Defense in 1961 he introduced the concept of 'cost-benefit analysis' to the study of efficiency within the Department of Defense. It is an extremely useful concept, particularly in those organizations which, like the Department of Defense, lack the goal of 'profitability' to guide them. Moreover, in a world of limited resources, getting the greatest benefit for the lowest cost must be laudable. I do not therefore wish to ridicule the concept; I merely note that its values are the values of capitalism. The usefulness of the technique was graphically publicized (Ansoff, 1969; p.167): 'Service leadership did not really know the total cost of supporting a B-70 [bomber]' It ultimately transpired that 'the

Polaris submarine, in fact, proved far cheaper to maintain for the same unit of retaliation effectiveness'. Following this revelation, the technique was adopted by every firm with any pretentions to sophisticated management. Yet it must be admitted that the idea of measuring costs versus benefits takes us into a philosophic quicksand. 'Costs' are not always simply measured in terms of money. 'Benefits' are even more difficult to define. Moreover, the people who gain the benefit are not necessarily those who pay the cost. the 'sophistication' of many managements was illusory. Such philosophic considerations are not the strong-point of the average manager. I do not suppose that those in Ford's American company were any more or any less blind to the limitations of 'cost-benefit analysis' than their counterparts in any other of the firms who so avidly adopted it. But it was the story of the Pinto car which was to reveal what can happen when, (to use Roethlisberger and Dickson's phraseology), the 'logic of efficiency' is not restrained by the 'logic of sentiment'.

16.3.5 Whether Ford used the technique of cost-benefit analysis in the initial stages of the design of the Pinto is not clear. However, in the interest of cost they certainly departed from their own safest manufacturing practice in the siting of its petrol tank. The model went into production and the incidence of death from incineration following accidents rose (Jacobson and Barnes, 1978). Courts in Florida (1975), Alabama (1976), and Virginia (1978) had awarded plaintiffs damages of $3.3m, $1.2m, and $0.625m respectively, following Pinto accidents in which the petrol tank caught fire. But not until 1978 was a case brought in which (p.4) 'lawyers were determined to press for a punitive judgement, which would involve convincing the jury that Ford had "consciously and wilfully" disregarded the safety of people who bought Pintos'.

16.3.6 Jacobson and Barnes comment (p.4) that 'the greatest damage to Ford's case was done by its own analysis of the price of building greater safety into Ford cars against the expected benefit derived from saving Ford owners from death or injury by burning'. These were contained in a company document entitled *Fatalities associated with crash-induced fuel leakages and fires*.

16.3.7 These calculations did not deal with the specific problem of the Pinto. The problem with the Pinto was that the petrol tank had been placed low down under the boot. It was therefore vulnerable to a crash in the rear. This was despite the fact that Ford's held the basic patent for 'a "saddle style" petrol tank placed above the car's back axle, out of the line of direct impact'. Such rear collisions were a more likely hazard than were the fires that might occur as a result of what was referred to as 'static rollover'. The prosecution produced the document to which I referred (in paragraph 16.3.6). It dealt not with the Pinto but with static rollover. However, the 'cost-benefit' conclusions it contained were clearly being used by the prosecution to infer the company's **attitude**, *inter alia*, towards the Pinto issue.

16.3.8

From official statistics Ford extracted the figure of 180 deaths per year from burns in rollover accidents...[and]...numbers emerging alive from such accidents but suffering severe burns, would also be 180 per year ... Based on the benefits of saving [this]...Ford put the total benefit of a design change at slightly less than $50 million. That was set against the costs – $11 worth of modifications per Ford vehicle sold – of $137 million. That, Ford's engineers observed, was almost three times greater than the benefits, 'even using a number of highly favourable benefit assumptions'. They could not envisage any developments which 'would make compliance with the rollover requirement **cost effective**'. (Jacobson and Barnes, 1978; p.4. My emphasis.)

16.3.9 Now it is the duty of managers to further the goals of the company. They must therefore look at problems from their 'professional' standpoint. That (as we saw in paragraph 1.2.7) is to foster the well-being of the firm as a matter of 'paramount' importance, and in the pursuit of this to avoid all known 'opportunity costs'. Yet on that basis Ford's managers and engineers were doing no more than their 'duty'. But managers cannot opt out of the obligations that they owe to their fellow-men. 'Cash payment', as the Victorian Thomas Carlyle said, 'is not the sole nexus of man with man.' **Yet I do not believe that the means exist within the value-system of capitalism to avoid the Ford-type nonsense.**

16.3.10 My reason for being a committed capitalist as I have repeatedly said, is two-fold. First I believe that market forces can more efficiently distribute and harness resources than can a centralized and therefore bureaucratic state. But secondly, and I believe more importantly, capitalism fosters democratic freedom. It does so as a natural consequence of the way it disperses economic autonomy to the individual commercial enterprise: a freedom which all states which have a centralized economic authority ultimately deny. *Yet I do not believe that the checks and balances upon the 'logic' of unrestrained capitalism can possibly be incorporated within the 'logic of efficiency' which governs capitalism. Such checks can only come from an appeal to the values of a separate and distinct system based upon the pre-eminence of humanitarianism.*

16.3.11 Those, and there are many, who cannot bear the ambiguities of life will try to claim the two can be incorporated into an integrated super-system of cost-benefit. **They cannot. If they could the whole Ford incident need never have happened. The irresolvable will not meld.** The manager is, in his own person, the unifying link. He owes allegiance to his profession, but he is not absolved from allegiance to humanity. If the first involves the logic of efficiency and gives a different answer from the second with its logic of sentiment, then he must allow his judgement to oscillate between these two frames of reference. Somewhere in that oscillation he must find the decision with which, as a manager and as a human being, he can live. It is an example of the process I described in Section 5.2. If he cannot do this, if he finds the 'stress' of such a totally ambivalent posture to be too great, he can only resolve it by taking President Truman's advice: 'If you can't stand the heat – get out of the kitchen!'

16.3.12 This is why Hayek is wrong when he quotes Milton Friedman with approval (Ansoff, 1969; p.239): 'If anything is certain to destroy our free society, to undermine its very foundations, it would be a widespread acceptance by management of social responsibilities in some sense other than to make as much money as possible. This is a fundamentally subversive doctrine.' I disagree. To suggest that in all circumstances the highest service that a manager can perform is to maximize the shareholders' profit is to maintain that when a manager accepts his responsibilities he also sells his soul. The trial judges of the Nazi war criminals at Nuremberg refused to accept that atrocities were excused because they were committed under orders. The court maintained, and rightly maintained, that those who committed such crimes were the keepers of their own consciences and responsible for their own actions.

16.3.13 If that were true of the Nazis, in a situation in which their very lives might have been forfeit for not conforming to orders, how much more is the manager responsible for his own morality? At worst he suffers the risk that his career prospects might conceivably be dented, at best his superiors might even respect him for his integrity (although, given the prevalence of Hayek's views, I offer no guarantees). On the other hand, if he does not, on what can he base his self-respect?

16.4 Organizational goals: minimizing opportunity cost or maximizing profit?

16.4.1 The mainstay of microeconomic theory is the assumption that all firms will try to 'profit-maximize'. Without this concept, virtually all the model-building of the microeconomist will fall to pieces. At one time I felt that the very real objections to this model of decision-making were so demonstrable that the myth could be exposed for what it is. I can now only wonder at my own naïvety. Now I am content to explain my standpoint and to leave it to the reader to accept or reject. I do so because I am now convinced that to attempt to argue the case is pointless and certainly tedious.

16.4.2 The basic problem of criticizing any belief system is that which we discussed in Section 2.2, namely 'How do we choose between the witch-doctor's truth and the physician's truth?' Our problem is that if we accept the witch-doctor's frame of reference then he can never be wrong. On the other hand, if we do **not** accept his frame of reference, then he can never be right. The way that we have attempted to solve this dilemma throughout this book has been (paragraph 2.2.6) to 'ignore the bedlam, and attain some degree of objectivity by tracing the divergent ways in which [opposing theorists] have developed from a single starting point'. This is not too difficult when the protagonists state their positions and hold to them. We have seen the elements that Taylor suppressed to give credibility to his view of 'economic man' and we have seen the elements that McGregor suppressed to give credibility to his 'self-actualizing man'.

16.4.3 However, the impossibility of arguing against those who claim firms will always seek to 'profit-maximize' is that they constantly move their ground. For example, a firm may go for growth rather than profits. This may be completely demonstrable in that it has cut its price to a level at which even the increased volume does not generate the net profit that could easily have been attained at a higher price, even though the higher price would have resulted in a lower volume of units sold. Surely this is an example of a firm which is not 'profit-maximizing'? 'Not at all!' says the microeconomist. 'True they have lost profit in the short term, but they have done so to profit-maximize in the long term.'

16.4.4 This example is only one of a great many that one could use to question the concept of 'profit-maximization' as the motivating force in management strategic decision-making. Here are a few more:

(1) Management does not have the omniscience to profit-maximize.
(2) Competitors will react and distort the hoped-for outcome.
(3) Maximization of profit may mean maximization of risk.
(4) All other management goals will not necessarily be subservient to this one.

Yet the microeconomist has a plaster for each of these sores. This is why it would be both tedious and pointless to try to disprove his claims. In fact we could never succeed, for 'profit maximization' is a portmanteau expression specifically designed to accommodate every circumstance by stretching and compressing its meaning to fit.

16.4.5 Consistent with his view that managers attempt to handle a 'vector' of objectives, of which profit is only one, Ansoff claims that firms should establish a 'threshold' level of return on investment (which is the minimum to keep them in the game), and a 'goal' level of return on investment which should be their target (commensurate with the achievement of the firm's other economic and non-economic goals). However, this does nothing to resolve the problem of the confused impotence that could be expected to result from such a vector of concomitant goals.

16.4.6 It would appear, both as a theoretical concept and as our practical experience of the real management world, that such conflicts can only be dealt with by managers demoting some goals and promoting others in a hierarchical structure of goal precedence. Moreover, since such knowledge as the manager possesses is so imperfect, he is quite devoid of the means of knowing how to arrive at the goal which microeconomic theory claims he is seeking. (*This is a particular state of equilibrium which will generate maximum profits.*) By contrast, the microeconomist has the same sort of advantage as the detective novelist. He starts from the solution and works backward, scattering clues and red herrings for the sleuth (manager) to pick up. I don't blame either the novelist or the microeconomist for doing this: after all they both need to do so to stay in business. But we should take into account the vested interests of both when they infer that the good sleuth (manager) can be presented with data and distinguish a clue from a red herring. This only happens in fiction.

16.4.7 Neither is this 'equilibrium' something, like the North Star, that is fixed. It is the product of the dynamics of a system which the manager does not fully understand, for which his data are questionable, and where other people over whom he has no power and whose actions he cannot forecast may change the rules or make unforeseen moves which upset all calculations concerning the position of the 'equilibrium'. But if the manager cannot home-in on this elusive target there is one thing he can do. He can attempt to avoid Scylla and Charybdis: the monster on the one hand and the whirlpool on the other.

16.4.8 It was not 'profit-maximization' that motivated our unanimous decision, when, in the earlier example of the photo-frame company, we decided to withhold our better frames from the large retailer. The trade-offs were beyond us. Luckily we **did** get his custom and even sold one million photo-frames to that one customer in the first twelve months. But what if we had failed? What if our tactics had actually lost us that vital sale? The trade-offs are incalculable. Yet we had no doubt that that our action was right: it was a unanimous decision taken in the full realization of the possible consequences. Why this unanimity?

16.4.9 The answer is simple. **If we had succeeded in getting the order at the cost of losing a suitable product-range that we could offer to other outlets, none of us would have had any further interest in the business**. It would have become captive to the whims of one large customer and if he were to let go of the handle all our eggs, which were in that one basket, would be smashed.

16.4.10 Now, by using his rubber yardstick, the microeconomist can turn my explanation into a proof that we really were, in one form or another, seeking 'profit maximization'. I do not wish to get into the tedium of this argument. For me, the issue was not the **positive** one of profit-maximization: it was the **negative** one of avoiding a perceived opportunity cost. So too was it with my colleagues. We did not want to live with reliance on one major customer. An order obtained on such terms would certainly have been Scylla. The reader may sense intuitively the rightness of my claim. If he were to talk to practising managers about it (having explained the respective models), I should be surprised if he did not find that they share my view. Each reader must make up his own mind. My claim is that, given the uncertainties of the situation, managers attempt to avoid opportunity cost because

(a) It sharpens up for them the hierarchy of objectives. *What they **most** wish to avoid conditions their **primary decision** and,* thereafter, successive 'opportunity cost-avoidance decisions' will help to determine how the remaining decisions will 'nest' within the hierarchy of objectives.

(b) It avoids the philosophic problem of having to suppose that, from the start, we know the end (goal), and therefore that we have only to seek **means** to attain it. Clearly this is untrue. It is more realistic to assume that we **avoid** certain ends and in so doing are driven, willy-nilly, into alternative strategies which narrow down the **means–end relationships** by creating 'goal-windows'.

(c) This makes it far more easy for managers to justify, as much to themselves as others, that the actions which they have taken, or propose to take, are not arbitrary.

16.5 The relationship of 'strategic', 'administrative', and 'operating' decisions

16.5.1 Ansoff, who is arguably the most significant theorist in the area of corporate planning, stresses the difference in kind between these three types of decision. *Operating* decisions are of a type that have an automatic trigger. Some icy February morning when only half the operatives for a conveyorized product layout have turned up for work, the need to make an operating decision **now** is very much borne in upon the poor production manager's consciousness.

16.5.2 By contrast, *strategic* decisions can be put off until triggered by catastrophe: and in badly managed companies they often are. It is at this juncture that we re-introduce the concept of 'systems' thinking. *I am not prepared to concede that 'classical' thinking was a closed system. Leverhulme displayed none of the 'clockwork gramophone syndrome' (paragraph 15.2.4).* Nevertheless, I do concede that there **is** a difference between responding **intuitively** to changes in the environment, and having a **conscious model** of the environment as **a place of change in which adaptation is a necessary response if a firm is to survive.**

16.5.3 Management consciousness of the need to adapt has enhanced by the concept of 'product life-cycle' concept, and enhanced yet more by the acceleration of the rate of technological and social change which has shortened the life-cycle of most products compared with the life-span of earlier products. (*We have already seen that the nineteenth century, for all the technical and social transformations that were wrought in those years, nevertheless permitted a life-cycle of sixty years to that most absurd of designs, the penny-farthing bicycle (paragraph 15.2.6).*) The typical product life-cycle is seen in Figure 16.5(a).

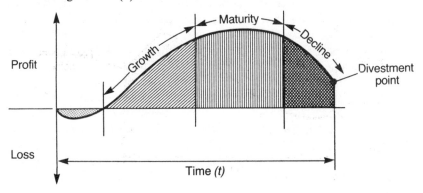

Figure 16.5(a) A typical product life-cycle

16.5.4 It is quite clear that it is in a firm's interest to extend the period of maturity in order to maintain profits for as long as possible, and this is usually attempted by means of a 're-launch' of the product. For example, Persil is a washing-powder which was originally developed early this century in Germany by the chemical firm of Henkel. It had a strong bleaching action and housewives, or their servants, usually soaked clothes overnight in Persil and then boiled them. Subsequently made in Britain by Crosfields and later by Lever Brothers, its formula has been progressively changed over the years to match the changing social and technological conditions, and by 1985 there were, in fact, two types of Persil on the market, one of which had been formulated for automatic washing machines. We see therefore that careful nursing and re-launches have kept the product sold under that name alive for three-quarters of a century, even if a housewife from 1910 would be unable to recognize today's products.

16.5.5 Yet all the re-launches in the world cannot save certain products, and when they reach the decline stage of the product life-cycle no amount of internal manufacturing efficiency can salvage the clockwork wind-up gramophone. Indeed, it can even be that a technological breakthrough for a competing product, **whether made by us or by our competitors**, may make our existing product obsolete overnight! In this case the typical product life-cycle illustrated in Figure 16.5(a) will never have the chance to run its course and the curve may well have the shape shown in Figure 16.5(b).

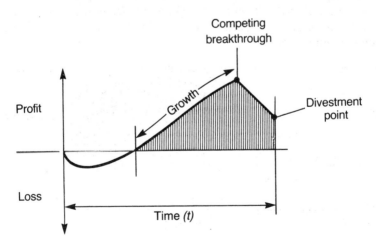

Figure 16.5(b) Frustrated product life-cycle

16.5.6 The 'product life-cycle' concept poses two problems for the firm. The first is that of recognizing where on the curves each product is currently located. The second is that of substituting another product for the one that is dying: for the loss of turnover resulting from a dead product can be very damaging, and even fatal in the case of a one-product firm. We shall return to this problem of recognition and substitution. For the moment we should notice that, unless some form of purposive stategic planning procedures are followed before the firm arrives at a crisis situation, any remedies will be likely to be too late, and also, because of time restraints, too ill-considered to be effective. Not to adopt formal strategic planning, in my view, is to rely upon luck to rescue the firm from the foolishness of its management.

16.5.7 *Administrative* decisions are prompted by the other two decision types. These are decisions concerned with creating the firm's structure and shape. However, in the absence of strategic decision-making, administrative decisions will only reflect the short-term administrative requirements of day-to-day operations. Many administrative set-ups have to be dismantled and rebuilt at great financial and social expense because they were created to serve the immediate needs of the firm and were totally inappropriate when the situation changed. Yet in many cases the later situation could have been foreseen by strategic planning, and so have enabled an administrative arrangement to be made which would have met the then-current needs and yet (progressively and without stress) could evolve to meet the firm's subsequent needs.

16.6 The relationship of long-term and short-term plans (1)

16.6.1 Successfully combining the requirements of the operating, strategic and administrative needs of a company requires far more than just a technique. It requires a marriage of the long- and short-term plans of the firm. This is a chicken-and-egg relationship. On the one hand, long-term goals are modified by, and subject to the constraints that will lie between where we now are and where we want to be. On the other hand, even the recognition of what we choose to call a 'constraint' is dependent on our seeing it as a hindrance to achieving our long-term objectives. We recognize the problem because we are capable of the 'figure–ground' oscillation of which I wrote in Section 5.2. Yet no such oscillation between the two is possible if one part of the company is concentrating upon the 'figure' and another upon the 'ground'. It follows that successful strategic planning demands that the organizational arrangements should **already** be such as to ensure that the same people are involved in both 'figure' and 'ground'. For this reason I regret that Ansoff, whose overall approach I admire, should have chosen largely to ignore the impact of the existing organization upon strategic decisions and upon operating decisions.

16.6.2 He is, as we shall see, far too good a scholar to ignore this aspect entirely, and we shall return to a quotation from a later article written by him (Ansoff, 1969; p.37) in which he demonstrates his awareness of this influence. In that article he advises that 'decisions should be made at the lowest levels [of the firm] at which the appropriate information is available'. Yet the goals of managers will be subtly conditioned by their own position in the organizational hierarchy, and by how that position affects both their own aspirations and their perception of what others expect of them. This situation could be expressed in the following aphorism: '*Pushing strategic planning down the hierarchy will alter the hierarchy of objectives of the planner.*'

16.6.3 All of this is somewhat at variance with the manner in which Ansoff wrote his first major work *Corporate Strategy*. There he writes as though his main objective (namely to create a formal approach to strategic planning) permits him to ignore such issues. I accept that he cannot cram everything into one small book, and that what he gave us is highly valuable. But he has obscured the manner in which the status of the decision-maker will change organizational goals, by such statements as that which follows. In making it he implies that (in attempting to create a formal approach) he is permitted the liberty of a dichotomy between those goals which relate to 'the firm as a whole' and those which relate to 'operational management': '...[W]e shall be concerned with objectives of the firm as a whole and shall not deal with the very important problem of the organizational hierarchy of objectives which are essential to the operating problem of the firm.' (Ansoff, 1968; p.36)

16.6.4 I shall challenge that dichotomy. Indeed, a statement that Ansoff makes in a later work implies that he too would equally do the same. However, before we deal with this later work of his, I need to explain terminology contained in it. This will probably be best done by first looking at what one might call the 'mechanics' of the strategic planning process. In doing this I am concentrating upon certain issues that appear to me to run as the main theme through Ansoff's approach. Yet I should be guilty indeed if I did not admit that I am offering a very simplified and highly modified version of the process. I have omitted some of the issues and changed the emphasis or nomenclature he imparts to the others. However, this to me is a tribute to Ansoff's genius: he has given to us a framework which we can adapt and modify. It supports us, but it is not a strait-jacket and we would be incomparably the poorer without it.

16.6.5 One further thing remains to be said of his work. Some writers attempt to explain the world as it is. In large measure this is what my present book has sought to do. For example, I have sought to show that, although the student's and the manager's perception of the widespread triumph of Taylorism may be obscured by ideological smoke-screens, yet Taylorism exists and it is the stuff of reality. I am not seeking to **change that particular situation**, I am merely seeking to **change perception and expose its existence**. By contrast, when Ansoff wrote his seminal book it did **not** reflect actuality.

16.6.6 Strategic planning was desperately haphazard or nonexistent as this example from my own experience shows. During the early 1960s I was surprised to learn that a certain multinational had made a bid for a particular company. (*To some extent the fact that I was surprised illustrates that I must have had in mind some of the criteria which Ansoff was later to codify: yet it certainly did not have the formalism that came from reading Ansoff. Nor, as I was to learn, did the procedures of the multinational.*) A close friend of mine was supposed to advise them in these matters. I asked him why he had suggested to them such a move. 'I didn't', he said. 'One of our directors dashed into my office and asked what I had on company X. So I gave him a file 6 inches thick. "Thank God for that!", he said, "We've just made a bid for it!".'

16.6.7 Now I do not say that such a thing would not happen today. What I do believe is that today's practice is far more likely to mirror the theory which Ansoff encapsulated into a technique. That being so, the number of firms committing such gaucheries is less.

16.7 An approach to the 'mechanics' of strategic planning

16.7.1 'The end product of strategic decisions is deceptively simple, a combination of products and markets is selected for the firm. This

		PRODUCT	
		Existing	New
MARKET	Existing	Market penetration ①	Product development ②
	New	Market development ③	Diversification ④

Figure 16.7(a)

combination is arrived at by addition of new product-markets, divestment from some old ones, and expansion of the present position.' (Ansoff, 1968; p.23.) So let us look at the basic options that are open to a firm by considering the **product/market** matrix as illustrated by Figure 16.7(a).

16.7.2 Basically the firm can consider four development options:

(1) To sell more of the existing product in the existing market.
(2) To sell a new product in the existing market.
(3) To sell the existing product in a new market.
(4) To sell a new product in a new market.

It is common practice now to refer to those moves which require us to move only **one** variable as representing 'expansion'. Thus both (2) and (3) above are **expansion** moves. They differ greatly from (4), where the product **and** the market variables are moved. This is the key aspect which identifies the act of **diversification**. This, as we shall see, is an important distinction, and diversification decisions are different in kind from expansion decisions.

16.7.3 We have already met the concept of **the product life-cycle**. Yet identifying where one is in that cycle is a difficulty. Decline usually first comes to light when we attempt to predict and to make plans for the next (say) 5 or 10 years and find that our initial calculations would lead us to forecast a future performance which falls short of our target aspirations. It is when we start to consider the realities behind this 'gap' that we begin to perceive the probable stage that each of the firm's products has reached in its life-cycle. I shall later come back to this point, because it shows the central importance of long-term budgets as problem-codifying agents and as triggers of strategic response. (*Moreover, we begin to see why I claim it would be wise to incorporate such personnel as produce those long-term budgets into our strategic planning team. For we need to elucidate the assumptions upon which they have operated. These can be far better challenged or modified when their authors are part of the team. Otherwise, willy-nilly we shall be absorbing their assumptions along with their data; and letting both go unchallenged. So, for both positive and negative reasons it is better that they be on the strategic planning team.*)

16.7.4 If the profit gap which has been thrown up by the long-term budget is to be closed, then there are methodological, psychological, economic and (I shall later show) organizational reasons for choosing the following sequence:

(1) improve via market penetration,

(2) improve via one or other forms of expansion, and
(3) improve via diversification.

The reasons are none the less valid for being mundane.

16.7.5 In a sense the question should be 'Why should one **not** exploit existing product/markets to the full before making a switch to other things?' Moreover, it is less likely to be risky and may well give a good return on investment, because money spent on releasing bottlenecks can be very productive indeed. Of course there will come a time when, in that graphic phrase, the manager could find himself 'flogging a dead horse'. In such circumstances it would be wise to consider expansion, either by selling existing products in new markets or alternatively finding new products for existing markets.

16.7.6 I have already suggested that expansion should precede diversification for economic reasons. It makes economic sense because of synergy. Let us imagine that we manufacture women's pantie-hose which we sell through lingerie outlets. Now let us suppose that we additionally get supermarkets to allow us to fix racks containing the hose by the check-out points and aimed at 'impulse buying' by the housewife who is queuing to pay for her groceries. Such an arrangement would be classified (see Figure 16.7(a)) as expansion via market development. Such 'market development' usually carries with it 'production synergy'. This arises because the increase in volume usually results in better utilization of plant and therefore a recovery of manufacturing fixed expenses that yields high profits, so creating this 'production synergy'.

16.7.7 Conversely, producing a new product that will be sold to the existing customers by the existing sales force usually produces 'marketing synergy'. This is because salesmen spend so **little of their time taking orders**, and so much time actually **travelling between customers**, that the same sales force might well be able to handle all the increase in business at no extra cost. Delivery too may be cheaper per unit sold.

16.7.8 Choosing the sequence (i) market penetration, (ii) expansion, and (iii) diversification also makes psychological sense. Not only are the expansion moves the ones which probably carry the least risk (after 'market penetration') but also they are the moves which are most readily visualized because of the relatively limited number of possible expansion options.

16.7.9 When market penetration and/or expansion have jointly closed the gap between the company's aspirations and its forecast performance, there is often a strong psychological pressure to halt the search for any additional increase in return on investment. Of course this is not always the case. Thrusting companies may feel that their original target aspirations must have been too low if they were so easily satisfied. Such a company might well raise its original expectations and create yet a further gap. Conversely, those companies which are not thrusters, and who failed to close the gap by using both market penetration and expansion, may well stop their search, despite the gap between their original aspirations and their later judgements. This leaves them with the psychological problem of dealing with this performance shortfall. They may well do this by convincing themselves that the former target was too high to be realistic anyway. (*This act of settling for something less than the real optimum because the manager thinks that what he can achieve by his present disposition of resources is 'good enough', is referred to by Simon as the act of 'satisficing'.*)

16.7.10 However, let us assume that the firm decides to go on and diversify. This brings with it a problem of quite a different nature to anything the management have so far experienced. For a start, whereas the opportunities for expansion were limited and obvious, the opportunities for diversification are infinite. How can we possibly cut these options down to manageable proportions without, in the process, inadvertently 'throwing away the baby with the bath-water'? Let me illustrate the problem another way. *If a personnel officer is faced with 600 applications for one job, his first task is to* **reject** *as many as possible.* This he frequently does by quite arbitrary decision rules, such as 'Throw out any application where the applicant is over 40 years old.' This gets rid of (say) 200 applications. Unfortunately, the ideal candidate's file is now in the waste-paper basket because he was 42.

16.7.11 The problem which faces the diversifying firm is similar. Given the embarrassingly wide spectrum of possible product/markets with which it can get involved, how can it discard some of these without inadvertently discarding a great opportunity as a result of employing some arbitrary decision-rule? *Clearly the problem cannot be solved without* **some** *decision-rules. The solution has to be to attempt to find decision-rules which will not be* **arbitrary**.

16.7.12 Here is the first 'rough-cut'. Listing by broad 'industry' category the areas into which the firm might move and identifying the characteristics that successful firms in that industry have displayed will give an **industry requirement profile**. Listing the capabilities of the company will give a **company capability profile**. Wherever we find a complete mismatch we can discard the possibility of entering that industry without fearing that we have 'thrown away the baby with the bath-water'. For example, if all the successful firms have assets of more than £50 million, and we don't have that sort of money, we can forget it. Similarly, no company of which I was M.D. would be likely to go into 'chemicals', since I am totally ignorant in that field.

16.7.13 Some industries would be discarded because the whole industry would appear to be coming to the end of its life-cycle. Alternatively, overcapacity could have ruined the industry's price structure. (*I should have the gravest doubts about any manager who even contemplated getting into the UK foundry business during the early 1980s. Demand had shrunk so rapidly that even the cut in overall production caused by some foundries closing did not compensate for this shrinkage. The result was that there was overcapacity throughout the industry, and this in turn led to firms accepting orders which were far from profitable, just to keep their plants active.*)

16.7.14 It should not be overlooked that if a company is thinking of diversifying in order to improve its overall return on investment **while still retaining its existing business**, this fact alone generates a need for the new company to achieve a tremendously high target-figure. Moreover, the smaller the new company is, the greater do its results have to be to fulfil its rôle and meet these expectations. For example, let us assume that an existing business makes 12 per cent return on investment (ROI) but the target for the new group, inclusive of the diversified business, is 18 per cent. It follows that, if the diversified business is the same size as the original one, then the diversified business must be able to make 24 per cent ROI. (*That is to say, since the first business is making 6 per cent less than target, and the businesses are the same size, the diversified business must make 6 per cent more than target to offset this loss on target.*) If, however, the diversified business were only one-third the size of the original business, then it must make 18 per cent better than targeted ROI to offset the 6 per cent loss on target of the original business. This means searching for a business of this size with an ROI of 36 per cent.

16.7.15 For this reason I am very sceptical of Ansoff's suggestion that firms may treat the act of diversification as a sort of 'make-weight' to an existing business, in order to close the profit gap. I believe such a policy would rule out too many chances to acquire firms which, considered independently of this rôle, would be good propositions. Nevertheless, it does highlight that we are probably safe to exclude from our area of search any industry in which the average company does **not** make a reasonably high ROI. In doing so we are unlikely to have 'thrown away the baby with the bath-water'.

16.7.16 Before we turn to consider what modifying effect the organizational context will have upon the above abstractly conceived technique, I should like to deal with two issues that crop up repeatedly in discussion on planning. *One is the question of how we can plan in uncertainty? If the future is so uncertain, doesn't that very uncertainty, which makes planning essential, also make it impossible?*

16.7.17 In part we have already seen that the approach is its own justification. *The reasons for diversifying are that the other courses of action are seen as inadequate to meet our aspirations.* Ansoff sees four basic reasons for diversification, and the three which I consider legitimate all fall within the category of attempting to meet aspirations. They are that (Ansoff. 1968; pp.113–114):

(1) Firms diversify when their objectives can no longer be met within the product–market scope defined by expansion.
(2) A firm may diversify because the retained cash exceeds the total expansion needs.
(3) A firm may diversify when diversification opportunities promise greater profitability than expansion opportunities.

16.7.18 The fourth reason for diversification is not, to my mind, legitimate. Fundamentally it is that management jumps into the next field because the grass looks greener and they are too ignorant of the situation to know better. In such circumstances they may happily vault the wall. They then find that the green quality was deceptive and that they are in a bog.

16.7.19 It should be self-evident that no management who contemplate diversification can be in total uncertainty. *They know enough to be worried about the need for change.* We are not living in a world of which we are totally ignorant. We live, says Ansoff, in 'partial ignorance'. Moreover, there are many social, technological, economic and political straws in the wind to give perceptive management some clues to future events. Even though I was chief executive of a factory making school uniforms that we have brought into reasonable profit, I advocated divestment because of two social straws in the wind. Straw number one (paragraph 3.2.33) was the imminent destruction of the UK grammar-school system. Straw number two (paragraph 3.2.34) was the probable pressures that would raise the manufacturing costs as women pressed for equal pay. In the event women are almost as disadvantaged as ever; but I was right about the destruction of the grammar schools and the virtual death of school uniforms. So we can and must plan, **irrespective of uncertainty**.

16.7.20 It seems to me that, to have no long-term objectives would be rather like steering a ship down Southampton Water and only when it reached the English Channel, to wonder whether to turn left or right because we have not earlier decided whether our ultimate destination was to be Amsterdam (left) or New York (right).

16.7.21 *The second issue that crops up repeatedly is the suggestion that 'planning limits opportunism'.* This is usually the position adopted by people who have made two fundamentally false assumptions. The first is that it is possible to recognize an opportunity without having done any homework. Let me correct this by a simple example. At the moment of writing this book I am considering moving home. When I started this exercise I had no idea of either what would be a reasonable asking price for the property I am selling, nor what I could reasonably get for the price I was contemplating paying. After some six months of desultory (but continuous) viewing of other properties I now know the market value of my own property, and when I find a property that I like but which by my calculation is underpriced, I shall buy it because it will be an 'opportunity'. *Yet it is my earlier 'leg-work' which will allow me to recognize an opportunity when I see it.*

16.7.22 The other false assumption is that 'planning' is the same thing as 'commitment'. *Whereas I am convinced that firms* **should** *arrive at diversification only after considering market penetration and then expansion, this does not mean that a firm should never diversify before having made moves in the other two areas.* We must not forget that a firm can only diversify using those resources that exist over and beyond what it uses elsewhere. Management can retrace their steps if (having looked at market penetration and the two types of expansion and possibly even having drawn up plans to take certain actions in these areas) the firm finds a marvellous diversification opportunity which it could not take up if it had previously committed resources to these other two areas. There is absolutely no reason why they should not put a halt to any of their earlier provisional expansion plans and concentrate their energies (and their resources in general) upon the diversification option. **This is quite different from jumping into diversification simply because of ignorance.** Moreover, nothing (other than the time spent in *considering* expansion) has thereby been lost; for none of the previous plans will have been executed.

16.7.23 Of course the time comes when such plans must be followed by an act of commitment. But such acts of commitment are necessary if the firm is to continue to operate. The only question is whether or not such acts have been preceded by intelligent appraisal.

16.7.24 The final issue that we shall deal with in respect of diversification is the question of whether it is done by taking over an existing business in the industry, or by starting up from scratch. The conventional wisdom is that this is a decision which is reached by trading off the costs of the one versus the other, and that the likelihood of buying an existing business is greater if the price and the potential are favourable. The ideal purchase, in terms of this wisdom, would be a company that is not doing well (and so is cheap), providing that this failure has been caused by some element which is missing from its 'capability profile' and which the purchaser can supply. If so, the resultant synergy could make their joint potential profit enormous. (The reader will note that this is a different form of synergy entirely from that described in paragraphs 16.7.6 and 16.7.7.)

16.7.25 However, in the next section I shall also maintain that any large concerns which are divisionalized by product (including multinationals) are likely to diversify by **buying** into any new area of interest and will almost never attempt to start in it **from scratch**. If I am correct in this view, it will be recognized that the implications of past administrative decisions are far wider than is generally credited. Past administrative decisions will then be seen to have a significant effect not only upon current operational decisions but also upon future strategy. Nor can we seriously believe that organizational goals can exist in some vague abstract form that is not subject to the influence of these other elements. So goals **too** are modified by the existing organization's format.

16.7.26 The importance of such a modifying influence is all the greater because, as we have already seen (e.g. paragraph 14.3.4), large firms are the major employers of all labour and the major holders of all capital assets. They must therefore be regarded as the most significant area of study for any text which is not deliberately slanted towards smaller concerns.

16.8 The relationship of long-term and short-term plans (2)

16.8.1 All planning involves an iterative process. We propose a certain objective, but from our existing circumstances we find that it needs to be modified, for it is unrealistic given our means. This iterative loop, which requires us to modify both ends and means until we have a relationship which is both acceptable and feasible, is part of all planning (Ansoff: 1968: p.35). 'The method has what Reitman calls "open constraint" property: both the objectives and the evaluation of the present position are subject to revision as a result of insights obtained in the process of solution.'

16.8.2 It follows that the organizational set-up must fail if it prevents this iterative loop from functioning. Of course, that may be the very reason for preventing such iteration by those who fear the outcome of such planning. In one academic establishment of which I know, the members of Academic Board voted **against** the integration of the Academic Development sub-committee and the Resources sub-committee. Consequently there was a continual mismatch between what the two sub-committees proposed. (*The purpose of an Academic Development sub-committee is to decide upon future academic objectives. The purpose of a Resources sub-committee is to decide how to allocate future resources. Clearly, for this arrangement to work these two committees should have operated in a continual iterative loop. It is pointless to plan academic programmes without knowing whether you have the resources and it is equally pointless to allocate resources to areas in which they are less urgently needed than in others.*) The result was that the unco-ordinated and separate reports they produced could never be actioned without requiring the intervention of Academic Board to clear up the mismatches that took place. This, to my mind, explains the original vote. It kept close control in the hands of Academic Board, though clearly at the cost of efficiency.

16.8.3 It follows that those who are performing the act of strategic planning must also be able to match requirements to resources and the future to the present if they are to make any coherent proposals. It is at this point that we begin to see how organizational structure can determine how such planning must proceed. The reason for having divisionalized a company is because the advantages of scale were being overcome by the disadvantages of the administrative burden that scale offered. Dependent upon circumstance these divisions will be either by 'product', by 'geography' or by 'function' (paragraph 14.1.9).

16.8.4 The future strategic planning of any company will be largely conditioned by the nature of these splits. I have come to the conclusion that in organizations which are divisionalized by product there is a strong, almost an inevitable, tendency for them to develop their strategic plans in a highly stratified manner. It is most common to discover in such organizations that:

(1)　the divisions will only seek expansion options,
(2)　the top management will employ experts specifically to seek for diversification options, and
(3)　such diversification options as are taken up will be pursued by the take-over of an existing business rather than by starting from scratch.

16.8.5 Indeed, it frequently happens that the very fact that certain products are similar, but currently handled by different divisions, has the effect of heightening rather than lessening this tendency to limit the areas of expansion into which each will go. Unilever presents us with a case in point. Batchelor's and Birdseye both produce convenience foods. Each is a separate division, and each is anxious to emphasize and legitimize its cherished separateness.

16.8.6 However, such legitimization demands that the other party practices a *quid pro quo*. It is conceivable that Batchelor's, whose products are basically dry or canned, could go into the frozen-food market. It is conceivable that Birdseye, whose products are basically frozen, could go into the dry or canned sector. However, such moves would frankly astonish me. The implicit 'live and let live' arrangement (which is doubtless rationalized as necessary to maintain a clear marketing image of each firm) would militate against them. Similar arguments apply to inhibit them from moving into other areas. Indeed, even in the matter of product development within the area of dry foods, Batchelor's chose to market their 'ready-meals' under the name 'Vesta'.

16.8.7 The whole ethos is therefore very limiting in terms of product development, let alone in terms of diversification. Moreover, the management of a product division have good reason to doubt whether their head office would endorse that they could keep control of any business that was so different from their normal activities that it warranted the name of 'diversification'. Indeed, to allow them to do so would go against the whole rationale of divisionalization by product. That rationale promotes the belief that the division's product/market can stand alone. No economies of scale would be obtained by amalgamating it with another part of the organization, and indeed, any such amalgamation would cause administrative diseconomies of scale. So even if a product division elected to divert talent and resources in order to give birth to such a child, *it would probably be taken away from them*. Such a situation does not encourage them even to consider diversification except when they are fighting for their lives.

16.8.8 Diversification therefore tends to become the province of the main board of the group, supported by analytical experts in strategic planning. Yet this is an influence that is likely to lead to diversification by acquisition rather than by going into some new product/market from scratch. For to start from scratch means finding management to do it. Of course if it is a product that has only just been thought of it will **have** to start from scratch; but the sort of business analysts that perform this function are not the creative/

entrepreneurial characters who think up a new product that the consumer has not yet dreamt of but would buy if it were on offer. No: the probability is that they see an existing company that has a good product which a further influx of administrative know-how and cash could exploit, and which enables them to use the nucleus of the existing staff in the business as a launch-pad.

16.8.9 There are other reasons which prompt such companies to buy rather than to start from scratch. One of the most simple businesses that one could possibly imagine would be to get bleach in bulk from a chemical company, dilute it to a level of concentration which is appropriate to use by the general public, and then bottle and sell it. Such a firm is Domestos which was bought by Unilever. (One could argue that such a purchase wasn't even diversification but product development in their existing soap and detergent market.) I do not suggest that they were wrong to do so. Clearly in acquiring the company they eliminated a competitor as well as gaining its market share, and this doubtless weighed more heavily than any consideration of the primitive production requirements, an aspect which would also give an impetus to buying in rather than starting up.

16.8.10 Yet a further reason for buying into a new area, rather than to start from scratch, is that the group may be almost embarrassed by the cash that it possesses and for which it needs to find an investment home. Indeed, the commonly used term for those divisions which are owned by the group which generate profits but have too doubtful a future to warrant further investment is 'cash cow'. It is one of the strengths of a large group that it can use its 'cash cows' to nurture its fledgling new ventures through their growing pains.

16.8.11 So for all these reasons it is highly probably that:

(1) Expansion, and only expansion, will be the province of strategic planning within the product division.
(2) Diversification, and only diversification, will be the province of top management and its advisors.
(3) Such diversification will be by purchase rather than by a process of starting from scratch.

6.8.12 That being so, it will surprise no one that the task of speaking of such matters within ICI to the 'City and Business' columnist of *The Mail on Sunday* (Barnfather, 1984) should have fallen to the ICI main board Financial Director, Alan Clements; nor that he should have said of his firm 'We need to buy... A big bid in the United States is most likely, with ICI's recent New York Stock Exchange quote easing the way. The attractive areas are speciality chemicals and pharmaceuticals. If we are to stay in the top five or six chemical companies in the world, while changing the group's structure we have to buy other companies.'

16.8.13 Commenting on this situation, the paper's City Editor, Maurice Barnfather, remarked that 'Low margins in much of ICI's businesses show why: 25 per cent of sales generate 55 per cent of profits. In short, three-quarters of ICI's businesses are not up to clip. They're cash cows, whose cash can and must be redeployed elsewhere if ICI isn't to continually fall foul of downturns in the chemical cycle.'

16.8.14 So at last we come to the later article written by Ansoff, and to which I referred earlier. What he says here I would agree reflects the way in which the affairs of existing divisions are handled. He says (Ansoff, 1969; p.37):

> In terms of observable behavior of firms, it is easy to see why in many firms strategic process can and does proceed with minimum participation from top management. So long as through the budgeting process, top management allocates resources for innovation, innovation can be managed at middle management levels. The transition between the respective stages of the logistic process becomes more permissive and automatic, strategic action is mainly confined to expansion, the strategy is an implicit one of 'natural' unplanned extrapolation of the firm's history.

16.8.15 The monitoring of such divisions by Head Office will clearly be largely a matter of budgetary control. Such 'innovation' as they undertake will doubtless be generated by the division. Such 'innovation' will be limited to 'expansion', and will be 'natural' unplanned extrapolation of the division's history. But that is to fail to recognizing that diversification can and does take place, and when it does, it is almost invariably the result of the main board's initiatives.

16.8.16 Clearly there are many issues that call out for development in the matter of company goals and that go far beyond what we have considered here. But enough has been said for the reader to see that the consideration of the goals of the firm forms an organic whole with all the other issues that we have discussed, from motivation to organizational structure.

Postscript

I hope and believe that the reader will recognize in this book a degree of holism. If so I shall be gratified, because I have spent my working life as a manager, as a consultant, as a lecturer, and (above all) as a human-being who believes in his responsibility to his God and his fellows, in trying to make sense of the conflicting social, technological, economic and political aspects of modern industrial life.

The authority given to managers makes their responsibility to this even greater than it is for non-managers... (and what a wholly Classical Theory concept that is!). Yet the complexity of theory and practice creates an apparently disjointed set of propositions. They appear to the newcomer like the separate islands of an atoll, for he only sees what sticks up above the surface. What I sought to do in this book was to invite the reader to put on flippers, aqualung and goggles, and join me below the surface. There he will have seen that the islands all rise from common foundations on the sea-floor. Some will say that the lenses of the goggles I have offered the reader created distortion. Well, it would be too much to expect that every reader will agree with my own personal philosophy. Marxists clearly will not, nor will those whose emotional attachment to neo-human relations ideas is stronger than my arguments against their consequences.

Nevertheless, even those who disagree may find some insights and/or may better understand certain relationships than they did. Students and managers, whether they identify with my views or not, can still use them to compare and contrast conflicting theories which previously seemed to have no obvious connection at all. Clearly it is in many ways a subjective book, but, in the words of Herman Minkowski, 'Je donne une oeuvre subjective ici; oeuvre cependent que tend de toutes ses forces vers l'objectivité' ('I am offering here a subjective work; but a work which strains with all its might for objectivity'). The sense of obligation to share my *Weltanschauung,* which led (after two and a half decades in the practice of management) to my becoming an *academic* in addition to my being a consultant, is the same impulse which led me to write this book. One can, and should comment to students upon the existing theories, but unless one's own views are part of the wider corpus of management literature there is a limit to the extent one may legitimately do so, no matter how valid such comment may be. Especially is this true when lecturing to students on courses which are externally examined, because then the examiner is not conscious of the input to which students refer. (It has been my good fortune to lecture mainly on internally examined courses run on behalf of professional and academic bodies enlightened enough to approve of some degree of unorthodoxy.)

However I had a subsidiary purpose in writing the book. In Europe by the mid-1980s the neo-human relations ideas of Douglas McGregor (which in the USA had been channelled into job-enrichment within the *mores* of capitalism) were threatening to change by law the precarious balance between management and union by increasing the level of enforced consultation: a proposal which would (if enacted) undoubtedly inhibit firms' capacity to change. The so-called 'Fifth' and 'Vredeling' Directives of the European Economic Community were to illustrate that although the Bullock Committee's proposals had long since died, much of their soul was busily marching on.

Management in Britain was clearly opposed to these Directives. Sir Terence Beckett of the Confederation of British Industry spoke out 'against' [these] 'social engineering' measures dreamed up in Brussels... because they place little or no emphasis on the need for maintaining or increasing competitiveness in industry... In the long term such schemes' will threaten employment, at a time when we desperately need to develop new new industries and create real jobs for the whole community'(*Management Today*, December 1984; p.74). The Director General of the Engineering Employers' Federation, James McFarlane, said (*Management Today*, December 1984; p.72) 'Such directives only lead to paralysis, not participation. They give power without responsibility and are a form of creeping expropriation.'

I would agree with them. Yet against the tide of neo-human relations sentiment such individual pronouncements are like Canute trying to keep back the sea. If the tide is to be stemmed, managers must be provided with the materials necessary for them to build a sea-wall. I refer to providing them with a strong, logical and morally acceptable counter argument to the sentimental nonsense in McGregorism. If the present tide continues to flow unchecked it could undermine both capitalism and parliamentary democracy. Why else should Marxists so frequently support 'industrial democracy'? I would need some convincing that they do so in order that capitalism will work more effectively. To date, liberals are far too charmed by what McGregorism does for their image to be aware of its inherent dangers. My hope is that this book will not only provide managers with the necessary logical and moral counter argument with which to stem McGregorism, but that it will also bring McGregor's followers to the realization that this woolly sentimentality could put our whole way of life in jeopardy.

Appendix
The neo-Nietzschean
élitism of Maslow

I wrote the following appendix before I ever came across The Journals
of Abraham Maslow *(Eds. Lowry and Freedman, 1982). As we might
expect from such journals, they offer a kaleidoscope of conflicting
ideas and emotions, including statements which appear democratic as
well as those which appear élitist.*

*Nevertheless, the overall balance of those journals is markedly
élitist, egocentric and amoral. In those journals Maslow makes it clear,
(10 September 1960), that he wants to replace 'Nietzsche's dominating
superman with healthy, loving, self-confident superman'. Of course
this is only possible if (like Maslow) one believes 'the inferior must
admire the superior without hostility, or else no society'. However, if
the inferior's admiration were not forthcoming Maslow has a solution.
(25 May 1966) he would 'jail and punish all civil disobedience. Such
punishment is necessary to bind society together at its bases for fear of
chaos. This is prepotent to "liberties", to rights, to **anything.'** [His
emphasis.]* 'The majesty of the law – if it can't be loved it must be
feared.' *He also believes, (30 August 1967) in a* hierarchy *of rights.
Absolute rights would only exist under the best conditions, otherwise
even minimal rights would be dictated not by any absolute moral code,
but by the rules of the game as nominated by the morality or immorality
of Maslow's opponents. He says, 'I'd have little hesitation in using **his**
rules of killing or torturing to get information or **whatever** he felt free*

to do to me:

Apart from offering the reader the contents of the above paragraph, the whole of this Appendix is based exclusively upon my analysis of the book (first published in 1954) Motivation and Personality *(Maslow, 1970). I could have reinforced my general conclusions from the wealth of examples in Maslow's journals. The reason that I did not is two-fold. Firstly, I wanted to show that the neo-Nietzscheanism which Maslow reveals in his journals **could and should have been deduced by the McGregorites, even from his earlier work.** Only if I left my original analysis totally unaltered did I feel justified in claiming this. Secondly, I felt some reticence towards using the random thoughts which a man confides to his diary (even if, as here, that diary were being deliberately kept for posterity). Maslow's journals show the same untrammelled ill-digested eclecticism as does* Motivation and Personality. *The chaotic ramblings of the journals show a brilliance all too flawed by lack of discipline: but they also show us, in the round, an admirable and sensitive human-being. Justice demands that the journal's elitist indiscretions should be read in context, or not at all.*

App.1 The first point in dealing with Maslow is to note that his modelling and his arguments are so confused that there is no statement I could make about his claims that could not be refuted by the reference to some portion of his text. I could, and shall, claim that this whole text is intended to have us take an optimistic view of Man, and therefore to invite anyone reading his book to hope that a utopian society is possible. He even gives a name to such an imaginary society, 'Eupsychia'. (Maslow, 1970; pp.277–278) '[A] Utopia in which all men are psychologically healthy... Eupsychia would tend to be more Taoistic, non intrusive, and basic need gratifying (whenever possible), would frustrate only under certain conditions that I have not attempted to describe, would be more honest with each other than we are, and would permit people to make free choices wherever possible.'

App.2 Elsewhere he makes the claim (Maslow, 1970; p.x) that his book
represented a different philosophy of human nature, a new image of man...
This new 'humanistic' *Weltanschauung* seems to be a new and far more hopeful
and encouraging way of conceiving any and every area of human knowledge:
e.g., economics, sociology, biology, and every profession: e.g., law, politics,
medicine, and all the social institutions e.g. the family, education, religion,

teaching. I have acted upon this personal conviction in revising this book, writing into the psychology presented herein, the belief that it is an aspect of a much broader world view and a comprehensive life-philosophy, which is already partly worked out, at least to the point of plausibility, and must therefore be taken seriously'.

App.3 Such writing predominates in the book. Despite all Maslow's contrary statements therefore, it invites us to believe that sufficient people will have been sufficiently 'perfected' to make this new society work. Yet the problems of society are not simply the problems caused by 'human nature' as an abstract concept. They include the practical and intractable problems caused by circumstance. What does Maslow have to say about these? Nothing: He merely hints that they cannot be ignored. Maslow (1970; 289) says 'The culture-personality relationship is usually studied as if culture were the prime mover, as if its shaping force were inexorable. But it can be and is resisted by stronger and healthier people. Acculturation and enculturation work only to an extent with some people. The study of freedom *from* the environment is called for.' (His emphasis)

App.4 The trouble with analysing or criticizing Maslow is that the bits of consistent logic are usually intertwined with another bit of inconsistent logic or another bit of inconsistent sentiment. To make a consistent system, something has to go. Unbridled individualism can make a Utopia for the unbridled individualist. It must however forgo the inhibitions of concern for others. This is a price that he is prepared to pay, but not prepared to **admit** to having paid. This is a wise decision in American democratic society. This is why the inconsistencies of logic and sentiment occur. In the above piece we can agree that the reformer must stand outside the norms of the society he wishes to reform. We can agree that society could stand a lot of reform. But the reformist is an interferer who is fortified by a strong moral code. Yet Maslow says elsewhere (1970; p.277) that he envisages a Utopia in which 'people will be...much less prone to press options or religions or philosophies, or tastes in clothes, or food or art or [sic] women [!] on their neighbours'. Despite which the reformer gets his licence to interfere, because 'adult human beings constitute a special case. The free choice situation does not necessarily work for people in general'. He does not spell out what constraints this will entitle his self-actualizing élitist to impose on others, yet we can infer that some societal constraints are 'good'. It is only the constraints that the non-self-actualizing try to use to trammel the self-actaulizer that are bad. A pattern is beginning to emerge and it is not, for all protestation, either democratic or co-operative. The naked egoism of Maslow's self-actualizer is unlikely to facilitate a conflict-free society, but it does explain why Maslow can ignore constraints upon that ego and still remain consistent.

App.5 We are left in little doubt by Maslow that his Utopia is achievable in the near future. It will be a tolerant society whose people will have healthy psyches; reflected in its name, Eupsychia. Maslow (1970; p.278) speculates about them: 'What kind of education would they choose? Economic system? Sexuality? Religion? I am very uncertain of some things – economics in particular. But of other things I am very sure. One of them is that this would be a (philosphically) anarchistic group...' One does not have to be a Marxist to complain that Maslow's suggestion that all these things are a matter of choice (including the economic system) is absurd. He has also ignored that that same economic system might impact upon the perception or interests of the parties. Is this because his society is made up of 'good' people? Here his images are again contradictory. He denies that he is basing his Utopia upon any such requirement, and indeed doubts (p.27) whether that is attainable. Yet he knows of a few people who (p.278) 'are not perfect but they certainly are as fine people as we can now conceive. Perhaps at this time and in this culture we just do not know enough about how perfect people can get. In any case ...individuals can be...much healthier than the culture.' Let us see if we can sort out some of these contradictions and inconsistencies in his expressions.

App.6 I would argue that there are three possible attitudes towards human nature, providing that one believed in such a thing as 'human nature' and providing that one believed in 'good' and 'evil' as objective things.

(a) Unless corrupted by circumstance it is essentially good.
(b) It is utterly depraved.
(c) It has both good and evil tendencies.

In the light of my experience I would deny (b) but commend (c) to the reader as being a 'true' interpretation of reality, which is supported both by everyday experience and by the insights of the Jewish and Christian religions. Let us now consider the manner in which Maslow treats the same options.

App.7 He is at pains from time-to-time to deny his belief in the perfectability of man. Thus (Maslow, 1970; p.xiii) 'we are all of us profoundly ambivalent about truth, beauty, virtue, loving them and fearing them too', a statement that seems to imply the universal shortcomings of man in Judeo-Christian belief. Elsewhere he seems to divide people into sheep and goats. For example, just prior to his last quoted statement he says

'Many people choose the worst rather than the better' and he therefore advocates a 'knowledge of psychopathology and of depth psychology' as a 'prophylactic against illusion'.

App.8 Whichever of these two attitudes had formed the basis of Maslow's thinking, I should have expected him to have subscribed to (c). Is this what he does? Not at all. Despite all his protestations about not believing in 'perfectability' he clings to (a), attacks (b), and never even mentions (c). Could this have been accidental? I did not think so. Yet what explanation could there be? Is he doing as the Marxists do, namely denying that he believes in 'perfectability' in order not to be accused of naïvety, and then quietly slipping back into that model later when nobody is looking. Let us see.

App.9 He starts (p.x) by advocating the aceptance of the new 'humanistic' *Weltanshauung* that I quoted in paragraph App.2 and which is essentially a 'perfectability' model. Then he switches to castigate any critics of this view. Ignoring completely the dual vision of Man to which most of us would subscribe, he sets up a false dichotomy by contrasting his vision with those who see human nature as **totally** depraved. On these imaginary foes he rounds with great ferocity. Who they are I cannot even guess.

> 'I must say a word about the irritating fact that this veritable revolution (a new image of man, of society, of nature, of science, of ultimate values, of philosophy, etc., etc.) is still almost completely overlooked by much of the intellectual community, especially that portion of it that controls the channels of communication to the educated public and to youth... Many members of this community propound an outlook characterized by a profound despair and cynicism which sometimes degenerates into corrosive malice and cruelty. In effect they deny the possibility of improving Human Nature and society, or of discovering intrinsic human values, or of being life-loving in general. Doubting the realness of honesty, of kindness, of generosity, of affection, they go beyond a reasonable skepticism or a withholding of judgement into an active hostility when confronted by people whom they sneer at as fools, 'Boy Scouts', squares, innocents, do-gooders, or Pollyannas. This active debunking, hating and rending goes beyond contempt; it sometimes looks like an outraged counterattack against what they consider to be an insulting effort to fool them, to take them in, to pull their legs.'

Then comes a wonderful piece of irony. For following the above incredible outburst Maslow says, 'The psychoanalyst would I think, see it in the dynamics of rage and revenge for past disappointments and disillusionments'.

App.10 This is where Maslow's modelling needs unravelling. His outrage at those who doubt the reality of honesty, kindness, and of generosity impels us to conclude that he is using a moral standard. Yet elsewhere (p.279) he wants above all, 'tolerance and freedom of taste and opinion'. There are references elsewhere in his book to 'responsibility'. Nevertheless, at this critical juncture where he is dealing with (in his own words) 'the key necessities' there is no mention of 'duty, honour, responsibility, or self-sacrifice'. Are these qualities inherent in what Maslow considers 'good'? What is his touchstone for identifying what he means by 'good' and 'evil'? Now although his modelling is often confused, this is one element of his thought in which we can have little doubt where he stands.

App.11 Maslow ponders (p.279) upon how any of us comes to know what is 'good' and asks the question in several ways: 'How can I be a good man?' 'How can I live a good life?' 'How can I be fruitful?' 'Happy?' 'At peace with myself?' He answers: If the organism tells us what it needs – and therefore what it values – by sickening and withering when deprived of those values, this is the same as telling us what is good for it' Now this is sheer naturalism. The sense is as muddled as all Maslow's writing. The 'good' of 'good man' implies goodness to others. The 'good' of the 'good life' could be anything from monasticism to hedonism, with more than a suggestion that the latter was intended as it shades off from 'good' life to 'happy' life. **But there is no doubt that it is essentially naturalism.** He continues, 'The key concepts in the newer dynamic psychology are spontaneity, release, naturalness, self-choice, self-acceptance, impulse awareness, gratification of basic needs'. They used to be control, inhibition, discipline, training, shaping, on the principle that the depths of human nature were dangerous, evil, predatory and ravenous.'

App.12 This basing of morality in the subjective intuition of individuals is a Hellenistic and not a Hebraic concept. Nugent (1983; p.13) points out that the difference between the two is 'revelation'. 'For the Hebrews, religion was a "given", a Law from without with which they were entrusted; elsewhere men were left to their own natural resources... [Yahweh's] people may not have always been more humane than the gentiles, but they were an historic people, perhaps the only historic people. As Nugent points out, this makes Yahweh a unique and 'constitutional' God. This is the God that Christendom inherited. And even though Christ's self-abnegating and atoning death was a further 'revelation' which transcended the Law of Moses, yet it most certainly did not abolish it. When St Augustine says 'Love God and do as you will', this does not abolish the Law. It implies that its precepts have been 'internalized' (if I may borrow that neo-human relations cliché).

App 13 So when Maslow (1970; claims that as a result of naturalism, he can take the words of St Augustine and render them as 'Be healthy and then trust your impulses [because] the dichotomy between selfishness and unselfishness disappears altogether in healthy people', this is clearly nonsense.

App.14 Based upon the Christian ethic of self-denial and self abnegation, what St Augustine says makes sense. But based upon the primacy of 'self-actualization' it must be quite false. The one thing that Maslow cannot accept is an obstacle in the path of the individual towards the goal of self-actualization. Of course, he is delighted if the self-actualizing person can achieve the loving relationships of which Maslow writes. But equally, if they do not, it seems to cause him little concern. 'Our subjects are capable of an extraordinary and unexpected ruthlessness. It must be remembered that they are very strong people. This makes it possible for them to display a surgical coldness when this is called for, beyond the power of the average man.' (1970; p.175.) Is this part of the Augustinian message? Not a bit of it.

App.15 I would concede that the world is a richer place because Paul Gauguin abandoned his wife and family in Paris and went to Tahiti to paint those disturbing and demonic pictures, I concur with Octave Mirabeau. He said, (Keller; 1980; p.242) that it seemed to him 'remarkable and exciting' that Gauguin should 'voluntarily flee civilization, seeking to forget and be in peace, to find himself and be able to hear his inner voice, which had been drowned here [in Paris] by the noise of our passions and quarrels'. Exciting it may be, understandable it may be, necessary it may be, but **moral in the Christian sense...?** 'Love God and do as you will'...? Hardly is it that. Yet it **is** self-actualization *par excellence!*

App.16 St. Augustine would have approved more of the abnegation of self for the benefit of others. This is not to say that selfless people are not fulfilled. On the contrary: but this is a special case and certainly not what Maslow is suggesting as the highroad to self actualization.

App.17 There is already in existence a philosophy that regards 'self-actualization' as the greatest duty that a person owes to himself, and which conveniently allows that person to fix his own morality. Indeed, the author of this philosophy actually wrote a book entitled '*Beyond Good and Evil*'. That philosopher is Nietzsche. Maslow is quite explicit that his subjects do not need to be bound by any fixed external moral code. With approval he notes that his subjects 'Have definite moral standards...[but] needless to say their notions of good and evil are often not the conventional ones.' (Maslow, 1970; p.168).

App.18 I feel sure that the thought of Maslow as a neo–Nietzschean will dismay many, and in particular those who cherish Maslow's pro-democratic inferences. For Nietzsche was essentially an élitist. Yet I shall show that there is a considerable amount of Maslow's thought that appears to be élitist in character, and indeed, it is the democratic bits that don't easily fit. For as Russell (1979; p.739) has indicated, Nietzsche's philosophy is 'unpleasant but internally consistent'. That being so, the pro-democratic element in Maslow appears to make his neo-Nietzscheanism **less unpleasant, but equally less internally consistent.** Indeed, when it comes to showing how democracy fits into his system, Maslow decides against any coherent argument. He suggests relationships without making syntactic sense. It is reminiscent of Stéphane Mallarmé who, as Leonard Bernstein (1976; p.239) put it, 'turned himself on with anti-semantic pills' to contribute to a type of poetry which had 'begun to show a remarkable disintegration of syntax, a diffusion of meaning or of logical continuity that intoxicates the mind... everywhere hovers a delicious vagueness, a highly charged ambiguousness of dreams, images and symbols'. Here is Maslow in full flight from syntax (1970; p.289): 'Theory of democracy, of anarchism. Democratic interpersonal relationship. The democratic leader. Power in a democracy and among democratic people and in the democratic leader. The motivations of the unselfish leader.' What does it all mean?

App.19 Moreover, there are so many other parallels to Nietzsche. Maslow's evident disgust at the inhibiting effect that seeking 'safety' would have upon the will to self actualize, mirrors Nietzsche's disgust with the inhibiting effect of Christian morality upon self-actualization. For Nietzsche objected to Christianity because it was a 'slave morality'. Russell (1979; p.733) singles out in particular this quotation from Nietzsche on the subject; 'What is it that we combat in Christianity? That it aims at destroying the strong, at breaking their spirit, at exploiting their moments of weariness and debility...until their will to power turns inwards, against themselves.' Idealizing the will also, Maslow similarly refuses to validate 'safety'. Yet it should be remembered that the fundamental drive for trade unionism cannot be understood other than in terms of 'safety'. For emotional and economic security are at the heart of informal group theory and Hoxie has shown us that trade unions must be seen as the coalescence of such group interests (paragraph 9.1.11). Are they all to be seen as neurotic? Maslow would seem to suggest so.

App.20 'The healthy and fortunate adult in our culture is largely satisfied in his safety needs. The peaceful, smoothly running, stable, good society ordinarily makes its members feel safe enough from wild animals, extremes of temperature, criminal assault, murder, chaos, tyranny, and so on...If we wish to see these needs directly and clearly we must turn to neurotic individuals, and to the economic and social underdogs, or else to social chaos, revolution, or breakdown in authority.' (Maslow, 1970; p.41). In the next quotation I should like to bring the reader's attention to the word 'only'. It speaks volumes. 'In between these extremes, we can perceive the expressions of safety needs **only** in such phenomena as, for instance, the common preference for a job with tenure and protection, the desire for a savings account, and for insurance of various kinds (medical, dental, unemployment, disability, old age.) (p.41). In the next quotation we should note how Maslow infers that there are no **real** threats, only the psychological imaginings of neurotics. It is virtually a replay of Mayo's 'obsession' explanation which reduced group norms to non-rational behaviour. 'Some neurotic adults in our society are, in many ways, like the unsafe child in their desire for safety... their reaction is often to unknown, psychological dangers in a world which is **perceived to be** hostile, overwhelming and threatening' (p.42).

App.21 Here again we get a whiff of élitism... 'economic and social underdogs'. So just how non-élitist is Maslow's thought? This is difficult to say because of the murky imagery. But there is enough élitism to complete the Nietzschean picture. For example, after urging us to study the 'culture–personality relationship' in terms of the 'freedom **from** the environment' of 'stronger and healthier people' – and how Nietzschean a thought that is – he says one of the most revealingly élitist things that I have ever read, (pp. 289-290). 'Opinion polling is based on the uncritical acceptance of a low conception of human possibilities, i.e., the assumption that people's votes will be determined by selfishness or sheer habit.' (I must confess I cannot for the life of me see why he should suggest that this is so. Nevertheless, let us accept that he does and that he deplores it. His next remark is the really significant one.) 'This is true, but only in the unhealthy 99 per cent of the population' (p.299).

App.22 Apparently therefore he is about to bring about his Utopia with the 1 per cent of healthy people. It would seem to me that that is quite an élitist concept. Yet in Nietzschean terms it would be possible to construct such a Utopia, at least as far as the self-actualizers are concerned. The only important thing is that they should not be inhibited from achieving what they willed. Perhaps now it at least becomes clear why this society should be, in Maslow's own words, Taoistic'.

App.23 Here is Russell on the topic (1979; p.732): 'Buddhism and Christianity, [Nietzsche] says, are both "nihilistic" religions in the sense that they deny the ultimate difference of value between one man and another, but Buddhism is much the less objectionable of the two... [for] ...Christianity, he argues, aims at taming the heart of man.' Taoism is a religious system with influences from Mahayana Buddhism that emphasizes the end of all striving. If the 99 percent are prepared to accept this then presumably it would indeed be a Utopia for the 1 per cent for whom striving is all. They would have a clear field: but it would not be a **caring** society.

App.24 Should it be so extraordinary a thought that Maslow of all people should, consciously or otherwise, have entertained ideas based upon Nietzschean concepts? Nugent would not have seen it as being so. He says (1983; p.125) that 'Nietzsche can be seen as a centre in which a number of diverse lines cross and sometimes intertwine, creating a strange spiritual coalition that defies the conventional political wisdoms: professors and soldiers, scientists and sadists, poets and robber barons, occultists and atheists, resurgent Hellenes, and – in the ethnic sense – deracinated Hebrews.' But I, for one, refuse to believe that an anarchistic society made up of self-gratifying people would be a Utopia that I should care to live in or to see others endure.

App.25 This leads on to my final question about Maslow's modelling. That is his use of the word 'higher' for self actualization. The Christian message that Nietzsche so despised was that 'love', in the sense of 'charity', was the highest goal to which we can attain. Whether Maslow is right in suggesting that the human psyche cannot develop into 'self-actualization' without having first experienced the support of loving relationships, I do not know. I suspect that he is.

App.26 But for me, and for many others, 'charity' is still the greatest virtue. Although Maslow does not create a model in which self-actualization must necessarily **exclude** 'charity', yet neither does his model necessarily **include** it. That being so, 'self-actualization, with its narcissistic overtones, is no basis for a loving, caring Utopia.

Bibliography

Ansoff, H. I., *Corporate Strategy*. Harmondsworth: Penguin, 1968 (first published 1965) [Refs. 16.1.2/12/13/14; 16.2.1/8; 16.6.3; 16.7.1/17; 16.8.1].

Ansoff, H. I., *Business Strategy*. Harmondsworth: Penguin, 1969 [Refs. 12.2.1; 16.3.4/12; 16.6.2; 16.8.14].

Aron, R., *Main Currents of Sociological Thought*, Vol. 1. Hardmondsworth: Pelican, 1968 (first published 1965) (Refs. 3.1.17; 6.1.6].

ASSC (Accounting Standards Steering Committee, Chairman Derek Boothman) *The Corporate Report*. London: Accounting Standards Steering Committee, 1975 [Refs. 2.3.23/24/25].

Bannock, G., *The Juggernauts*. Harmondsworth: Pelican, 1973 [Refs. 13.2.25; 16.1.20].

Baran, P. A., and Sweezy, P. M., *Monopoly Capital*. Harmondsworth: Pelican, 1968 (first published 1966) [Ref. 11.1.12].

Barnfather, M., *The Mail on Sunday*, 22 April 1984 [Refs. 16.8.12/13].

Beckett, T., *Management Today*, December 1984. B.I.M. [Ref. Postscript].

Bernstein, L., *The Unanswered Question*. Cambridge, Mass.: Harvard University Press, 1976 [Ref. App. 18].

Blake R., and Mouton J., *The Managerial Grid*. Houston: Gulf, 1964 [Ref. Introduction].

Bronowski, J., *The Ascent of Man*. London: British Broadcasting Corporation, 1973 [Refs. 2.4.3; 3.1.7; 5.1.19; 10.2.6].

Brown, W., *Exploration in Management*. Harmondsworth: Pelican, 1965 (first published 1960) [Ref. 10.1.8].

Bruns, W. J., and DeCoster D. T., *Accounting and its Behavioral Implications*. New York: McGraw-Hill, 1969 [Refs. 10.3.19; 12.4.4].

Bullock, Lord (Ch'man), *Report of the Committee of Inquiry on Industrial Democracy*. London: HMSO, 1977 [Refs. 2.3.7/8].

Burns, T., *New Society*, 31 January 1963 (Available in Pugh, D.S., ed., *Organization Theory*. Harmondsworth: Penguin, 1971 [Ref. 3.1.4].

Burns, T., *Industrial Man*. Harmondsworth: Penguin, 1969 [Refs. 8.2.4; 9.4.25/26/27; 15.7.6/7].

434   Bibliography

Burns, T., and Stalker, G., *The Management of Innovation*. London: Tavistock, 1966 [Refs. 15.7.8; 15.12.7].

Clark, K., *Civilization*. London: British Broadcasting Corporation, 1969 [Refs. 8.2.11; 11.1.35).

Coser, L. A., *The Functions of Social Conflict*. London: Routledge & Kegan Paul, 1972 (first published 1956) [Refs. 9.4.22/23].

Cyert, R. M., and March, J. G., *A Behavioural Theory of the Firm*. Englewood Cliffs: Prentice-Hall, 1963 [Ref. 16.1.4].

Dalton, G., and Lawrence, P., *Motivation and Control in Organizations*. Homewood, Ill.: Richard D. Irwin, 1971 [Ref. 10.2.4].

Del Mar, D., and Collons, R. D., eds., *Classics in Scientific Management*. University of Alabama Press, 1976 [Refs. 7.1.22; 7.2.13; 9.3.4/5/7/9/10].

Drucker, P., *The Practice of Manasgement*. London: Pan, 1968 (first published 1955) [Refs. 13.2.9; 15.5.2].

Eccles, T., *Under New Management*. London: Pan, 1981 [Refs. 11.1.27/28].

Feuer, L. S., *Ideology and the Ideologists*. New York: Harper & Row, 1975 [Ref. 2.4.5].

Galbraith, J. K., *The New Industrial State*. Harmondsworth: Penguin, 1974 [Refs. 14.2.11; 14.3.4; 16.1.21].

Galbraith, J. K., *The Age of Uncertainty*. London: Book Club Associates, 1977 [Refs. 11.1.37/38].

Gellerman, S., *Behavioural Science in Management*. Harmondsworth: Pelican, 1974 [Refs. 4.1.21/22].

Giddens, A., *Capitalism and Modern Social Theory*. Cambridge: Cambridge University Press, 1971 [Refs. 6.1.6; 8.2.5].

Giddens, A., *New Rules of Sociological Method*. London: Hutchinson, 1976 [Ref. 2.1.5].

Goldthorpe, J. H., Lockwood D., and Bechhofer, F., *The Affluent Worker*. Cambridge: Cambridge University Press, 1968 [Ref. 13.1.8].

Gouldner, A., *The Two Marxisms*. London: Macmillan, 1980 [Refs. 8.2.6 (footnote); 11.3.3/9/10/11].

Haire, M., *Organization Theory in Industrial Practice*. New York: [Ref. 12.3.2].

Handy, C. B., *Understanding Organizations*. Harmondsworth: Penguin, 1976 [Ref. 9.5.15].

Haraszti, M., *A Worker in a Workers' State*. Harmondsworth: Pelican, 1977 [Refs. 11.3.13/14].

Herzberg, F., 'One more time: How do you motivate employees?', *Harvard Business Review*, Jan–Feb. 1968 [Refs. 4.1.19; 10.4.21].

HMSO, Cmnd. 3627, *Payment By Result Systems*. London: HMSO, 1968 [Ref. 8.5.13].

Hobbes, T., *Leviathan*. (Everyman's Library Edn.) London: J. M. Dent & Sons, 1973 (first published 1651) [Ref. 2.2.10].

Hobsbawn, E. J., *Industry and Empire*. London: Weidenfeld & Nicholson, 1968 [Ref. 8.2.9].

ILO, *Introduction to Work Study*. Geneva International Labour Office, 1957 [Ref. 7.2.50].

Jacobson, P., and Barnes, J., *Sunday Times*, 12 January 1978 [Refs. 16.3.5/6/7/8].

Jenkins, C., *Financial Times*, 8 January 1977 [Ref. 2.3.14].

Jones, H. G., *Management Today*, February 1983 pp.78–82 [Refs. 4.2.9/10].

Kakar, S., *Frederick Taylor*. Cambridge, Mass.: The MIT Press, 1970 [Refs. 8.3.26/27/28/29/30; 9.1.8/15/16].

Katz, D., and Kahn, R. L., *The Social Psychology of Organizations*. (2nd ed.). New York John Wiley & Sons, 1978 (first published 1966) [Refs. 3.1.3/5; 11.3.16; 16.1.1].

Keller, H., *The Art of the Impressionists*. Oxford: Phaidon Press, 1980 (first published 1975) [Refs. 9.5.14; App.15].

Keynes, J. M., *The General Theory of Employment Interest and Money*. New York: Harcourt, Brace, 1936 [Ref. 1.3.4].

Kidder, T., *The Soul of a New Machine*. Harmondsworth: Penguin, 1982 [Refs. 3.1.25/26/27/28/29/30/31/32].

Koestler, A., *The Act of Creation*. London: Picador, 1975a (first published 1964) [Ref. 10.3.27].

Koestler, A., *The Ghost in the Machine*. London: Picador, 1975b (first published 1967) [Refs. 3.1.6/8/9/10; 15.3.7; 15.9.2].

Koestler, A., *Janus – A Summing Up*. London: Hutchinson, 1978 [Refs. 3.1.19/20/21; Figure 3.1(a); 8.4.10].

Koontz, H., and O'Donnell, C., *Management – A Book of Readings*. New York: McGraw-Hill, 1976 [Ref. 1.1.2].

Laing, R. D., *The Divided Self*. Harmondsworth: Pelican, 1965 [Ref. 2.3.21].

Likert, R., *New Patterns of Management*. New York: McGraw-Hill, 1961. [Refs. 12.4.5; Figure 12.4(a)].

Likert, R., *The Human Organization*. New York: McGraw-Hill, 1967 [Refs. 12.4.8; Figure 12.4(c)].

Luthans, F., *Organizational Behaviour* (3rd ed.). Kogakusha: McGraw-Hill, 1981 [Refs. 10.3.27; 11.2.8/9; 14.1.2/9/15; 15.11.3].

McCarthy, W. E. J., ed., *Trade Unions*. Harmondsworth: Penguin, 1972 [Refs. 5.2.14; 6.2.1; 9.1.11/12/13; 10.3.9/11/12; 11.1.16].

McFarlane, J., *Management Today*, December 1984 [Ref. Postscript].

McGregor, D., *The Human Side Of Enterprise*. New York: McGraw-Hill, 1960 [Refs. 3.2.14; 4.1.16; 6.5.4; 7.1.5; 10.3.16/18/21/25/26/28/32/33/34/35/36].

MacRae, D. G., *Weber*. London: Fontana, 1974 [Refs. 8.5.9; 9.5.8].

Magee, B., *Popper*. London: Fontana/Collins, 1973 [Refs. 2.1.7/8; 2.3.12].

Magee, B., *Men of Ideas*. London: British Broadcasting Corporation, 1978 [Ref. 2.3.6].

March, J. G., and Simon, H. A., *Organizations*. New York: John Wiley & Sons, 1958 [Refs. 12.4.3; 12.5.10; 14.1.8].

Marx, K., and Engels, F., *Selected Works*. Moscow: Progress Publishers, 1970 (Preface to: *A Contribution to the Critique of Political Economy*, first published 1859). [Ref. 9.4.21;11.1.6/8].

Maslow, A., *Motivation and Personality*. New York: Harper & Row, 1970 (first published 1954) [Refs. 6.5.2; 10.2.1/6; App. 1/2/3/4/5/7/9/10/11/13/14/17/19/20/21].

Maslow, A., (abridged and edited by Lowry R.J., and Freedman, J.) *The Journals of Abraham Maslow* Brattleboro, Vermont: Lewis, 1982 [Ref. Appendix].

Merkle, J. A., *Management and Ideology*. Berkeley: University of California Press, 1980 [Refs. 7.2.7/8/9/10/11/12/17/18/19; 8.3.9; 9.1.18].

Midgley, M., *Wickedness*. London: Routledge & Kegan Paul, 1984 [Ref. 10.1.5].

Morison, S. E., *The Oxford History of the American People*. Oxford: Oxford University Press, 1965 [Ref 7.1.8].

Nugent, C., *Masks of Satan*. London: Sheed & Ward, 1983 [Refs. App. 12/24].

Optner, S. L., ed., *Systems Analysis*. Harmondsworth: Penguin, 1973 [Refs. 15.12.4/6].

O'Shaughnessy, J., *Business Organization*. London: George Allen & Unwin, 1969 [Refs. 12.6.8; 14.3.5; 14.4.22; 15.7.5; 15.12.12].

Pears, D., *Wittgenstein*. London: Fontana/Collins, 1971 [Refs. 2.2.5/6; 5.1.5].

Pugh, D. S., ed., *Organization Theory*. Harmondsworth: Penguin, 1971 [Refs. 8.3.4; 15.7.10; 15.9.6; 15.11.2].

Pugh, D. S., Hickson, D. J., and Hinings, C. R., *Writers on Organization* (2nd ed.). Hardmondsworth: Penguin 1971 [Ref. 9.1.1].

Reich, B., and Adcock, C., *Values, Attitudes and Behaviour Change*. London: Methuen, 1976 [Ref. 7.2.15].

Robinson, J., *Economic Philosophy*. London: C.A. Watts, 1962 [Ref. 11.1.33].

Roethlisberger, F. J., and Dickson, W.J., *Management and the Worker*. Cambridge, Mass.: Harvard University Press, 1970 (first published 1939) [Refs. 9.2.3/5/68/ 9.2.6/12/14/15; 9.3.8; 9.4.2/6/7/11/12; Figure 9.2(a)].

Rose, M., *Industrial Behaviour–Theoretical Development since Taylor*. Harmondsworth: Penguin, 1978 (first published 1975) [Refs. 4.1.11; 9.3.3/12; 9.4.22; 11.3.17].

Russell, B., *History of Western Philosophy*. London: Book Club Associates, 1979 (first published 1946) [Refs. 10.3.23; App. 18/19/23].

Sampson, A., *Anatomy of Britain*. Sevenoaks: Hodder & Stoughton, 1962 [Refs. 13.1.2; 13.2.2/3].

Sampson, A., *The Changing Anatomy of Britain*. Sevenoaks: Hodder & Stoughton, 1982 [Refs. 7.2.31; 10.4.13].

Scanlon, H., *Sunday Times*, 23 July 1978 [Ref. 2.3.16].

Schein, E. H., *Organizational Psychology* (2nd ed.). Englewood Cliffs: Prentice-Hall, 1970 (first published 1965) [Refs. 3.1 intro. 3.1.2; 9.1.4; 12.3.4; 15.1.9].

Shields, B. F., *The Evolution of Industrial Organization*. London: Pitman, 1930 [Ref.12.2.2].

Simon, H. A., *Administrative Behaviour* (2nd ed.). London: Macmillan, 1957 [Ref. 12.5.5].

Simon, H. A., *The New Science of Management Decision*. New York: Harper & Row, 1960 [Refs. 12.4.1; 15.3.3].

Sirota, D., and Wolfson, A. D., *Personnel*, May/June 1972 [References in text are to version in Gellerman (1974) listed above] [Refs. 4.1.21/22].

Smith, Adam, *An Inquiry into the Nature and Causes of the Wealth of Nations*. (Everyman's Library Edn.) London: J. M. Dent & Sons, 1970 (first published 1776) [Ref. 4.2.2; 7.2.27].

Sofer, C., *Organizations in Theory and Practice*. London: Heinemann, 1972 [Ref. 13.1.4].

Stern, W. M., *Britain Yesterday and Today*. London: Longmans, Green, 1962 [Ref. 3.2.28/29].

Stewart, R., *The Reality of Organizations*. London: Pan, 1972 (first published 1970) [Ref. 14.3.5].

Tannenbaum, A. S., Kavčič, B., Rosner, M., Vianello, M., and Wieser, G., *Hierarchy in Organizations*. San Francisco: Jossey-Bass, 1974 [Ref. 3.1.3].

Tawney, R. H., *Religion and the Rise of Capitalism*. London: John Murray, 1926 [Refs. 8.2.13/14].

Taylor, A. J. P. Preface to *The Communist Manifesto*. Harmondsworth: Pelican, 1982 [Ref. 11.1.11].

Taylor, F. W., *The Principles of Scientific Management*. New York: Norton & Co., 1967 (first published 1911) [Ref. 7.1.9; 8.3.21/22; 9.1.19].

Trist, E. L., Higgin, G. W., Murray, H., and Pollock, A. B., *Organizational Choice: Capabilities of Groups at the Coal Face under Changing Technologies*. London: Tavistock, 1963 [Ref. 4.2.12].

Udy, S. H., *Work in Traditional and Modern Society*. Modernization of Society Series. Englewood Cliffs: Prentice-Hall, 1970 [Refs. 3.2.6/7/8/14/18/19; Figure 3.2(a)].

Van de Vliet, A., *Management Today*, December 1984 [Ref. 11.1.42].

Vroom, V. H., *Work and Motivation* New York: John Wiley & Sons, 1964 [Ref. 11.2.5].

Whyte, W. H., *The Organization Man*. Harmondsworth: Penguin, 1960 (first published 1957) [Ref. 11.1.46; 13.1.6].

Wilson, C., *The History of Unilever*, Vol. 1. London: Cassell, 1954 [Ref. 15.2.4].

Woodward, J., *Management and Technology*. London: HMSO, 1958 [Refs. 8.1.1; 15.8.2].

Index